SUMMER
WITH
DURHAM

SUMMERS
WITH
DURHAM

TIM WELLOCK

FOREWORD BY STEPHEN HARMISON

CABOODLE BOOKS LTD

A Catalogue record for this book is available from the
British Library.

ISBN-13: 978-0-9559711-6-7

Typeset in Bembo by www.envydesign.co.uk

Printed in the UK by CPI Cox & Wyman, Reading

The paper and board used in the paperback by Caboodle Books
Ltd are natural recyclable products made from wood grown in
sustainable forests. The manufacturing processes conform to the
environmental regulations of the country of origin.

Caboodle Books Ltd
Riversdale, 8 Rivock Avenue, Steeton, BD20 6SA
Tel: 01535 656015

With thanks to:

The Good Pub Guide,
The Northern Echo for photos and in particular Nick Loughlin
Barry Goodwin for front cover
Durham Handbooks compiled by Brian Hunt
Wisden for statistical references

All opinions are those of the author.

CONTENTS

FOREWORD

WHEN I made my Durham debut, aged 17, in the last match of the 1996 season we took such a hammering that people must have wondered if Durham had made any progress at all in five years. We lost by an innings and 251 runs against Leicestershire. They were the champions and we finished bottom for the third time.

If I had been making my debut for any other county that could have been the last that was heard of me. I missed the whole of the next season with a back injury, but Geoff Cook kept in touch and suddenly I found at the start of the 1998 season that the legendary David Boon wanted me in the team. He was brilliant for me and for the club. I can't say I've never looked back, nor can Durham. There have been a few setbacks, but the general trend has been upward and to come from that 1996 humiliation against Leicestershire to being champions 12 years later has been a fantastic journey.

Durham came into first-class cricket to provide opportunities for North-East lads like me. We are proud of our roots and if it sometimes seems that I don't travel well I'm not the first from this neck of the woods. Although the leagues have always been strong and there's always been plenty of talent, not too many went away to become stars in the first-class game.

Riverside has a special place in my heart. I get a good reception from the fans and I always try to put on a bit of a show for them. Even though we needed to bring in a few outsiders to help us to the top, there's still a family atmosphere. I love playing in the same team as my brother, Ben, and we weren't the first pair of brothers to play for the county. That honour went to Andrew and Gary Pratt, and we now have Gordon Muchall's brother, Paul, in the academy.

It's a lovely environment to play in, and to parade the county championship trophy in front of the fans was absolutely brilliant. I'm delighted that this book has been written to celebrate the triumph.

Stephen Harmison

INTRODUCTION

THIS is a fascinating story. Whether or not it is well told is for you to judge, but the story of how Durham grew from minor to major, winning the County Championship in their 17th season, deserved to be fully recounted. It could have been Miner to Major given that the county once housed 147 coal mines, and equally the title of this book could have been Pits to Prizes. That would have been a slightly more sophisticated version of Chumps to Champs, which is too tacky for my taste, and as this is a personalised account of Durham's first-class life it had always been my intention to call it Summers With Durham. It would eventually have been written in more relaxed and reflective circumstances, but after the glorious triumph of 2008 it suddenly became essential to seize the moment.

The book, therefore, can be seen as a celebration. It is a celebration not just of a team's climb from adversity, but of the warmth, eccentricity and especially the humour which surrounds English county cricket. I have tried to bring as much humour as possible to the book. It was in its early stages at a time when the England team's involvement in the Stanford Challenge in Antigua coincided with the outcry over Jonathan Ross and Russell Brand for a foul-mouthed radio broadcast, which was meant to be funny. While cherishing the hope that these equally vulgar events would spark a return to this country's more traditional values, it seems important to hang on to good, old-fashioned humour.

What do I mean by that? Well, I once heard a female Durham fan say: "I've just realised who Jack Russell reminds me of. It's him out of the Woodentops." I suspect she meant Bill (or Ben) the Flowerpot Men. Or younger readers might appreciate more the supporter who said of Shoaib Akhtar: "Rawalpindi Express? He's more like the Rawalpindi Rickshaw."

The fact that I am amused by such quips will be at odds with how some Durham officials and players perceive me. When, for example, I write in this book that there was a period when stadium development took priority over team building some will see that as a negative comment, when it is intended purely as a statement of fact. Supporters have a different viewpoint and are more likely to tell me I am known for my trenchant views, which they seem to like. But I see myself as neither negative nor trenchant. Negativity is often mistaken for truth and realism, and to me it is important that this should be the full "warts and all" story. It is a heart-warming illustration of how triumph can emerge from adversity, and of how it is worth battling through all the muck and bullets to savour the magic moments.

In terms of expressing opinions I have never seen any point in being bland. So, for example, in giving my opinion of Twenty20 cricket, an "abomination" seems a fitting description. It sometimes seems that the last bastions of civilisation in this country are cricket and country pubs, in their old-style, unblemished versions, of course. My sentiments might best be summed up by quoting Rupert Brooke and Hilaire Belloc:

Stands the church clock at ten to three

And is there honey still for tea?

These lines from Brooke were written about his home village of Grantchester and were not about cricket. But they sound as though they ought to have been, while Belloc wrote:

"When you have lost your inns, you may drown your empty selves, for you will have lost the heart of England."

Village greens have linked cricket and pubs for generations, and as I find I am not alone in appreciating both, this book is also a celebration of the best ancient hostelries I have discovered in cricket's first-class shires. I've even crossed into Shropshire, Suffolk, Cheshire and Devon to find those which cock a snook at brasserie-style modernisation and maintain the old traditions.

On my first day in journalism, at the Whitley Bay Guardian 35 years ago, the editor called me into his office and said: "There are three things you need to know about journalism. The first is accuracy, the second is accuracy and the third is accuracy." That was it until a couple of weeks later he angrily pointed out that by typing out the wrong week's tide tables I was in danger of incurring the wrath of fishermen, not to mention visitors to St Mary's Island. Dougie Blackhall was a meticulous man who checked everything. It could be argued that as a weekly paper editor he had time to do that, whereas tight morning newspaper deadlines do not allow it. So, like everyone, I have made mistakes. But despite the cynicism in this country which persuades Australians to label us Whingeing Poms, I have never set out to be deliberately negative, only to convey an accurate picture. As we all know, the truth sometimes hurts and I like to think I have made some allowances for that.

The humour may have faded during the 17 years of first-class cricket covered by this book, or perhaps that's simply a reflection of the increasing professionalism which carried Durham to the title. They were, of course, swept along by the general trend which increasingly seemed to demand success. It created the ridiculous dichotomy whereby county cricket's primary function of producing England players was compromised by an influx of overseas players. In winning the Friends Provident Trophy in 2007 and the championship the following year, Durham were perceived to have got the balance right. Yet even their shrewd South African captain, Dale Benkenstein, could see that the scales were becoming overloaded with imports.

The Durham story has its share of strife, painfully so during the two years under the captaincy of Michael Roseberry, and the season under Nick Speak, which are outlined in detail to emphasise the sympathy both deserved. The fact that Roseberry hardly ever won the toss seemed to sum up his misfortunes. It was during that time that the local press coined the phrase "curse of the Durham captaincy."

When looking at the bigger picture, however, it is clear that Durham have been lucky, first in getting into first-class cricket when they did, and secondly in achieving division one status just as the split was about to become profound. Once Durham had been accepted it wasn't long before people began to say that the talent was spread too thinly and some of the first-class counties should amalgamate. Then the split into two divisions in 2000, designed to bring the cream to the top and provide tougher competition, began to have a real impact five years later with the reduction to two up and two down. That was when Durham were promoted under the captaincy of Mike Hussey, who began by making 253 as Durham won at Grace Road by an innings and 216 runs. For most of their previous first-class life they had been routinely thrashed by Leicestershire, but it subsequently became clear that the sudden change in both counties' fortunes marked a significant shift within county cricket. Deciding that their best chance of silverware lay with the Twenty20 Cup did Leicestershire no favours and over the next few years they became one of a quartet of counties who appeared to have little prospect of escaping the championship's second division.

Durham's rise had to involve transformation off the field, as well as on, which is why we reporters went from being housed in a leaking cabin to a palatial media centre. The early years might have been tough for us all, but they were generally great fun and I hope the book reflects that.

The fun may have stemmed partly from an embattled region's sheer joy in staging first-class cricket. The attitude of Don Robson, the man who did more than anyone to make it happen, was always: "Isn't it marvellous", even when the cutlery drawer was starting to bulge with wooden spoons. I don't think he lacked the ambition to take things further, but when fellow directors jokingly started referring to him as the Ayatollah it was clear that he was determined to do things his way and wasn't always getting it right. The club's first two chief executives lasted less than four years between them and one director who probably expected to have a bigger say resigned in the second year. Perhaps Robson had little faith in his fellow board members, and the fact that none of them, himself included, had any background in first-class cricket was undoubtedly a handicap.

Robson was the leader of Durham County Council, a body in which socialist attitudes inevitably prevailed, and that may have had a very slight bearing on the selection of Geoff Cook as Director of Cricket. He was always a huge believer that the Durham ethos was to provide local lads with the opportunity to play first-class cricket on their doorstep, and if they were from what might be termed an under-privileged background so much the better. To some extent he has been proved right in querying the cricketing ambitions of those from wealthy families. Nicky Peng is the outstanding example, while Robin Weston could be another, although there was a political element to his release. It is slightly incongruous that the wealth of the Weston and Roseberry families acted as the catalyst for Durham's first-class application, as will be outlined, yet they were unable greatly to influence matters once it was achieved. Despite a long association with the club as a minor county, Mike Weston declined to get involved, while Mattie Roseberry was on the board but vanished from the scene after his son, Michael, stepped down towards the end of his second season as captain.

Michael's appointment certainly seemed like a good idea at the time, bearing all the hallmarks of the prodigal son returning to herald a bright new dawn. But if Geoff Cook suspected that there was an element of the heart ruling the head, he was proved correct. A man of steel, proven at the top level, was needed, and Cook personally flew out to Tasmania to get his man. Yet, after three years of progress under David Boon, things were allowed to slip as the club again tried to build a home-grown team topped up by a few cast-offs from other counties. Finally, with Martyn Moxon as head coach, the management accepted that the production of local talent, however admirable, was not enough to win trophies.

That was how it came about that the team which clinched the championship included six players born overseas, even if five of them did have EU passports. Cook continued to say that the next challenge was to bring more young players through. But a cast list which includes Steve Harmison, Paul Collingwood, Liam Plunkett and Phil Mustard, who have all played for England, plus Graham Onions and Mark Davies, who are knocking on the door, is better than most counties can boast.

If Cook still believes in the hungry fighter syndrome, he need look no further than Collingwood as a vindication. At under 19 level he would have lagged behind Robin Weston and Nicky Peng, who were outstanding schoolboy batsmen. But they would have had far more time and expense lavished on their coaching and ultimately possessed nothing like the hunger to succeed on a cricket field which drove Collingwood to the heights of England one-day captaincy.

Sadly, his England commitments meant he had little involvement with Durham winning the championship. But Harmison played a huge part and was very prominent in a thrilling climax, which is why I asked him to write the foreword for this book. In his younger days he wasn't always the easiest to deal with, but it was a measure of his progress as a person that throughout 2008 he spoke willingly to the media and always from the heart. No-one enjoyed the triumph more than he did.

CHAPTER 1

CHAMPIONS

STUFF of dreams, astounding achievement, call it what you will. There was indeed a fairytale element about Durham winning the County Championship in their 17th season in first-class cricket, but what made it truly remarkable was that only four years earlier they had finished bottom of the pile for the fifth time. When Steve Harmison found himself bottom of the pile at 11.44am on Saturday, September 27, 2008, it represented a moment of sheer ecstasy. He had just taken the final Kent wicket on a glorious Canterbury morning to seal the innings win which would leave Durham top of the table.

In 17 seasons of following their first-class fortunes I had never witnessed such an unforgettable sight as the players falling in a joyous heap after Harmison bowled Martin Saggers first ball. Some might have thought it unsightly, too redolent of football. But it wasn't meant to happen and the sheer spontaneity of it created a photographer's dream and an image which would last forever.

That it stemmed from Ben Harmison failing to hit the brakes after leading the enthusiastic rush to embrace his brother made it all the more poignant. The Bedser twins probably never reached such heights of ecstasy when capturing any of their seven successive titles at Surrey in the 1950s, but this was a genuinely historic moment.

Liam Plunkett, the 12th man, ran on to join the heap, from which one photograph showed Harmison's left arm sticking out in protective fashion (see front cover). It was in plaster because of a crack just above the wrist, resulting from an attempted gully catch, but if ever there was a moment when the pleasure was worth the pain this was it.

Although they had to wait several hours for confirmation, Durham knew that Nottinghamshire weren't going to beat Hampshire and the County Championship trophy would be coming to Chester-le-Street. The actual moment of confirmation, some four hours later, was slightly delayed. At that point Durham were watching Sky's transmission from Trent Bridge on the team bus, and just as the lbw appeal against last man Charlie Shreck went up the coach entered the Dartford Tunnel. When it emerged at the other end the last stragglers were trooping off at Nottingham and Durham knew they were champions. They alighted at their Riverside headquarters five hours later, still in their playing kit, a little the worse for wear.

There had been more snakes than ladders since Durham embarked on the journey in 1992. For their original chairman, Don Robson, and the others who realised the dream, just to have first-class cricket in the North-East was a reward in itself. Robson often recalled how, when the first season ended at Gateshead Fell's windswept ground, a stream of fans came up to thank him for a wonderful summer, even though Durham finished bottom, as they did in three of the first six years.

The captain for the first two years was David Graveney, who co-wrote with Jack Bannister the last book about the county (Durham CCC: Past, Present and Future), published in 1993. Graveney, who always had an excellent rapport with the press and public, concluded his account of the inaugural season with a moving tribute to the fans, particularly Malcolm Rooney, a promising player who had been crippled in a car accident. "Malcolm will always be my inspiration to play for Durham and be as successful as I can," wrote Graveney. "He is the epitome to all the players of the sheer passion and unique support they enjoy from the people in the North-East. The members and supporters are an inspiration. That is why Durham will be successful, and I only hope the first trophy comes during my time. If it doesn't I can assure them it will not be for lack of effort or planning. They deserve the best because they are the best."

If those words were to resonate 15 years later, what about the book's revelation concerning Clive Leach, who at the time was the Tyne Tees and Yorkshire Television chief executive? The book described how in the 1959 match against India at Sunderland Leach had opened the batting for Durham with 17-year-old Colin Milburn, who made a century. While the Milburn legend undoubtedly played a part in Durham's ascent to first-class status, it could equally be argued that the appointment of Leach as club chairman in 2004 kick-started the assault on the summit.

The highlight of that inaugural 1992 season was the first match, a Sunday League game against Lancashire. Had there been any rafters at the Racecourse people would have been hanging from them as 6,000 packed into the Durham University ground. Ian Botham opened the batting and after charging down the pitch, only to be stumped, he passed Dean Jones on the way in and told him: "This will be the slowest pitch you've ever played on."

No matter, Jones scored 114 and became an instant North-East legend as Durham won a thriller by nine runs. Botham running out Warren Hegg to seal the victory remains one of the magic moments in Durham's history, and despite the first championship win at Cardiff a few weeks later it was some time before it was upstaged.

It was in 2007 that Durham really became a major force, winning the Friends Provident Trophy and finishing second to Sussex in the championship. That was the year when 38-year-old Ottis Gibson indelibly etched his name in Durham folklore. He truly was the man with Hants in his pants as he took wickets with the first two balls of Hampshire's innings in the FPT final a few weeks after taking ten for 47 against them at Riverside. Gibson was only the third bowler in 50 years to take all ten in a county championship innings and he finished the season with 80 wickets. It was easily a Durham record and, despite a glut of home-grown seamers, there was some concern that he would be sorely missed when he took up the opportunity to become England's bowling coach.

In the event, the fact that Steve Harmison was available for much of the 2008 season, after being dropped by England, compensated for the absence of Gibson. Although he had no part in selection, Gibson observed at the end of the season that being axed in New Zealand had done Harmison good.

The bowler himself wouldn't have put it so bluntly, but he admitted that he had been rock bottom and that his determination to get his England place back had driven him on. He also acknowledged that because of the help Durham gave him he felt compelled, after being persuaded out of one-day international retirement, to go back to them at the end of the season and help them to the title.

Harmison's heartfelt words as he accepted two awards at Durham's Player of the Year dinner confirmed that here was a man on top of his game. To speak as he did confirmed how much his whole demeanour had recovered from the dark days of the previous winter. Referring to the immediate aftermath of that final wicket at Canterbury, he said: "The greatest pleasure for me was to see the joy on the young lads' faces. My brother Ben was the first to reach me, then the others piled in and we collapsed in a heap. I was just so pleased for them – it meant more to me than personal achievement. It was brilliant for the club and for the region.

"I love playing with Ben and the other young lads, but I also had a goal to get back in the England team, and I knew if I did that it would mean I'd helped Durham to have a good season. To be dropped by England hurt a lot. And when people started speculating that I might never play Test cricket again I was on the floor. I go out and perform as well as I can for any team. No captain has ever questioned my commitment. It's very amusing when you hear people like Bob Willis saying Durham are punching above their weight and I would never play for England again. I was determined to get back in the England team, but I wouldn't say I was motivated by wanting to answer my critics."

While Will Smith got the Durham members' vote as Player of the Year, Harmison received the accolade from his team-mates for his 60 championship wickets and all-round contributions. Injuries had always been a big setback for a paceman who needs to keep bowling and maintain his rhythm and confidence, and at the start of the season he was still struggling to find his best form. In the second game at Old Trafford, in which Durham suffered their only big defeat, by 232 runs, he had match figures of one for 100, while Jimmy Anderson had nine for 76 and Andrew Flintoff seven for 42.

Three wickets in each innings in the easy home win against Yorkshire which followed began the renaissance. Harmison barely looked back, other than in having to take a short break after bowling in pain from a foot injury suffered at Hove, where his hat-trick helped to secure a vital win.

"Staying fit is the key. I can't stress that enough," he said. "Having a good physio in Nigel Kent is a big help, and as you get older and wiser you know what you have to do. As long as I'm fit and my confidence is high I can just try to enjoy my cricket and believe anything is possible. When you are winning the little niggles don't hurt. I owed Durham so much for helping me back on my feet. I really wanted to come back after the one-day internationals and win the championship."

It was undoubtedly the wettest season in Durham's first-class existence, and while some might have felt that made the championship something of a lottery, the fact that Durham finished in the top four in all competitions meant it was widely acknowledged they were the best team. They were blessed with brilliant sunshine for their final day of glorious triumph. Even though it took the team only 74 minutes to wrap up the victory which saw them crowned champions, the 200 or so fans who made the trip to Kent would have a Canterbury tale to last a lifetime.

Among them was the most loyal supporter, 60-year-old Jim Kay, from

Tanfield Lea, near Stanley, who had missed only half a dozen games, home and away, in 17 seasons.

"This is the best day of my life since Sunderland won the FA Cup in 1973," he said. "I've stopped watching football – there's too much hassle. This is far more relaxing and there's a much better atmosphere."

Even before taking early retirement 18 months earlier, the ex-civil servant used to spend his entire holiday entitlement watching Durham. "Sometimes I drive, but on the longer trips like this I take the train. Everywhere I go I wear my Durham shirt in town and there's always someone wanting to talk cricket."

Also present were Tony Huzzard and his son, Geoff, from North Shields. They had risen at 2am and driven down, returning once the action was over. Two days later they were at Riverside when the team paraded the trophy in front of the fans to the strains of We Are The Champions and Tony said: "We wouldn't miss this for the world. People have told us we were mad for driving down to Kent through the night, but that's what it's all about. And the whole Durham story's a bit mad anyway."

The supporters at Canterbury had gathered in front of the pavilion after the victory, keen for any glimpse of their heroes, who soon emerged for photographs and to sign autographs. Few gave any credence to the remote possibility that Nottinghamshire could snatch the title by scoring 442 to beat Hampshire. But some retired to the bar, where the Trent Bridge match was being shown on television, and every time a wicket fell a huge roar went up from the Durham faithful.

When the great day had dawned it seemed the biggest threat might come from fog. That would have been the final kick in the teeth after a season in which Durham at one point saw eight championship days out of 11 washed out at their Riverside base. There had been a few wry smiles when fog delayed the start at Trent Bridge the previous day. Surely it couldn't happen in Canterbury? By 10.30 the ground was bathed in sunshine and while there was an autumnal tinge to the leaves of the replacement for the famous old lime tree there was a spring in Durham's step.

With five wickets to be taken the first was in the bag after ten minutes. Then came 55 minutes of defiance from Kent. It was during that period that I decided to forsake the homely old press box and savour the sunshine and the occasion in solitude. That was when I met Durham's coach, Geoff Cook, prowling the boundary alone, and I was neither surprised nor disappointed when he declined to discuss any celebrations. "There's still a lot of cricket to be played," he said.

Ten minutes later it was all over, the initial breakthrough being greeted by a rapturous jump for joy from Bob Robinson, of Cleadon, near South Shields, who was attending his fifth away game of the season with his wife, Margaret.

"We've been members since 1992 and it's been wonderful," he said. "We were at Lord's last year to see Durham win the Friends Provident Trophy. But I'm a four-day man, so this is better."

After Kent were all out for 204, with Callum Thorp taking a career-best seven for 88, another stalwart member, Quinton Phillips, of Aycliffe village, said: "I've enjoyed every minute since 1992, but I'm unexpectedly delighted about this because last week I didn't think we were going to do it. I was angry that they batted out time for a draw against Sussex instead of going for a win. I wondered are they men or boys? But they have really proved themselves here."

It had taken less than 20 years for the dreams of a handful of influential Durham cricket fans to be realised beyond their wildest imaginations. Two of the original six-man board, Bob Jackson and Tom Moffat, were still involved and both were at Canterbury, where Moffat said: "I never thought I'd live to see Test match status awarded to Chester-le-Street, and I certainly never thought I'd live to see this. It's a great thrill."

The same sentiments were echoed by Geoff Cook, although he pronounced them in the more studied manner which had been his trademark since the Durham dreamers appointed him as Director of Cricket in 1991.

Middlesbrough-born, the former England batsman had been a successful captain of Northamptonshire, although they were one of three counties, along with Somerset and Gloucestershire, beaten to their first championship by Durham.

Cook said: "I have been in the game for 36 years and the things I have stood for are based on traditional values of behaviour, team ethos and individual ambition. The culmination of all this has always been to win the county championship, so for us to do it with as nice a group of lads as you could possibly have means this is one of the sweetest moments of my career.

"It's always been a key element to have the sort of people who are turned on by the environment we were trying to create. If they are quality cricketers as well then you have a real chance. We have played some wonderful cricket. There was some inconsistency in the middle of the season with the variety of cricket we were having to play, but we got to two cup semi-finals and finished third in the Pro40 League. It's a tangible reward for players who have shown stamina, professionalism and desire to perform for a club that tries to do them proud.

"We played some dashing, outstanding cricket to win the Friends Provident Trophy last year, and that was a great moment for the spectators and players. But after 96 days of cricket this season we had to come out and play really well to give ourselves a chance of winning this title, and we did that when it really mattered.

"Individuals have improved. Ben Harmison has made an all-round contribution, Will Smith has been consistent in all competitions, and for Michael Di Venuto to score over 1,000 championship runs when he has often had to bat in tricky conditions is terrific. Callum Thorp has been very professional. He knows what he can do with his natural skills and we have reaped the benefit."

It was fitting that Cook should be back at the helm for this moment of triumph. The struggles in the early years had seen him adopt a less conspicuous role, concentrating on the academy with obvious success. But his return to senior duties at the start of the 2007 season came about only because Martyn Moxon, who had been the first team coach for six years, decided to take up the offer to return to Yorkshire. He had turned them down a few years earlier, saying he had unfinished business at Durham, and it was largely for family reasons that he eventually went back to his roots at a time when he must have suspected his work at Riverside could be about to bear fruit. His part in the story has tended to be overlooked, but he was always highly regarded at Durham and played an important role in laying the foundations for success.

Apart from Cook and two directors, one other official who had been ever-present was David Harker, initially as a young accountant and since 2000 as the club's chief executive. He travelled down to Canterbury after finishing his shift at Riverside the previous evening, along with events manager Richard Dowson, to witness the 74 minutes of action on the Saturday morning. The club's media manager, Yvette Thompson, had also arrived, to orchestrate the plethora of interviews.

Harker praised Cook for his role, among other things, in bringing the captain, Dale Benkenstein, to the club in 2005. "An agent had put Dale's name forward and Geoff said he knew a bit about him and thought we should go for him. We asked him to play a couple of games in the second team. It was a bit embarrassing getting a player of his calibre to play at that level, but he did and it confirmed Geoff's opinion of him."

Harker also stressed the huge impact made by Clive Leach, who had been head-hunted to come in as chairman in 2004. He had played for Warwickshire in the late 1950s and for Durham as a minor county while with the Bishop Auckland club.

"Getting Clive involved was about raising the funds to develop the stadium," said Harker. "But he made it very clear from day one that if we were to have any credibility we had to invest in the core business. The development of the ground didn't make sense otherwise. We didn't have the working capital to finance team building, so it was risky. But he was adamant, and with the confidence that came from his success in business he was comfortable with taking the risk. It gave Geoff the opportunity to recruit players who have helped us win the title, so Clive's commitment to cricket has been massively influential."

For many regular observers, however, the greatest influence in the transformation from pits to prizes had been Benkenstein, who in his third season as captain was determined to bow out at the top and announced afterwards that he would be standing down.

He said: "It has been unbelievably enjoyable with this group of players. That's what makes it a great team – they are a fantastic group of people to work with. It helps you to get through the bad patches you have in any season. We have a mixture of experience and youth, and you have to have the experience there for the youngsters to learn from.

"We lost in the semi-finals of the Friends Provident Trophy and the Twenty20 Cup, and the disappointment drains you, so to come back and win the main event is really special. It's been brilliant working with Geoff Cook. He has been the real heart and soul of the club and a lot of the success is down to the effort he has put in over almost 20 years. We are the end product of that."

Benkenstein, who was made captain of Natal at 22 and won several trophies in his eight seasons at the helm, jokingly added: "To me this feels quite normal, but for the fans and the management it's the ultimate. There are a few counties who have never won it. Since I have been here we have always been moving forward. We have changed the mental approach so that from ball one this season we have been saying we could win every competition and everyone believed it."

CHAPTER 2

THE REPORTER'S
LOT

SO, that's chapter one out of the way. That was the easy bit. It was a re-hash of my reporting of Durham's County Championship triumph, which provided the catalyst for a book I had otherwise planned to write in semi-retirement several years down the line.

Having adopted the usual policy of putting the highlights first, should I now follow the standard procedures of slipping seamlessly back to where it all began, continuing on a chronological path thereafter? Or, by way of contrast with chapter one, should I continue with the sort of ramblings not normally permissible in concise, factual newspaper reporting? Something more personalised, which is what people seem to like. As a lover of getting off the beaten track, the book will be littered with meanderings.

I'm also a firm believer in the therapeutic value of a good chortle, so I often wish I could spend time among the wags in the crowd like the one who responded to the news of David Boon's signing by saying: "It's Daniel Boon we need."

The public address announcers often provoke a titter, especially the one who began one day: "For anyone interested in cricket." Those at other counties have occasionally been set up and the Lancashire players once arranged for the Old Trafford announcer to put out a message for someone who was supposedly from Upper Ramsbottom. No, there isn't a Lower Ramsbottom, either.

Umpire Barrie Leadbeater once became irritated by having his name pronounced "better" rather than "beeter" every time he was welcomed on to the field at Darlington. When he kept complaining the other umpire, Alan Whitehead, suggested he should have a word. On the final morning they walked out to hear: "Please welcome our umpires, Barrie Leadbeeeeeter and Alan Whiteside."

Announcing a new bowler is among the duties, and as the Indian all-rounder Manoj Prabhakar was about to deliver his first ball for Durham in 1995 the PA man asked the scorer, Brian Hunt: "Is this John Wood?"

Fond of a laugh himself, Brian is an invaluable source of amusement as well as statistical information, and if he personally doesn't feature at regular intervals in the following pages he will always be there in spirit, lurking between the lines. Only he, and perhaps devoted fan Jim Kay, quoted in chapter one, have seen as much Durham cricket as I have. Brian had been Durham's part-time scorer since 1975 and was 44 when he became the youngest "chalker" on the first-class circuit in 1992, since when his only absences have been when he has been required for international duty back at Riverside.

When he made his England debut, in the one-day match against the West Indies at Riverside in 2000, he had to travel overnight from Leicester then be back with Durham at Southgate the following day. Still, it would be worth the effort to score for England, wouldn't it? I asked. "No" was the swift reply from a Bishop Aucklander who has always delighted in his duties with Durham. He wasn't exactly thrilled about the six bottles of wine he received for 25 years' service, but was paid the ultimate accolade for a scorer of being awarded a testimonial in 2009.

If chapter one seemed overloaded with quotes, it was because I consider them exceptionally good quotes, far better than the standard nannies (from nanny goats), as we often call them in the newspaper trade. If you're not sure you agree, re-read those quotes and compare them with the bland, bog-standard statements of the obvious from footballers and their managers which, for reasons beyond my comprehension, occupy vast tracts of our newspapers.

Most of chapter one's quotes were gathered exclusively by me on that final morning at Canterbury, the exceptions being some of those attributed to Steve Harmison and Dale Benkenstein. They were quizzed by a posse of Sunday newspaper correspondents for whom the unlikely realisation of the Durham dream provided a welcome break from their obsession with the England team.

With Harmison they still wanted to fit it into an England context as he had recently made his comeback in the final Test of the series against South Africa, then came out of one-day international retirement, and faced a busy winter beginning with the Stanford Challenge match in Antigua. Benkenstein, open and honest as ever, confirmed what he had told me on a wet day at Taunton two weeks earlier that he wished to hand over the reins to Will Smith. He raised a few eyebrows among the Sunday correspondents when he said he felt Smith could go on to captain England.

Benkenstein is his own man, otherwise this might have been construed as a classic case of toeing the Durham line by accentuating the positive. It was such an ingrained trait during Don Robson's chairmanship that I suspected the induction course for members of staff might involve an element of brainwashing in a dark room somewhere in the bowels of Riverside. We never saw that room, but there also appeared to be a determination to keep the press in the dark, even about matters of general public interest.

This, of course, goes hugely against the grain for those seeking truth and honesty. I don't like having the wool pulled over my eyes, partly because I believe the members have a right to know what's going on. I can accept a reluctance to discuss a potential signing in case it scuppers the deal, but putting a positive slant on things in a deliberate effort to distort the truth smacks too heavily of politics.

Robson had played football for Doncaster and Gateshead, plus Tyneside league cricket, and made some money from the construction industry and sports shops. But he was primarily a politician. He was affable, polite and always returned telephone calls, but he seemed to harbour a general distrust of the press and this helped to foster the impression among many of the staff that the local media were negative.

We always remarked how it was only the negative bits they seemed to see, and now I can tell them that out of darkness comes light. In order to appreciate fully the euphoria of the title-clinching moment it was necessary to have witnessed the years of struggle, shared the agonies and reported them accurately rather than coating them in a superficial, meaningless gloss.

We tread a fine line between upsetting players, possibly harming their confidence, and giving the readers what they want. A letter writer to The Northern Echo once suggested it was time to end my "cosy relationship" with Durham. This was after I took an admittedly sympathetic line when they lost a 1999 NatWest Trophy tie on a pudding of a pitch in Holland. As Dutch cricket writers are a little thin on the ground, it fell to me to decide the Man of the Match, which wasn't difficult as Feiko Kloppenburg performed a decisive role with bat and ball.

It's one of those names you don't forget, nor have I forgotten how eloquently the Holland captain, ex-Somerset seamer Roland Lefebvre, spoke afterwards about how much the victory would lift Dutch cricket. In hindsight, his words were not exactly prophetic, but his passion, sincerity and faultless use of the English language earned him a place on my list of cricketers to whom it has been a pleasure to speak. I can't imagine saying the same about people tainted by football's degrading culture.

Many county cricket club members, probably more so at Headingley than Riverside, do expect to see their team pilloried in print if they perform badly, and without pandering to their wishes the reporter's role must lean more towards pleasing the punters than providing a public relations service for the club.

I have been well aware since Minor Counties days of how easily some players are offended. I had played with or against most of the team from the late 1970s and early 80s and enjoyed their company, particularly the opening batsmen, Steve Atkinson and Paul Romaines. But things soured during later years, when the captain, Neil Riddell, preferred to surround himself with veteran former first-class players such as Steve Greensword, Peter Kippax and Paul Newman rather than promising youngsters. He even took a gamble, which backfired, on Middlesex reject Jamie Sykes. Any hint of criticism did not go down well.

In 1992 I was naïve enough to think professionals would be more inclined to accept the criticism alongside the praise because they were being paid. But even a seasoned pro like Wayne Larkins was not as thick-skinned as might be imagined. He took me to task for reporting that he had scored a "magnificent" century against the Australians on a "featherbed" pitch at the Durham University ground.

"What's a featherbed?" he asked, implying that use of what I now admit is a pretty meaningless word had undermined his achievement, and adding that it hadn't been a featherbed when the tourists batted because Simon Brown bowled them out. My protests that Brown took his seven wickets through swing, needing no help from the pitch, cut little ice.

Generally I got on well with the man known as Ned and will always consider it a great privilege to have watched him bat. The same could be said of John Morris, an affable character who unfortunately reached his greatest heights in his Tiger Moth sortie with David Gower in Australia. I am by no means alone in feeling that Morris had sufficient talent to have enjoyed a successful Test career, but he didn't like it when anyone suggested he had under-achieved, insisting that with more than 20,000 first-class runs his record bore comparison with any of his contemporaries.

He played for Durham at a difficult time in their evolution and in 100 first-class matches he scored 14 centuries and averaged 32.77. It is partly a reflection of the climate and the pitches that while Durham have produced a plethora of seamers, no spinners of great note have emerged and few batsmen. The only Englishmen to have averaged better than Morris over more than a few games for Durham are Larkins (the best at 37.52), Paul Parker, and Paul Collingwood. But Morris endured long barren periods and his popularity with the members slowly waned.

In his fifth season he was averaging 19 in the championship when it was announced that he would have a benefit the following year, which had been agreed when he initially signed his six-year contract. The members felt he was jumping the queue ahead of Simon Brown and when Morris scored a century shortly afterwards against Glamorgan he raised a V-sign towards a section of the crowd on reaching three figures.

He had been barracked from that area when fielding on the boundary the previous day, but insisted there was nothing offensive in his gesture, which was caught on camera. "I was gesturing to a mate who had bet me £20 I wouldn't score a century," he said. He even named the friend and added: "If the members think I was gesturing at them, I apologise. I have no quarrel with them."

It didn't look good and he would obviously have preferred it not to be publicised, but I had to point out that the freelance photographer who had captured the moment on film would be selling his picture as widely as possible, so I could hardly hush it up. Local television also had some footage of it.

Quoting him as I did, without comment, was an example of letting someone put his own side of the story and leaving the readers to make their own judgement. I wasn't born yesterday, but Morris was so plausible and self-assured in his explanation that he had either been tipped off that we were coming to ask him about his gesture or he was telling the truth. Or possibly he was much quicker at thinking on his feet than I had suspected.

Either way, he shot himself in the foot when he returned to Riverside with Nottinghamshire two years later. His one-day record for Durham was surprisingly poor but on this occasion he made 73 before falling to a brilliant catch by Ian Hunter. Instead of departing humbly, he kept looking across at Hunter as though he couldn't believe he was out, which is probably what prompted a shout from a spectator. Morris again responded with an offensive gesture, which was again caught on camera, and this time he said: "I just waved back at the crowd as I left. They gave me a bit of a send-off, so I waved back at them. It wasn't malicious on either part. If people have a problem with me having a bit of fun, then so be it."

Perhaps therein lay the problem. Everyone knew from his Tiger Moth jaunt that Morris likes a bit of fun, and we shouldn't blame anyone for that – unless it offends others.

Whether my reporting of those incidents turned him against me I'm not sure, but Morris is one of two players who have waved their bats in my direction on reaching 50. Both got out immediately afterwards, mission apparently accomplished. In Morris's case it was for Nottinghamshire in a one-day match at Trent Bridge. He had the game in his pocket, but got out carelessly two balls later and his team scrambled to victory off the last ball.

The other player who offered me a triumphal "up your's mate" gesture was Phil Bainbridge, probably in response to me criticising his selection when he had already announced he would be retiring at the end of the season. A gritty all-rounder whose batting average for Durham was almost identical to Morris's, he got out the very next ball. So the message must be that either waving at Press boxes is bad for your concentration or the pen is mightier than the bat.

I once heard of a footballer grabbing a reporter by the throat and pinning him up against the wall, demanding: "How dare you describe me with that word you used last week?" "What word was that?" gasped the reporter. "Ubiquitous," was the reply. Such extremes do not occur in cricket, although there was a look of menace on Kevin Shine's face when Dermot Reeve, as Somerset coach, once brought him and Graham Rose to our press cabin. I had written that the visitors appeared to lack back-up bowling and as he marched in Reeve said: "I'd like to introduce you to two of my back-up bowlers."

I pointed out that they were frontline bowlers and my report was referring to the fact that they had had to bring on the innocuous medium pace of Michael Burns for nine overs. Reeve, though bumptious, was pleasant enough and said it hadn't particularly bothered him, but the two lads were upset about it. Judging by the look on his face, Shine was the one who had really taken exception.

It was towards the end of the inaugural season in 1992, during which I stayed with the team, that I was twice verbally accosted in the hotel bar by Phil Bainbridge. We laughed about it later, and just before he retired in 1996 he presented me with one of his benefit ties "to show there are no hard feelings". The gesture was appreciated and he seemed pleased to see that I was wearing the tie when we later bumped into each other at Bristol. But, unwittingly, he had already done me a huge favour four years earlier by persuading me that, in addition to my general dislike of hotels, it was probably not a good idea to stay with the team.

That enabled me to expand my voyage of discovery round the first-class shires, staying in the sort of rural retreats which have greatly enhanced my summers. Sheepscombe (Gloucestershire), Watterow (Somerset), Ockley (Surrey), Dedham (Essex) and Over Haddon, overlooking Lathkill Dale in Derbyshire, top the list. Then there's Alresford, where John Arlott lived in Hampshire, Kislingbury outside Northampton, plus several north Cheshire villages easily accessible from Old Trafford. They are all delightful places where lovely people provide bed and breakfast in peace and great comfort at rather less then hotel prices. Some of these places, notably Sheepscombe, Ockley and Kislingbury, boast beautiful cricket grounds, ideal for a few gentle early-morning laps to sweat out the remnants of the previous night's beer and develop an appetite for the freshly-cooked breakfast which awaits at 8.30.

The starting time is, of course, a big advantage. Only when there has been a specific reason to do so have I arrived at grounds much before 11am, knowing I might not get away until 8pm. I often travel 20 miles or more in preference to staying in a functional, but soulless, lodge alongside the ground. My longest journey is from the Wenlock Edge Inn in Shropshire to get to Edgbaston. Traffic has increased since I discovered it to the extent that a 45-minute drive now takes an hour, but it's still worth it.

Sadly, I cannot claim to have seen every ball of Brian Lara's 501 not out in 1994 because I was a few minutes late that day, having dawdled in from Wenlock Edge knowing that on its final day the match had nowhere to go. That, of course, was why Lara was able to do what he did. It ought to have been one of those "I was there" occasions, but I don't look back on it with any more fondness than Durham's wicketkeeper Chris Scott. He dropped Lara on 18 and said: "I suppose he'll go on to get a hundred now."

My discovery of Wenlock Edge came courtesy of the Good Pub Guide, along with the one other pub I still stay at, if the opportunity arises, the Lathkil. (Yes, it is spelt with one L, even though there are two in the name of the Derbyshire dale it overlooks, and if you ask the friendly landlord, Robert Grigor-Taylor, why this is so he will explain over an excellent pint of Hartington, or black pudding if he is serving breakfast at the time).

I initially used the Good Pub Guide for a couple of years before realising there was greater comfort and better value to be had from country B and Bs, which in any case usually have a good pub nearby. The Butcher's Arms at

Sheepscombe is the perfect example, while near Alresford is the Bush at Ovington, with its beer garden running down to the crystal clear waters of the River Itchen. Near Ockley is the Parrott at Forest Green, overlooking another idyllic cricket ground in the Surrey Hills. Those hills also house Coldharbour, where the Plough Inn has its own Leith Hill Brewery, named after the county's highest summit. Access to this is via a forested track opposite the pub and halfway up, in a sudden clearing, is the village cricket ground. The pub at nearby Friday Street seems to be more of a restaurant now, but is worth visiting for the sylvan setting and the sheer adventure of finding it.

This is quite a contrast from the terraced houses of the Durham village called No Place, but that's the setting for the wonderfully old-fashioned pub I always recommend to visitors to Chester-le-Street. It's called the Beamish Mary and has provided beer, bed and lashings of good food at exceptional value for several appreciative cricket writers.

On my way home from Riverside I tend to call at the Crown at Manfield, where the ever-changing choice of immaculately-kept real ales takes some beating. But if I had to nominate my favourite pub it would be the Royal Oak at Luxborough, in Somerset's Brendon Hills, where I have to stoop slightly after lifting the latch to pass through the doorway. The cosy, stone-flagged bar, with logs stacked ready for winter next to the big open fire, serves those excellent local beers, Cotleigh Tawny and Exmoor Gold, and is the sort of dedicated drinking area which is all too rare these days, and of which I heartily approve. A modern, and very tasteful, extension is provided for the purpose of sampling food which could not be faulted on my last visit.

On a brief sortie into Devon I was hugely impressed by the Nobody Inn at Doddiscombsleigh, but that was a one-off a few years ago. So, having become reacquainted with Somerset following their promotion, I can confirm that the Globe at Appley remains top-notch. Tucked away in an intricate network of sunken lanes, it is another lovely old pub in an area I greatly missed visiting during the two years it took Somerset to follow Durham into division one. Which reminds me that the downside of that glorious title-clinching day at Canterbury was that Kent were relegated, robbing me of my annual visit to wonderful Whitstable.

With the Bat and Ball opposite the entrance gates, Canterbury is one of the few grounds (Hove is another) where there is still a temptation to nip out for a quick one at lunchtime, or to congregate with fellow scribes at close of play. Advancing years have given me the power to resist more often than not, which is regrettable as there is much to be said for the old traditions and it is one of life's pleasing coincidences that cricket and real ale have a strong bond. There's nothing like a pint of Adnam's Broadside for fuelling debate about the game's intricacies, unless it be Barnsley Bitter or one of Timothy Taylor's brews, or Brakspear's or Wadworth's or Jennings'. It must be something to do with rural tradition: cricket on village greens, played by blacksmiths who bowled fast and supped hard in the adjoining boozer afterwards.

Sheepscombe had a legendary paceman named Frank Mansell, who opened the bowling for nearby Miserden at 14 and was said to have been persuaded to switch clubs in 1946 with the help of cider. This is Cider With Rosie country, the book written by Laurie Lee, who became a great friend of Mansell's and was in such regular attendance that Sheepscombe's ground is named after him. As the village is in a steep-sided valley with little flat ground in the bottom, the Laurie Lee Field sits high on the southern slope, where it begins to level out.

There are magnificent views of Painswick away to the west, and across the sort of valley where plumes of woodsmoke should be a permanent feature. In early morning the only sound is birdsong and the chiming church clock. Even the cricket ground is by no means flat, yet Mansell apparently always bowled uphill, with only his head visible at the start of his run-up. Such is the climb that he could have been forgiven had he dubbed the crease Base Camp Three, yet he took 141 wickets in 1964 and 135 in 1967, and played for the club for 30 years. Some said he could have played for Gloucestershire, but Bristol probably didn't appeal.

Perhaps I digress, but it was at Laurie Lee's local, the Woolpack in Slad, that I celebrated one of the great days of Durham cricket with a couple of pints of Uley bitter. It was Saturday, May 15, 2004 and I was moving on for a one-day match at Worcester from the final day at Taunton, where Durham had needed 450 to win and were 95 for five when Gareth Breese went in. The little Jamaican made 165 not out and they won by one wicket.

Happy days, indeed, but into every life a little rain must fall. By way of explaining that there's always a price to pay, or a cross to be borne, or that Sod's Law is never far from the surface, I will remember Saturday, July 26, 2008 for all the wrong reasons. In an otherwise sodden summer Durham suffered their worst couple of hours in glorious sunshine on Twenty20 finals day at the Rose Bowl, and I drove there and back in the day (600 miles) to witness it.

In truth, I didn't want to go, chiefly because in my view Twenty20 is an abomination. It is cricket's contribution to dumbing down when this most civilised of games ought to be doing its bit to maintain standards. It will also be the death of bowlers, but on the day in question it served to embarrass the batsman who would a few weeks later be named International Player of the Year, Shivnarine Chanderpaul. The dapper craftsman's game is ill-suited to this form of kamikaze cricket, which he had not previously played for Durham.

They didn't come into first-class cricket to play this nonsense, but in their determination to cast off the worst Twenty20 record among the first-class counties they had signed the big-hitting South African, Albie Morkel, as their official overseas man for the middle part of the season. Having helped them to reach the semi-finals, he was no longer available and Chanderpaul's 48 from 47 balls proved inadequate. Durham scored 138 for six, then Tyron Henderson blasted seven sixes in thrashing an unbeaten 57 off 22 balls before also contributing with bat and ball as Middlesex won a tense final against Kent after amassing 187 for six. Henderson, a burly South African, was well known to Dale Benkenstein, who in an aside to me after the official press conference said: "He's just a slogger."

On the way back to the media centre on the opposite side of the ground from the pavilion where the conference had been held, I was delayed by a line of men wearing wigs, skirts and false breasts doing the conga. There are circumstances in which I might have found this very amusing, but not when I was anxious to reach the car and get the hell out of there.

In the early days there were three newspapermen and a BBC radio reporter covering Durham full-time, but since around the turn of the century I'm the only one who has travelled, thanks to The Northern Echo's editor possessing the wisdom to realise I provide value for money. I always enjoyed the company of Jeff Brown, then of the Newcastle Journal and Chronicle and latterly a TV man, and Tim Rich, an Essex boy taken on by the Sunderland Echo specifically to cover Durham until he deservedly graduated to higher things.

We enjoyed a lively camaraderie in the rickety old cabin which served as our press box until the Riverside's extremely plush media centre was built to cater for the hordes who arrive for Test matches. There was something of the absent-minded professor about Filthy Rich, as he was known by the players, although they would have been shocked to discover how little he earned. His photographic memory was a great help to us all, but he was also quick to see the humorous side of things, nicknaming another county's particularly miserable scorer the Cheerful Chalker.

In those early days the evening paper men were still required to file a report around noon and when Durham were playing at Portsmouth in 1994 I glanced over Rich's shoulder an hour into the first day to note that he had begun: "The only Victory Durham will see here is the one moored in Portsmouth harbour." And they accuse me of being negative! Durham almost won that match thanks to young Jimmy Daley, middle name Arthur, making 159 not out in the second innings, convincing everyone that he could be Durham's No 4 for the next 15 years. Sadly, it wasn't to be.

I remember that among the scribes impressed by Daley's debut was Dicky (D J) Rutnagur, who wrote for The Daily Telegraph from 1966 to 2005. He was always a very agreeable companion, as was The Guardian's David Foot, who had an uncanny ability to wrap up a day's play in a lovely, lyrical style without missing any of the essential details. I once went with those two, plus Ivo Tennant, of The Times, to a Hampshire hostelry which, according to the Good Pub Guide, offered unusual dishes such as kangaroo and ostrich.

As I was reminded when seeking out the GPG's Gloucestershire Dining Pub of the Year for 2007, only to find it boarded up, any guide can quickly become outdated. In the Hampshire case it was immediately obvious that the pub must have changed hands as the specials board offered bangers and mash. Tennant, who also writes about wine, had presumably not considered this possibility when he asked to see the wine list. The landlady replied: "We've got house white and house red."

She seemed determined, however, to compensate for these limitations and fussed around us very attentively throughout a very convivial evening. No doubt she was cajoled by Dicky, who retained much of his youthful charm.

After retirement, he wrote in the 2007 Wisden of how, in his early days "county press boxes had at least six occupants on any given day, almost every one a true character." He would find it bemusing that nowadays some of them bury their heads in the internet throughout the day, apparently worried about missing useful titbits of information. Dicky went on to talk about the entertainers of 30–40 years ago out in the middle, observing: "Colin Milburn became a legend before he had played five seasons. As a person, warm and modest, and as a cricketer, dashing and chivalrous, he was a priceless asset to English cricket. When there was all that fuss about Freddie

Flintoff's girth and his fondness for a pie and a pint, one wondered if there would have been a place in today's cricket for that dearest of fat men."

Phil Mustard might have had a tendency towards porkiness were it not for modern fitness requirements. He has been one of Durham's modern characters, offering Milburnesque strokes and revelling in the nickname "Colonel" after Colonel Mustard of Cleudo fame.

One of the older characters in the press box these days is Norman Harris, a man with an eye for the offbeat angle. He left London for the wilds of Northumberland a few years ago and covers Durham's home games for The Times. It was reassuring to hear that some of the old standards still apply when he received a call from the desk at 10.30 one night asking where the dagger which goes alongside the wicketkeeper should appear in the Somerset scoreboard. Regular keeper Rob Turner had retired hurt and been replaced by Michael Burns. It was tempting to suggest they should ask Colonel Mustard, who might have proposed a dagger for Turner and a candlestick for Burns.

To return to Jimmy Daley, he was a polite and unassuming character from the former pit village of Eppleton, and he epitomised what Durham's elevation to first-class status was supposed to be all about. The county's history was littered with home-loving lads who failed to flourish elsewhere, and here was one in his late teens who suddenly had the opportunity to realise his potential on his doorstep.

Daley was the members' favourite batsman, but he suffered a series of broken fingers on early Riverside pitches and was further sidelined by the panic which gripped the Don Robson regime after Michael Roseberry's reign as captain ended in disappointment in its second season in 1996. Bringing in David Boon to succeed him was a master stroke, but to sign Jon Lewis from Essex, Martin Speight from Sussex and Nick Speak from Lancashire at the same time was over the top. There was no room for Daley and when he did eventually get a chance and scored a nice 50 at Darlington I asked Boon if that had earned Jimmy a run in the team.

This was a captain we had been told had been brought in with carte blanche to do as he liked, but the muttered response from underneath that famous moustache was along the lines of: "You can't print this, but it's political." There were threats of physical violence if those words got into the papers, and while the threat may have been lighthearted I knew I'd get no more assistance from Mr Boon if I didn't heed his words. Ten years later I'm prepared to risk him sending round a hit-man.

Back on a lighter note, in those early days we still had to dictate our reports to copy-takers, which was a regular source of amusement. Players who retire and move straight into the media are not always well received and in Simon Hughes' first season of reporting he came to Durham's opening match at Chesterfield. As he dictated his first few paragraphs, which amounted to a lavish description of the ground's foliage, one illustrious wordsmith rose to his feet and bellowed: "What's this. Nature notes?" Another began his report: "Durham are looking a much better side now they have cleared out the dead wood," Hughes having retired at the end of the previous season. He's a thick-skinned character, who shrugged it all off and went on to create a very good career for himself. Some more famous players have found it's not as easy as they imagined.

Derbyshire press boxes invariably had the best craic and it was there that one of our members once accused the Benson & Hedges Cup caterers of supplying deep-fried roofing felt in the lunchtime buffet. When we didn't eat whatever it was, it reappeared at tea-time, prompting the observation: "Caterers enforce follow-on."

The best copy-taking laughs arose from the howlers which appeared at the other end, and among those which got past the sub-editors was a reference to a bowler exploiting a "lamp post" on the pitch. It should have read "damp spot". The best may be apocryphal, but it's worth repeating. A Yorkshire Evening Post reporter at Scarborough dictated: "the ball flew over the slips and into the deep for three." It appeared in the paper as "over the cliffs and into the deep blue sea."

Which leads me seamlessly on again to my favourite grounds. Scarborough, with its amphitheatre-like quality and seaside atmosphere, earns my vote for the best viewing arena, and it always saddens me that whoever programmes the fixture computer at Lord's can't make it see the absolute sense of staging the Yorkshire v Durham match there on a regular basis. My favourite headquarters ground is Worcester, not so much for the cathedral, which is no match for Durham's, as for the delightful ladies' tea pavilion, where a refreshing brew and scrumptious home-baked cakes are served in mid-afternoon just when my full English breakfast has worn off. Is it the ladies who are delightful, or the pavilion? Both, of course.

Having tolerated a leaking cabin for 12 years, I'm quite prepared to put up with the lack of facilities at outgrounds, where we often watch from a tent. But I bemoan the fact that the pitches are rarely conducive to four-day cricket. Horsham and Arundel in Sussex are a delight to visit, as are

Cheltenham College and Chesterfield, but trips to Blackpool, Basingstoke, Tunbridge Wells and Kidderminster have been infuriatingly brief because of the clatter of wickets.

Sadly, Durham haven't used an outground since a pitch panel was convened after the match against Kent at Stockton in 2006. As the visitors topped 400 in their second innings, the good people of Stockton could scarcely believe the lengths, and the expense, to which the panel went to decide that the pitch was below average but not worthy of a points deduction. No club in the country, in my experience, has been more hospitable.

Durham were involved in the last match in the public park at Weston Super Mare in 1996. That's why I know that the last bowler to take a first-class wicket there was the same man who was bowled first ball by Steve Harmison to complete the win at Canterbury which clinched the championship. At Weston the man in question had been a Durham player, and while he went on to play for England I wonder if there was a pang of jealousy as Durham celebrated his first-ball demise 12 years later in such joyous fashion. Knowing the gratitude he felt towards Durham for giving him a belated first-class opportunity at the age of 24, I suspect that the ex-Norfolk bowler Martin Saggers might even have been tempted to join in.

CHAPTER 3

GRASS ROOTS

IT is often said that Durham is divided by the A1. To the east lie the remnants of the mining and shipbuilding which formed the backbone of the county's industry; to the west lie the moorlands and the dales. In Teesdale, where some still claim a Yorkshire birthright, many of the villages have cricket teams. But further north in Weardale village cricket has been all but extinct for years.

Not that the farmers thereabouts have no interest in the game. One of them showed his knowledge in memorable fashion when he visited Darlington for Durham's 1984 NatWest Trophy match against Northamptonshire. Like most farmers from his locality he was in the habit of ending each sentence with the words "tha knaz" (a colloquialism for "you know".)

His recollection of the last time Durham had played Northants, in 1977, went something along these lines: "Northants had four Test players, tha knaz. They had David Steele, tha knaz. They had Mushtaq Mohammad, tha knaz. They had Bishen Bedi, tha knaz. And they had Sarfraz Nawaz, tha knaz."

He might have added that, despite all that talent, Northants were given an enormous fright by Durham, or more specifically by Stuart Wilkinson, the man who had clean bowled Geoff Boycott in the famous Gillette Cup victory at Harrogate in 1973. A bowler of genuine pace, Wilkinson shot out Roy Virgin, Peter Willey, Steele and Mushtaq as Northants slumped to 17 for four in reply to 151. But they more than any other county had tapped into the North-East's rich seam of talent and their Hartlepool-born wicketkeeper, George Sharp, saw them to a three-wicket win with 35 not out.

Hartlepool is part of long stretch of coastline which was formerly blighted by industry but has produced plenty of first-class cricketers. Peter Willey learned his cricket at Seaham Harbour, Bob Willis was born at Sunderland, and Bob Carter, part of Worcestershire's pace attack from

1961-72, came from Horden. From 1986-90 four youngsters from Boldon went into the first-class game, among them Simon Brown, who would return to play such a prominent role with Durham and earn an England cap. He was joined at Northants by his school friend Gareth Smith, who dismissed Sunil Gavaskar with his second ball on his debut and later moved on to Warwickshire. The other Boldon boys were Andrew Robson, who went to Surrey, and Martin Thursfield, who signed first for Middlesex then Hampshire.

Boldon, Horden and Seaham Harbour are Durham Senior League clubs in an area where the character of the people and the landscape was largely fashioned at the coalface. Their cricket was characterised by down-to-earth humour, such that if a pompous paceman from Durham City marked out a long run-up he would be told: "We don't go that far on our holidays." And when he delivered the ball he would be told he carried it faster than he bowled it. Or if he were a spinner he'd be told he couldn't turn a mangle. Batsmen on Durham club grounds have often been distracted by a sudden flurry of pigeons being released from their cree directly behind the bowler's arm. It only seems to happen to opposing batsmen, particularly those with fancy gear.

As a player, I once received a hot reception at Blackhall for being foolish enough to write in my North Yorkshire and South Durham League column that they would again be cast in the role of doormats. Once we'd had a few beers afterwards in a boozer down Ninth Street (or was it Fifth or Sixth Street?) we parted on amicable terms and a couple of years later they brought in Desmond Haynes as their professional. He liked it well enough to return and was followed by Roger Harper then Clayton Lambert, who was in his fifth season with the club when he was called up to replace Gordon Greenidge in the 1991 West Indian party. Another former West Indian Test player, Derek Parry, kept returning to play at Horden for more than ten years.

Also hidden away along that coast for the latter part of his life was the legendary Alex Coxon, who set up an indoor cricket school near Sunderland, where he had been the club professional. He was said to be brilliant with youngsters, but maintained the same hostility towards adults which was ever-present in his bowling. Born in Huddersfield, he overlapped briefly in the Yorkshire team with Fred Trueman and could also bat, taking him into the England team at Lord's in 1948, when he was convinced he had Don Bradman lbw for nought. What he said to the umpire who rejected his appeal is not recorded, but it was reported that he had a fight with Denis Compton in the dressing room. He was not selected again and two years later, after taking 131 wickets in the season, he was sacked by Yorkshire.

He moved to Durham, but even his career with them ended badly, against Lancashire seconds at Old Trafford in 1954. Roy Collins was flaying the bowling on a wet wicket when Coxon called for sawdust. A young groundstaff boy asked where he would like it and Coxon reportedly said: "Put t'bugger there," pointing to a spot on a length where he was aiming to pitch the ball. The sawdust was duly deposited and a team-mate observed: "It was more like a butcher's shop than a cricket pitch." The only fielder not amused was the Durham captain, Bill Proud, who hailed from Bishop Auckland but had been educated at Winchester and Oxford. He had a heated conversation with Coxon along the lines of "I never thought anybody could be so daft" and Coxon never played for Durham again.

He died, aged 90, in 2006, the same year as Arthur Austin, after whom Austin's bar at Durham's Riverside ground is named. He lived to be 97 and was an altogether different character who wore a cravat when batting and was known as the perfect gentleman. A wicketkeeper who stood up even to Coxon, he stumped almost as many as he caught and went on to join the committee in 1951, serving as chairman from 1975 until first-class status arrived when he was 82. In recognition of his services he was made club patron.

Even in his 80s Austin clearly recalled playing in the 1936 side which beat All India by five wickets in a two-day match at Sunderland's Ashbrooke ground. From early in the century until 1962 Durham played the touring team 26 times, but this was their only victory. The Indians included batsman V M Merchant and wicketkeeper D D Hindekar, who both returned with the Test team ten years later. Austin recalled how the Indian captain, Maharajah Sir V A Vizianagram, always fielded in a brown trilby hat.

Austin also played in the 1938 match, when 26,000 packed into Ashbrooke to watch the Australians, and almost as many turned up when they returned ten years later with a team which included Keith Miller and Neil Harvey. Although it was decided in 1991 that the Ashbrooke square wasn't suitable for first-class cricket, it had long been regarded as Durham's headquarters and it was there that 17-year-old Colin Milburn, in his only appearance for the county, scored 101 against India in 1959.

From 1864 to 1991 there were 120 Durham-born graduates to the higher level, but 35 of those played in first-class matches only for the Minor Counties or for Oxford or Cambridge Universities. So the idea of a constant supply going off to play for first-class counties is something of a myth. It has long been my belief that the myth was perpetuated by the legend of Milburn. Prior to 1992 seven other Durham-born cricketers had played for England, but only Willey, Willis and A E (Andrew) Stoddart had more than ten caps. And Willis lived on Wearside for only six weeks before his father, who had emerged from mining stock to become a journalist with the Sunderland Echo, took a job in Manchester.

During his pomp, Milburn was described by John Arlott as "the best-loved cricketer of modern times" and was remembered as much for his Falstaffian bulk, and for his cavalier approach as an opening batsman, as for his actual deeds. Although he hit two brilliant centuries and averaged 46.71 for England, he played in only nine Tests and was often overlooked by selectors looking for greater mobility in the field.

Milburn might have played in more Tests had he not been robbed of the use of his left eye in a car accident on May 23, 1969. He returned to play 25 more matches for Northants in 1973 and 74 as a middle order batsman and medium pace bowler, but his top score was 57 and he reluctantly gave up the struggle.

Standing 5ft 9in and weighing 18st, he was known in Durham as the Burnopfield Basher after the village in the north-west of the county where he was born. He was opening the batting for Burnopfield in the Tyneside Senior League by the time he was 13 and as a 17-year-old he scored 156 not out for Chester-le-Street against Horden in the Durham Senior League. In 1960, aged 18, he left Stanley Grammar School two months before he was due to take his A-levels and joined Northants because they offered ten shillings a week more than Warwickshire. In those days beer was about a shilling a pint, or 5p for younger readers.

It was the year Frank Tyson retired, aged 30, but there were other famous names in the side such as Raman Subba Row and Keith Andrew. There were also two other players from Durham, all-rounder Gus Williamson (from Stockton, but later Bishop Auckland's professional) and left-arm spinner Malcolm Scott, from South Shields, who also played football for Newcastle and Darlington. Willey joined in 1966, making his debut against Cambridge University aged 16 years five months and scoring 78 in the second innings.

By 1962 Milburn was a regular in the Northants side as an all-rounder, taking his career-best six for 59 against Glamorgan at Swansea. He was capped the following season, when he topped 1,000 runs for the first time, and from that point his bowling was rarely used. He made his Test debut against Garfield Sobers' West Indians at Old Trafford in 1966 and hit 94 after England followed on 317 behind.

The second Test at Lord's produced what Sobers apparently felt was the outstanding innings of his career, overshadowing a magnificent contribution from Milburn. West Indies were 95 for five in their second innings, only nine runs ahead, when Sobers was joined by his cousin, David Holford, playing in only his second Test. When the declaration came at 369 for five Sobers was on 163 and Holford 105, and England needed 284 to win in four hours.

Milburn went for it, but after an interruption for rain England lost Boycott, Barrington, Cowdrey and Parks to Wes Hall and Charlie Griffith. Tom Graveney went in nursing a thumb badly bruised by Hall in the first innings and was content to play safe for 30 not out while Milburn continued to play in the only way he knew. He finished unbeaten on 126 out of 197 for four.

When Sobers and Holford had reached their hundreds they were hoisted aloft by West Indian fans, and when Milburn arrived at three figures a spectator ran on and tried to give him the same treatment. But the Burnopfield Basher could not be budged.

Milburn's final Test was the last one of the 1968 series in Pakistan, for which he was not selected. He was flown from Australia for the Karachi Test and played what Wisden described as "a storming innings" of 139 in a match which had to be abandoned because of a riot. Milburn also made an enormous impact in Australia, where he hit a century in 77 minutes for Western Australia at Adelaide. He also scored 243 against Queensland, of which 181 came in two hours between lunch and tea. That was his highest score in a first-class career which brought 13,262 runs at an average of 33.07.

The accident which virtually ended his career happened on a country road at Moulton, near Northampton. His car bounced off a lorry and was in a more serious collision with a van. It was reported that when a nurse in Northampton General Hospital was selecting a false eye to match the brown right one Milburn told her to find two – "one to match it now and a bloodshot one to match it in the mornings." The minutes of the hospital management committee noted: "Colin endeared himself to all who looked

27

after him and somehow his infectious good humour and indomitable spirit raised morale for the hospital."

Milburn was found guilty of driving without due care (did he ever do that at the crease?) and was fined £10, which came to look like a pathetic gesture in the face of the enormous price still to be paid. Cricket was Milburn's life and when it was all over he went back to live with his parents in Burnopfield. He played for two seasons as a club professional, first for Chester-le-Street then for Lowerhouse in the Lancashire League.

After that he settled for a few knockabouts with the Lord's Taverners, and was always happy to be involved in raising money for charity. He was also in great demand as an after-dinner speaker and was often called upon as a Man of the Match adjudicator. He maintained a jovial exterior, but those closest to him felt that beneath it all he was a sad figure when he collapsed and died in the car park of the North Briton, in Aycliffe village, on February 28, 1990, at the age of 48.

The similarities between Milburn and a batsman who came from Northants to play for Durham after an all-too-brief Test career are uncanny, although the latter always maintained a reasonable level of fitness. Much more of Wayne Larkins later, but at this point it is worth digressing briefly to ponder the difficulty which the more ebullient types experience in adapting to life after cricket. Although he has always been fond of a drink, personality-wise ebullient is probably the wrong word for Larkins. But it would have applied to Yorkshire's David Bairstow and, presumably, to another who committed suicide, the aforementioned Andrew Stoddart.

Born at Westoe, near South Shields, in 1863, he apparently became very fond of the London social scene, often carousing through the night, when playing for Middlesex from 1885-90. Obviously a hugely talented sportsman, he captained England at rugby and cricket. In the course of 16 Test appearances, he led two tours to Australia but shot himself 20 years later.

Of the other Durham-born Test cricketers, Jim McConnon was also born at Burnopfield. An off-spinner who also played football for Aston Villa, he was with Glamorgan from 1950-61. He took 100 wickets in a season three times and played in two Tests.

Three Test players were born at Stockton, or more precisely nearby Norton in the case of Richard Spooner and D C H Townsend, and Eaglescliffe in the case of Cecil Parkin. Spooner, usually known as Dick, was a wicketkeeper who played for Warwickshire in the 1950s and appeared in seven Tests, while Townsend was the last player to represent England who did not appear for a first-class county. An Oxford blue, he went on the 1934-35 tour of the West Indies and opened the batting in three Tests. Four generations of the Townsend family played first-class cricket, with David's grandfather, Frank, and father, Charles, both having long careers with Gloucestershire. David's son, Jon, played for Oxford University in 1964. Parkin, an off-spin bowler, played one match in 1906 for Yorkshire, who thought he was Yorkshire-born, before switching to Lancashire for a 12-year spell during which he played in ten Tests.

Others who distinguished themselves in the first-class arena included Ossie Wheatley, born at Low Fell, Gateshead. He took 100 wickets in a season five times and was captain of Glamorgan from 1961-66. Bishop Auckland produced Paul Romaines and Bill Blenkiron, who bowled for Warwickshire from 1964-74 and whose son, Darren, was part of Durham's original first-class squad. Romaines also hoped to be in that squad after starring as an opening batsman in Durham's Minor Counties days before spending nine seasons with Gloucestershire. He was appointed commercial manager instead, but it wasn't what he wanted and he lasted only five months before returning to Bristol.

Another exile who was taken on was all-rounder Ian Smith, born at Chopwell, near Blaydon. He had been released after nine years with Glamorgan but was still only 25 and hoped that returning to his native county would bring the best out of him.

The elevation to first-class status came too late for Steve Greensword. Realising in 1991 that at the age of 48 he had no further part to play he switched to Northumberland and had the honour of captaining the Minor Counties. Born in Gateshead, he had a spell with Leicestershire in the 1960s before making 190 appearances for Durham from 1970-90 and proving their most outstanding all-rounder. He amassed 7,802 runs, leaving him second to Neil Riddell in the county's list of highest scorers, and finished fourth in the bowling list with 427 wickets.

Greensword won three Man of the Match awards for Durham in the Gillette/NatWest Trophy, although the honour went to Brian Lander, the captain, in the 1973 win against Yorkshire, which is as much a part of Durham folklore as Sunderland's FA Cup final win against Leeds in the same year. Two humiliating defeats by minnows from up the road was almost too much for Yorkshire folk to bear, and Durham players recalled how badly opponents such as Richard Hutton took it. One exception was Chris Old, whose brother Alan was in the Durham side.

The Olds were from Middlesbrough and Alan, better known for his feats in an England rugby shirt, was the only person on either side not playing for his native county. He remembered the day as the highlight of his cricketing career and recalled how Chris walked straight into the Durham dressing room after the match.

"He knew most of the Durham players and wanted to share in our celebration," said Alan. "He certainly didn't fancy the dressing-down waiting for the Yorkshire players from Mr Boycott. It was not a fluke result. It was pure adrenalin on Durham's part. We were a good team and we played right at the peak of our form and sustained it for the whole game."

Stuart Wilkinson bowled Boycott for 14 and years later wicketkeeper Bobby Cole recalled: "Boycott had just hit a four through the covers and he tried it again, but the ball came back through the gate. It was like a dream. We were on a high from that moment."

Colin Johnson, with 44, was the only man to pass 20 as Lander took five for 15 in 11.4 overs to dismiss Yorkshire for 135. Another Durham legend, Russell Inglis, led the reply with 47 and with Greensword making 35 not out Durham won by five wickets.

A former county cricketer, writing for a Sunday newspaper, visited Lander's club, Durham City, and asked to face him in the nets. Pads would not be necessary, the reporter said, and immediately received a painful rap on the shins.

It was a man from a daily tabloid who had egg on his face the day Durham beat Derbyshire at Derby in the NatWest Trophy in 1985. After about an hour's play he received a call from his office telling him to nip across to Trent Bridge, where a giant-killing was on the cards. Off he went to witness Paul Johnson haul Nottinghamshire out of the mire against Staffordshire, while back at Derby the host county slipped rapidly into it.

Durham gambled on the left-arm spin of Ashok Patel and, helped by some rash strokes, he took three quick wickets as Derbyshire slumped from 83 for two to 99 for six. They were all out for 171 and Durham's only fear was the pace of Michael Holding, who quickly forced David Jackson to retire after a blow on the helmet. Holding's hostility continued, but Durham survived, with Darlington's John Lister leading the way. Relishing the chance to prove a point to the county who released him from a three-year contract in 1979, the day after he scored a double century for their second team, Lister hit 42 of Durham's first 62 runs. He paved the way for Greensword, Patel and Riddell to steer Durham home with seven wickets and 4.2 overs to spare.

They had been the first minor county to beat a first-class side and now they were the first to do it twice. They also shared with Buckinghamshire the distinction of winning the title the most times since the Minor Counties Championship had been established in 1895. Durham's nine titles came in 1895, 1900, 1901, 1926, 1930, 1976, 1980, 1981 and 1984.

They also finished second in 1979 and took up their option to challenge the top side, who always had home advantage and knew that a draw would secure them the title. On that occasion it was Suffolk and Sir Bobby Robson, then managing Ipswich, turned up to watch his native county's challenge. Obviously playing for the draw, batsman Simon Clemence was playing almost every ball from leg-spinner Peter Kippax with his pad, and as soon as Kippax saw Robson he pointed to Clemence and shouted: "This is the man you want to sign."

The draw denied Durham on that occasion, but it was on the basis of their nine titles, plus the cup wins against Yorkshire and Derbyshire, that talk of applying for first-class status gathered momentum.

Before Steve Harmison came along, the most famous cricketer born in Northumberland was Tom Graveney, who hailed from Riding Mill, near Corbridge. A little further up the Tyne valley, Hexham was the birthplace of the former Kent bowler, Norman Graham, who during the early 1980s returned to work as Northumberland County Cricket Club's commercial manager.

During that time he floated the idea of a joint Durham-Northumberland team applying for first-class status. A feasibility study was started, but the idea fizzled out when it was decided it would be impossible to generate enough income to run a first-class team. But Durham businessmen Mattie Roseberry and Mike Weston had already reached a decision to build an indoor cricket school, which would ultimately prove the catalyst in persuading Durham to go for the big time.

Roseberry and Weston would be entitled to claim that without their efforts neither their sons nor Durham would have had a first-class future. Michael and Andrew Roseberry, and Philip and Robin Weston all went to Lord's for coaching from around the age of 12. They were all products of Durham School, a famous sporting establishment. The Lord's coach, former Yorkshire spinner Don Wilson, realised there must be others with similar ability in Durham but without the means to develop their talent. He suggested to Mattie Roseberry, who was in the construction industry, that he should build an indoor school.

Mike Weston, the former England and British Lions rugby player who also became England manager, had made his debut for the Durham County cricket team at the age of 17. His younger son, Robin, was to beat that when he became the county's youngest player, aged 15, in their final season of Minor Counties cricket, 1991. Weston senior went into partnership with Roseberry and with the help of Sports Council and county council grants they built the McEwans Centre at Rainton Bridge, near Houghton-le-Spring. It was opened in 1985 by former England captain Sir Gubby Allen.

John Hampshire became the coach and he also played a role in Durham's first-class application after seeing eight boys in one year go from the indoor school to other counties. Mattie Roseberry recalled: "John said it was ridiculous they couldn't play on their own doorstep. I had discussions with some potential sponsors and local authorities, then John and I went round the Durham committee members individually and won their support to go for first-class status." He claimed that the only man not in favour was Neil Riddell, who was captain of the Minor Counties as well as Durham.

Roseberry was co-opted on to the committee, and in late 1988 it was decided that the major responsibility for preparing Durham's case would be left in the hands of newly-installed president Ian Caller, Tom Moffat and Don Robson. Caller and his brother, Roy, ran the Callers Pegasus travel company based in Newcastle and for ten years had brought Test stars from all over the world to play in the Callers Pegasus cricket festival at Jesmond. The enormous popularity of the festival had always suggested that the North-East public would support first-class cricket.

Moffat, who had kept wicket for the county, ran a publishing company near Chester-le-Street and was chairman of the Durham Small Business Club. The key figure was Robson. As leader of Durham County Council and chairman of the National Cricket Association, he had all the necessary power and connections. He also had a tremendous will to succeed, born of a deep love of the game and a determination to see Durham placed firmly on the map.

This intrepid triumvirate could have been excused for feeling like three men cast afloat in a leaking boat, rowing against a tide of public scepticism. With so many first-class counties losing money, how could Durham hope to stay afloat? But Roseberry had already had some encouraging response to his enquiries about sponsorship, so it was decided to launch a major appeal, while setting about the whole task as professionally as possible.

"We began in early 1989 and for almost two years it was a big part of our lives," said Moffat. "We set out to impress upon people that this was a major regional development, which would provide all kinds of opportunities for small businesses and create jobs. Television exposure and marketing potential would benefit the region, tourism would be increased, catering and hospitality facilities would be developed and would be used all year round."

Leading accountants Price Waterhouse were commissioned to draw up a business plan, which was to be much more than a projection of financial viability. It took 18 months to prepare, ran to more than 70 pages and made a very favourable impression on the Test and County Cricket Board.

It was also decided at an early stage that if Durham were to be the first county to be accepted into first-class cricket since Glamorgan in 1920 they would need a permanent home. It was envisaged that there would be housing and a business park alongside, helping to secure financial viability.

The perfect site alongside the River Wear at Chester-le-Street was quickly earmarked. It provided easy access, being just off the A1(M) and was overlooked by the imposing Lumley Castle. It was easy to imagine television coverage of the cricket helping to give Durham a new image. But the initial plans for the 107-acre site created something of an outcry, largely because of the amount of housing and office space envisaged in an environmentally-sensitive area. The land was council-owned and, although some of it was used for farming and sport, it was mostly open ground where families went for picnics and walked their dogs. The county's structure plan laid down that the area should not be developed, and protestors also pointed out the riverbank was the habitat of some rare species of flora and fauna. Botanist David Bellamy became involved, along with locally-born MP Jack Cunningham, as a Save Our Riverside action group was formed.

They drew up a protest petition and collected 18,000 signatures, although some cricket club officials claimed they knew of some people who signed ten times. The same officials were accused of feathering their own nests and of environmental vandalism, and even though the initial plans were toned down, the arguments raged on. The council justified the breach of the structure plan on the grounds that the scheme held regional significance, and they also promised to provide an athletics track, nature conservation area and a walkway by the river.

Demands for a public inquiry still hung in the air when the TCCB accepted Durham's application, which was announced at Lord's on December 6, 1990. Don Robson and Arthur Austin were in London to receive the news, and it was Robson who telephoned the Callers-Pegasus offices in Newcastle, where the Durham committee, Olympic 10,000 metres medallist Brendan Foster, sponsors and media men awaited the historic announcement. Caller had the call put through on full volume so that the television microphones could pick up Robson's words. "Great news. We've been accepted unopposed into all competitions in 1992. Wonderful, isn't it?"

Joyous scenes erupted as the champagne was cracked open and Caller said it was the best Christmas present he'd ever had then went before the television cameras. "The TCCB gave us a very searching examination, so we must have done a good job," he said. "Their working party saw for themselves the strength of feeling for cricket in Durham. They are aware of the strength of our leagues and have seen our cricket centre. We can all be proud of the wonderful background Durham cricket has got. My dream now is to see a boy from Burnopfield, Blackhall or Billingham play for Durham and then England, just as Colin Milburn did. I find that the most thrilling aspect of all."

Some time later, Tom Moffat went in search of something solid to soak up the bubbly. But there was no time for a proper meal. It had to be something quick and it was when I bumped into him eating fish and chips in the street that I asked him who he would like Durham's first signing to be. Quick as a flash, he replied: "A 29-year-old Alex Coxon."

Coxon would have been 75 at the time, but after Moffat's quote appeared in the following morning's Northern Echo he received a call from someone who enquired: "Do you think you'll get Alex Coxon?"

Coxon's renowned reticence was in marked contrast to the joviality of Moffat and his companion as they ate their fish and chips on that December evening. The moment was all the more poignant because his companion was Jack Iley, Durham's secretary for 45 years. Not known as a jovial man, Iley was in amazingly buoyant mood as he told how he had once hit Coxon for two sixes in an over. It was a memorable scene – two of Durham's greatest stalwarts excitedly reliving happy days as a Minor County as they celebrated the county's arrival in a brave new world.

For Jack Iley there was to be no first-class life. He died the following June with Durham's County Championship debut still ten months away. He was only the third secretary in the county's history following William Wilson (1894-1906) and Tom Bulmer (1906-1946). Some said he felt frozen out because once Durham had appointed their six-man board and a chief executive, there was nothing left for him to do. In truth, he had been ill for some time, but even at the age of 80 he had continued working until his death and still wanted to be involved with Durham.

Iley died shortly after being made an honorary life vice-president and Arthur Austin said: "No-one has been a greater servant to the club. He carried a tremendous workload for many years and there's no doubt his greatest thrill was when Durham knocked Yorkshire out of the Gillette Cup."

One of the conditions of the TCCB's approval was that planning permission for a 10,000 capacity stadium must be secured. This was as good as rubber-stamped a week later when Chris Patten, the environment secretary, announced he would not be calling a public inquiry.

It had been necessary to scale down the plans to win an important battle, and the business park never materialised. But the financial aspect seemed less important as sponsorship began to roll in, partly as a result of a highly professional video produced to promote Durham's cause.

Tom Graveney was brought in to front the video, which also featured Brendan Foster, whose company, Nova International, was commissioned to handle sponsorship and marketing. Foster argued that just as Gateshead International Stadium had generated enormous interest in athletics in the region, Durham's first-class plans would provide a tremendous shot-in-the-arm for cricket.

Perhaps the star of the show was a schoolboy named Brendan McCreesh, picked virtually at random from the boys being coached at the indoor school. He spoke passionately about how it would be a dream come true for local lads like him to play first-class cricket for Durham, and the film ended with him walking out supposedly to bat for England in the first Test to be held at Chester-le-Street. Substitute Collingwood for McCreesh and the video's fanciful notions weren't that far out, although Tom Graveney later admitted that he never for one moment believed it would happen.

The video was presented to local firms, together with a package offering incentives for various levels of sponsorship. Durham had set a target of £500,000 a year in sponsorship for five years, by which time they hoped the new stadium would make them self-financing. Newcastle Building Society were the first on board, followed by the Co-operative Bank and

British Gas. Seeking maximum publicity for each sponsorship, Nova International brought in Graham Gooch for one announcement. He was England captain at the time and was playing in a world single wicket challenge at the Gateshead Garden Festival. Steve Cram announced another sponsorship at half-time during a Sunderland football match.

While various other sponsorships were flowing in, the biggest deal was being negotiated amid speculation that it involved Ian Botham. It was reported that Newcastle Breweries wanted Botham to be involved just as Kevin Keegan was when they initially sponsored Newcastle United. But when their offering of £325,000 a year for three years was announced, links with Botham were strenuously denied as Durham sought to maintain their stance that they could not be seen to be making illegal approaches for contracted players. All that mattered for the moment was that the initial target of £500,000 had been surpassed, although it had to be raised when they realised the annual turnover was likely to be almost £1m.

CHAPTER 4

COOK'S RECIPE

WHILE preparing their application for first-class status, Durham appointed Geoff Cook to oversee the final stages. It was a fairly loose arrangement. But clearly they had something more permanent in mind for a man who, as secretary of the Cricketers' Association, had contacts throughout the game. He also had a strong affection for the North-East, having been born and brought up in Middlesbrough before beginning his 19-year career with Northamptonshire, where he was captain from 1981-88.

Cook set about assessing the talent in Durham and also discovered there was already a lot of support for their entry into the first-class game. This took the form both of counties promising their vote and of individuals expressing interest in playing for Durham.

The business plan was circulated round the counties and its sheer professionalism and far-sighted approach to many of county cricket's administrative problems created a big impression. Durham also circulated a glossy brochure, giving details of the county's achievements and of the grounds they proposed to use while their stadium was being built. There were messages of support ranging from Bob Willis to cricket-loving writer Lesley Thomas. As the author of Virgin Soldiers, Thomas might be supposed to have known a thing or two about stepping into the unknown.

With the 17 first-class counties, plus the MCC and the Minor Counties, getting a vote, Durham's only worry was about how hard-up counties would react to having to split the TCCB share-out 20 ways instead of 19. But in the week before the meeting a Northern Echo survey revealed overwhelming support for Durham, and in the event the voting was 16 in favour and three abstentions.

Among the conditions of acceptance were the appointment of a chief executive and a head groundsman and there were more than 200 applicants for the former post. As with Cook, who was to become Director of Cricket, Durham looked towards Middlesbrough for their groundsman. Keith Boyce, who had transformed the Acklam Park square from a minefield into a batsman's paradise before moving on to Headingley, might have been a candidate. But he considered his work with Yorkshire was unfinished, leaving the way clear for his Acklam Park successor, Tom Flintoft, who had joined Hampshire in 1985.———

Flintoft had been Groundsman of the Year in 1990 for his work at Southampton, where his wife Mary had worked as a receptionist for the county club and was to prove a valuable secretarial assistant for Durham. Then aged 57, Flintoft said: "We are happy to be coming home, but I also applied for the job because I thought it would be very exciting to be involved with the launch of a first-class county. I was even more convinced when I met the committee. Their enthusiasm rubbed off on me."

Mike Gear, a 45-year-old former assistant secretary with the TCCB, was appointed chief executive. He had played for Surrey and Essex seconds, then taught PE and turned out for Bedfordshire and Buckinghamshire as an opening batsman. One of his tasks at Lord's had been to draw up the first-class fixture list and he said: "When I first started I used to spend six to eight weeks moving pins around in a board in the wall. It was an absolute nightmare. Then we wrote a computer programme to do the job."

The programme had to be changed to accommodate Durham and one of Gear's early tasks was to visit Lord's to make sure Durham were not given too many trips up and down the country. Even in 2008 that was still a problem as they twice flew back from the south to give the players time to prepare for a home game.

Gear felt that in many respects Durham would act as a model for other counties looking to cast off outdated policies. "Knowing how parochial and how money-minded the counties are, the fact that they were prepared to give up a slice of the financial cake was a reflection of how professional Durham's presentation was. I think the idea of operating as a limited company with a six-man board is very forward-thinking. Some county committees are so unwieldy it's amazing they ever get anything done. Durham's set-up could be a blueprint. We don't have to go along traditional lines. We have an opportunity to do things differently and set up a structure for the 21st century."

These were fine words from Gear, but he lasted for only half of his four-year contract and, as it happened, the structure of which he spoke needed to be overhauled 15 years later when Clive Leach came in as chairman and set about the transformation which took Durham to the top.

The biggest step towards setting up the original first-class structure came at the 109th annual meeting on March 21, 1990, at Durham City CC. No time was wasted in dissolving the old club and transferring its assets to the new set-up. Some observers felt it was done with almost indecent haste, and for some of the older members it provided a foretaste of Don Robson's penchant for getting things done. In the next few years he proved adept at completing the business of annual meetings in around an hour, usually followed by complaints that there had been no opportunity to ask questions.

Although he had not been a particularly prominent member of the old committee, it had already been agreed that Robson would be chairman and at the 1990 annual meeting he explained that the board of the first-class club would be elected immediately afterwards. He and Tom Moffat were assured of places as nominee directors, which left four more to choose from five candidates. They included Neil Riddell, who had now accepted that a first-class future was assured. He was elected, along with Mattie Roseberry, Bob Jackson and Bill Milner.

It transpired that the man who failed to make it was not Mike Weston, who chose not to stand, but Frank Strickland, a Sunderland building society director who had given many years' service as a committee man and treasurer. Another established committee man who chose not to stand, as he was still working full-time and felt he wouldn't be able to devote sufficient time, was Hartlepool's Ken Gardner. He joined the board in 1998, however, and was still involved in 2008.

There was much talk about how the directors would use their different fields of expertise to create a successful blend, but it always looked a volatile mixture. Roseberry and Riddell were self-made businessmen who had had their differences and would continue to do so. Riddell had just stepped down after 11 years as captain and was a man who liked to be in charge. But it quickly became apparent that Robson would be very much in charge and after little more than a year Riddell departed.

Milner, an accountant, was an affable character from the Stockton club, who had earned his stripes as a hard-working county committee member since being co-opted in 1985. Jackson, a genial Geordie, was well known through his work as secretary of the Durham Cricket Association and of the Tyneside Senior League.

It was announced at the AGM that Sir Don Bradman, at the age of 83, had agreed to become Durham's overseas patron, which had come about through the efforts of Milner. His father had made contact with Bradman while working in Australia in 1957 and asked the great man to sign two Australian cricket caps he had bought for his sons, but Bradman declined on the grounds that they were the wrong make. Instead he sent the Milner boys two autographed photographs of himself, plus a letter.

"I sent him a copy of that letter when Durham agreed that I should approach him," said Bill Milner. "He wrote back immediately expressing his surprise and interest, and congratulating Durham. He said he didn't know why we wanted him to be a patron at his age, but if it pleased the committee he would be delighted to oblige."

Bradman's letters were to form part of Durham's memorabilia collection, which Milner was putting together. It would also feature what was believed to be the world's biggest cup, a 4ft solid silver trophy donated by the Durham Light Infantry, whose second battalion football team won it in India in 1927. It was decided that Durham and Yorkshire would compete for the trophy every year in their County Championship match, and it once stopped play at Headingley because the sun glinted off it and dazzled the batsman.

Other than assembling a team, the greatest problem for Durham in their early years was always likely to be producing adequate playing surfaces. Shortly after announcing their first-class ambitions they had suffered a setback in their 1989 NatWest Trophy match against Middlesex at Darlington. The Feethams ground had staged such matches in the past without complaint, but certain members of the press seemed intent on using this occasion to pour scorn on Durham's aspirations.

Newspapermen were accommodated on a couple of tables, with a few telephones, outside the pavilion. Unfortunately play had hardly begun before a light shower caused pandemonium, with a few notebooks getting slightly damp. The Times had sent a freelance who immediately dismissed the organisation as an absolute shambles, with a few expletives thrown in. His report the following morning criticised the lack of stewards, proper sightscreens and media facilities and queried whether Durham were fully aware of the basic requirements for first-class cricket. "There are few, if any, more inhospitable places in cricket than Feethams," he added.

The Independent mentioned the slowness of the pitch and went on: "This, plus the organisational inadequacies, were a decidedly poor advertisement for Durham's claims for first-class status." And the Daily Telegraph wrote: "The railway to Stockton put Darlington on the map, the Football League took it off, and after yesterday's NatWest Trophy match at

Feethams few of the first-class cricket fraternity would thank the TCCB for putting it back." The bit about the Football League was a reference to the fact that Darlington had just been relegated to the Vauxhall Conference, from which they were to bounce straight back.

With Riverside not expected to be ready until 1995, Durham had to find several grounds which could be brought up to standard for three or four-day cricket. Sunderland was rejected by the TCCB, mainly because of a ridge where the bowlers arrived at the crease, and those approved were Darlington, Stockton, Hartlepool, Gateshead Fell, Durham University and the Chester-le-Street club ground. Improvements were carried out, but the TCCB might well have had cause to agree that Feethams was one of the most inhospitable places in the game when, on one of their inspection visits, their working party was ordered off the square by the groundsman. The club had forgotten to tell him they were expecting VIP visitors.

In order to maintain good relations with Northumberland, it was agreed that their headquarters at Jesmond would stage a Benson & Hedges Cup tie against Derbyshire in 1992. It proved a one-off, however, largely because of the ease with which John Morris twice chipped David Graveney into the adjoining cemetery in the spinner's only over.

It was decided that first-class life would be launched at the University ground, known as the Racecourse. Although beautifully situated alongside the River Wear, with the magnificent cathedral in the background, the facilities had changed little over the years. There was no scorebox and the students were still hanging tins on a board. But being part of a complex of playing fields, the ground offered plenty of space for bringing in all the necessary equipment, including temporary seating. The pitch was good and had the advantage over the other grounds that it was sparingly used. The others were club grounds suffering from a surfeit of cup cricket on midweek evenings.

The Sports Council awarded a grant of £45,000 for improving the grounds, but each club recognised they would have to spend much more than that. Local council grants helped, but they also set about raising money themselves. Darlington began by spending £8,500 on a new electronic scorebox, £6,000 on an umpires' room plus refurbishment of the dressing rooms, £4,000 on new covers and £3,000 on a watering system. This had been completed by the time of the 1991 NatWest Trophy match against Glamorgan when a mobile Press box was brought in, the sun shone all day and the comments from the national press were entirely favourable.

Durham also had an encouraging response when they asked which clubs would like to stage second X1 games, with 19 coming forward. Some of these were prosperous clubs who, at times, had been accused of neglecting their facilities in order to pay huge amounts to star professionals such as Wasim Raja and Lance Cairns. This was not the case at Seaton Carew, the small resort south of Hartlepool which in 2007 became famous for a canoeist who came back from the dead.

The North Yorkshire and South Durham League's closed shop policy, which was still operating going into the 1990s, had prevented ambitious Seaton from gaining promotion from the B Division, in which professionals were not allowed. The club had therefore invested in their facilities and had one of the best pitches around, although this cut little ice with Dickie Bird after they were awarded two second X1 matches in 1992. The backdrop of heavy industry may not have helped, but the biting wind off the North Sea rendered the famous umpire so cold that he suspended play.

While looking forward to becoming the only living person to have laid a square for first-class cricket, Tom Flintoft worked with the groundsmen at each club after an early reminder that the growing season was not as long as in Southampton. The spring of 1991 was too cold to encourage grass growth and served as a chill warning to Flintoft that he faced climatic disadvantages working in Durham compared with Hampshire.

For a man born at Fryup in the wilds of the North York Moors, however, acclimatisation presented no great problem and for Durham's two biggest matches of the summer he supervised the preparation of run-laden strips. In the NatWest tie against Glamorgan at Darlington 650 runs were scored, while the match against Victoria at Durham University produced 1,106 runs for the loss of 11 wickets in the first three innings before the pitch began to take spin on the third afternoon.

There had been some speculation that Durham might have an outfield of artificial grass at Riverside, but Flintoft said: "If they want to roll out a plastic outfield they can keep on rolling it into the River Wear and roll me in with it. If we tried to take a roller across it would create a huge wave before we got halfway to the wicket. And the way fielders throw themselves around these days they could suffer some nasty burns."

On the team-building front Geoff Cook, then 39, always insisted he would not be playing in 1992, but he led the side in their final season of preparation. Apart from the usual Minor Counties matches, games were arranged against Yorkshire, Victoria and a League Professionals' X1, which included four Test stars turning out for North-East clubs. Durham were also invited to play in the Tilcon Trophy at Harrogate and the Joshua Tetley Trophy at the Scarborough Festival, and were awarded a one-day match against Sri Lanka at Hartlepool.

Cook quickly identified a lack of bowling talent and was to be frustrated in his search for it after making Simon Brown his first signing. The left-arm swing bowler was still only 21 and had declined the offer of a new contract from Northants, where he felt he was going nowhere. The next two signings were 17-year-old Darren Blenkiron and Gary Brown, a former Middlesex batsman who was working at the McEwans Cricket Centre and playing as Sunderland's professional.

Cook was prepared to give a chance to local players in their late 20s, such as Paul Burn, Andy Fothergill and Ian Conn. But he stressed that, if offered contracts, they would be ten years behind in terms of first-class experience. Burn, from the Philadelphia club in North-East Durham, had topped the averages in 1990 with 582 runs at 64.66 and was considered by many to be the most likely to make the first-class grade.

Fothergill, the Darlington wicketkeeper, had come in as a late replacement for the 1985 win against Derbyshire, who invited him back for a trial. But he had settled for a happy-go-lucky existence, trying various jobs and playing Northern League football for Bishop Auckland.

Conn, a medium pace bowler from Burnmoor, had played for the Minor Counties and Cook said he was surprised he had slipped through the first-class net. But at 29 he had a career as a chemist, which created indecision on both sides and in the end no contract was awarded.

During winter nets Cook had picked out two schoolboys who would be given summer contracts during their holidays. One was Robin Weston, who had captained England Under 15s in 1990 and won the Sir Jack Hobbs Trophy as the country's most outstanding under 16 schoolboy. The other was Paul Henderson, who was born at Stockton but played for Middlesbrough and had been approached by Yorkshire. A pace bowler who could also bat, he had also played for England Under 15s.

Two more youngsters who were interesting Cook were offered places on the Lord's groundstaff for 1991, but would be made available if he wanted to give them a game. They were Jimmy Daley and Gary Wigham, a 6ft 5in bowler from Bishop Auckland, while Middlesbrough batsman John Glendenen would be available on his return from playing in Australia. He was known to be a player of enormous ability who was let down by his lack of concentration. He had been with Yorkshire seconds from 1983-86 and also had trials with Somerset and Gloucestershire, so at 26 this would be his last chance.

Simon Brown was taking an electrician's course and was unavailable in early season, when none of the bowlers made an impression. It was particularly disappointing for Hartlepool's Ashley Day, who had burst on to the Durham scene in 1988 by taking five for 15 on his debut against Bedfordshire, aged 19. He quickly had a posse of counties on his trail, but on the first day of a trial with Derbyshire he contracted pleurisy. He saw Durham's elevation to first-class status as his last chance to realise an ambition, but it was not to be.

The third match saw the introduction of a burly pace bowler named John Wood, from Bradford League club Spen Victoria. He had been recommended by Peter Kippax and immediately impressed Cook, who felt he could step straight into first-class cricket without looking out of place. He wasn't wrong, as Wood's debut the following year proved. But Cook also came to realise, as did Lancashire after they signed him in 2001, that Wood's ability to create an impression was not matched by a huge desire to sustain it. This need not be seen as a harsh judgement as professional sport generally is increasingly littered with victims of an affluent society. If they don't need to go through a pain barrier, mental or physical, they won't.

Another who flattered to deceive was Mark Briers, a 23-year-old batsman and leg-spinner from Leicestershire, who had taken a job as professional for Thornaby in the North Yorkshire and South Durham League specifically with the intention of trying to earn a first-class contract. He had played for Leicestershire and Worcestershire seconds and impressed Durham while playing against them for Bedfordshire in 1990.

Briers made his Durham debut in a benefit match for Paul Romaines, who brought a strong Gloucestershire side to his home club, Bishop Auckland. Romaines was out first ball and Briers took two wickets as the visitors were restricted to 199 for six in 50 overs, then Glendenen and Gary Brown put on 112 for Durham's first wicket. Despite suffering a broken toe late in his innings, Glendenen went on to make 86 and Briers chipped in with 25 not out, but Durham finished 18 short on 181 for three.

Weston, ten days short of his 16th birthday, became the youngest player to have appeared for Durham against Hertfordshire at Hartlepool, when Wigham also made his debut. Weston made six in the first innings and on the second day Cook discovered the difficulty of preparing for first-class cricket in a contrived two-day match as Hertfordshire fed Durham easy runs to prompt a declaration.

There were no easy pickings for Weston, however, as his arrival at No 4 prompted the return of the pacemen and he was out for two. Durham lost by four wickets in the final over, then tackled the three-day match at Stockton against the League Professionals' X1, who were captained by former Indian Test player Madan Lal and also included West Indian off-spinner Clyde Butts. He took five for 37 as Durham were obliged to follow on 244 behind. They had drafted in Ijaz Ahmed, then the Redcar professional, after deciding to use him as their overseas player in the forthcoming NatWest Trophy tie. He hit 151 in the second innings, but Cook's 71 was the only other significant contribution in a three-wicket defeat.

Simon Brown made his first appearance in the Tilcon Trophy, as did Phil Bainbridge, who had left Gloucestershire the previous season and was now playing for Leyland in Lancashire while setting up a hospitality business. This was Durham's first visit to Harrogate since the 1973 Gillette Cup win against Yorkshire, but they were greeted by traditional Tilcon Trophy weather.

This was the competition which pioneered the single stump contest in 1985 and had witnessed both semi-finals and the final settled in this fashion in 1987. When Durham's match against Leicestershire was abandoned all 11 players on both sides had two balls each at one stump. Like the animals entering the ark, the Leicestershire players came out two by two, protected by an umbrella, and managed only one hit through No 3 batsman Ben Smith. Durham, scenting victory, braved the elements and gathered round to encourage each other. But the result was the same, with Darren Blenkiron on target. The bizarre contest then went to sudden death and both sides had 17 misses each before Ijaz Ahmed struck the winning blow for Durham.

They played Surrey in the final, for which Ijaz was not available because Redcar had first call. The start was delayed until mid-afternoon and in a 32-overs-a-side game Darren Bicknell hammered 149 not out off 111 balls, including six sixes. Replying to 242 for five, Durham were 95 for eight before Simon Brown helped Cook to complete a century off the penultimate ball in a final total of 164 for nine.

In the NatWest match at Darlington, Durham quickly removed Alan Butcher and Ravi Shastri, but those were the only wickets they took. Matthew Maynard gave Hugh Morris 25 overs' start and finished 25 runs ahead of him on 151, which included seven sixes. Blenkiron made a pleasing 50 in reply, but it was Glendenen who kept Durham in the game with an innings which clearly had the stamp of a first-class player. He left to a standing ovation after being caught at long-on for 109, and although Durham finished 40 short on 305 for nine it was easily a Minor County record for what was still a 60-over competition.

Paul Henderson made his debut in the next match, away to Staffordshire, beginning a successful run in the side, while Briers also impressed in a run of four games leading up to the Sri Lankans' visit to Hartlepool's compact, tree-lined ground. Against a side featuring four spinners, including Sanath Jarasuriya, Durham were all out for 149, Bainbridge top scoring with 62.

Paul Burn had struggled for an hour for ten, and despite having hit five half-centuries in that season's Minor Counties matches, he was not selected again. Cook cast his net a little wider by introducing 22-year-old left-handed opener Stewart Hutton, from Guisborough. He was on his way to breaking the NYSD League record for runs in a season by an amateur, previously held by Glendenen.

Hutton scored 69 on his debut at Norton against Denmark, who were dismissed for 95, with Henderson taking four for 13. He again took four wickets in the first innings as almost a century of Minor Counties derbies drew to a close with the visit of Northumberland to Gateshead Fell. Hutton made 52 and Briers 90 in a total of 338 for nine and only a defiant 42 not out by their former stalwart, Steve Greensword, prevented Durham from winning by an innings.

Seaton Carew were delighted to stage a county match for the first time when Lancashire seconds, led by Trevor Jesty, were the visitors. Steve Titchard scored 120 and Jesty 94 in a 55-over total of 277 for five, then Robin Weston opened the reply and overcame a slow start to make a highly impressive 93. He lacked the power to hit boundaries, managing only three fours, but used his feet well against the spinners and found the gaps for ones and twos as Durham reached 259 for six.

Another 16-year-old was introduced against Norfolk in the shape of Durham City's Quentin Hughes, an off-spinner who could also bat. With David Graveney watching, Hughes took three for 61 in the first innings and after a century by Hutton the visitors were set a target of 286 in 74 overs. They needed seven off the last over, bowled by Hughes, with one wicket left. Only one came from the first two balls then off the third former Derbyshire player Roger Finney was sent back halfway through a second run. The whole Durham team felt Bainbridge's throw had beaten him by a yard. But he was given not out, then hit the next two balls for two and four to complete his century and win the match.

Had Durham won they would have clinched the Eastern Division in their final season by winning the last game against Suffolk at Stockton, which they duly did. This time the visitors were set 299 and once former Middlesex and England batsman Roland Butcher had gone for 43 they subsided to 250 all out. Quentin Hughes again bowled well, but although he was to feature in Durham's second team for several years batting became the main string to his bow and he was never offered a contract.

In the Tetley Trophy at Scarborough, Durham put Essex in and in the second over Fothergill took a one-handed catch diving to his right off Simon Brown to get rid of Graham Gooch for a duck. Brown then bowled Paul Prichard to make it three for two, only for Salim Malik to launch into a glorious array of strokes on his way to a 78-ball century. John Stephenson also made a hundred and Nasser Hussain 81 not out in a total of 323 for five.

The reply began with an extraordinary opening over from Steve Andrew. The former Hampshire bowler sent down six wides in his first eight balls, then delivered a no-ball, which caused square leg umpire Don Oslear to collapse in fits of laughter. Andrew eventually completed a 14-ball over then had Glendenen caught at slip in his second over and went on to finish with four wickets as Durham were dismissed for 169.

The visit of Victoria in mid-September was important to Durham, both as a final chance to gain experience against first-class opposition and as a test run for the Racecourse ground's ability to stage a first-class match. In terms of organisation the match against Norfolk on the same ground a month earlier had not been a great success. A volunteer had to be found to put the tins on the scoreboard, which was obscured from the view of most spectators by a hot dog stand. The scorers' view was often interrupted by the comings and goings of the caterers' van, and there was a general rumble of discontent. There was no telephone available, but fortunately the only reporter covering the match knew there was a phone on the bar of the splendid Dun Cow, just around the corner.

Such were the joys of covering Minor Counties cricket. But by the time Victoria arrived it was a whole different ball game. Seating for 3,000 had been installed, plus two hospitality marquees. There were mobile caravans for the scorers and the press, complete with umpteen telephones. A proper scoreboard had been erected on the bank overlooking the ground, where everyone could see it. There were extra toilets, plenty of stewards, and even facilities for the disabled. And still the ground looked a picture.

The teams first played a one-day game, which was badly interrupted by rain. But the three-day match which followed was blessed by lovely early autumn weather. Victoria included three Test players in Dean Jones, Merv Hughes and skipper Simon O'Donnell, plus a highly-rated 21-year-old left-hander named Darren Lehmann. They batted first and scored 402 for five with Jones scoring a majestic 144 on the day he officially signed as Durham's overseas player for their entry into first-class cricket.

On a pitch which might have had bowlers contemplating suicide, Durham reached 354 for three on the second day, declaring immediately when Glendenen reached 200. He still hadn't been offered a contract, but this innings appeared to dispel any lingering doubts about his powers of concentration. The only other player to have scored a double century for the county was Sunderland's Edgar Elliot, an England rugby international, who hit 201 against Northumberland in 1903 and 217 not out against Lancashire seconds in 1906.

Victoria declared at 350 for three in their second innings, with Lehmann making 137 not out – the first of many centuries he took off Durham, against whom he had a phenomenal record for Yorkshire. With the pitch finally taking spin, Durham struggled to 172 for eight in their second innings to complete an excellent four days, which had been well staged and well supported. Victoria were at the ground early each morning for a rigorous work-out, and most of them stayed for an hour each evening to practise Australian Rules. Asked if his team-mates had enjoyed it, Jones said: "The Vics have had a ball. I could not be happier with the way I have been treated and I just hope I can repay everybody next year. I'm really looking forward to it."

It was a happy note on which to end the season, whetting everyone's appetite for the return to the Racecourse the following spring.

CHAPTER 5
BOTHAM UNVEILED

AS soon as Durham announced their intentions to apply for first-class status they were not best pleased to find newspapers linking them with Ian Botham, who lived just south of the county border in Ravensworth, near Richmond. While not denying they would have to be interested in a player of Botham's quality if he became available, the publicity immediately put Durham officials on their guard. It triggered an almost paranoic fear that reports that they were approaching contracted players would annoy other counties. This fear was understandable as they needed all the support and good will they could get to be accepted into the first-class fold.

Geoff Cook was always very discreet in his dealings with players, but there were leaks about his early interest in Phil Bainbridge and Ian Smith, and the speculation increased once Durham had their first-class ticket. They would say nothing about Botham other than that he was contracted to Worcestershire, even when it was reported that the major sponsorship deal being lined up with Newcastle Breweries was dependent on Durham signing England's greatest star.

When the sponsorship was unveiled on April 18, 1991, a written statement came from Botham, which said: "I am a contracted professional with Worcestershire until the end of 1992 and I wish to confirm I have had no discussions with Durham County Cricket Club with regard to representing them. In common with everyone in the world of cricket, I wish them all the best in the first-class game and particularly look forward to playing in the North-East. I also wish to point out I have had no discussions with Newcastle Breweries with regard to sponsorship or promotional activities. But, once again, I applaud their tie-up with Durham and their subsequent link with the first-class scene. It's a most welcome addition to the sport."

The Breweries' managing director, David Stephenson, said: "We have had no discussion or meetings with Ian Botham, but if he were to become available and the club felt he would lead them into the promised land, naturally we would be pleased."

Don Robson added: "The fact is we haven't even discussed Ian Botham. We're not at the stage where we can look at signing anyone other than an overseas professional."

That was the position on April 18, but three months later the speculation became so rife that it was clear something was in the wind. It was also clear that most Durham officials were in the dark. At a board meeting after the Sri Lanka match on July 26 Robson ordered that only he would be allowed to speak to the press on the subject of Botham. He emerged to say they were amazed by all the speculation.

The following morning Worcestershire announced that Botham would be released from the final year of his contract, and Robson, who was at the Edgbaston Test against the West Indies, told a Press Association reporter: "We will be putting in an official offer as soon as we can. We are certainly not going to allow the grass to grow under our feet."

Robson undertook to conduct negotiations himself. He said it was a unanimous board decision to go for Botham, and Geoff Cook was also happy about it. It was understandable that, being new to the game, Durham should remain solidly on the back foot for fear of not doing things by the book. But they obviously had nothing to fear from Worcestershire, whose secretary, Mike Vockins, said: "We had a formal approach from Durham some time ago. Everything has been done exactly in line with regulations."

He added: "We decided to let Ian Botham go because he asked us to. He has done a splendid job for us and is still doing so. But at this stage of his career if he wants a new challenge we felt that in view of what he has done for us we ought to be sympathetic to his request."

Botham refused to divulge which county he would be joining, except to say he would prefer to play nearer home, partly because beer was only about 90p a pint in the North. Robson said Durham expected to have to compete with other counties for Botham's services, but the player himself, when he eventually signed, said he never had any intention of joining anyone else

The signing took place in Newcastle Breweries' offices on September 28. Botham said he hoped he would still be playing in five years and expressed a wish to play alongside his son, Liam, who was then 14, in the Durham team.

If the Botham experience put Durham on their guard, so did a report that they were interested in signing Paul Jarvis. As a former Redcar player, the paceman had strong North-East connections and appeared to have grown disillusioned with Yorkshire. As Cook had identified a lack of bowling talent within Durham and was already finding it difficult to sign any, he was furious that this leaked out, saying: "We won't get him now." Yorkshire persuaded Jarvis to stay for two more years before he headed for Sussex.

The lack of bowling had prompted speculation that Durham might go for an Australian paceman, Craig McDermott or Merv Hughes, as their overseas player, or even the West Indian, Patrick Patterson. But in confirming that Dean Jones was about to sign, Cook said: "We will have to get a solid base and stabilise ourselves, and the best way of doing that is to get some runs on the board. Dean is one of the best one-day cricketers in the world. Batsmen of his calibre win one-day matches virtually single-handedly."

The contract had been sent to Jones, but it was decided to wait until he came over with the Victoria squad in September to stage the actual signing. In the meantime, Durham were shocked to hear that Australia were planning a tour to Sri Lanka in 1992 and would be assembling their players in late July for a training camp.

It was suggested that if Jones were available for only half a season it would make more sense to sign Richie Richardson. He had put himself in the shop window to play county cricket and had said he was disappointed not to have been approached by Durham, where he had spent two happy seasons as a club professional. But as doubts about the Sri Lanka tour persisted well beyond the date of Jones's signing Durham accepted there was nothing they could do about the situation.

When Jones arrived with Victoria he was met at Newcastle Airport by the Durham president, Ian Caller, who presented him with a copy of "Larn Yersel Geordie." Jones signed at lunchtime on September 17, the first day of the three-day match, shortly after hitting a six to reach his 50. He was hastily hustled into a marquee to face the cameras of his sponsors, Tyne Tees Television, who announced they would pay the overseas player's salary for four years. They accepted a replacement would probably have to be found for Jones in 1993, when he was expected to tour England with Australia. But they hoped he would return for the following two seasons. Whether they had any further say in the matter is not recorded, but the question of Jones's return became an annual bone of contention.

Cook had decided by mid-season to offer a contract to John Wood, but the other members of the 1991 squad without contracts would have to wait until the end of the season for a decision. The announcement was to be made in the week after Durham's appearance at the Scarborough Festival, where Andy Fothergill did his chances no harm. Also in his favour was his lively personality as Cook felt the wicketkeeper should keep a team on its toes and raise their spirits when the going got tough.

Fothergill was very friendly with John Glendenen and although both had worked as salesmen neither had any particular career mapped out, so there was no choice to make when, at a Press conference at the McEwans Centre, it was announced that both would be awarded two-year contracts. With Wood, Simon Brown and Darren Blenkiron already signed up, the same offer went to Mark Briers and Paul Henderson.

As his headmaster at Billingham Campus would not let him out of school, Henderson was unable to attend the meeting, which Fothergill turned into something of a one-man sideshow. He didn't seem at all perturbed when Cook revealed that another wicketkeeper had been signed to give him competition.

"Andy has been an exceptionally talented wicketkeeper in the Minor Counties for a few years," said Cook. "He is well aware of his deficiencies and we hope the challenge of playing every day will give him the chance to make himself a better keeper. But we will have to bring in someone with first-class experience to give him the necessary competition."

In fact, Chris Scott had already been lined up following his release by Nottinghamshire, where he had spent ten years as Bruce French's understudy. He made his Durham debut the following week against Victoria.

Cook also spoke of how Glendenen had earned his contract the hard way, doing well in the matches against first-class opposition. Now he had to strive for consistency. "This season has shown we need a lot of experience in vital positions. But these lads represent the ethos of what Durham was all about when it was admitted to first-class cricket. We want to give as much opportunity as possible to players in the North-East. These players have been given a wonderful opportunity and it's in their hands to make a success of it."

Sadly, none of them were really temperamentally suited for it. Barring injury to Scott, at 29 the role of understudy was likely to be as good as it got for Fothergill and he was delighted just to have that chance. He and Henderson lasted three years, one more than Glendenen and Briers.

Cook said Robin Weston and Quentin Hughes would be playing a lot of schoolboy representative cricket in 1992, but Durham very much hoped they could be seen as part of the future of the club. Cook also added that Durham had been swamped with offers of players from other counties and approaches from individuals. They even had a call from customs officials at Heathrow, saying that a Mr Shakir Khan had flown in from Pakistan claiming to have been offered a trial by Durham. "We had to tell them we'd never heard of him," said Cook. "I hope he doesn't turn up with another county one day and take eight for 17 against us."

The search for bowlers brought rejections from former Durham University man Paul Allott, who chose to stay with Lancashire, and Joey Benjamin, who went from Warwickshire to Surrey. But David Graveney's appointment as captain was confirmed as Somerset were happy to let him go, despite having been their leading wicket-taker after taking up a one-year contract following his release by Gloucestershire. There was a slight North-East connection as David's father Ken, like Tom, was born just north of the county border at Riding Mill. David was born at Bristol in 1953, joined Gloucestershire in 1972 and was captain from 1981-88.

Cook said Graveney had been his target as captain since early in the season, when his assessment of the local talent had shown him that slow bowlers were at a premium – a situation which has steadfastly refused to change. "David is still a top-class bowler," he said. "He is also a man who can gel people. Gloucestershire did well under him with limited resources. A lot of people think after a spell of captaincy they would like another crack at it, so they can do it better. He has that chance."

Cook signed another slow bowler in 24-year-old off-spinner Phil Berry, from Redcar. He had been released from the last year of his contract by Yorkshire and hoped that Durham's pitches would dictate that he had plenty of opportunity to bowl in tandem with his captain.

Cook decided to offer a contract to Ian Smith and also took on the two Durham boys on the Lord's groundstaff, Jimmy Daley and Gary Wigham. Then Wayne Larkins, who had played in ten Tests and 18 one-day internationals, signed in October, a month before his 38th birthday. Cook had often admired his ability from the other end during their opening partnerships for Northants and felt Larkins' final years in the game could be of great benefit to Durham. Larkins admitted it was a wrench, but the excitement of the challenge proved too much to resist, and it was much the same for Paul Parker. At 35, he had been asked to stand down after four years as Sussex captain and when he told his family of his decision to join Durham, his son said: "Oh, good. You can get Ian Botham's autograph."

Stewart Hutton, who had a job with ICI, finally decided to take the plunge, and after several months of considering his options Simon Hughes signed in mid-November, a month before his 32nd birthday. He spoke in his column in The Independent the following day of the 92p pint in the Dun Cow, where the cutting was passed round with raised eyebrows the same evening as the landlord continued to charge his usual £1.20.

Whatever the price, Hughes made the point that it would be preferable to drinking in the Lord's Tavern, just as playing on small grounds in front of an excited throng would be preferable to playing at an almost deserted Lord's. As a Durham University graduate he would bring with him some local knowledge, as well as contributing to a think tank which included seven players with captaincy experience.

The final piece in the 22-man jigsaw was another seamer, Steve McEwan, who had been released by Worcestershire and recommended by Botham. He had taken 52 championship wickets in 1989, but was overlooked in 1991 and had begun an accountancy course, which ruled him out of Durham's four-week trip to Zimbabwe in the February prior to their first-class baptism. Jones, Botham and Hughes were also unavailable and Blenkiron was with England Under 19s in Pakistan.

Prior to the tour the players were given individual fitness programmes following rigorous tests carried out by the sports department at Newcastle Polytechnic. At 5ft 9in and 12st 3lb, Blenkiron was considered overweight and was put on the sort of healthy diet which was likely to come as a shock to someone who had been known to skip the main course at cricket lunches and opt instead for a large bag of crisps.

John Wood, 6ft 3in and 16st, was also told to lose weight and began swimming every day. But it was a sign of things to come, cruel though it was, when he suffered a back injury in the nets a week before the tour. He was replaced by 16-year-old Neil Killeen, who was taken out of school to go on the trip and whose father had to drive hurriedly to Glasgow to pick up a passport. Killeen, who had played for Englnd Under 15s, was a member of the Tyneside Senior League club Annfield Plain. His family lived alongside the ground and he had played there since he was eight.

As interest in Durham was huge at the time, I secured enough work to fund the trip, writing for The Northern Echo, Daily Telegraph, The Times, Daily Express and Hartlepool Mail. I was joined by fellow scribe Jeff Brown, and five of the directors were present, with their wives, while a few spectators completed the happy throng.

We emerged at Harare Airport at 6am on February 2 to be greeted by brilliant sunshine. The only rain we saw in four weeks came on that first afternoon, cutting short the players' practice session at Graeme Hick's old club, Old Hararians. It was the first rain since December and made the front page lead in the following day's Zimbabwe Herald. More rain was forecast, but instead the drought warnings increased as the temperatures soared, causing a few problems for several Durham players.

Although Robert Mugabe was not as hostile to British journalists in those days, Jeff and I had to spend a couple of frustrating hours securing accreditation on the second morning, causing us to miss the start of the first match at the delightful Harare South ground. Durham were pitched straight into their toughest matches when they played two 50-over games against the full Zimbabwe X1, who then played South Africa for the first time before both squads flew off to the World Cup in Australia and New Zealand.

Zimbabwe treated the Durham games as the start of their World Cup preparations and won the first by 123 runs. Apart from the heat, the altitude of 4,500 ft also had Durham fighting for breath and they managed only 151 for eight in reply to 274 for four. Young left-handed opener Andy Flower made 90, while his brother, Grant, was entrusted with the task of driving the Durham directors and fans around in their mini bus as he had a wrist in plaster at the time.

The following day at Harare's Alexander Park Durham might have won had Graveney not been injured with the match nearing a thrilling climax. Making a diving stop at short extra cover, he split the webbing between the third and fourth fingers of his left hand, and in his absence Zimbabwe passed Durham's 206 for four with one over and two wickets to spare. Bainbridge scored 64 and Glendenen 49.

Durham still had no official vice-captain as Cook intended to speak to Botham about it before making a decision. Parker took over in Graveney's absence and led Durham to a six-wicket win against Zimbabwe Under 19s. Wigham took three for ten, then Briers (63) and Henderson (36) saw Durham home in an unbroken stand of 105.

Graveney had insisted that the club's newly-appointed physio, Sheila Job, should go on the tour and he wasn't the only one requiring early treatment. She was kept busy throughout, treating injuries, dispensing large quantities of anti-diarrhoea tablets, supervising pre-match loosening up as well as the tough fitness regime, and occasionally providing a motherly shoulder for some of the younger members. Notably absent from all this was young Killeen, who took everything in his stride and was one of the last to call on Sheila's services when he turned an ankle late in the tour.

Such problems were of no great concern to Cook, who wanted the tour to stretch his players mentally and physically so he could see exactly what they were made of. He saw it as an essential exercise in preparing the newcomers to the first-class game for the rigours of constant playing and travelling. What he hadn't bargained for were the hiccups such as the one which saw his squad happily relaxing by the pool at the delightful Wise Owl Motel at Mutare, only to be told they were at the wrong hotel.

Africa time also caused some problems as the locals' laid-back approach to life meant, for example, that if the team bus was asked to come early it rarely did so. One bus, a rickety 1956 Mercedes, caused momentary panic when its engine burst into flames, forcing a rapid evacuation.

There was also a nasty scare for scorer Brian Hunt when he was trapped in a lift for 50 minutes in a Harare hotel. His cries for help were finally answered by two members of the South African squad, Hansie Cronje and Andrew Hudson, who broke open the door with a cricket bat.

Such incidents provided excellent material for Paul Parker's tour song as the Cambridge classics graduate displayed another string to his bow by leading the team singing with his guitar. One verse went: "Lenny is a tight-fisted get, he hasn't bought a round as yet."

Lenny was the nickname given to Stewart Hutton, while Phil Berry was Chuck, Simon Brown was Chubby and Chris Scott was George. Team spirit thrived as the winner of the Dick of the Day competition was forced to wear a bow tie each evening. On one occasion it went to Geoff Cook for advising the whole party to take a sweater on a trip to Victoria Falls, where the steamy heat proved almost unbearable. A fines system was also operated and Graveney was asked to cough up for trying to swallow the ball after being struck a nasty blow in the mouth.

This happened on the first day of a three-day match against a Manicaland X1 at the beautiful ground at Mutare in the Eastern Highlands. Graveney still had stitches in his left hand, and again trudged off to hold a huge block of ice to his swollen lips. He was able to return after an hour and took four for 39, while Wigham had four for 36 and seemed to be emerging as the find of the tour.

Briers batted for four hours for 74 the following day and when the hosts were left with 30 minutes' batting in their second innings he was brought on to bowl the seventh over. His leg spinners pitched mainly halfway down the pitch and Nigel Hough took 16 runs off an over. It must have whetted his appetite because the 28-year-old poultry farmer thrashed 200 not out the next day, hitting five sixes and scoring his second hundred off 66 balls. Durham were set a target of 207 in 70 minutes plus 20 overs and Larkins, with 56 runs in four innings behind him, rose to the challenge with 119. Smith was unbeaten on 55 when a seven-wicket win was secured with nine balls to spare.

Durham left Mutare in high spirits, but were brought back to earth on their return to Harare when they were all out for 120 against a Zimbabwe X1. Graveney stood down for the next match when Durham fielded a young side against fellow tourists Buckinghamshire, risking a potentially embarrassing defeat against the county with whom they shared the record of nine Minor Counties Championship titles. But Durham won by 70 runs with Killeen taking his first wickets of the tour.

The latter part of the tour featured two sensational bowling spells by 17-year-olds, although only the Zimbabwean would go on to enjoy a successful career. First came a hat-trick by Paul Henderson in a four-day match against Zimbabwe B, which also featured centuries for Hutton and Parker as victory was achieved by an innings and 90 runs. Then on the final leg of the tour Durham came up against young Heath Streak, who suddenly took five wickets in 17 balls.

After an early morning flight down to Bulawayo the previous day most of the players had spent the rest of the day relaxing at the farm of Streak's father, Denis, a former Zimbabwe player. It seemed such an idyllic existence at the time, highlighting the tragedy which has unfolded there since. Heath later spent a summer playing Durham Senior League cricket for Durham City before going on to enjoy an excellent Test career while also playing for Warwickshire.

He missed the second match at Bulawayo, the final one of the tour, because he had to go back to school. Otherwise it was the same opposition that Durham had already beaten by four wickets and this time Briers scored an unbeaten 132 on the first day and there was a nice little innings of 47 from Scott, making the most of his first real chance with the bat. After three declarations, the hosts' target was 257 in 130 minutes plus 20 overs and at the start of the final hour anything was possible, including a tropical storm.

Drought warnings were everywhere in Bulawayo and the delicately-poised match was of minor importance to the locals as a storm brewed in the distance. Thunder and lightning crept closer and the fans which had brought comforting relief for the perspiring scorers were rendered redundant by a swirling wind. The game looked certain to be washed out, but amazingly the storm passed by and the last pair survived for four and a half overs on 205 for nine to deny Durham a farewell victory.

Cook's verdict was: "The tour has achieved all its objectives. Everyone who has been on it appreciates how necessary it was. The cynics said four weeks would be too long, but on a two-week tour people can hide their deficiencies. Four weeks has stretched our youngsters mentally and physically and given them an insight into what's in store.

"We have tried to get it across to them that they were better than their opponents here in terms of inherent ability. But the Zimababweans provided good opposition because they always give blood and guts, and that's the sort of consistency of commitment we are looking for because it creates a winning team."

He added that he wanted Parker to be vice-captain, a decision which was ratified at a board meeting shortly after the tour. Whether the directors were unanimous on this point is not known. At least one was concerned about Botham's reaction, and it would not have been surprising had there been some argument. It became clear on the tour that some directors were starting to resent the way Robson was running the show. If he was aware of this he displayed the skin of a rhino in rising above it and continued to slip easily into the role of joking Geordie, decisive organiser or eloquent communicator as the situation demanded.

When it leaked out during the tour that Paul Romaines had quit as commercial manager, Robson dealt with a query about the matter by launching into a speech which quickly defused any potential controversy and developed into a eulogy about all the good things which were happening. Romaines, originally so keen to be involved, had returned to Bristol at a crucial time for Durham and there was a danger that other stormy waters might have to be negotiated. Or would those doing the stirring decide it was best not to rock the boat?

CHAPTER 6
THE CLUB GROUND
YEARS (1992-94)

FOR the first 15 years of first-class life I wrote a weekly Durham Diary in The Northern Echo. Cricket's penchant for throwing up off-beat, and occasionally bizarre, stories meant that such columns were quite popular in newspapers, both local and national, until the growing obsession with football helped to consign them to the scrapheap. The diaries form a useful looking glass through which to summarise the first three seasons, during which Durham played on club grounds. This inevitably meant that some of the amateur spirit still prevailed, which was no bad thing in terms of having fun, developing a rapport with the members, and picking up the anecdotes around which much of the following narrative is woven.

First things first. A double first at Oxford, in fact, for John Glendenen. On his first-class debut he made Durham's maiden first-class century, narrowly beating opening partner Paul Parker, who, for the record, had faced the first ball. They put on 222, which was by no means the biggest opening stand during the six seasons in which Durham began the season at the delightful venue of The Parks. David Boon put a stop to it on the not unreasonable grounds that the cricket was too soft to provide serious preparation for a county season. Glendenen wasn't to know it, but having etched another mark in the Durham record books following his double century against Victoria it was to be all downhill from there. John Wood also made his first-class debut, Steve McEwan went into his Durham debut without any sleep after witnessing the birth of his daughter, Tom Graveney was there to watch and five sessions were lost to the weather.

The gaps in play allowed the Durham press corps to discover the Lamb and Flag, one of Oxford's many delights, although in later years I would head out through Woodstock to Church Enstone, or Great Tew, where edge-of-Cotswolds scenery combined with Hook Norton beer to help the summer off to a lovely, gentle start.

Long before I fell for the wonders of Whitstable, the Durham Diary was launched from Canterbury, where I was staying in the team hotel in early May, 1992. Alcohol's prominent role in North-East culture was evident as I observed that the Durham team couldn't be accused of not supporting their major sponsors because their hotel had run out of Newcastle Brown. The same column noted that it wasn't just the Durham attack which surprised Sussex seconds in the visitors' two-day defeat at Sunderland. There were also a few raised eyebrows when Vaux's horse-drawn dray wagon arrived at the Ashbrooke ground with its morning delivery.

Having lost their inaugural championship match at home to Leicestershire, despite second innings centuries from Paul Parker and Ian Botham, Durham drew the rain-affected match at Canterbury then went to Cardiff. Centuries by Wayne Larkins and Parker, plus 94 from Dean Jones, saw them amass 521 for nine declared and they clinched a three-day victory on May 16 by an innings and 104 runs. There was a dream debut for Paul Henderson, who scored 46 and claimed the scalps of Viv Richards, Matthew Maynard and Hugh Morris in Glamorgan's first innings.

If ever a debut flattered to deceive this was it. Someone foolishly dubbed him Young Beefy, but Henderson never bettered his 46 and totalled ten wickets in five first-class matches. He had a few injury problems and lost his away swing, but despite the lack of any obvious alternative employment he was never convinced that he wanted to be a professional cricketer. He was released at the end of the 1994 season, having made no senior appearances for two years.

Botham held an outstanding slip catch to get rid of Richards in the second innings at Cardiff as Simon Brown reached 20 wickets in the third game by taking five for 66.

The following week Stockton made its debut as a first-class venue and when a member of the groundstaff saw Northamptonshire's Curtly Ambrose inspecting the pitch before play he enquired: "Do you like what you see?" Ambrose replied: "Do I look a happy man?" He was happy enough when Allan Lamb chose to bat and Northants made 420 for nine, and Durham were the ones wearing a frown when the 6ft 7in Ambrose delivered the ball from above the sightscreen.

This prompted another diary observation two weeks later when they had the same problem with Somerset's Andrew Caddick at Darlington. That match produced Durham's first home win after Chris Tavare declared and set them a target of 213 in what turned out to be 42 overs. Wayne Larkins and Dean Jones opened up with a stand of 175 and the diary noted that they couldn't believe their luck when Caddick opened at the football ground end, with the whitewashed stand behind him. During the first innings he was delivering the ball from the background of an open window and Jones sent 12th man John Wood to ask if the window could be closed. The request was apparently declined on the grounds that the residents wanted to watch the match from there.

When Jones was dropped during the second innings run chase, his wife earned a gentle rebuke from the Durham club chaplain, Brian Rice. As the ball was in the air she shouted: "Drop it, drop it, drop it" and the chaplain, listening nearby, said: "By all means pray, but please do it quietly." Durham's second win took them to fourth in the table and Henderson had again performed creditably in the absence of Botham on Test duty. But, as was often the case with Wood, he was reduced to 12th man duties by injury following a sensational championship debut. He had removed Tony Middleton with his first ball at Southampton and David Gower with the sixth on his way to figures of five for 68.

The next stop was Chesterfield, where the first day was washed out and wicketkeeper Chris Scott went home to Nottingham to please his wife. "I'd only been in the house two minutes when she took me shopping," he said. "Within half an hour of play being called off I was in Marks and Spencers wondering how on earth I'd got there."

On to Hartlepool for the visit of Essex, coinciding with the announcement of Ian Botham's OBE. There was a less happy event for Dean Jones, prompting a query as to whether an Australian really needs a Sheila when he's been struck down under. Sheila Job, the physio, scuttled out with some pain-killers, only for Jones to turn his back on her.

Russell Hart had been looking forward to the best view of that match from the balcony of his house overlooking the ground. As chairman of the borough council's policy and resources committee he had been instrumental in many of the improvements to the ground. But he awoke on the first morning to find his view from behind the bowler's arm totally obscured by a Sky television gantry. Graham Gooch made 113 and 86 for Essex and was called upon to present Simon Brown with his Whittingdale Young Player of the Month award. It was a Gucci watch.

Next stop Horsham, where Stewart Hutton became the next to be incapacitated by a blow where it hurts most and, by pure coincidence, Dean Jones came out with a theory about battered balls. He was talking about cricket balls going out of shape and suggested it was because the cork being used was of a poor quality. Most of the world's best cork, he added, was used in the manufacture of footwear when platform soles were all the rage.

From Horsham it was a short hop to Gatwick for a flight to Dublin for a NatWest Trophy tie. Durham had been warned to beware of Irish hospitality before the match but had hoped to make the most of it afterwards. They weren't best pleased to discover they were booked on a flight home at 8.40 the following morning. Nor was I best pleased when, having persuaded our hosts at the Clontarf club that a telephone was essential they fed one out through a clubhouse window and suspended it behind a trellis covered with flowers. I had been asked to phone the score to the Press Association every half hour, but couldn't even see the scoreboard from there. Perhaps my query about whether the Irish side contained any turf cutters had not gone down well. I was referring to men who dig peat for a living, but the query fell on soggy ground because, apparently, in Irish cricket a turf cutter is a ball which shoots along the ground.

Back at Stockton, for the visit of Gloucestershire, an unusual ceremony took place in the bar one lunchtime. On the receiving end was Tony Day, then one of Durham's most ardent supporters and nicknamed Jesus because of his long hair and wispy beard. He had been banned from nearby Redcar Cricket Club on the grounds that his dog had allegedly fouled the square, but they said they would lift the ban if Tony would carry a poopa scoopa, which was duly handed over. His reaction? "It's not big enough to clean all the crap out of Redcar Cricket Club."

On to Lord's for the first time, and the battle of the OBEs. Someone had suggested Mike Gatting's stood for Obese Branston Eater and another unkind soul made a similar suggestion following Ian Botham's award. But Beefy obviously felt himself the slimmer of the two because he quickly stamped on plans to spread the field when Gatting arrived at the crease, saying: "No, no – close in. Don't let this tub of lard get any." This little snippet came to me from the resident Lord's reporter, Norman De Mesquita, via the umpires.

Scorer Brian Hunt had the task of ringing in advance to let Lord's know Durham would be bringing a female physio. "I spoke to a woman who sounded like Penelope Keith and she said it would be impossible. But I eventually got through to the MCC secretary, Lt Col Stephenson, who said it would be no problem." Getting on to the field was a problem, however, and Botham had to endure much pain after a blow on an already damaged thumb before Sheila Job could find a way past the steward on the gate to administer treatment.

Durham lost the match by seven wickets, but it was a personal triumph for Phil Berry, who was called up because Graveney was injured. The ex-Yorkshire off-spinner took ten of the 13 Middlesex wickets to fall and also enjoyed a career-best with the bat, making 76 and 14 not out. It was another of those hugely misleading occasions when a player seemed to have arrived, only to disappear rapidly from view.

In early August the Durham University ground which had previously seemed a batsman's paradise suddenly produced a clatter of wickets and Yorkshire's Mark Robinson, renowned as one of the world's worst Nó 11s, almost missed his turn to bat. Having been a six-wicket hero the previous day, he had been given permission to go shopping in Durham City when Yorkshire resumed their innings on 56 for two. When wickets began to tumble a frantic and fruitless search was mounted, but he arrived at the ground just in time to see No 10 Jeremy Batty walking to the crease. Robinson just had time to get his pads on before Batty was out, but the pitch reverted to type and 19-year-old Sachin Tendulkar scored his only century for Yorkshire in the second innings to win the match.

Durham had their first taste of the pyjama game under floodlights in the Flamingo Land Trophy at Sheffield's Don Valley Stadium. It was the brainchild of Scarborough businessman Don Robinson, who once wrestled as Doctor Death. Every time a batsman was out the giant scoreboard flashed up: "Gotcha" and at one stage it told us that B Bainbridge was batting. Could it be Phil, or was it Beryl?

Back to Hartlepool for the visit of Glamorgan, with Viv Richards. "What's the best rain dance in the world?" he asked as he surveyed the soggy ground on the Saturday evening. Answer: "When Glamorgan get in a winning position."

The next big name to visit a Durham club ground was David Gower, whose autobiography was released ahead of schedule while he was at Darlington. It caused a bit of a rumpus, but he didn't have a copy with him, explaining that the publishers had sent him nine copies of a book on how to play tennis, by mistake.

Jones's final appearance on Durham soil was at the Chester-le-Street club ground, where he scored a century in both innings against the Pakistanis in mid-July. "Deano, Deano" had become a popular cry and as he left the arena to a standing ovation after his second hundred of the game he turned to give a final wave of the bat. It was a hugely emotional moment. He finished third in the national averages with 1,179 runs at 73,68 and topped the Sunday League averages with 656 at 82.0, but a broken finger ended his season a week before he was due to leave for Australia's tour of Sri Lanka at the end of July.

Durham had already lost their early impetus, but now they went into freefall and finished 36 points adrift in the championship, a rare bright spot being the debut innings of 88 by Jimmy Daley at Taunton.

At this late stage in the season speculation was mounting about who Durham would sign for next year and Chris Broad's name entered the frame when he rang the Darlington clubhouse and asked to speak to David Graveney. The man who answered the phone was club stalwart Tom Hendrick, uncle of Mike Hendrick, who as Nottinghamshire's manager had just sacked Broad. In the event, Durham signed Graeme Fowler instead and, with Jones expected to be in the Australian touring squad the following summer they failed to reach agreement with New Zealander Martin Crowe and changed tack by going for a bowler, West Indian Anderson Cummins.

1993

Jones was not selected in the Australian squad and on the day the Ashes series opened he was otherwise occupied in the unlikely setting of Felling. He had agreed to look after the Durham second X1 in their match against Surrey at the South Tyneside ground, having come over for an extended holiday. Asked about the Australians, he said they had a real trump card in Shane Warne and he had bet Geoff Cook £20 that the leg-spinner would take 15 wickets in the series. "He's an unbelievable bowler," said Jones. "Australia have used him very carefully so far. He hasn't bowled his wrong 'un or his flipper to any Test batsman yet." In the event, Warne reached 15 wickets in the first two Tests.

According to his entry in the 1993 Cricketers' Who's Who, down-to-earth Geordie Ian Smith, who had been in and out of the Glamorgan team for several years, was taking an Open University degree in social psychology and listed wine, music and theatre among his relaxations. His favourite cricketers were listed as Viv Richards, Ian Botham and Mike Fatkin, who as Glamorgan's cricket secretary had filled in the form for Smith before he left the Welsh county. In reality, the sociable Smith liked nothing better than a pint and a fag with Ned Larkins, which may have been his downfall.

Following an innings defeat at Grace Road in early June, and no victories of any kind, there were signs that skipper Graveney, always a popular man in Durham, was becoming desperate. He was almost pleading for any observations which could help him turn Durham's fortunes around and bemoaning his own ill luck when he asked: "How can Laurie Potter take four wickets and I only get one?" The answer was that the Durham batsmen surrendered to Potter's left-arm dross through poor strokes.

Cook, meanwhile, had been re-titled executive director following Durham's decision to part company with chief executive Mike Gear. Signs that Cook was also feeling the strain came when a national tabloid reporter asked him what was Durham's problem and he replied: "We are victims of the vagaries of cricket." It wasn't quite what the reporter wanted to hear.

Drawn away to Wiltshire in the NatWest Trophy, it seemed Durham might come up against Steve "Piggy" Malone, the nickname coming from a devious character in The Two Ronnies. The former Hampshire bowler had played Minor Counties cricket for Durham during an undistinguished season as Darlington's professional in 1986. Threatened with dismissal if he didn't improve, he insisted he was bowling a county length and everyone else in the league was getting it wrong.

When Kent came to Darlington the sightscreen again proved inadequate against an opening attack of Alan Igglesden, 6ft 6in, and Martin McCague, 6ft 5in. More successful was Durham's idea of selling what they called "club hospitality" at a reduced price on the third and fourth days. "It's going really well," said a marketing man. "When the Kent hierarchy saw the club people getting mushy peas they wanted some as well."

A few days after Llandudno was hit by devastating floods, Durham had to play Glamorgan at nearby Colwyn Bay. One of the host club's players was Andy Puddle, then the Wales captain, and he reported that all was shipshape. There was a strong Durham contingent in the crowd and they were amazed to discover that they could have saved £12 by taking out Glamorgan membership, which had been reduced from £38 to £15. The daily admission fee at Colwyn Bay was £5 for the four-day match and £7 for the Sunday League. There was a fine range of beers in the clubhouse, where former Durham captain Brian Lander was heard to remark: "The Bass is wonderful, the Tetleys is magic and the Guinness is superb." Lander visited his aged mother shortly after this quote appeared in The Northern Echo and was told: "I see you've been drinking again."

Stockton played host to Worcestershire, where Botham scored a wonderful century against his former club. A visiting official recalled how he once took a call at New Road from a young lady asking for Botham. "She said she was from an organisation called Dreams Come True and knew a little boy who had leukaemia and had three weeks to live. He wanted to meet Ian before he died. Ian was in Australia, but I rang his agent who said he was coming home for three days to do a Baked Beans commercial. He visited the little boy while he was over."

There was another lament from Graveney after Durham lost in two days at The Oval on a pitch prepared to suit Surrey's quicks. With neither Graveney nor John Glendenen able to bat after being struck by Waqar Younis, Durham were 29 for seven in their second innings before Chris Scott and Simon Hughes put on 91. Struck just above the elbow, it sadly proved to be the end of Glendenen's first-class career, and Graveney was not pleased when he heard that Oval groundsman Harry Brind, the Test and County Cricket Board's inspector of pitches, had admitted the surface was prepared to suit the home attack, adding: "You have to win matches." Graveney said: "It means even the man in charge is guilty. One of the top young spinners in England, James Boiling, isn't getting a game, and we are not getting the benefits of four-day cricket. It also means over-rates are very slow."

The latter point meant a very late finish on the first day, when The Times' esteemed correspondent, John Woodcock, had to catch a 7.30 train and phoned in his copy before the close. "No Durham bowler has taken five wickets in an innings this season, nor do any of them look like doing so," he reported. No sooner were the words spoken than Phil Bainbridge bowled Joey Benjamin to claim his fifth scalp.

Brind, meanwhile, pulled no punches when asked why Sunderland wasn't staging first-class cricket. "If they had done the work I suggested three years ago there would be no problem," he said. "The playing surface is OK, but you can't have bowlers running up, suddenly climbing nine inches at the crease then going down again."

Botham had been expected to quit at the end of the season, following a match against his old pals from Somerset at Hartlepool, but he announced his immediate retirement on July 18 in the middle of the match against the Australians at Durham University. It seemed that the failure of his century at Stockton to get him back into the England team had finally convinced him his Test career was over, and without that incentive the drudgery of county cricket had no appeal. He scored 32 as Larkins' 151 helped Durham to 385 for eight declared then took none for 21 in six overs and was off the field for much of the Australian innings as they were dismissed for 221, with

Simon Brown taking seven for 70. It was the first time in their first-class history that Durham were able to enforce the follow-on, and it was no mean achievement against a top six reading: Taylor, Hayden, Boon, S Waugh, Martyn, Border.

At his farewell press conference on the final morning of the match, Botham said: "I have had about ten operations and the last two years have been tough. I'm like a battered Ford Escort – you might find one panel that's original. It also seems like a good idea to leave when my son Liam is just starting. He's got a game with Hampshire seconds this week. I think he will do well."

A crowd of 3,000 turned up for that final day, when rain delayed the start until 2.30, and the Australians closed on 295 for three. Botham finished by briefly keeping wicket after bowling 11 wicketless overs, which featured an impersonation of former Aussie paceman Jeff Thomson. There was talk of him continuing to play in the Sunday League, but he didn't and Durham won their next six games in that competition.

What did the Aussies think of Durham City? "A very nice village," was the verdict of one player. Whether they graced the cosy front bar of the Dun Cow is not recorded. But it became one of the cricket circuit's favourite watering holes and a couple of weeks later the landlord, Alan Whitfield, noted: "The Sussex lads were never out." When the first day of the subsequent match against Derbyshire was washed out the players and umpires retired to the Dun Cow, ostensibly to watch the Test match on television. "I organised a sweep on the lunchtime score," said Alan. "Dickie Bird said he never gambled, but the other umpire, Bob White, won it." His winnings didn't make White any better disposed towards the Durham players as he gave six of them out lbw the following day.

It was also in the bar of the Dun Cow that I heard a Durham member suggest that a certain nicely-coiffured former England player signed from Lancashire used a shampoo called Slog And Go.

The following week it was off to Northampton, where I bumped into Colin Milburn's mother, Bertha. Who was she supporting? "Why, Northants of course. They treat me like a queen here." This was more than 20 years after her son had given up the struggle to resurrect his career following the loss of an eye. And what did she think of that morning's play, when Northants scored 70 in 38 overs? "I hope it picks up. It wouldn't have been like that in Colin's day."

There was another sad farewell at the end of the season as Paul Parker, who was always a pleasure to deal with, reluctantly accepted the offer of a teaching post at Tonbridge School. Equally sad, although more for reasons of unfulfilled promise, was the release of John Glendenen, along with leg-spinner Mark Briers.

1994

Although David Graveney was to play for one more season, Phil Bainbridge had taken over as captain, John Morris had been signed on a six-year contract from Derbyshire, Jon Longley had arrived from Kent, Mark Saxelby from Nottinghamshire, and Alan Wright, a BBC local radio presenter, had been appointed as chief executive. He reported that at a TCCB meeting a list of banned drugs was circulated. Observing that marijuana was not listed, Yorkshire's Chris Hassell light-heartedly asked if it was OK to use it. To which Derbyshire's Reg Taylor replied: "No, Chris, it stunts your growth. As Hassell stood about 5ft 2in this brought a rare ripple of laughter.

Whatever his shortcomings in a role in which he lasted less than two years, Wright could be trusted to pass on amusing tit-bits and he announced that Durham were expecting a visit from a United Arab Republic delegation. After winning the ICC Trophy to book a place in the World Cup, the UAR had decided to build a cricket stadium in Dubai. "They have expressed an interest in what we are doing," said Wright. "Their unit of currency is the dirham and out of dafter things have great sponsorships arisen."

Not surprisingly, nothing more was heard of this, and as Wright hailed from Hartlepool one wonders whether he had been associating with someone else who enjoyed rubbing shoulders with the super-rich, the town's MP, Peter Mandelson. Perhaps it was simply good spin on Wright's part, but out in the middle left-arm spinner Graveney, hitherto the club's best PR man, suddenly produced his best figures for Durham with six for 80 at Trent Bridge. Bainbridge's form, meanwhile, nosedived but at least he began with a resounding championship win at Chesterfield, where Saxelby made 181, Morris 90 and Longley his only first-class century in a total of 625 for six. Mohammad Azharuddin stroked a majestic second innings double century for Derbyshire, but Durham won by seven wickets.

It was a triumphant start for Saxelby, who gave no hint of being anything other than a pleasant, level-headed, intelligent character until shortly after he asked to be released 16 months later. He sent me a strange note, outlining why he was disenchanted with county cricket and suggesting how it could be improved. Some of it was quite bizarre. Saxelby played for Cornwall and Cheshire, qualified as a teacher and signed for Derbyshire in 2000. He made only two appearances and on October 12 that year he committed suicide by drinking weed-killer. He was 31 and had been suffering from clinical depression.

In late May Gateshead Fell staged what seemed certain to be its final first-class match as it had been allocated only one game for the season, and Riverside was due on stream the following year. Having observed the previous season that Jack Foley, the long-serving Kent scorer, had refused to sit in the dilapidated scorebox, I commented on the irony of Fell's new £12,000 scoreboard being completed just in time to preside over their final first-class game. Along with an observation that they put up their beer prices by 10p, it didn't go down well.

It seemed the other Durham clubs also put up their beer prices for first-class games as they felt it was the only way they could make money out of it. The Gateshead Fell chairman, Ian Rae, said: "What we have spent to bring county cricket here has left us £12,000 out of pocket. It's a lot of hard work, but we are prepared to do it to bring county cricket here because we think Tyneside deserves it." Unfortunately for the good folk on the Fell, their ground was never the prettiest, and it was the quality of the pitch which earned them their five first-class games.

The pitch had pace and bounce, so much bounce on the first morning against Gloucestershire, in fact, that Courtney Walsh initially looked unplayable. He blew away all Durham's top six apart from Larkins, who became the first player to carry his bat for the county, making 158 out of 305. While others surpassed it numerically, it was undoubtedly the finest first-class innings played for Durham until Mike Hussey made 253 not out on his debut on a seaming pitch at Grace Road. Walsh told Larkins afterwards: "Man, you were awesome" and Durham won by 108 runs to continue their encouraging start.

The Fell pitch could never hope to be as run-laden, however, as the Edgbaston strip for Durham's visit in early June. Morris made 204 and Graveney his Durham best of 65 in a total of 556 for eight declared. When Brian Lara went in to bat he was almost out first ball, toe-ending an attempted hook off Anderson Cummins just out of the bowler's reach. On ten Lara was bowled by a Cummins no-ball, on 18 he was dropped by Chris Scott off Simon Brown, yet he went on to make his world-record score of

501 not out. In the process, he became the first player to score seven centuries in eight first-class innings, a sequence which had begun with his 375 against England in Antigua.

Lara, on 111 overnight, was able to bat all day because after the third day was washed out Warwickshire began the final day on 210 for two aware that had they declared Durham would not be setting a target on such a flat pitch. That was partly because Graveney was unfit to bowl and their other spinner, David Cox, was making his debut. He emerged with figures of none for 163, but said: "I only bowled about ten bad balls. It whetted my appetite for first-class cricket and I'll be sick if I'm not picked for the next match."

With no result possible, play was due to be halted halfway through the final 20 overs and Lara was not aware of this until there were only three balls left. He was on 497 and the next ball was a bouncer from Morris, which struck his helmet. The next, like so many before, was driven to the extra cover boundary. Larkins had volunteered to bowl with Lara on 363 and said later: "Bowling properly at him wasn't getting us anywhere, so I deliberately set out to bowl a pile of garbage. The first ball wasn't quite meant to be aimed at his head, but not far off. I also pitched some balls halfway down the pitch. Ian Botham got wickets like that for years."

Four days later Scott had regained his sense of humour. When Northants' Russell Warren was out for 11 after being dropped on three by 18-year-old paceman Steve Lugsden, Scott said: "Don't worry, Lugsy, it only cost us eight runs. My last miss cost us 483."

In a NatWest Trophy tie against Cheshire at Bowdon, Durham came up against Geoff Miller, who 13 years later would become chairman of selectors. At the time Simon Brown was nudging the selectors and he bowled Miller first ball, taking all the wickets in reducing Cheshire to 28 for five. A week later Durham faced Kevin Shine, the man who raised many an eyebrow by becoming England's bowling coach, in a Sunday League match at Lord's for which Middlesex rushed back Phil Tufnell following a court appearance in which he was fined £1,100 for assault and motoring offences. With last man Alan Walker on strike, Durham needed 11 off the last over, bowled by Shine, and after missing the first ball Walker won the game with two balls to spare and Shine had conceded 73 runs off 7.4 overs.

It was also during that trip that a colleague and I adjourned to the Lord's Tavern at lunchtime on the third day of the championship match knowing that Durham would be following on immediately afterwards. We speculated over how Larkins would approach the task. "Head down," I ventured. "All guns blazing," said my colleague just before we departed five minutes after play had resumed. As we went through the Tavern door we passed Larkins on the way in, having been dismissed second ball. Around three hours later a Tannoy message asked Larkins to return to the dressing room. We could only guess they wanted him to act as a runner for the injured John Wood.

This was the year when fantasy leagues were launched in newspapers, and Morris reported that when he was out to Andy Afford at Trent Bridge the Nottinghamshire spinner cursed him. "What's the matter?" asked Morris. "You're in my fantasy team," was the reply.

A few weeks after turning down a tabloid request to be photographed with a pack of butter in his hands after dropping Lara, Chris Scott made his maiden first-class century against Surrey at Darlington. But he was upstaged by Alistair Brown, who straight drove three of his five sixes over the stand into the Feethams football ground. Darlington chairman Brian Dobson, who had been associated with the club for 40 years, said the only hitting he could recall to match Brown's had come from the Saltburn professional Bill Pincher, later to become the Scarborough groundsman. "Bill put two over the stand, two into the River Skerne and one into the United bus sheds."

Back at the Racecourse base, 20-year-old Alamgir Sheriyar, making his Leicestershire debut, completed his side's innings win with their second hat-trick of the match. The first was by Vince Wells and Chris Scott featured in both. Umpire Jack Bond was standing at the bowler's end for both hat-tricks and said: "I've never seen or heard of two hat-tricks in one game before."

For the Sunday League clash, Durham's mascot, Chester-le-Lion, introduced with a fair amount of fanfare earlier in the season, was conspicuous by his absence. The reason given was that his head was at the cleaners.

Going into August, the members were threatening a Yorkshire-style revolt when word went round that Graveney would be lost to them at the end of the season. "He has been the finest ambassador for Durham on and off the field," said Fred Gill, from East Herrington. Graveney was touched, saying: "It wasn't like this when I was at Gloucestershire. Just the opposite, in fact."

August 2 saw the Riverside ground's debut in a second X1 match against Middlesex. Around 2,000 turned up, including Clement Freud, and most of them seemed to be congratulating 60-year-old groundsman Tom Flintoft, who had seeded the square two years earlier. Durham were captained by Graeme Fowler, trying to find some form, and included a triallist in Jamaican paceman Franklyn Rose, who was being considered as next season's overseas man. He bowled the first ball but failed to impress on a pitch which offered variable bounce but generally played quite well.

Asked if he preferred it to Shildon, where the seconds had played the previous week, scorer Peter Foster said: "Well, I like Shildon. But this is quite canny." Some members were not happy about Ramside Catering charging £1.50 for hamburgers. One burger victim, who had arrived at 9.30 with his deckchair only to be told to move ten yards back from the boundary, said: "I've no money left and I could do with the Jodrell Bank telescope to see the play. Apart from that, I'm quite happy." Chairman Don Robson was cock-a-hoop, saying: "It's a dream come true. But this is only the beginning. It's a miracle when you think that in 28 months we have come from being a Minor County with an annual turnover of £25,000 to spending £3m on this."

Four days later Durham suffered their sixth successive championship defeat, losing in two days on a Taunton pitch well-suited to the pace and bounce of Andre Van Troost, the Flying Dutchman. Apart from the rock cakes served in the tea-room, one of the delights of Taunton is the chance to watch from behind the arm from some old cinema seats in one of the older stands. It was from there that I witnessed an absolute brute of a ball from Van Troost break Larkins' arm. Resistance swiftly crumbled after that.

The match started on a Thursday and a Durham director who travelled straight down after work on the Friday turned up at the ground the following morning, not knowing the game was over. With a Sunday League game to be played, the free Saturday gave me the opportunity to discover the Royal Oak at Luxborough, explore Lorna Doone country and enjoy an evening round of golf on the scruffy links at Minehead. Just in case they are offended, I should add I'm a huge fan of scruffy links and the whole day convinced me of West Somerset's charms. And that's without being sufficiently daring to get stuck into the Scrumpy.

Anderson Cummins thrashed 46 off 20 balls to propel Durham to a last-over win in the Sunday League game. The Barbadian was a reasonably successful overseas player, but at this stage the members were demanding the return of Dean Jones for the following season, with one saying: "If he wants more than Durham are willing to pay I'll go round with a bucket." Having been proved wrong in their expectation of Jones being selected for the 1993

Ashes squad, Durham were now uncertain whether Cummins would be in the 1995 West Indies touring party. My Durham Diary noted: "Although he is a regular member of the West Indies squad, at 28 Cummins has played in only three Tests and there must be a danger of him being overtaken by the likes of Glamorgan's Ottis Gibson." Much more of him later.

After a seventh successive championship defeat at Canterbury, the rot was stopped by Morris, after a lean run, making his first century since the last win against Northants at Hartlepool. On the return to Hartlepool, Durham beat Glamorgan by three wickets to ensure the Welshmen would relieve them of the wooden spoon. The public address man inadvertently raised a laugh when he welcomed Hartlepool Borough Council just as Durham were taking the field. It had nothing to do with the fact that they were being led out by a Meyer – umpire Barry Meyer – but this, of course, was the town where they later elected a man in a monkey suit to wear the chains of office.

Larkins returned after a three-week absence to plunder 131 out of 220 in a ten-wicket Sunday League win at Portsmouth. His unlikely partner, Jon Longley, finished on 72.

South African all-rounder Craig Matthews suddenly emerged as the leading candidate to be the 1995 overseas man, but at roughly the same time as Geoff Cook told me there had been no developments, Alan Wright was telling other media men terms had been agreed. He had been brought in as chief executive partly to improve press relations, but his desire for openness obviously contradicted the policy of concealing interest in players until the contract was signed and sealed.

Graveney officially announced his impending retirement on August 22, saying that the final three of his 23 years in the first-class game had been his happiest. "It's odd to get a cult following at 41, but the people who come to watch Durham have been brilliant to me. They just ask that you give 100 per cent every time you wear a Durham shirt, and they are the most understanding and supportive fans, particularly of the younger players, I have witnessed." Don Robson said: "The standards David has set this club will never be lost. You can't measure what he has done for us. He will always be welcome here. We think he still has a role to play in the game." How right he was.

Twelve months earlier Robson had supervised a rather shambolic handover of the captaincy to Bainbridge, whose form had suffered badly and who was now facing a shoulder operation. Around this time Ian

Botham's autobiography was published, in which he described his move to Durham as one of the worst decisions of his life. Perhaps he thought it would help to sell more copies, but for such a fun-loving fellow it seemed a strangely churlish thing to say. A week later he accepted an offer of life membership, which had also been awarded to Graveney, Paul Parker, Simon Hughes and groundsman Tom Flintoft. Graveney was presented with a crystal decanter to mark his retirement and said: "Despite what other people might say, I think coming here was the best move of my life. Meeting the people here has enriched my life."

A few days later, however, Graveney was deprived of the chance of a farewell performance after the first five sessions of Durham's final match of the season were washed out. The game was at Worcester, where his uncle Tom was president. Both had been sacked in acrimonious circumstances by Gloucestershire, and this little reunion promised to be a happy occasion. David's son, Adam, had been granted a day off school to watch him. But in the truncated game, with no prospect of the pitch taking spin, Durham opted for an all-seam attack, which was pulverised by Tom Moody. A fan in a Toon Army baseball cap, just back from watching Newcastle in Antwerp, visited the press box to voice his outrage.

Graveney's greatest cheerleader had been a character known as Gilly, who was often seen wearing a string vest, drinking from a can, and shouting: "Haway Davy, son." It was an incongruous sight, given that the recipient was a fairly posh southerner, educated at Millfield School, but there is probably no more fitting epitaph.

Craig Matthews, who had found himself involved in a tug-of-war between Durham and Yorkshire, decided not to play county cricket and Durham were briefly linked with New Zealander Dion Nash. They wanted an all-rounder and it soon transpired that their main target was the Indian Manoj Prabhakar, who was duly signed. Unfortunately, he never saw eye-to-eye with the man who took over as captain, Michael Roseberry.

CHAPTER 7

THE ROSEBERRY YEARS (1995-96)

THERE were great expectations that, after three nomadic years, everything was coming together perfectly for Durham as they moved into their magnificent new home. Michael Roseberry was welcomed home like the prodigal son to lead his native county after ten seasons with Middlesex. In Durham's first season, 1992, Roseberry had scored 173 against them at Lord's and was the country's joint leading run scorer with 2,044 first-class runs, which earned him an England A tour to Australia. In 1994 he scored 152 against Durham and, as he had also smashed every batting record in the book at Durham School, they had every reason to want him in their side. "It wasn't easy to leave Middlesex, but the captaincy swung it," he said. "It has always been an ambition to come back here as captain."

Newcastle Breweries had renewed their sponsorship with a three-year deal worth £500,000 and as the Under 19s had reached the previous year's national final with a team in which one of the lesser lights was Paul Collingwood everything was looking rosy.

Graeme Fowler had been released, but another ex-Durham University man, James Boiling, arrived from Surrey as the senior spinner in succession to David Graveney. Another Surrey man, David Ligertwood, arrived as reserve wicketkeeper in succession to Andy Fothergill.

Roseberry said he was "absolutely gutted" to get out for 90 in the opening match against Oxford University, but the disappointment was to become a lot more intense. He made 145 not out at The Parks 12 months later, but his highest championship score in his two years at the helm was 60. The perfect marriage of new home and new Durham-born captain was doomed to failure partly because of the Riverside pitches, which the Durham batsmen rapidly came to dislike. Roseberry maintained a cheerful exterior, and was always approachable and polite, but he admitted that the one thing he never anticipated was losing his own form. The pain of that, and of leading a struggling side, was obvious.

Manoj Prabhakar arrived from 37 degrees C in Delhi to something close to 37 degrees F in Chester-le-Street and asked Geoff Cook at his first press conference: "Have you turned the heating on?" He said he was known at home as "Fighter" and added: "I fight all the time with journalists." Given that he had already fallen foul of the Indian authorities and would subsequently be implicated in match-fixing allegations, he probably wasn't joking. But after an early display of his obvious talent we had little reason to speak to him again as he increasingly took the attitude that the only way to bat at Riverside was to slog. Anderson Cummins, meanwhile, would have been available after all as he was not in the West Indies tour party.

With the first match at Riverside scheduled for May 18, Durham began the season at Stockton by slumping to 39 for six in a Benson & Hedges Cup tie against Leicestershire. Mark Saxelby then made 88, putting on 69 for the last wicket with Simon Brown, and Durham won by 50 runs. In the championship match against Hampshire which followed at the same venue visiting seamer James Bovill had match figures of 12 for 68, but with Prabhakar scoring 84 in the second innings Durham won by 26 runs – their first championship win in seven attempts at Stockton.

The bubble burst at Old Trafford as Mike Atherton scored match-winning centuries in both the Sunday League and the championship, then the inaugural match at Riverside brought no joy for Durham, other than that the ground was up and running. Or rather crawling, at least on the first day, as Warwickshire's suspicion about the pitch prompted openers Nick Knight and Andy Moles to dig in. They put on 172 as the visitors reached 240 for two in 96 overs. David Graveney and Paul Parker were among the guests, along with TCCB officials Alan Smith, Dennis Silk and Tim Lamb, plus MCC secretary Roger Knight and Newcastle United chairman Sir John Hall. Tom Graveney hadn't needed an invitation, saying: "I got up at 4am and left behind the West Indies at Worcester to be here. It's a very important day for me. It's absolutely fabulous and it's almost certain to stage Test cricket."

Warwickshire eventually amassed 424 at 2.63 runs an over and, despite John Morris becoming the ground's first century-maker, Durham lost by 111 runs. They were all out for 145 in the second innings with Jimmy Daley unable to bat after receiving an early taste of how the Riverside pitches would blight his career, suffering the first of his seven broken fingers.

For the members the occasion was spoilt by the cost of parking in the pay and display area outside the ground, which was run by Chester-le-Street council. Having parked where the stewards directed me, I was issued with a £50 ticket in mid-afternoon on the second day, but should point out that we were soon allocated our own dedicated parking area adjacent to where we work. In the Durham Diary I noted that had I received £1 for every time the words "historic occasion" had appeared in reports I would have been able to pay my parking fine.

It had been the same when Durham played their inaugural first-class match at Oxford, but the significance seemed to be lost on the umpire who stood on both occasions, Chris Balderstone. "I hadn't thought of that," he said. "They are all historic occasions with Durham." His colleague, John Hampshire, swiftly changed the subject to more immediate matters. "Put us a bet on," he said. "Red River Valley in the 6.50 at Hamilton." It won at 2-1.

Durham decided that the ends at Riverside should be known as Lumley, even though Lumley Castle was over extra cover, and Finchale, even though Finchale Abbey was about a mile and a half upstream. Still, it was preferable to "petrochemical end," which had been coined by one national newspaper at Stockton, despite ICI Billingham being barely visible.

With pace pair John Wood and Steve Lugsden ruled out for the rest of the season by stress fractures of the back, and Alan Walker also injured, Durham had to rush through the registration of 19-year-old Neil Killeen so that he could make his debut in a Sunday League defeat away to a Leicestershire side which featured Hansie Cronje.

Aravinda de Silva was the first to decide that the best approach at Riverside was all-out attack as he cracked 79 off 68 balls for Kent in the next championship match before he was halted by an enormous hailstorm. Wayne Larkins dropped down to No 5 and said: "It was my idea. We needed to bolster the middle order and it will give us the chance to bring on a young opener. I'm fit and my eyes are still good. It will be a sad day when I finish, but I don't like to think about those things. I only look as far ahead as tomorrow." It was just as well he didn't know what the next day had in store as, after two washed out days, Kent fed Durham 72 runs from 3.5 overs, Roseberry and Jon Longley the beneficiaries, then forfeited their second innings to set a target of 200. Roseberry was delighted with his efforts in negotiating that, but Durham were all out for 85.

The parking saga rumbled on with news that a sponsor's guest, assured by his hosts that parking was free, received a £50 fine. The council reduced the daily fee from £3 to £2 and promised season tickets at £50. By the end of the season they had not materialised.

Things threatened to look up courtesy of willing workhorse Alan

Walker, who might have wondered if he had a first-class future when he began the season by taking none for 43 in eight overs against Oxford University and was then injured. He was in the team at Chelmsford and at 32 the former Yorkshire miner took the third five-wicket haul of a career which had begun 12 years earlier with Northants. He went on to finish with eight for 111 and followed up with six more in the second innings of a match in which Darren Blenkiron also starred. With a total of seven runs from three previous first-class innings, the 21-year-old left-hander made 94 off 99 balls, but Durham still suffered their sixth successive championship defeat by 179 runs. The Sunday League match was tied, with the final ball involving Jon Lewis and Walker, later to become fellow members of Durham's coaching staff. With Essex needing two to win, Lewis ran that last ball down to third man but in going back for the second was well beaten by Walker's throw.

Back to Riverside for the visit of the West Indians, with everyone wondering whether Brian Lara would play. Durham had developed a nationwide reputation for leading the way in feeding the press at lunchtime but starving them of information. When I rang at 5pm the day before the match to ask for the West Indies team I was told there was no-one there who could authorise the release of the information. A quick call to City Printers in Chester-le-Street, who printed the programmes, brought a prompt and courteous response, and the information proved to be spot on. The news, therefore, that Lara would be playing, which surely helped to swell the crowd, came courtesy of the printers. Their boss came to see me in the press box to let me know that he had received a rollicking.

On arrival on the first two mornings of the match, the vexed issue of parking raised its ugly head again as I was turned away from what we thought had become our established slot. The Durham Diary observed: "Perhaps someone at the club thinks the ground can be filled without the benefit of publicity. Could it be the same person who implants such distrust of the press in the staff that they are worried about getting into trouble for telling us the West Indies team?

A dog would have been parted from his bone more readily than Lara departed the crease when adjudged lbw to Melvyn Betts after making 91 off 90 balls. The tourists amassed 462 for five with centuries by Richie Richardson, wicketkeeper Courtney Browne and opener Sherwin Campbell, who would become Durham's overseas player the following season. The team also included Ottis Gibson, and with the Benjamins,

Winston and Kenny, injured he was to make his Test debut at Lord's a few days later.

Durham ended their run of defeats by exchanging bottom place with visitors Derbyshire in an eight-wicket win in a match which was all over inside seven sessions. Shaun Birbeck, a 22-year-old all-rounder from Eppleton, made 75 not out, only to succumb shortly afterwards to injury and fade from the scene.

Proof of how far Durham had come in bridging the gulf between Minor Counties and first-class cricket came in a 207-run home win against Herefordshire in the NatWest Trophy. Roseberry and Stewart Hutton put on 255, beating by seven the record opening partnership in what was still a 60-over competition. This was late June and Durham had not taken a championship wicket with spin on a home ground since August 1 the previous year, but James Boiling took four for 22 as Herefordshire were dismissed for 119.

Prabhakar made his only century in the next match at Swansea, but it was two local lads who clinched a six-wicket victory on the sort of day Durham officials might have envisaged in their wildest dreams. Blenkiron made his maiden century and put on 177 with Hutton as Durham cruised to their target of 341. Blenkiron rang his father, Bill, the former Warwickshire player, and was told the Teletext at home in Bishop Auckland had almost worn out. An excellent trip for Durham was completed by Roseberry making 94 in a Sunday League win, but Blenkiron returned home to find one newspaper had illustrated his maiden century with a picture of Darren Bicknell. Just as everyone thinks we write our own headlines, he obviously thought the reporter was responsible for selecting the picture. "You dozy pillock," he said.

It surprised me that the Swansea ground best known for Sir Garfield Sobers' six sixes in an over off Malcolm Nash in 1968 bore no recognition of the feat. Glamorgan's historian, Andrew Hignell, said there was a painting of Sobers, signed by both Sobers and Nash, in the players' dining room. He took me to see it, but only a blank wall existed where it had once hung. We searched all bars, lounges, dining areas and committee rooms but found nothing. "Gone with the wind," said Hignell, meaning that was what the painting was called because Nash claimed he would be famous and they would probably make a film about him.

I had a meal one evening in a restaurant on the Mumbles with Hignell and Fred Raffles, a well-known blind cricket fan who often kept the company of the travelling Glamorgan press corps. That also included the legendary former bowler Don Shepherd. Fred told how on their first meeting he didn't realise he was speaking to Don when asking him where he came from. "The Gower peninsula," said Don, to which Fred had replied: "Ah, that's Don Shepherd country."

The waitresses fussed endlessly round Fred's guide dog and as things were fairly lively outside the restaurant when we left, Fred recalled how the dog had once stood on some broken glass. "He had his paw wrapped in a bandage and someone came up to me and said 'do you realise your dog has lost three of its socks'?"

Everyone eulogises about the Gower, so I stayed there and in perfect midsummer weather it was absolutely blissful. My room was on elevated ground in the middle of the peninsula with a stunning view down over the genuinely golden sands of Oxwich Bay. It's a matter of deep regret that Durham have never been back.

James Boiling ended Durham's home spin drought by taking five wickets in Worcestershire's first innings at Darlington, but the visitors made 424 for eight declared and won by ten wickets after Roseberry lost the toss for the seventh successive championship match. Meanwhile, England had suffered a three-day defeat against the West Indies at Edgbaston, so Graeme Hick was available for the Sunday League match, also at Darlington, and hammered a 68-ball century. His team-mates had turned on the television specially supplied for them in their dressing room on the Thursday just in time to see him trudging back to the pavilion at Edgbaston, where the West Indies had exploited steep bounce.

There was none of that at Feethams, but the pitch had played well and questions were asked about why Durham couldn't have stayed there for the home NatWest tie against Gloucestershire three days later, especially as their record at Darlington was quite good. The answer revolved around hospitality packages and the like at Riverside, although those staying for tea had little else to look forward to as Durham were dismissed for 117 and lost by 159 runs.

Roseberry and Larkins and were both adjudged lbw by Hartlepool-born umpire George Sharp, who in those days rarely did Durham any favours. Larkins looked astonished to be sent packing by his former Northants team-mate, although there were no excuses from Roseberry, who said: "We batted like absolute idiots." His misery deepened a few days later at Harrogate, where Peter Hartley remorselessly exploited the steep

Above: First-class at last! The news was received in the Callers Pegasus Travel offices in Newcastle on December 6, 1990 by: Mattie Roseberry, Bob Jackson, Ian Caller, Tom Moffat and the late Jack Iley (then secretary).

Below: Durham's original first-class squad in 1992: back row: Paul Henderson, Ian Smith, Mark Briers, Phil Berry, Stewart Hutton, Jimmy Daley, Darren Blenkiron, Chris Scott. Middle: Geoff Cook, Sheila Job (physio), Steve McEwan, Andy Fothergill, John Wood, Gary Wigham, Simon Brown, John Glendenen, Gary Brown, Brian Hunt (scorer) Front: Simon Hughes, Phil Bainbridge, Paul Parker, David Graveney, Ian Botham, Wayne Larkins, Dean Jones.

The Northern Echo

SPORT
on MONDAY

MONDAY, APRIL 20, 1992

Durham make a first class start

Page 3

SPORT QUIZ ON PAGE 16

Front page news. Magnificent shot could refer either to the stroke being played by Wayne Larkins or the picture taken by The Northern Echo photographer. The Echo devoted the front page of its sports section on April 20, 1992, to Durham's winning start at the university ground, presided over by Durham Cathedral.

Ground-breakers. Chairman Don Robson and chief executive Alan Wright prepare to cut the first sod as construction work begins at snowy Riverside in February, 1994.

Above: Wickets pitched. Groundsman Tom Flintoft puts the stumps in for the first day's play at Riverside on August 2, 1994. Durham seconds played Middlesex.

Below: Here they come. The players emerge on that opening day, having changed in the scorebox.

Above: Work goes on. Construction of the pavilion continued throughout that first match.

Below: The Riverside ground in its early days.

Above: Durham's first academy intake (1996): back: Marc Symington (Norton), Simon Birtwisle (Durham City), Ian Hunter (Sacriston), Phil Carlin (Lanchester), Paul Lyndsey (Gateshead Fell). Front: Chris Hewison (Burnopfield), Stephen Harmison (Ashington), Michael Gough (Hartlepool), Ian Jones (Sacriston). It was announced they would earn £50 a week for the two years they were members of the academy. Six out of nine went on to play first-class cricket.

Below: Snow joke. David Boon poses with a snowball on the opening day of the 1999 season.

Still chilly. Martyn Moxon needed gloves and exercise to keep warm when he began his six-year stint as coach in 2001.

Happy days. Stockton – the last of Durham's outgrounds. In this 2005 match Andrew Caddick, pictured bowling to Gareth Breese, took 12 wickets and scored a half-century to no avail. Durham won by four wickets.

bounce available at one end. He struck Roseberry on his right index finger twice in an over, chipping a bone and ruling him out for two weeks. It was around this time that the phrase "curse of the Durham captaincy" was coined. Yorkshire were merciless to the end, with Darren Gough evoking memories of Harold Larwood as he posted three short legs to Durham's last man, Melvyn Betts, who at that stage of the season had a batting average of 2.4. He was a better batsman than that, however, and made 14 before Yorkshire sealed victory by 211 runs.

The pitch had favoured Yorkshire's seamers, but back at Headingley for the Sunday League match a sluggish surface saw the Tykes dismissed for 133 and Prabhakar's muck-or-nettles approach won the game for Durham. Simon Brown took a Sunday best four for 20 in front of his first coach, Alex Coxon, who was among a crowd of Yorkshire's golden oldies who paraded on the ground at tea-time. "I didn't know he was here. I haven't seen him for years," said Brown. No-one ventured to ask the reclusive Coxon for his views as he was known brusquely to decline requests for autographs, never mind interviews.

Not long after his return to action, Jimmy Daley was sidelined again after suffering another hand injury at Riverside in a one-day match against Denmark. He was struck by Soren Vestergaard, who was then on the Warwickshire staff.

Going into August with six fewer batting points than any other county, Durham were dismissed for 148 on the first day at Northampton, with Anil Kumble taking five for 26, and went on to lose by an innings and 76 runs, despite a second innings century by Larkins. At the same time Ottis Gibson was hitting a 69-ball century for the West Indians at Taunton. It was to be his only first-class century until his 151 at Headingley saved Durham from relegation in the final match of 2006.

Larkins' ton back on his old stamping ground earned a standing ovation as it meant he had completed the full set of centuries against all other counties. It was something he cherished and his usual after-match drink turned into such a celebration that he was deemed unfit for play in the following day's Sunday League match. Don Robson was present and was reported to be rather dischuffed, although he would be much cheered by the sight of one of his Tyneside Senior League products, Neil Killeen, becoming the first Durham bowler to take a five-wicket haul in the competition. Northants left out their five internationals and included Yorkshire cast-off Michael Foster, later to join Durham, plus Redcar-born seamer Mark Bowen, who had turned them down. Durham won by 28 runs.

Mike Gatting had words of sympathy and consolation for Roseberry, his former team-mate, after the Riverside pitch showed its Jekyll and Hyde character during Middlesex's 386-run victory. It appeared so docile on the third day that Gatting batted on until the lead was 500, then Richard Johnson and Dion Nash proved almost unplayable. "They had no chance at all," said Gatting. "Perhaps Durham have started playing here too soon. The fans here will have to be patient. If they expect their team to do well they have to play on decent pitches and from what I have heard they have not had them here. Now I have seen it for myself I have a lot of sympathy for Mike."

In those days championship matches were still scheduled to finish on a Monday and when Durham resumed their second innings on 82 for two they were all out for 114 in 12 overs. Geoff Cook said: "The behaviour of the pitch was inexplicable. It was covered by matting during the Sunday League game, but any dampness should have gone by the time we started play." Jason Pooley, who had faced the first ball on the ground during the previous season's second X1 match, took six catches at short leg.

Following such trauma the last man Durham would have wanted to face in the following match, also at Riverside, was Andre Van Troost. He had broken West Indian Jimmy Adams' jaw two weeks earlier then been ordered out of the attack for intimidatory bowling against Kent. To add to Durham's woes their list of injured seamers rose to nine and James Lawrence, an 18-year-old left arm bowler from Darlington who had played in only two second X1 games for Durham, was summoned for what proved to be his only first-class appearance on the day he received his A-level results.

Lawrence opened up with three maidens and in 16 overs in the first innings took two for 44, his first victim being the prolific Peter Bowler. Perhaps Lawrence's mistake was to take up a place at Durham University as Durham never showed much interest in signing players from what may have been regarded as an elitist institution. It was usually a sign of desperation when ex-university men were signed and none was a great success until Will Smith suddenly flourished.

Robin Weston also made his first-class debut against Somerset, only to be out first ball, and Chris Scott made what most believed was a long overdue return behind the stumps after losing his place in early season to David Ligertwood following a back spasm. Cook felt Ligertwood was a technically superior batsman, but in his previous ten innings he had totalled 79 runs.

The nightmare continued for Roseberry as he was out fourth ball and shouted back at a member who barracked him on his way up the pavilion steps. "I went to see him later and asked him if he could imagine how much it hurts me," said the captain. "I'm having a horrendous season and I nearly didn't play in this match because of my chipped knuckle. But I decided to carry on and I have to live or die by that."

Stan Ross, of Tudhoe, revealed himself as the man to whom Roseberry had spoken and explained: "As Mike was coming off the field somebody suggested they should take his big sponsored car off him and give him a Reliant Robin. I said 'never mind a Reliant, give him a bike.' He came over and told me how frustrated he was. I feel sorry for him but there was no need for him to shout at me."

Van Troost bowled poorly and took more stick than he dished out, being hit by both the first two balls he faced from Neil Killeen. He followed Killeen back up the pitch and told him: "You are very slow." The pitch proved very much to the liking, however, of Andrew Caddick, making his comeback after a lengthy absence with shin splints. He took eight for 69 in the first innings then Durham were set a target of 500 for the second successive Saturday and Somerset won by 286 runs. John Morris was struck by the second ball of his innings, and responded with a 36-ball half-century then discovered that his thumb was broken.

With a month of the season left, Durham announced the release of Mark Saxelby at his own request. Forced down the order by Roseberry's arrival, he had begun the season with a Gold Award winning performance against Leicestershire in the Benson & Hedges Cup but scored only 194 runs in ten championship innings before being dropped. Cook said: "No decision of this nature is ever easy," but even he could not have been fully aware of Saxelby's troubled nature.

Two Teessiders rubbed Durham's noses further into the dirt as Paul Jarvis and Bill Athey starred in Sussex's victory by an innings and 50 runs at Hartlepool. Weston, who had been scoring centuries for fun in the second team, lasted a total of five balls in his two innings, while Paul Collingwood took five for 20 for the seconds against Leicestershire at Riverside. When Weston returned a few years later with Derbyshire, Collingwood greeted his arrival at the crease by announcing: "This lad averages about three on this ground."

Larkins was still hoping to hear he would be awarded another two-year contract, but was disgusted with his second innings dismissal against Sussex. "Bounced out by Giddins," he said scornfully.

At 19, Collingwood made his senior debut the following week in the Tetley Bitter Trophy against Kent at Scarborough. Going in with the match as good as lost at 116 for five in the 31st over in reply to 328 for seven, Collingwood made 74 off 56 balls, which included five powerfully-driven sixes. Kent had relaxed by then, but the innings still provided a very strong hint of Collingwood's mettle.

The next stop for Durham was Bristol, where the greatest interest surrounded Andrew Symonds, who was due to announce whether he would tour Pakistan with England A. He declined to do so, then made six off five balls before slogging a catch to square leg. But after losing a day and a half to rain Durham still contrived to slump to their seventh successive defeat after being handed a chance of victory when set a target of 256 in 65 overs. They reached 127 for one after 34 overs then kept going for victory when wickets began to fall and lost by 19 runs.

Durham admitted that they had spoken to Chris Lewis, who had been released by Nottinghamshire, for whom he had scored 247 at the Chester-le-Street club ground two years earlier. Meanwhile, the annual dilemma over whether to bow to members' demands to re-sign Dean Jones had again run into trouble, apparently because of his financial demands. In the event, the offer of the captaincy lured him to Derbyshire, while the lure of bright lights took Lewis to Surrey after the Nottinghamshire team he was leaving allowed Durham to end the season on a high. Although the luckless Roseberry lost the toss for the 11th successive time in a championship match, centuries by Larkins and Morris helped Durham to win by an innings and 14 runs. It meant they finished next to the bottom, with the wooden spoon going to Kent.

His 59th first-class century was not enough to save Larkins, however. At 41, his career was over and Cook, his opening partner at Northampton for many years, said: "This is one of the most painful decisions I have had to make. We are hoping to announce the signing of an overseas batsman and it would be difficult to justify a place for Wayne, especially when opportunities have to be given to youngsters." Larkins' average had come down from 41.73 the previous season to 32.04, and as he was at the age where the deterioration was likely to accelerate his release made sense, despite his four years of excellent service. But he took it very badly, drowned his sorrows heavily and refused to accept condolences.

He continued to live in Sedgefield for a few years, and played as Richmond's professional while also appearing for his native county, Bedfordshire. But when former Yorkshire captain David Bairstow committed suicide a headline appeared in the News of the World saying "It could be me next, says Larkins." To me it stank of the sort of journalism which preys on people's insecurities, but it seems Ned could never quite get used to life without cricket and at 54 he made a comeback for Bedfordshire. At least he was still with us and I know most Durham members would agree that those of us who were privileged enough to see him in full cry will always cherish the memory.

What had probably sealed his fate was the signing, announced a few days later, of Sherwin Campbell, who had scored 454 runs at 45.4 in that summer's Test series. As it turned out, he had flattered to deceive.

1996

Durham brought in Norman Gifford as coach after a six-year stint as Sussex manager had been terminated towards the end of the previous season. "I know Geoff Cook very well and our views on cricket are very similar," he said. "I have always enjoyed working with youngsters and this is going to be a young side. The emphasis has to be very much on youth development." To that end, Cook took charge of youth development and was rarely seen with the first team for the next ten years. For a few months he also had extra administrative responsibilities following a parting of the ways with chief executive Alan Wright.

More than half the staff were now local lads, with Collingwood having been awarded a contract, along with wicketkeeper Andrew Pratt and 6ft 4in paceman Colin Campbell, who had played for England Under 19s. Yorkshireman Michael Foster, released by Northants, was handed a trial.

Roseberry had enjoyed a fruitful opening partnership with a West Indian before, namely Desmond Haynes at Middlesex, and was hopeful of another one with Campbell, saying: "I'm certain he'll get a lot of runs, I'll score more runs and so will John Morris. And people like Stewart Hutton and Jimmy Daley are ready for a big season."

It was the usual pre-season optimism shared by all sportsmen everywhere, but unfortunately it proved utterly ill-founded, despite Roseberry and Hutton sharing an unbroken opening stand of 334 in Durham's annual opener in The Parks. The Oxford attack featured Mark Wagh and Iain Sutcliffe, who would go on to enjoy county careers as batsmen. It was the biggest stand in Durham's history, beating the 251 shared by Charlie Adamson and George Hickman for the third wicket against Yorkshire seconds at South Shields in 1935. Although he didn't play, Collingwood was present, as was Geoff Arnold, who had been taken on as a part-time bowling coach.

With Sherwin Campbell unavailable for the start of the Benson & Hedges Cup, Durham began with a 104-run defeat at Chesterfield as the new Derbyshire captain, Dean Jones, made 67 and Chris Adams 100 not out. Derbyshire finished second in the championship that year, only for Jones to depart amid a fair amount of acrimony the following May.

A seven-wicket defeat at Old Trafford followed, with Michael Atherton continuing his century habit against Durham, who then began their championship campaign with a home match against Northants. Despite still being plagued by a no-ball habit, Melvyn Betts now looked a real prospect as he took four wickets for the first time in an innings, but the match will always be remembered for Collingwood scoring 91 and taking a wicket with his first ball in first-class cricket.

I wrote at the time: "Dream debuts have a habit of flattering to deceive. But in Paul Collingwood's case there is every reason to hope it is the start of a glittering career." The first-ball victim was David Capel, who was yorked to bring in Tony Penberthy, who himself had removed Australian captain Mark Taylor with his first ball in first-class cricket in 1989.

Collingwood went in with the score on 44 for three, but while Roseberry dug in at the other end the youngster was never afraid to attack, even against former England spinner John Emburey. His first boundary was a hooked six off Paul Taylor and afterwards he said: "It doesn't matter who's bowling, if the ball is there to be hit I'll hit it. Kevin Curran and David Capel gave me a bit of stick but it just made me more determined." Roseberry also showed great determination in batting 239 minutes for 59 as Durham drew the rain-affected game. They lost the Sunday League clash by eight wickets with Collingwood making 54 not out, 37 more than any of his team-mates, on the day when Campbell arrived, fresh from a double century against New Zealand.

It was a week before Collingwood's 20th birthday when Durham moved on to Lord's, which he decided had narrowly usurped Shotley Bridge as his favourite ground. Sitting prettily alongside the River Derwent in North West Durham, Shotley Bridge CC was five minutes' walk from the Collingwood household and Paul's father, David, and elder brother, Peter, have a long association with the club. "I was there every night in summer as a boy," said Paul. "Dad taught us to do things properly from an early age. He's a very correct opening batsman and he tells me off for playing attacking strokes. But that's the way I like to play. My hero as a boy was Ian Botham."

In the first innings at Lord's Collingwood was adjudged lbw for seven to a ball which hit his thigh. What did he think of the decision? "No comment." Campbell flashed a catch to point as Durham flopped with the bat after Betts had again bowled well, as did Michael Foster. As in the previous year's game at Riverside, Mike Gatting batted Durham out of the game, completing the full set of centuries against the other 17 counties with his 90th first-class ton in the second innings. Then came Durham's darkest hour. They were bowled out for 67, filleted by Follett.

Seamer David Follett hailed from Newcastle, but not the one on Tyneside, and had been playing for his native Staffordshire two years previously. Turned down after trials with three other counties, he was already 27, but his sensational figures of eight for 22 did not herald the start of a bright career as he was barely heard of again. Roseberry had put on 19 with Campbell when he fell lbw to Follett's first ball. Campbell made 23 before he played across Follett's quicker ball and had his middle stump removed. Stewart Hutton fell to a magnificent slip catch by John Carr, Collingwood padded up and was lbw third ball, Jimmy Daley nicked a short one, Chris Scott chased a wide one, Foster repeated Campbell's mistake and it was all over when Betts gloved a leg-side catch to the wicketkeeper. Angus Fraser and Phil Tufnell took one wicket each.

Roseberry said: "We had three very good days then a nightmare. We just have to make sure this doesn't affect our confidence, but I don't think that should be a problem."

It was at Lord's that Don Robson made an extremely rare visit to a press box, which in those days was at fine leg, to announce that 48-year-old Mike Candlish was Durham's new chief executive. A long-distance runner with Steve Cram's club, Jarrow and Hebburn, he had been regional operations manager for a multi-national building materials company. A very affable character, he also proved a success in the job, although there was little he could do to improve matters on the field.

After the Lord's debacle the Durham press corps adjourned to the Sun Inn at Marston Trussell, which had become a much-favoured place to stay for any match at Leicester or Northampton. Although the food was excellent, I came to appreciate that a rather quaint old village pub had, in fact, been spoiled by the addition of a modern accommodation block.

After the record low the previous day, Durham made their biggest B & H total of 287 for five at Grace Road, John Morris making their record one-day individual score of 145. But they lost by four wickets with burly left-hander Jon Dakin hitting an unbeaten century.

Durham had their first sight of Martin Saggers when he played for the Minor Counties in a B & H match at Riverside and removed both Roseberry and Campbell in an impressive spell. He was invited to play in a second team game the following week. Durham beat the Minor Counties by five wickets, but the championship visit of Yorkshire brought further gloom as Richard Stemp and Chris Silverwood shared a last-wicket stand of 110. Campbell, out third ball at Leicester, suffered the same fate when he was lbw to Darren Gough, and was pinned by a shooter from Peter Hartley in the second innings. Pre-season confidence had been helped by the impression that Riverside pitches had improved, but Jimmy Daley suffered his third broken finger as Yorkshire won by 144 runs.

A Durham member offered consoling words to Campbell as he emerged from a long session in the nets. Putting his arm round the West Indian, he said: "Divvent worry if tha's card, bonny lad. Ah've lived here all mi life and ah's frozzen."

Rather more cultured vowels were heard in the press cabin through a visit from Henry Blofeld, who had a brief contretemps with groundsman Tom Flintoft when walking his dogs round the perimeter of the ground. A few choice phrases were exchanged, but the ones with the plummy tones did not come out on top.

It was not all gloom as Brown and Betts were the country's leading wicket-takers at the end of May, when it began to emerge that Durham were operating a tough regime, possibly inspired by Gifford. Stewart Hutton was suspended for three weeks for a "non-cricketing matter" and after scoring a century on his return to the team at Portsmouth, Darren Blenkiron revealed he had had a slap on the wrist. "When I wasn't selected for the first match my attitude went to pot," he said. "I got a bollocking and was told to work hard." Collingwood made 80, but after getting the better of a rain-ruined match Durham had to settle for a draw.

Campbell finally came good by making 118 at Trent Bridge, but was upstaged by Blenkiron hitting 130 in a total of 455. They dismissed Nottinghamshire for 269 but after following on the hosts made 408 for three. It was so tedious a steward was heard to remark: "If this was a dying dog it would be put down."

Blenkiron had obviously left an impression as when Durham arrived for the third day a magazine picture of a fat, ginger-haired weekend cricketer was pinned on their dressing room door. On it was written the word Darren. He suspected Chris Cairns was the culprit because they had played together as eight-year-olds at Bishop Auckland, where Chris's dad, Lance, was the club professional. Further inquiries, however, pointed the finger at Paul Johnson.

David Lloyd, then the England coach, was at Trent Bridge mainly to watch Simon Brown. He hinted he would like both Brown and Alan Mullally in the England team and his former Lancashire colleague Graeme Fowler, who was present for the Sunday Telegraph, said: "He'd have any left-armer wearing size 28 boots in the team just to rough up the pitch."

At that stage in his career Blenkiron had made three centuries in 19 first-class innings, plus his 94 at Chelmsford, but after racing to 20 with supreme confidence in the next match at Hove the turning point in his career arrived with the introduction of Ian Salisbury. It was one of those days when the leg-spinner bowled well. Trying to fathom the mysteries of a type of bowling he had barely encountered, Blenkiron's runs dried up until he edged down the pitch and was stumped by Peter Moores. Having looked set for a lengthy and prosperous career, Blenkiron barely made another run.

From 119 for two Durham collapsed to 159 all out with Salisbury taking six for 15. They trailed by the small matter of 393 as Bill Athey had batted for almost six hours in making his fourth century in successive seasons against Durham. Keith Greenfield and Alan Wells also made centuries and a Sussex reporter mused: "When was the last time three of our batsmen made hundreds in one innings?" In best Smart Alec style, I was able to reply: "Last year at Hartlepool." Just as my colleague was checking this in his records, a steward popped his head through the door and said: "Everyone out here wants to know when Sussex last had three century-makers in an innings." The reply was instant: "Last year at Hartlepool – Athey, Hall and Lenham."

Sussex won by an innings and 67 runs with Danny Law taking five for 33 in the second innings. He also hit an unbeaten 47 off 25 balls in the Sunday League win, alerting Durham to the talent which persuaded them to sign him a few years later. This was the last season of championship games starting on a Thursday and ending on Monday after the Sunday League match. Durham fans claimed that their memberships came complete with DCMs, which stood for Don't Come Monday, but the match at Hove was taken into the final day by a last-wicket stand of 103 between Melvyn Betts and David Cox. The seventh ball on the Monday saw Cox bowled by Ed Giddins for 67. Durham member Kenny Harrison, a former shipyard worker from Sunderland, was left clutching a can of cider at the end and said: "I'll still have a good day, even though we've lost. I'm off down the beach."

Three years earlier there had been talk of how Betts and Lugsden could become a fearsome pair of opening bowlers and after all Lugsden's injury problems they were reunited for the following match, at home to Lancashire. But Betts was still plagued by no-balls, bowling 16 in his opening six overs, while Lugsden looked as quick as any English bowler but bowled 12 wides. He claimed the scalp of Michael Atherton, but there were echoes of the previous season as 18 wickets fell on the first day then the pitch flattened in Lancashire's second innings. They won by 345 runs.

Although an eight-wicket defeat by Surrey followed, there was some relief for Durham as they escaped to Stockton and made 377 in their first innings. Mark Butcher and Darren Bicknell then put on 245. In the Sunday match the man nicknamed Jaws treated Durham like a shoal of sprat as David Ward, left out of the four-day team, hit eight sixes in 14 balls on his way to a 55-ball century. His second 50 took only 13 balls and Durham lost by 59 runs in a game which saw 19-year-old Blaydon paceman Colin Campbell make his senior debut. There was also an appearance from 16-year-old Michael Gough, who acted as 12th man on the first two days at Stockton and said: "It has definitely whetted my appetite to be a first-class cricketer." A week later it was announced he would be joining Durham's newly-formed academy.

John Morris, at that stage averaging 19.1 in the championship, made a century as Durham beat Scotland by 92 runs in the NatWest Trophy, then 15 wickets fell on the first day against Gloucestershire at Riverside. The visitors included Nick Trainor, from Gateshead, who had done well in Durham's second team, but not well enough to earn a contract. Lugsden tore a hamstring delivering his fifth ball and when Colin Campbell replaced him he bowled Tony Wright with his fourth ball in first-class cricket. Stewart Hutton batted for eight hours in the second innings to make 143 not out and Phil Bainbridge scored 83, his highest for three years, against his former team. Gloucestershire needed 395 to win but rain ruined the final day and they closed on 150 for two.

A trip to Maidstone provided a welcome chance to explore pastures new, but not for Collingwood, who was left out as Roseberry returned from injury and lost the toss for the sixth successive time in the championship. He moved down the order to No 5 and made 60, but Carl Hooper's stunning 78-ball century in Kent's second innings helped them to an 83-run victory. He confirmed his liking for the Mote with an unbeaten 76 in the Sunday League victory.

Durham moved on to Chelmsford for a NatWest Trophy tie and the man called Horse decided he would have a foot in neither camp. Geoff (G G) Arnold had been dividing his time as a bowling coach between Durham and Essex but took the day off. His earlier work with Durham appeared to have been in vain as Essex recovered from 43 for three to amass 361 for seven with blistering centuries from Stuart Law and Ronnie Irani. Betts' ten overs cost 87 runs and Alan Walker had two for 13 off his first eight overs but conceded 45 off the remaining four. Durham looked out of it at 109 for four but Roseberry briefly rekindled hope until more wickets went down and at 208 for seven he settled for respectability. He completed a 103-ball century, but Durham were all out for 294.

Without a win of any kind against first-class opposition, Durham's season was effectively over in mid-July and Roseberry was showing the strain. Geoff Cook said: "There's nothing wrong with him other than a broken heart." Winning the Costcutter Cup at Harrogate brought tongue-in-cheek suggestions of an open-top bus ride, but it was scant consolation.

Simon Brown stepped up his selector nudging by taking three for none in nine balls to reduce Worcestershire to 11 for four. But the hosts recovered through Graeme Hick's 150. He survived the simplest of chances on 77 to Morris, who was then out first ball to 20-year-old seamer Scott Ellis. Durham lost by nine wickets early on the Saturday, leaving a party of ten from Durham City soaking up the sun and pondering how to spend the rest of the day. Among them were Brian Lander, the ex-captain, and Ray Pallister, a former Durham Senior League president.

"We are not dispirited because we have grown used to failure," he said. "But we think the whole business is awful. The people at the top have to take the blame." Pallister had formerly been one of Durham's public address announcers and added: "We were never sure what we were supposed to do. It seems to be the same throughout the club." Along with everyone else, however, he was amused to find that Worcester's public address men had passed the special test for incompetence which most county cricket clubs seemed to set. It was announced that the tea break would be 40 minutes when everyone else in the ground knew it had been 20 since before the sliced loaf was invented. It was also stated that Hick had been bowled by Melvyn Betts before the bit about the catch by David Ligertwood was falteringly added.

Brown's England call-up for the first Test against Pakistan at Lord's the following Thursday was announced at a time when he had 56 championship wickets and was 12 ahead of his nearest rival, Leicestershire's David Millns. Brown had always seemed indifferent to his England prospects, saying: "If it happens, it happens." But on hearing of his selection he said: "Everyone who plays county cricket wants to play at Test level and I'm no different." The fact that he was so well known to the chariman of selectors, David Graveney, however, probably didn't help him as his laid-back nature almost certainly contributed to him joining the list of one-cap wonders.

In Brown's absence for the match against Essex at Hartlepool, and with three other seamers injured, Durham rushed through the registration of Martin Saggers. He suffered heavy punishment in the first innings but bowled better in the second, when he had Graham Gooch dropped at slip just after Gooch had reached 1,000 runs for the 20th time. Durham could reflect that they had grown used to Sod's Law and Murphy's Law but there was little they could do about Stuart Law as he took advantage of the small ground to score 172. Essex won by 292 runs, but after going a year without a Sunday League win Durham cruised to an eight-wicket victory on the back of Sherwin Campbell's Sunday-best of 77.

Former Essex seamer Don Topley was in the middle of a brief spell as our local BBC radio reporter at the time and told us he had captained Saggers in Essex seconds. So what could we expect of him, we enquired, when Saggers came in to bat at No 11 with Durham needing 28 to avoid the follow-on. "He makes Peter Such look like Don Bradman," was Topley's reply, which seemed a little harsh when Saggers presented an immaculate straight bat then blasted Such over extra cover for four.

Brown took five for 88 when the Pakistanis played Durham at Riverside then revealed that the type of ball used in the Lord's Test hadn't helped him. He had been selected for his swing bowling but then had to use a Reader ball for only the second time that season. The Reader had developed a reputation for not swinging, except in the hands of reverse swing experts when scuffed up. "Durham always use a Dukes, and the only time we've had a Reader this season was in the high-scoring draw at Trent Bridge," said Brown. He added: "I was kicking myself for getting Saeed Anwar out with a no-ball in my first over. I only bowl about two a season."

Roseberry made 93 not out and 48 in the seven-wicket defeat by the Pakistanis, but it did not signal any change of fortune for him or his team. On the trip to Edgbaston which followed he tried to protect a broken finger by standing down from the Sunday side but Durham, captained by Brown for the first time, were all out for 99 on a blameless pitch. It was a measure of their desperation that James Boiling went in at No 3 and the only consolation from a 282-run championship defeat came from the form of David Cox. On the ground where he took none for 163 on his debut two years earlier he became only the fourth bowler to take ten wickets in a first-class match for Durham.

Cox continued to shine as he cut and carved his way to 95 not out at Weston-super-Mare, but hopes of a Weston super score were scuppered as Robin Weston was out for two, taking his tally to 44 in 11 first-class innings. He consoled himself with the knowledge that his brother, Phil, found it tough to become established at Worcestershire, despite a similarly illustrious schoolboy career. "We have always been very close and I talk to him about it a lot," said Robin. "He says he found it tough until he made a good score."

A crowd of 2,000 turned up for the first day of what proved to be the final Weston Festival, which had been going since 1914 in a public park which staged no other cricket. But the rest of the match was ruined by rain, which merely underlined the inadequacy of the facilities and left Dickie Bird feeling a little disgruntled.

Phil Bainbridge brought forward his intended end-of-season retirement, saying: "The mind is still willing but the body isn't. The captaincy was a highly-pressurised job and I was probably a bit naïve in thinking it wasn't. But it was a great honour. I had two years in the wilderness, but I've finished the way I wanted to, by showing I could still play."

Saggers took six for 65 at home to Glamorgan, but Durham were all out for 114 in their first innings and when they lost inside three days Roseberry resigned with three weeks of the season remaining. He denied any knowledge of moves to bring in an overseas captain, although it transpired that Geoff Cook was on his way to Tasmania to speak to David Boon.

Roseberry said: "I just wanted to finish now. I wanted to do it on the first morning of this match, but the chairman was in a meeting and I couldn't speak to him until Friday. He was very sympathetic. Every time we were being beaten it started to hurt more and more. As captain you are the figurehead and it reflects on you. The only reason I left Middlesex was because I wanted to captain my home county. I had ambitions but without doubt it was harder than I expected."

His father, still on the board, blamed the local press for undermining his son's position, saying: "Are you happy now? Have you got what you want?" But Michael remained his usual courteous self and added: "I can't pinpoint one particular reason for our struggles, but these are difficult pitches to play on. As a batsman they put doubts in your mind."

With vice-captain Morris's form also having suffered, the captaincy was handed to Brown for the rest of the season. He began with a defeat by Glamorgan which confirmed Durham would finish bottom of the Sunday League. Things did not improve. In fact, they got worse and it was into this impossible situation that 17-year-old Steve Harmison was pitched for the final home game against title-chasing Leicestershire. His first five-over burst cost 49 runs and he finished with none for 77 in nine as the visitors made 516 for six and won by an innings and 251 runs in two days.

Phil Simmons made what was then Riverside's highest individual score of 171 and shared Leicestershire's record sixth wicket stand of 284 with Paul Nixon. In the Sunday match Simmons hit an 86-ball century, which was eclipsed by Darren Maddy reaching the target off only 54 balls. The total of 344 for four was the second highest in the history of 40-over cricket.

Prior to the final match at Derby some kind of end-of-season party was held, which was surprising enough. But it transpired that two club cars were damaged afterwards and the police became involved. Shaun Birbeck and Darren Blenkiron were suspended, although Birbeck was to be released in any case.

Cox, left out of the previous two games because Durham favoured an all-seam attack at Riverside, scored 91 at Derby to finish top of the batting averages. But Durham suffered their 12th defeat of the season and became only the fourth team since 1946 to go through a season without a championship win. They had won once in the Sunday League.

It was announced that 35-year-old Boon, who had retired from Test cricket, had signed a two-year contract. As it turned out, he needed a third season to complete the task of dragging Durham from the depths of despair.

CHAPTER 8

THE BOON
YEARS

AFTER years of worrying about whether their overseas target would be available for the full season, Durham had no such fears about David Boon. At 36, he had retired from international cricket after scoring 7,422 runs in 107 Tests and he had captained Tasmania, who were also relative newcomers to the first-class game. Renowned as someone who never knew when he was beaten, he was also a man whose wealth of experience would allow him to shoulder the troublesome burden of the Durham captaincy without it affecting his own form.

Mike Candlish, the chief executive, flew to Tasmania to spend a week with Boon discussing the way forward. The result was that he was virtually given carte blanche to run the cricket side of things, which effectively meant demotion for Geoff Cook, although with nine boys in the newly-established academy it gave Cook the opportunity to concentrate further on youth development. Steve Harmison was among those nine, but a back injury restricted him to playing for Ashington seconds as a batsman that season. After his harrowing debut at the end of 1996 he didn't seem particularly interested in Durham, but Cook stayed on his case.

There was a clear argument that a leader of Boon's stature was all Durham needed, but so disastrous had the 1996 season been that there was an element of panic in the signing of three others who would bat in the top six. Jon Lewis, from Essex, was an instant hit, went on to captain the team for four years and finally joined the coaching staff. Nick Speak, from Lancashire, never recovered the form which had seen him score 1,892 first-class runs in 1992 and his one season of captaincy at Durham was terminated in fairly acrimonious circumstances. Martin Speight, who had missed a season through illness, was similarly unable to recapture former batting glories, although he did well enough behind the stumps after moving partly because he had lost the gloves to Peter Moores at Sussex. Speight's arrival meant there was only one more season on the staff for David Ligertwood, who had rather controversially taken over from the popular Chris Scott, who was released at the end of the 1996 season.

The new signings gave Durham a new-look batting order in which there was no room for Michael Roseberry, Jimmy Daley, Darren Blenkiron, Stewart Hutton or Robin Weston. As Boon was arriving with no first-hand knowledge of the players' ability, selection for the opening Benson & Hedges matches seemed to be largely in the hands of Norman Gifford, who preferred James Boiling to David Cox. Both had played in seven championship matches the previous season, with Cox topping the batting averages with 434 runs at 48.22 and taking 26 wickets at 33.96. Boiling scored 79 runs at 11.28 and took eight wickets at 66.5.

Doubtless Cox's batting average was a fluke as he had cut and carved most of his runs and the more astute captains, like Matthew Maynard, quickly had him caught at gully. Perhaps Boiling was also seen as the sounder character and a tighter one-day bowler, but Boon tended to stick with the team initially selected for him and this effectively spelt the end for the unfortunate Cox. The same applied to Blenkiron. He may have finished the previous season under a disciplinary cloud, but he was still on the staff and, having scored three championship centuries, clearly expected some opportunities. They didn't materialise, he grew frustrated and in August was told he and the club did not appear to get on and he was free to go.

Paul Collingwood began the season as an opening batsman. It may not have done him any harm, but it was not a role to which he was suited, while Lewis immediately nailed down the top slot after previously considering himself a number three. Continuing the Durham tradition of big opening stands at The Parks, they put on 290 and after Collingwood fell for 107 Lewis went on to make 210 not out. He said: "Batsmen around the country will say I'm greedy, but the captain and coach insisted no-one should give his wicket away." It was little wonder that Boon decided this annual trip was a waste of time as the students slipped to 37 for seven after he declared on 353 for two.

The first championship game was at Old Trafford, bringing a reunion for Boon with Lancashire's chairman of selectors, Jack Simmons, who had described Durham's new captain as "the son I never had." Flat Jack was godfather to Boon's five-year-old son, also named Jack, with the relationship dating back to when Simmons first went to Tasmania in 1971-72. He returned every winter for 12 years and was captain when Boon first got into the team, having had him signed up at 14 because he was so confident in his ability.

"Like Durham, I felt Tasmania had to build from the bottom upwards and I used to go into the schools," said Simmons. "That's how I first discovered David. He's a very nuggety character. Richie Benaud said no-one had ever worn Australia's baggy green cap with greater pride. He is not the flamboyant type and he's fairly quiet compared with a lot of Australians, but they have looked to him to lead them in many ways. I am sure there's a lot of talent in Durham and he will convince the players of their abilities."

Boon had an early taste of a problem which had frequently afflicted Durham, namely knocking over the tail. Even Lancashire's No 11, Peter Martin, had scored a century at Gateshead Fell in 1992 and this time he put on 156 for the last wicket with Glen Chapple. Boon looked as immovable as Ayers Rock as he scored 85 not out, the previous highest championship score by a Durham captain being 67 by Phil Bainbridge. The last two days were washed out, then Boon scored a century in his first competitive match at Riverside to earn a Benson & Hedges win against Northants.

With the pitch playing well, things were clearly looking up. But Simon Brown, who took six for 30 against Northants, may have got a little carried away on the B & H trip to Scotland which followed. Returning to his Forfar hotel in the wee small hours, some fanciful notion drove him to inspect the contents of a builders' skip. He tried to balance what he assumed was an empty paint can on his head, only to discover it wasn't empty at all as a coating of gloss deposited itself on his cranium. An attempt to cut his hair off left him with a few stray tufts and he was a comical sight when play began in Lochside Park, where the distant Grampians reminded the Scots of the mountain they had to climb to compete at this level. They made 150 for eight and Durham raced home by eight wickets in 24.3 overs with Michael Foster hammering an unbeaten 73.

There was a break for snow in the next B & H match, at home to Leicestershire on May 5, and the new Duckworth/Lewis method came into operation. Durham fell 19 short of the revised target it set them and their hopes of quarter-final qualification vanished.

In the final first-class match at Hartlepool, injuries provided an unexpected opportunity for Alan Walker, who responded with seven for 56 against Nottinghamshire on what he described as a "plug-away pitch." Speak batted for five and half hours for 93, but rain robbed Durham of a deserved victory.

If that was annoying there was heartbreak to follow as a one-day match against the Australians at Riverside was called off at 10am following torrential rain. More than 1,000 people were already in the ground for the prestigious occasion, which also involved Kevin Keegan opening a new £2.3m stand. "The queen came to open the first stand, so to have me here is a bit of a come-down," he said.

It was still too wet the following day for the match against Worcestershire to start, which probably created more newspaper space for the revelation that Shropshire had banned former Warwickshire player Paul Smith for admitting in a Sunday newspaper that he had taken drugs throughout his first-class career. As a native of Newcastle, he had often been linked with Durham.

The respite did nothing for the casualty list and the new ball against Worcestershire was entrusted to Martin Saggers and Steve Lugsden, who bowled nine wides. Durham followed on 219 behind, but did much better second time around and Worcestershire had to score 114 to win in 25 overs. The scores finished level as they struggled to 113 for eight, with Saggers taking five for 57.

After making his maiden championship 50 against Worcestershire, Foster scored his only championship century in the next match at Cardiff, fearlessly winning an intriguing tussle with Waqar Younis. When Durham were in a hopeless position on 81 for five in reply to 597 for eight, Foster put on 140 with Boon and said: "I think it's OK to hook Waqar on a slow pitch. The skipper was happy for me to do it as long as I left the quicker one, which goes over your head."

Durham lost by an innings and eight runs, despite a second innings 149 from John Morris, who had been working over the winter with Graham Gooch and said: "I put a lot of hard work in. I had a kick up the backside, which was quite frightening, last year and I don't want it to happen again." In the next match he scored 124 at home to Sussex, but Durham ended up hanging on for a draw on 269 for eight, 38 short of their target.

Jimmy Daley was included for a trip to Cambridge University, but had to sit with his pads on for four hours while Boon and Speak put on 203. There were no moans from Daley, who denied that he had been approached by other counties and said: "I wouldn't really be interested anyway. I would die for Durham. Playing for them is all I've ever really wanted to do. I have had a few chats with David Boon and he has encouraged me to be positive. He wants us to be one big unit working together."

It was back to the usual line-up for the next match against Kent at Darlington, where Boon and Speak both made ducks but Durham recovered from 127 for seven on a blameless pitch through Lewis and Boiling. They put on 120, of which the latter made 28 as Lewis became the second player to carry his bat for Durham, making 158 out of 251. Wayne Larkins had also made 158 in carrying his bat against Gloucestershire in 1994 and Lewis was surprised to be mentioned in the same breath. "I remember playing against Ned at Chelmsford when he hit Neil Foster's first ball of the match over extra cover for six," he said. "I'm known more for bloody-mindedness."

When Kent batted Melvyn Betts bowled fast away swing to take seven for 29 and Durham beat the leaders by 135 runs to record their first championship win for 24 games. Bowling his rarely-used off-spin only because of poor light, Boon took the last wicket with 5.4 overs left, having Martin McCague caught off bat and pad by Morris.

"I had to bowl to keep us on the ball-park and we should give credit to the umpires for not coming off," said Boon. Coach Norman Gifford admitted victory was a huge relief and added: "David is a quiet general. When a wicket fell he did not rush over and hug the bowler, he would go over last, tap him on the shoulder and offer a word of encouragement. He has a very calming influence. When he says something he means it, and people listen because of who he is."

It transpired that during an earlier rain break Gifford had tried to stop the players watching a television re-run of Australian Bob Massie taking 16 wickets in the Lord's Test in 1972. It would do them no good to watch some of the poor strokes played by England, he said, and they realised what he meant when they saw the last man out, having a huge waft outside off stump, was none other than Gifford.

Momentum was lost as the four-day match against Hampshire at Riverside, scheduled for July 2-5, was totally washed out, then Collingwood's season was ended by a hand injury suffered in the second team. In ten championship innings as an opener he had averaged 16.9, and Michael Roseberry now had a chance to return to the team.

The next stop was Scarborough for the Northern Electric Trophy, the festival having been brought forward to mid-July from its time-honoured early September slot in an effort to pep it up. There was a perceived need to attract a younger audience, so music and dancing girls were introduced, although it struck me that no-one had told the seagulls about the change of date. Their raucous cries were all part of the tradition, but they failed to flock to the festival in their usual numbers, prompting speculation that the council had gone ahead with a planned gull cull. Perhaps these not-so-gullible creatures simply objected to the threat of being drowned out by the razzmatazz.

Batsmen walked to the crease to the accompaniment of music of their choice, John Morris selecting Sex and Drugs and Rock n' Roll, while Simon Brown went for Two Pints of Lager and a Packet of Crisps. Yorkshire's Darren Lehmann opted for Wild Thing, which at least had a smidgen of musical merit. But none of this went down particularly well with the festival die-hards and, mercy of mercies, it continues to thrive in early September. That's despite the scandalous ruination of the bar at the Royal Hotel, where the Tetley's Bitter used to be unsurpassed. Still, it's not bad at the Albert, just up the road from the ground, and if you need to clear the head in the morning there's nowhere better for a gentle jog than the firm sand in South Bay. That demands to be followed by a coffee in the wonderful Harbour Bar, which is akin to a 1950s American ice cream emporium.

Yorkshire skipper David Byas, back on his home ground, must have been humming Green Green Grass of Home when the covers for the championship clash at Scarborough were removed. After a series of high-scoring draws at the ground, the ends of the pitch for this match had been shaved to suit the spinners, while the 15 yards in the middle would have produced a decent crop of hay. This suited a seam attack of Darren Gough, Chris Silverwood, Peter Hartley and Craig White rather better than Durham's lighter infantry. White forced Roseberry to retire after a blow on the helmet. He returned two and a half hours later and was given out caught behind off the next ball by George Sharp. Roseberry stared back down the pitch for several seconds, clearly astonished both by the decision and the continuation of his own misfortunes. Sharp said he would report him.

Durham lost by an innings and 56 runs early on the third day and Boon said of the pitch: "I have never seen anything like it in my 20 years in first-class cricket. If England are trying to produce Test cricketers by playing four-day cricket, why produce a false sense of security about someone's ability by playing on something like that?" Byas said his only concern was to win games for Yorkshire.

While it seemed that even Boon might be in danger of becoming ensnared by the cricketing equivalent of the Bermuda Triangle – the Durham captaincy – his opposite number at Gloucestershire was clearly thriving. With another festival, this time in the tented splendour at Cheltenham, failing to lift Durham's spirits, Mark Alleyne took five for 14 to dismiss them for 86 then scored 169 as his team replied with 471 for six. After various ailments, Durham had selected John Wood for this match and a travelling fan asked him on the second morning: "Are you fit and raring to go, John?" The reply of "No, I've been vomiting all night" wasn't quite what the spectator wanted to hear, but Wood was the victim of a bout of gastro-enteritis which afflicted several players.

Durham fared better in the second innings and when they resumed on 321 for seven on the third morning they lost an early wicket then Wood stroked a glorious four through the covers. Morris tried to claim some of the credit, saying: "I've just been giving him a bit of coaching. He gets his head too far across and for someone with his ability he doesn't get enough runs." Seconds later Wood drove a catch straight to extra cover just as light rain was starting to fall and two overs later it was all over. The drizzle was just turning to heavy rain, which persisted for the rest of the day.

With a Sunday League match to hang around for, having a free Saturday afternoon provided a chance for exploration. Even in the rain, the deep valleys in the south-west corner of the Cotswolds placed the emphasis more firmly on the landscape than in the rather twee area better known to the tourists around Stow and the Slaughters. I had decamped from a pub at Oddington to a lovely old house offering bed and breakfast at Winstone, ten miles south of Cheltenham and just north of the delightful Duntisbourne Abbots. It was a few miles west of there that I discovered Sheepscombe and I have never missed an opportunity to return since. The fact that the landlord at the Butcher's Arms was in chatty mood that afternoon may have helped. I subsequently found that he was rarely behind the bar, but perhaps nowhere's perfect.

Durham went into August bottom of the Sunday League and with only their next visitors, Derbyshire, below them in the championship. There was some evidence that the variable bounce was back at Riverside as 16 wickets fell on the first day and 17 on the second. Simon Brown had nine in the match and Durham began the third day on 48 for three, needing a further 209 to win, with Stewart Hutton having been pinned lbw by a shooter for the second time in his first appearance of the season.

Horizontal bounce seemed to have left Durham with a vertical task, but as in the season's one other championship win, against Kent at Darlington, Jon Lewis found a durable companion in James Boiling. The nightwatchman completed his maiden half-century as they put on 204 and Lewis remained unbeaten on 160. If Derbyshire hadn't previously realised that Lewis was strong through the off-side off the back foot, they should have done long before Durham's victory was achieved by six wickets. The innings took Lewis past 1,000 first-class runs for the season.

With Speak averaging 16.11 in the championship, a chance was finally given to Robin Weston at The Oval, where he made 21 and 18 before twice being snared by Saqlain Mushtaq in a nine-wicket defeat. Boon said he had been impressed by Weston, who would be given another chance, but it was the end of the road for Blenkiron after being left out of the second team since early July. He was told in mid-August he was being released. He was still only 23 and had not grown out of his headstrong ways, which he admitted when he said: "They don't like it when someone stands up to them. I know I can be hot-headed, but we can't all be robots."

Harsh judgements over discipline were not uncommon during Norman Gifford's time at the club, and another who two years later would be accused of chucking his toys out of the pram was Melvyn Betts. But he looked set for a long and prosperous career with Durham, and possibly England, when he produced a sensational spell to take nine for 64 at Northampton. As in his seven for 29 against Kent, he bowled fast away swing in dismissing the hosts for 144. Three of his victims were bowled and five fell to edged catches, then Boon made a century and Hutton 95 in building a lead of 232. Betts had turned an ankle and as the press waited to speak to him Alan Walker emerged from the physio's room first and said: "He won't be long. He's just having an ice pack applied to his head, it's swollen that much."

Betts defied his injury to take four more wickets in the second innings, but Durham's hopes that Boiling and Cox would spin them to victory did not materialise as Northants crawled to 309 for nine to earn a draw. The spinners' failings clearly riled Gifford, who sent me away with a flea in my ear when I went to question him about it. I had obviously picked a bad time and was told that negative publicity wasn't helping the team. It was the only time I felt the sharp end of Norman's tongue, but I suspect some of the players weren't so lucky.

Weston made 36 and Boon a century in a rain-ruined home match against Middlesex, which was preceded by a minute's silence following the death from cancer of director Bill Milner, aged 49. The Middlesex team did not include David Follett, who had routed Durham at Lord's the previous year. He was now playing for Northants seconds and took two for 65 in 12 overs against Durham, with Michael Roseberry scoring his second successive second X1 century.

Home defeats by Warwickshire and Somerset followed, the former being notable for Nick Knight and Mark Wagh putting on 206, beating the highest opening stand at Riverside of 172, also set by Warwickshire in the ground's inaugural first-class match two years earlier. For Somerset, Mushtaq Ahmed began what would become many years of torment for Durham when he took three for four in 13 overs in the second innings.

That was the final home match of the season and there were rumblings among the members that Jimmy Daley would be leaving as his only appearance had been at Cambridge. One of the more vociferous members, lifelong devotee Mervyn Hardy, said: "We have a crown that is not exactly jewel-encrusted, but I understand we are letting the brightest star go. You wouldn't treat a sewer rat the way Jimmy has been treated. It's absolutely appalling. Apart from his ability, his demeanour has always been a credit to the club, and to his upbringing." Another member, Fred Gill, said: "We understand there will be an announcement at the end of the season, when we have all gone home. The same sort of thing happened when the captaincy was taken away from David Graveney and when Wayne Larkins was sacked. But this is even more emotive because Jimmy's a local lad. Seeing lads like him succeed is what Durham coming into first-class cricket is all about for most of us."

Daley himself was uncertain what to do as he had been approached by another county but still had a year left on his contract. He was finally selected for the last match of the season at Grace Road, taking the place of Weston, who had just heard that he was to be released. Daley contributed 36 in the second innings to a stand of 83 with Boon, which threatened to carry Durham to a target of 328. In the end they lost by 17 runs, Daley said he had enjoyed batting with Boon and decided to stay. Yet it seemed extremely odd that, other than Blenkiron, Weston was the only player to be released. He had had only 19 first-class innings, many of them on dodgy Riverside pitches and had made an impressive 36 there a few weeks earlier. His father's decision not to get involved with Durham at first-class level, after previously serving on the committee, undoubtedly created a political under-current which ultimately did Robin no favours.

He signed for Derbyshire and was second in their batting averages in each of the next two seasons, scoring three championship centuries in 1999.

But that was a time of great unrest at Derby and at the end of that season they lost five players they would rather have kept, Weston among them. He joined Middlesex at the same time as Michael Roseberry went back there in 2000. As boys they had gone to Lord's for coaching, prompting their fathers to build the McEwans Cricket Centre and create Durham's first-class platform. And now they were back at Lord's, but only briefly did it threaten to be Durham's loss as Weston averaged 41.93 in 2001, again hitting three centuries. Roseberry never could regain his form, while Weston faded in competition with Strauss, Joyce, Shah and Hutton and his career ended in 2003.

Durham finished the 1997 season third from the bottom of the championship, which equalled their previous highest in 1994. But among the young players only Betts and Foster had progressed, with Alan Walker playing in most of the games while four young seamers, Wood, Lugsden,.Campbell and Killeen, managed 14 first-class appearances between them. Boiling played in every championship match, and while contributing with the bat to the two victories, he took only 17 wickets at 49.7. With Cox's face clearly not fitting, Gifford's influence saw the bespectacled off-spinner Nicky Phillips signed from Sussex for the following season. It proved to be the end for Boiling and Cox, neither of whom played another first-class game.

1998

WHO was this mystery man in the line-up for the pre-season photo-call? He hadn't been named in the published staff list, but it transpired that a one-year contract had been quietly awarded to Steve Harmison. David Boon had needed to see him bowl only a few balls in the nets before demanding that he should be in the team.

The other new local lad on the staff was Michael Gough, whose signing had been trumpeted over the winter as he was the first player to be promoted from the academy. Ten years later, still only 28, he was promoted to the full umpires' list for 2009, having stopped playing at the end of the 2003 season because he wasn't enjoying it. This seemed incredible for someone who, on being awarded his initial contract, said: "I had offers from two other counties but I've wanted to play for Durham ever since they went first-class. I've been brought up to appreciate things and I certainly appreciate this opportunity I have been given."

A 6ft 2in opening batsman from Hartlepool, Gough captained England

Under 19s and was considered a definite England prospect. His father, also Michael, had played for Durham as a Minor County and Gough junior was always keen to stress the parental support he received. With a stable background, an apparently level head, and a deep love of the game there wasn't the slightest reason to suspect it would end as it did. It is sometimes said that the passion for sport in the North-East brings a level of media attention which creates its own pressure. It seems to have been that pressure, plus the expectation he placed upon himself, which drove Michael to seek a different first-class avenue.

In 1998 he had the added benefit of working with Graham Gooch, who had been taken on by Durham in a consultancy role. The general feeling was that it was now Boon or bust, with the Australian captain needing to build on the groundwork of his first season.

Gooch had said there was too much "dead wood" in county cricket, and although he wasn't referring to John Wood it was certain that the burly paceman was in the Last Chance Saloon. After six injury-plagued years he had worked hard on his fitness and also claimed to have learned how to swing and seam the ball instead of relying on pace and bounce. With Simon Brown troubled by a knee problem, Wood, Harmison and Melvyn Betts were selected for the first match at Edgbaston and the national press descended to see if Brian Lara could inflict further punishment on Durham.

Wood had him caught behind for a duck in the opening day's fourth over, prompting the Guardian's David Hopps to observe: "That will be the highlight of Durham's season." Shortly afterwards the national scribes were wondering why on earth Harmison was in the team as he opened with a full toss and a long hop, both hit for four by David Hemp.

Harmison settled down and took two wickets, while Betts took five. But Neil Smith rode his luck with 113 off 123 balls to carry Warwickshire to 336. Durham slumped to 45 for five before Paul Collingwood, who had opened before his injury the previous season, strode out to score his maiden championship century, which he reached with a pulled six off Ed Giddins. Boon also scored a hundred and Collingwood said: "He doesn't say a lot, but his sheer presence is very reassuring." The last remaining Durham record involving Ian Botham was expunged as his sixth-wicket stand of 152 with Anderson Cummins against Worcestershire at Stockton in 1993 was beaten by 41.

It was in Warwickshire's second innings that Harmison really made people sit up and take notice. He spreadeagled the stumps of Nick Knight and David Hemp, while Wood again saw off Lara for 13. Durham needed 219 to win and when rain ended play they were 90 for five, with Nick Speak having raced to 50 with batting of a quality not seen the previous season. He scored 41 of the 46 runs they added after lunch before the rain arrived at 2.30.

Back at Riverside, Harmison took the first four Gloucestershire wickets in a 12-over spell in which he conceded only 21 runs. He went on to complete his first five-wicket haul, then went in at 126 for nine with 12 needed to avoid the follow-on. A straight drive for four was followed by an attempted hook off Courtney Walsh, which brought a richly-acclaimed single, in what must have been the finest innings of 12 in Durham's history. Boon observed: "I have said throughout my career that if there's one bloke thou shalt not hook it's Courtney Walsh, but Steve has done it. He obviously has no thought process about getting flattened." Speak threatened to guide Durham to a victory target of 248, but he fell for 74 and they lost by 46 runs, Walsh finishing with six for 42.

Durham recorded their first away win in any competition against county opposition since August, 1995, when they beat Derbyshire by six runs in the Benson & Hedges Cup. They then needed a half-century from Martin Speight to scrape home by two wickets against Scotland, and 54 from Mike Foster helped them to a similarly narrow win at home to Worcestershire. He also took three wickets as Durham reached the last eight for the first time. But there was a danger they would go into the quarter-final at Headingley without Boon, who had suffered a broken toe in the nets, and vice-captain John Morris. There had been some extra fitness work over the winter and after following a thigh strain with a torn calf, Morris said: "I'm pulling muscles where I didn't have them before." Old stagers would have observed that many a true word is spoken in jest.

Speak took over the captaincy and proved quite innovative in leading Durham to victory in a Sunday League match at Nottingham in which James Boiling took five for 23. But, having lost his championship place to Phillips, who was faring no better, he announced in mid-May that he would be retiring at the end of the season to take up teaching and was ignored thereafter.

With Jon Lewis also succumbing to a pulled muscle, Gough made his debut at home to Essex and batted for 17 minutes short of five hours in making 62. "I knew my mum and dad were by the sightscreen and there were so many emotions going through my head when I got to 50," he said. "I can't express how much it means to me."

The match also witnessed the start of Jimmy Daley's first run in the team since Boon's arrival and his second innings stand of 65 with Speak helped Durham into a winning position, despite Danny Law taking Riverside's first hat-trick. He had Foster and Phillips caught at second slip and pinned Betts lbw. Betts had the last word, taking six for 83 as Durham wrapped up a 95-run victory, and Geoff Arnold was greatly impressed. The bowling coach had spent the previous two seasons dividing his time between the two counties, but was now with Essex full-time. "Betts could play for England," he said. "I have worked a lot with him and I have a lot of time for him." Of Wood, he said: "He looks a different bowler. He's hitting a length instead of trying to bang it in halfway down. At 27 he has seen the light, but he should have been doing it when he was 24."

In the Sunday League clash Durham handed a debut to Andrew Pratt, the 23-year-old wicketkeeper from Crook, and he went in at No 11 to score five runs off the two balls he faced in a tied game. Daley made 69 out of Durham's 194 for nine.

Gough had been selected ahead of Stewart Hutton, for whom the 18-year-old's success was further bad news. They opened together in the next match at Cambridge University and both made centuries, but it proved to be Hutton's last appearance. In 66 first-class matches he had a batting average of 29.56, which in Durham terms wasn't bad. But he was never quite a fixture in the side and could be seen as a victim of the influx of imports prior to the 1997 season.

Gooch was present at Cambridge and said of Gough: "He showed great application on his debut last week in conditions which were not easy. The Cambridge attack is not the greatest but you still have to apply yourself and he has again proved he can bat for a long time, which bodes well for the four-day game."

Dickie Bird took the players off for tea two minutes early with Hutton on 99 and Gough on 96. On his last appearance at the ground, the umpire had an important function to perform during the interval, cutting the cake which marked the 150th anniversary, to the day (May 16), since Cambridge first played cricket at Fenner's.

Cambridge were captained by Quentin Hughes, the off-spinner who had made his Durham debut aged 16 in their last Minor Counties side seven years earlier. What little bowling he did in this match confirmed how much his batting had taken over. He had looked highly promising, as had Jason Searle, another off-spinner from Bath taken on to the staff at the age of 17 in 1993. He also played in this match, but was released at the end of the season and the difficulty of developing spin bowlers on seaming North-East pitches has remained unresolved.

Marc Symington, an 18-year-old all-rounder from Norton, made his debut at Cambridge and took a wicket with his sixth ball when Sussex's James Pyemont edged to second slip. Although it was known that Simon Brown would eventually need a knee operation he appeared in this match with a view to playing in the B & H quarter-final, and took six for 17.

Brown wasn't risked in the next match at Canterbury when, still without Boon, Durham lost by an innings and 27 runs after Robert Key scored his maiden century before being bowled by Steve Harmison. They became friends at the inaugural ECB Academy and ten years later they were the only survivors from the 1998 clash in the 2008 match which saw Durham clinch the championship.

Durham gambled on the fitness of both Boon and Brown for the B & H match at Headingley. Brown bowled straight through his ten-over allocation, taking one for 28, only for his knee to give way in the field. His season was over, and so was Durham's interest in the cup as Yorkshire recovered from two for two through a Darren Lehmann century and won by 102 runs. A few days later, however, Durham went into June looking down from the giddy heights of third in the championship after an eight-wicket win at Trent Bridge. On a well-grassed pitch Betts took five for 59 in Nottinghamshire's first innings, then Durham were rescued from 98 for six by a stand of 110 between Collingwood and Foster. The youngster was happy to play second fiddle, but when three more wickets fell Collingwood cut loose, racing from 50 to 97 in 34 balls of thrilling strokeplay. He was left stranded three short of his century when Harmison fell lbw to Zimbabwean leg-spinner Paul Strang. Needing 167 to win, Durham were guided home by an unbroken stand of 120 between Speak and Boon.

Foster had also taken four wickets in Nottinghamshire's second innings and was continuing to look a strong all-round presence in the side. It seemed that he would fulfil his obvious potential with his third county, but within a few weeks a chronic back problem was to re-surface, effectively ending his career. His hitting prowess had first come to light in a 70-ball Sunday League century for Yorkshire at Grace Road in 1993, which included eight sixes, and it was underlined when Durham next went to Lord's. In thrashing 70 in the Sunday game he lifted one of his three sixes on to the pavilion's south turret, which had last been cleared more than 100 years previously by Albert Trott, an Australian who played for Middlesex before becoming a member of that notable band of cricketers who have taken their own life.

Foster apart, Durham's Sunday performance was very much a case of after the Lord Mayor's Show as the previous day had witnessed a thrilling one-wicket championship win. Justin Langer was greatly impressed as Betts and Harmison took four scalps each in Middlesex's first innings, becoming the first two bowlers in the country to 25 wickets. Betts followed up with five in the second innings and Harmison three, and after Gough's 56 set them on the way to a victory target of 240 the two bowling heroes came together with 12 still needed. The target was nine off two overs when Betts launched Phil Tufnell into the new Grand Stand over mid-wicket then turned the next ball to fine leg to finish on 29 not out.

The opening day's proclamation that Wood removing Lara for a duck would be the highlight of Durham's season had been proved utterly wrong and I wrote at the time: "It was simply the best day's cricket I have seen – a perfect advert for four-day County Championship cricket and another kick in the teeth for the two-division lobby." As Betts scampered the winning runs his team-mates were dancing jubilantly on their dressing room balcony and it was said that Boon jumped on someone's back. But, phlegmatic as ever, he emerged an hour later to tell the press: "We must not get carried away by this."

He added: "There were no heroes because everybody contributed. The good sides are the ones that win the tight games and these boys are learning very quickly. The success has come far quicker than I expected. The ones who are really coming through are the local lads. That's an enormous plus for the county and the region."

That proved a memorable last visit to the old Lord's press box. The new media centre, already dubbed the Steel Gherkin and looking like something out of ET, was taking shape at the Nursery End. While the two electronic scoreboards offered oodles of information, the umpires found they were too remote from the scorers to see whether their signals were being acknowledged. As if to prove that technology didn't have all the answers, Durham's Brian Hunt visited the kitchen for the solution and spent the match waving back at the umpires with a large tea towel.

Northamptonshire came to Riverside with a seam attack which included Devon Malcolm, David Follett and Franklyn Rose, who had bowled the first ball at the ground when on trial with Durham seconds. But none impressed in a rain-ruined match in which Durham reached 249 for four in reply to 163 all out, with John Wood having taken five for 52, his best figures for four years. Unfortunately, the fact that they were deprived by the weather of their fourth win in five games seemed to burst Durham's bubble. They were second in the table in mid-June, but in the end only the three teams they had beaten, plus Northants, finished below them.

It was also a turning point for Collingwood, who went into the next match at home to Yorkshire with a championship average of 50 but was bowled for a duck shouldering arms to Paul Hutchison. Boon scored an unbeaten 139 in a total of 337, to which Michael Vaughan responded with 177 out of 319. It was the highest individual score at Riverside at the time and was followed by Durham being dismissed for what was then the lowest total on the ground. In an attack shorn of Darren Gough, Chris Silverwood and Craig White through injury, left-armers Hutchison, Ryan Sidebottom and Richard Stemp shared the wickets as Durham inexplicably folded for 74. Faced with five overs' batting before lunch they had taken 16 runs off the first three overs to stretch their lead to 34 and the perfect four-day match appeared to be unfolding. Then Jon Lewis and Nick Speak were given out to successive balls from Hutchison and TV replays suggested that both of the decisions by umpire Trevor Jesty were highly questionable.

It was not the first time I had observed that Durham had cause to ask who put the jest in Jesty? This time he clearly did them a huge disservice as their encouraging form abruptly deserted them. The pitch was blameless as Yorkshire cruised to a nine-wicket win. Boon said: "It was a huge day as far as the learning process of this club goes. It showed that complacency and just expecting things to happen cannot be allowed to creep into your game."

Another extraordinary aspect of the game was that it was the first time more than 100 overs of spin had been bowled in a match at Riverside. Durham had tended to favour an all-seam attack there and the previous year the first wicket they had taken with spin at their headquarters went to James Boiling on August 22. Since replacing Boiling, Nicky Phillips had bowled only 32.4 overs in three games at Riverside, yet in Yorkshire's first innings he sent down 52 and took four for 89. Richard Stemp bowled 46 overs in Durham's two innings and Phillips brought up the hundred when Yorkshire batted again.

It was the first time Phillips had taken four wickets in a championship innings and he said: "Despite the wet weather, the pitch was quite dry. It also helps to have a left-arm seamer creating rough outside the off stump, and with Paul Hutchison getting close to the stumps it gave me a good patch to aim at."

He followed by winning the Gold Award in a NatWest Trophy tie against Norfolk at Lakenham, a Norwich ground with a thatched pavilion, owned by the Colmans mustard family. Phillips' figures of 12-4-16-2 were the most economical by a Durham bowler in the event since first-class status was achieved, although former Kent seamer David Halfyard had recorded 12-5-11-2 for Durham against Oxfordshire in 1972.

David Boon walked to the crease at Lakenham to the accompaniment of the lager-fuelled chant of: "You fat Aussie, you ate all the pies." But as far as he was concerned the only pies were those purveyed by the Norfolk bowlers as he made 80 not out in an eight-wicket win marred by injuries to Mike Foster and Michael Roseberry. They weren't serious, but the cumulative impact of their various mishaps meant that time was running out for them both.

Talking of pies, their arrival at Darlington was always guaranteed to have the press corps salivating whenever Durham played at Feethams. On this occasion we were also delighted to receive a consignment of Mars bars from Pat Walton, who has been with Durham throughout their first-class life, intially as the cricket secretary then in a more senior role.

Feethams was usually a happy hunting ground, but Durham's habit of playing like chickens against the Leicestershire Foxes resurfaced after Darren Maddy scored 162 out of the visitors' 414. There was another five-wicket haul for Wood, but Phil Simmons then took seven for 49 as Durham were routed for 134. This beat the West Indian's previous best figures of six for 14, also taken against Durham, and this was the man who had bowled appallingly for them in a NatWest Trophy tie at Old Trafford in their Minor Counties days, when he was the Guisborough professional.

Durham succumbed for 177 in their second innings to lose by an innings and 103 runs to a team pursuing their second title in three years. Jimmy Daley, finally drafted in because Michael Gough had sprained an ankle, top scored in both innings with 30 and 42 not out.

John Morris had been promoted to open in Gough's absence and in the first innings against Leicestershire he took 46 balls to get off the mark as he concentrated on surviving some excellent bowling from Alan Mullally. There was apparently a dramatic shift in the tone of the conversation as his batting partner, Nick Speak, kept enquiring after his well-being. After eight overs the reply was "Yes, I'm fine, I'm enjoying it." Two overs later it was much the same, but two overs after that it had changed to: "For god's sake get a single and let me get down that end."

Half an hour before going in to bat at number ten, John Wood heard that his wife had given birth to a son. He proceeded to blast 36 off 35 balls before being spared the lengthy post-mortem as he rushed off to see the new arrival. It serves as a reminder of how attitudes would quickly change as a few years later Durham would bat with ten men so that James Brinkley could be present at the birth of his child.

Leicestershire included former Durham second team all-rounder Dominic Williamson, from Esh Winning, in the Sunday League match and he took two for 22 as they won by five runs.

It was around this time that it became clear that the writing was on the wall for David Cox. He was left out of the second team to accommodate Steve Chapman, an all-rounder from Bishop Auckland who had been tried in the second X1 several years earlier but had since converted from left-arm seam to spin. Cox, in fact, did not play again and was released, without explanation, in mid-July. Naturally tubby, he probably didn't live up to the required work ethic, but a career which had promised much was finally ended by some remarks he made out of sheer frustration. What rankled with the members was that James Boiling had been preferred to Cox in the previous season, with no long-term benefit for the club.

Memories of Cox's last-wicket stand of 103 with Betts at Hove two years earlier had faded, especially as at this stage of the season Betts had recorded six ducks in the championship, and three in the Sunday League, in which his average from six innings was 0.6.

Norman Gifford's belief that he could turn Chapman into a first-class spinner proved over-optimistic. A dedicated cricketer who later became a coach, Chapman was handed a contract, but was 27 when he made his debut and after three first-class games he was released at the end of the 2000 season.

For their NatWest Trophy second round tie against Middlesex, Durham went to Southgate, where the stewards were rather more pleasant than the officious jobsworths at Lord's. One of them asked me very politely if I would mind not walking in front of the sightscreen, so I equally politely pointed out that this requirement applied only after play had actually begun. Around an hour after play started Henry Blofeld arrived in the press tent. Why so late? "My dear old thing," he explained. "I would have been here on time but I thought the match was at Uxbridge."

Nick Speak made 73 out of Durham's 240 for eight and they seemed to be coasting to victory when Middlesex were 129 for seven. But an exemplary performance in the field disintegrated as soon as Keith Dutch put bat to ball. He put on 49 in eight overs with Alistair Fraser and scored the final 66 runs in seven overs with Richard Johnson.

Other than Daryll Cullinan scoring 200 not out, Riverside's first double century, the visit of the South Africans was unremarkable. Hansie Cronje's delayed second innings declaration killed the game, but at least he had some kind words to say about the hosts. "They are the first county who have put out their strongest side against us and it was the best county attack we have faced. I would not be in the least surprised to see Melvyn Betts get into the England team. The ground and facilities are excellent and we would be happy to come back here for a Test match."

A Taunton pitch with a tinge of green offered steep bounce and while Steve Harmison took four wickets in Somerset's first innings and impressed Andrew Caddick it was the Somerset man who took ten in the match as his side won by ten wickets. It was all very reminiscent of the collapse against Yorkshire as Durham made 259 and competed on equal terms until they allowed the last two Somerset wickets to add 104 runs. Durham then folded for 128 and Boon had no complaints about Caddick persistently bowling short from round the wicket. Caddick had taken his tally against Durham to 51 wickets in seven matches.

Having played in all Durham's championship games, Harmison was now required to play for England Under 19s at a time when Justin Langer was quoted in The Cricketer magazine as saying: "This kid is seriously quick. He is capable of bowling a cricket ball as quick as anyone in the world." And Caddick told the Western Morning News: "He's quick and gets bounce because of his height. I hope they use him wisely and don't burn him out while he's still learning."

Durham's demise was true to form as the wheels traditionally came off in July. The only championship matches they had won in July were at Chelmsford in 1993 and Swansea in 1995, which began on June 29. Another unscheduled Saturday off in Somerset offered some consolation, of course, and it was while wondering down the main street in Dunster that I bumped into Brian Lander and Ray Pallister, who had bemoaned a similar scenario at Worcester two years earlier. Of the previous day's play, they observed: "The sad part about it was that it was so predictable."

County cricket's public address men are not renowned for their wit, but the one at Taunton caused a ripple of laughter when he announced: "Would those people high in the Ian Botham stand….I'm sorry I mean high up in the Ian Botham Stand…." Botham had recently been refused admission to the United States because of his long-forgotten drugs offence.

At a time of year when they might have expected Nicky Phillips to come into his own on dry southern pitches, Durham moved on to find another green-top at Southampton. They left out Phillips for the first time and brought Steve Lugsden into an all-seam attack. Alex Morris took four for 30 as Durham were dismissed for 203, and his pony-tail prompted the observation that he was a most unusual product of Barnsley. It is rare indeed for people from the south Yorkshire town to christen their sons Alexander Corfield and Zachary Clegg, and Yorkshire had released them both the previous season. Durham's Morris, christened John Edward, made his top championship score of the season to date, 48, but the presence of Graham Gooch in his consultancy role worked against Durham.

He was also an England selector at the time, and after scoring a superb 134 Robin Smith said: "I was really inspired by the fact that Graham was here. I hope my innings has given him and the other selectors food for thought."

Lugsden, Betts and Wood took three wickets each, but Durham trailed by 193 and were saved by rain after Martin Speight made his best score for the county, 97 not out. He had gone into the match with a season's average of 16.8.

It was an oddity, caused partly by the weather, that Hampshire at that time remained the only county not to have beaten Durham in the championship, yet Durham were regularly thrashed by Sussex, who were not a great side. The next port of call on this southern tour was the Saffrons ground at Eastbourne and, having played no spinners at Southampton, Durham opted for two here, handing a debut to Steve Chapman. Harmison was back, but Betts had succumbed to an Achilles injury and Foster had just played his final first-class match because of his back problem.

It appeared that Durham were gambling on winning the toss, but in glorious weather they lost it and Sussex scored 460, Chapman taking none for 79 in 29 overs. He said: "This is all I've ever wanted to do. If it's the only game I play no-one can take it away from me. I used to bowl left-arm aerosol, spraying it everywhere. I had a bad action and it was giving me injuries. After I changed to spin I wrote to Norman Gifford and asked if I could come to the nets. He has been brilliant. At the start of the year my bowling was very raw and rough at the edges, but Norman has refined it."

He added: "The lads told me before the start not to expect it to turn, and it didn't. Bowling on something so unhelpful is not funny."

Despite unbeaten half-centuries in the first innings from Speight and in the second from Collingwood, Durham lost by an innings and 81 runs.

The tour had reinforced my dislike of hotels. Having stayed in my usual lovely cottage B and B in Somerset, the three-day gap before Hampshire offered a chance to explore a county not on the first-class circuit, Dorset. I had my family with me on the first part of the trip and thought a couple of days at the seaside would be nice. We booked for two nights in a Weymouth hotel, but stayed only one as it was unspeakably awful. Why stay there when there was an old vicarage in the Piddle Valley offering B and B at a cheaper rate, or a farmhouse in the heart of Thomas Hardy country? Lyme Regis in the middle of a hot afternoon was a disappointment, largely because it was so busy. But an almost deserted Lulworth Cove just before sunset was as sublime as a Tom Graveney cover drive, especially after a visit to the nearby Weld Arms. On top of the Weld? Well, almost.

Being a lover of promenades, unless they are as tacky as Blackpool's, cricket at seaside resorts presents a dilemma, especially in Sussex, where the Downs are in such proximity. But having not visited Eastbourne before, I decided to give a sea-front hotel a try. I felt rather inconsiderate when passing the Zimmer frames on the way out for my early morning jog in the bracing sea air, but the hotel was tolerable for me and clearly much better than that for the vast majority, being of advancing years. As at Hove, the cricket ground was much less inspiring than Sussex's inland venues at Horsham and Arundel.

Two threadbare attacks resulted in a high-scoring draw when Glamorgan visited Riverside, handing a championship debut to 19-year-old Simon Jones. With Harmison and Gough on England Under 19 duty, Durham gave Lugsden another chance but were in big trouble when Betts collapsed in agony after four balls of Glamorgan's first innings. A torn groin muscle ended his season, and with Lugsden taking two for 151 in 29.2 overs the end of his career was nigh.

Boon and Glamorgan's Tony Cottey, a regular thorn in Durham's side, scored first innings centuries then John Morris made 163 as the match petered out with Durham reaching 385 for seven second time around.

This run-fest, in which 1,267 were scored for the loss of 27 wickets, was followed by the fall of 20 wickets on the first day of Lancashire's visit, for which Neil Killeen and Jason Searle had been drafted in, while Andrew

Pratt made his championship debut because Martin Speight was ill. Killeen took five for 49 then in the midst of all the mayhem Jon Lewis became the first player to carry his bat twice for Durham, making 70 out of 158. Second innings centuries by Neil Fairbrother and Graham Lloyd exposed Durham's limitations, Lugsden taking one for 62 in 13 overs in his final appearance, while Searle had three for 92. It wasn't a bad effort, but he too would shortly find himself on the scrapheap. Nick Speak was unable to bat against his former colleagues after suffering a bad groin strain in taking a diving catch, and with Wasim Akram and Glen Chapple taking four wickets each Durham folded for 122 in their second innings to lose by 350 runs.

Pratt top-scored with 34, otherwise Lancashire were held up only by John Barnes's car. Playing for Newcastle at the time, the footballer had to be summoned from training on an adjacent ground to move his Toyota Lexus because the glint off the windscreen was dazzling the batsmen. This was also the match in which a Wasim Akram six smashed a headlight on the car belonging to Radio Lancashire commentator John Gwynn. Subsequently better known for his enthusiastic darts commentary, Gwynn on this occasion was to be seen dashing out of the press box to shake his fist at Wasim, who had looked every inch a world-class all-rounder throughout the match.

Both attacks were also depleted at Derby, where Marc Symington's bustling medium pace earned three wickets in the first innings on his championship debut. He claimed Australian Michael Slater, lbw for 54, as his maiden scalp. Speak's injury allowed Michael Roseberry to come in and he eclipsed his previous top championship score for Durham of 60 by making 97. But Jimmy Daley took the honours by erasing four years of disappointment since his 159 not out at Portsmouth by making 157 out of 434 for six. It was not enough to force a victory following the first day's washout as Derbyshire reached 269 for nine in their second innings, Robin Weston making 45. Nicky Phillips completed his first five-wicket haul, but Symington suffered a side strain, opening the door for Martin Saggers to stake a belated claim for his retention.

It was too late, however. With Killeen also injured, Saggers was selected for the visit of Surrey, but it was merely an opportunity to put himself in the shop window. With Gooch heavily involved in the contract talks, Durham had decided that Killeen was a better prospect as back-up to Brown, Harmison, Betts and Wood. There were also two highly promising seamers in the academy in Mark Davies and Ian Hunter. It was announced that Saggers, Lugsden, Searle and Colin Campbell would be released, in addition to Boiling, Cox and Hutton, who had already gone. Alan Walker's playing contract would not be renewed, but he would be awarded a coaching role.

Morris made another century against Surrey as Durham reached 231 for three in reply to 323 before rain washed out most of the third day. Durham needed 19 more runs for the bonus point which would guarantee their highest championship finish and they were duly handed those runs in one over of dross from Jon Batty on the final morning. At the end of that over the press box door was flung open and a fan fumed: "Put it in the Echo that they're robbing the members."

Some of those members reckoned they knew from the moment the first ball was bowled precisely how things would unfold. They remembered Riverside's first taste of declaration bowling designed for Durham to be the beneficiaries of a generous target. On that occasion they were shot out by Kent for 85, and this time they needed a last-wicket stand of 33 in order to reach 91.

As often happened after the pitch had sweated under covers, the ball seamed alarmingly and 37-year-old Joey Benjamin took six for 35 and Durham lost by 121 runs, having been set a target of 213 in 61 overs after they fed Surrey 142 runs in 15.4 overs. Jon Lewis claimed his only first-class wicket as he had Mark Butcher stumped by Speight.

The victory kept Surrey on Leicestershire's tail in the title race, but they were bottom of the Sunday League, one place below Durham, and the places remained unaltered despite Surrey's victory by 101 runs. After two years as the AXA League, the competition was to be replaced by two divisions of a 50-over National League.

For the final game at Worcester, Kent's coach, John Wright, was present to watch Saggers, who bowled well and took three for 47 as the hosts made 310. Harmison took four wickets to pass 50 for the season and Durham's haul of 65 bowling points was only three short of the maximum and was matched only by Gloucestershire. After shouldering a huge burden for six years, Simon Brown had not been unduly missed as Wood finished with 61 wickets. Only Brown had taken more in a season for Durham, with 66 in 1994 and 69 in 1996. Boon was the only batsman to reach 1,000 runs, passing the landmark in that final match, which Durham lost by 155 runs after leading by 32 in the first innings.

Jimmy Daley, who played in ten games, finished second to Boon in the championship averages with 554 runs at 32.58 and signed a new two-year contract.

Harmison had begun to show the first signs of the sore shins which were to trouble him for some time, and he was pulled out of the second Under 19 Test against Pakistan. But he and Betts were selected for the England A tour to Zimbabwe and South Africa, while Michael Gough, Marc Symington, Ian Hunter and left-arm spinner Graeme Bridge were in the England Under 19 squad.

Harmison said: "If anyone had told me at the start of the season I would be going on an England A tour I would have laughed in their face. Last year there were times when I thought I would never play for Durham again. But I was given a fitness programme and worked really hard at it. This season has been a long slog, but the more I play the more I enjoy it. Going on the A tour will not be as big a step as it was going from Ashington to Pakistan with England Under 19s."

Harmison picked out Boon as the biggest influence in his development, saying: "He really looks after everybody. Everything in the club revolves around him. As a young lad you couldn't ask for anyone better."

Little wonder, then, that Durham persuaded Boon to return for a third season.

CHAPTER 9
BOON OR BUST

HIS work unfinished, at 38 David Boon had given himself one more season to get Durham into the inaugural division one with the championship due to be split in 2000. John Morris had handed over the vice-captaincy to Nick Speak, Michael Roseberry had opted out of the last two years of his contract to return to Middlesex, and 11 of the trimmed-down staff of 20 were from the North-East. Three others were from Yorkshire, but one of them, Michael Foster, was obliged to retire in mid-season through injury. As a genuine all-rounder of considerable talent, he had given Durham a better balance when fit the previous season and it was a sad day when he had to quit, aged 26.

Graham Gooch was still there in his consultancy role and on his recommendation a Lord's groundstafff boy, Muazam Ali, a batsman who had played for Essex seconds, was taken on to the staff. Marc Symington also had a contract, as did Nicky Hatch, a 6ft 8in seamer from Darlington, and former Yorkshire Academy all-rounder Ryan Robinson, who hailed from Huddersfield and was a cousin of Alan Walker.

The start of the season was brought forward to April 13 because of the World Cup and, much to their annoyance, Durham's first three matches were at home, starting against Worcestershire. At 11am on the first morning Riverside was covered by an inch of snow, which at least allowed Boon to pose in a woolly hat, tossing up a snowball, for what became a famous photograph. When it appeared a year or so later in the picture quiz on Question of Sport, one contestant got his moustaches mixed up when he mistook Boon for Merv Hughes.

It was not exactly a baptism of fire for the new groundsman, David Measor, who had taken over on the retirement of Tom Flintoft. He also had to prepare for Riverside's international debut with two World Cup matches coming to the ground – Pakistan v Scotland on May 20 and Australia v Bangladesh the following week. Measor had worked for 12 years at Seaton Carew and four at Hartlepool before joining the Durham staff in 1995.

"When I got up the sun was shining and the ground was dry," he said on that first morning. "It started to drizzle, then it turned to sleet and by 9.30 it was snowing. All the preparation we have put in has gone down the drain. It's been a wet winter, but we put some new drains into the wetter areas and there has never been any standing water. Now we'll have to wait for the snow to melt."

Mike Candlish, the chief executive, said: "We usually make six or seven requests with regard to fixtures which might, for example, include playing Yorkshire at the height of summer. But this year we made only two and one of those was to start away from home. We were particularly keen for that to happen."

A seam attack of Brown, Betts, Harmison and Wood was predicted to be as good as any in the country and it was Brown, back after his knee operation, who led the way with six for 25 the following day as the snowy wastes were transformed into a green and pleasant land. As the sun disappeared the threat of a return to icy conditions saw Bradford-born David Leatherdale provide some Yorkshire grit by making 85 out of 152. No-one else passed 15.

Only 100 overs' play was possible on the first three days, but Jon Lewis, John Morris, David Boon and Paul Collingwood all made half-centuries before Durham declared on 303 for six. They had 66 overs to dismiss Worcestershire and had them reeling on 68 for six before two showers interrupted their progress. The visitors finished on 137 for seven.

With sponsors Newcastle Breweries promoting their Fosters brand, Durham began life as the Dynamos, their new one-day moniker, looking like 11 cans of amber nectar. It was barely appropriate on another perishing day, interrupted by showers. The Duckworth/Lewis method left them needing four runs with three wickets standing when the last over began in near darkness at 7.55. But four balls later they were all out – there were two run-outs – and their chance to beat Surrey for the first time in any competition had finished two runs short.

The visit of Hampshire provided first-day evidence that the potency of Durham's seam attack might now be blunted by mellowing pitches. Tom Flintoft knew Durham had played on his square too soon and always insisted it would eventually be full of runs. Will Kendall scored a century in Hampshire's total of 366 then Durham reached 73 for one before Hampshire's gentler bowlers, Simon Renshaw and John Stephenson, found something in the docile surface. Durham were all out for 167 and, following on, collapsed again from 172 for three to 264 all out after half-centuries by Gough, Daley and Boon. Hampshire won by eight wickets to cast off the unwanted tag of being the only county not to have beaten Durham in the championship.

The batting woes continued as Daley made 90 out of 189 in the next National League game, at home to Middlesex, for whom Roseberry scored an unbeaten 77 in an eight-wicket win. It was a throwback to his previous existence with Middlesex, when he hardly ever failed to make runs against Durham. Why he couldn't do it for them is a mystery he will take to his grave, although he let it be known when he left that he was not impressed with some aspects of their management.

With the World Cup coming up, Durham decamped to Stockton for their next match. But first they played Scotland at Riverside and won by only two runs as Gavin Hamilton made 91 and James Brinkley 40. Both would later join Durham and they were also the only batsmen to pass 20 – Hamilton made 76 – when Scotland lost to Pakistan a few days later by 94 runs. This was the first visit to Riverside for Shoaib Akhtar, another future signing, and he took three for 11.

Harmison had impressed on the England A tour over the winter, but there were clear signs now that he was struggling, as was Betts, who seemed to have lost his away swing. But Durham persisted with their four-man seam attack, and no spinner, when they played Kent at Stockton. The first day was washed out and the visitors were 15 for three when Andrew Symonds came in to blast 78. Alan Wells survived a simple chance to John Morris at mid-on on nought to make 111. Kent seemed to have a better understanding of how the pitch would play than Durham as they preferred the gentle seam of Dr Julian Thompson to the hostility of Martin McCague. They also included the left-arm spin of Min Patel, who took five for 18 as Durham subsided for 93. Following on, Lewis and Gough then simply concentrated on keeping out Patel, who had none for 19 in 26 overs when Durham closed the third day on 153 without loss.

Lewis, who had followed his excellent first season for Durham with a moderate one, went on to make 132 and Gough 67. But Thompson, a gynaecologist, breathed new life into Kent with a spell of five for 19. He finished with a career-best seven for 89 as Durham collapsed from 268 for two to 325 all out. Boon rarely prospered on Durham's outgrounds and he seemed to lose sight of the full-length in-swinger which bowled him first ball. Kent needed 118 from 24 overs to win and skipper Matthew Fleming saw them home with five balls to spare after they slipped to 86 for five.

It was beginning to look like a season too far for Boon when he was out second ball to Chris Silverwood at Headingley and Durham were dismissed for 114. For the third successive match they threatened to follow a debacle with a second innings recovery, but from 107 for one they slumped to 211 all out and lost by nine wickets. Lewis again top-scored with 74, but Collingwood, like Boon, was struggling and was lbw first ball to Craig White. As with Lewis's effort at Stockton, such a heavy defeat was deeply unjust for John Wood, who exploited variable bounce to take a career-best seven for 58. Wood always tended to bowl well against Yorkshire, who rejected him after one trial match, and against Lancashire, who were interested in signing him.

Ian Jones, another seamer from the same Sacriston club as Melvyn Betts, had always dreamed of making his first-class debut at Chester-le-Street. But he didn't expect it to be for the opposition. Durham's original academy boy, he had been released after the 1997 season and joined Somerset, who were captained by Boon's fellow Tasmanian, Jamie Cox. It was not a Sacriston reunion, however, as Betts was dropped, with Neil Killeen coming in.

Harmison had just become a father to his first daughter, Emily, and he took three wickets in reducing Somerset to 126 for seven. But Rob Turner survived a routine chance to fellow wicketkeeper Martin Speight on 17 and went on to make 95. Matthew Bulbeck contributed 76 not out and Jones, batting at 11, was unbeaten on 18 in a total of 300 for nine declared. In the second innings I Jones might almost have been Indiana as he cracked the whip with menacing intent in making 35. He took only one wicket, however, as John Morris made a century in a rain-ruined draw.

It was a high-class innings from Morris. He had developed a reputation for getting out to ordinary bowling but rising to the challenge against the better performers. Here he won an intriguing joust with Andrew Caddick and his critics in front of the press box were prepared to offer grudging praise when he hit two successive fours to reach 100. There was one ball left before lunch and he clipped it straight down long leg's throat. "If you weren't here to see it, you wouldn't believe it," proferred his sternest critic. "On the stroke of lunch he goes and does a daft trick like that."

As Durham Academy seamer Ian Hunter was also from Sacriston, it began to look as though the former pit village five miles south-west of Chester-le-Street was taking over from Boldon as the county's richest seam of bowling talent. But Jones made only two more first-class appearances for Somerset, both at Taunton against Middlesex and New

Zealand, while Hunter's early promise faded and after being released he was taken on by Derbyshire.

Durham at this stage were well adrift at the foot of the table and a year had elapsed since their last championship win, on that glorious day at Lord's when Betts was the hero. Now he was out of the team and it looked as though the England A tour had done him no good. Although it appeared that he was more open-chested, which might have explained the loss of away swing, he denied that coming under the coaching of John Emburey in Zimbabwe had changed his action. "I've looked at the tapes from last year and this season and they're not much different," he said. "I'm just lacking rhythm."

While the Betts were off in Sacriston, Melvyn's malaise had paved the way for dancing in the streets of Annfield Plain, a similar settlement a few miles north, which was home to Neil Killeen. Given that there were four seamers ahead of him, he might not have fancied his chances at the start of the season, but at 23 he had realised he needed to make some progress and had worked hard to develop his bowling over the winter. Figures of six for 20 at Northampton cemented his place in the team, and he retained it for the rest of what would prove to be his best season. Killeen began by having a frenzied Mal Loye lbw when trying to pull and took the rest of his wickets with full-length balls. Matthew Hayden got a leading edge to short extra cover after making 68 and, with a rest in the middle, Killeen took his last four wickets without conceding a run in 23 balls. The other four wickets all went to Harmison.

All out for190, Northants trailed by 127 but then reduced Durham to 110 for seven before a disciplined innings of 72 by Collingwood, at a time when he was averaging 13.8, took the total to 216. It looked as though Durham would be thwarted as 42 overs were lost to rain at the start of the final day, but they clinched victory by 45 runs with three overs left. Brown took five wickets and Harmison the last two, both gleefully caught at fourth slip by substitute Nicky Phillips. Durham had put down four slip catches in the match in the absence of Boon, who had been hit on the hand by Devon Malcolm.

Boon sat out the following day's National League match at Hove, where Durham had their first sight of his Tasmanian team-mate Michael Di Venuto, who hit an unbeaten 72 in a seven-wicket win for Sussex. It was Durham's sixth straight defeat in the competition and it became seven when they were all out for 137 at home to Northants.

As they concentrated on building a four-day team, which was their reason for coming into first-class cricket, Durham had not had a good one-day side since the first season and this became even more evident in the NatWest Trophy trip to Holland. The Dutch Masters left Durham on the canvas in an embarrassing five-wicket defeat in the Amsterdam suburb of Amstelveen, where the pitch was the slowest the professionals had encountered. Unsure what a good score would be when they were put in, several perished trying to force the pace and they were all out for 194. It was still expected to be enough, but with Holland on 11 for two in came South African Kenny Jackson, a former professional at Annfield Plain, where he had played with a young Neil Killeen.

Jackson was eventually caught at slip off Killeen, but he had made 36 in a third-wicket stand of 74 with Man of the Match Feiko Kloppenburg and by that time Holland were cruising. Kloppenburg, a 24-year-old student, made 61 but was outshone by Luuk van Troost, whose unbeaten 59 off 68 balls saw his team home with three overs to spare.

Norman Gifford, the Durham coach, said: "It's a very poor result for the players, for the members on this trip and for the members back home. I wish I knew what has gone wrong. Our championship form is good, but in one-day cricket we are failing to do the right things and it's honesty time for all of us."

For vice-captain Nick Speak it was his first senior game since his injury on August 19 the previous year and he was given out lbw for one when he had nicked the ball on to his pad. He did have one surprise for his opponents, however, courtesy of the fact that his wife's parents were Dutch. "They were getting a bit smarmy," he said. "They got quite a shock when I let them know I understood what they were saying."

The match had been switched quite late from Deventer, who suddenly asked for more money than had been agreed in order to prepare the ground. Tickets and posters had been printed, but Deventer were told that unless they stood by the initial agreement the match would be taken elsewhere. The switch caused a good deal of inconvenience for Durham fan Stephen Hodgson and his wife, Lucy, who were unaware of it. They bought The Times and the Daily Mail at Amsterdam Central Station on the morning of the match and noted that while the Mail listed the venue as Amstelveen, The Times still had it as Deventer.

"Which one would you believe?" asked Stephen. "We got to the Deventer ground at 9.30 and they made us very welcome. They gave us coffee and the groundsman showed us his wicket, of which he was very proud. They also showed us the indoor cricket school they are building. The next train back was at 11.14, arriving in Amsterdam at 12.20. We then took a tram to Amstelveen, but couldn't find anybody who knew where the ground was. We went to the police station, they called a taxi and even the driver had to ask for directions. We arrived at 2.15, just as the Durham innings was finishing."

Having thus far relied on four seamers, plus the occasional over of off-spin from Michael Gough, Durham handed Graeme Bridge his debut at The Oval. Having begun life as a seamer with the Ryhope club, Bridge still trotted in at Derek Underwood pace to bowl his left-arm spin and had ten maidens in his 29 overs, taking one for 60. This was commendable given that the Surrey showboats crash, bang, walloped their way to 174 for six before the dredgers down the order steered them to 335.

Harmison finished with five for 76, but whereas six years earlier Surrey had prepared a pitch to suit their far more potent seam attack, which included Waqar Younis, this time they were banking on the spinners. Ian Salisbury took four wickets in the first innings and Saqlain Mushtaq finished with match figures of 12 for 110 as Durham lost by 226 runs.

Surrey were without their Test players and this match coincided with Alex Tudor making 99 not out against New Zealand. Collingwood and Daley showed their inexperience of playing high-class spin, while Speight's attempts to sweep almost everything ended when he was bowled round his legs.

The Oval's resident reporter at that time, David Llewellyn, had christened the Durham press corps PODs (prophets of doom). But he was greatly amused when my prediction that Speight would be out attempting a reverse sweep swiftly came true.

On the first day we had a visit in the press box from the identically dressed Bedser twins, Sir Alec and Eric, who were then 80 and spoke almost in stereo. They had climbed the stairs to the fourth floor rather than take the lift and had missed the fall of Surrey's sixth wicket. "Who else has chucked his wicket away?" asked Sir Alec. "Did you see the way Ben Hollioake got out in the over before lunch? We would have been sacked for that."

What did he think of Steve Harmison? I asked. "They're all open-chested. That's why they can't swing the ball properly. Look at that field he's bowling to. You'd think he was Ray Lindwall."

I pointed out that the modern way was often to encourage an open-chested delivery to prevent stress fractures of the back.

"There were no stress fractures in our day," was the inevitable reply. "We were digging our dad's allotment when we were nine and when we joined Surrey we did manual work in the winter. One year we used to come at 6am every day to shift an embankment with pick axes and shovels. Nowadays Surrey second team players have sponsored cars."

The match was umpired by John Hampshire, who had been with Tasmania when Boon made his debut 21 years earlier, aged 17. "It was obvious then that he was an outstanding player," said Hampshire, who was also down to umpire what would be Boon's final first-class match at Grace Road. "I'll be there with my boots blacked," he said. "I'll be at the party afterwards, but I'll be sorry to see another summer gone and another great career ended."

In the following day's National League game at Lord's, with his father watching from the committee balcony, Roseberry scored 87 as Durham lost by 25 runs. The one bright spot was an innings of 33 off 40 balls by Ryan Robinson. From a Durham perspective, things didn't look any better for being viewed from the new £5.2m media centre. With its superb view from behind the arm, its bar, air conditioning and overall comfort it felt like something from the space age compared with our cabin at Riverside. But it was cut off from the outside world, so there was no chance to record any quips, complaints or general observations from the punters.

Still, Durham would have to build something like this if Riverside were to compete as a Test venue, and shaving a few bob off the wage bill might help. At this point, in early July, with Durham bottom of both tables, they announced that 23-year-old Western Australia left-hander Simon Katich would be their overseas player the following season. The initial approach had been made by Graham Gooch, who said: "The club's obvious requirement is for a quality run scorer. Signing players who are on the up has worked well for other clubs, such as Essex when they first took on Mark Waugh. Simon is very highly regarded in Australia and is viewed as one of the next generation of Test batsmen."

The headline would be Top Kat if he were a success, or Katichoo if Durham caught a cold over the signing. Although they would be replacing their experienced Australian captain with a relative unknown, the news appeared to give Durham's youngsters a shot in the arm as things immediately began to look up. Katich was to form a close bond with

Collingwood, and he was the first to emerge from the doldrums, swiftly followed by the recalled Betts.

On what intially looked a poor Riverside pitch, lacking pace and with variable bounce, an experimental 12.30 start was probably to Durham's advantage against Nottinghamshire as they didn't have to wait long for the afternoon sun to take effect. Lewis was bowled for his first single figure championship score of the season and Morris retired hurt after a blow on the arm. But Gough made 62 and Collingwood put his struggles behind him with a perfectly-constructed century. Speak made 41 after being preferred to Jimmy Daley, whose omission on the day Robin Weston scored his third century of the season for Derbyshire was noted by the members.

Despite glorious weather, there was no great stampede to take advantage of free evening admission as play went on until 8.20. Cricket fans are creatures of habit, and one regular congratulated Collingwood on his hundred then admitted he had missed the second 50 because he had to leave at the usual time. His tea, presumably, would be on the table. Durham repeated the experiment only once.

With Wood now injured, Betts took four wickets and Killeen three as Durham earned a first innings lead of 39, then Lewis carefully compiled a flawless century and Morris made 78. They declared at 304 for eight and Nottinghamshire, needing 344 in 83 overs, had the target down to 104 off the last 14 with five wickets left. Tim Robinson had gone for 80 but Paul Johnson was steaming along at his irrepressible best against an attack which had reverted to all seam – other than Gough. He had already taken two wickets and it was when Chris Tolley drove Gough to long-on that the final capitulation set in. Vasbert Drakes gave Gough a return catch and Harmison cleaned up as the last five wickets went down for four runs in four overs, leaving Johnson stranded on 70. It was the first time Durham had taken maximum points since the equivalent match four years earlier, and 1,297 runs had been scored in the perfect four-day game.

The win sparked a reversal of Durham's usual fall from grace in July following a decent start and Boon said: "This result gives us a realistic chance of pushing for a place in next season's first division." He wasn't wrong, and the light at the end of the tunnel was further brightened by Riverside's first floodlit match witnessing the end of a run of eight National League defeats.

The start was delayed by rain for almost two hours, but just over 4,000 attended, some no doubt attracted by the obligatory bouncy castle, the face painting for children, the Southern Fried Chicken, the music and the fluorescent orange stumps. Whether they fully appreciated the wiles of bespectacled off-spinner Nicky Phillips is another matter, but he took four for 13. After Michael Slater made a 54-ball half-century for Derbyshire, they collapsed to 143 for nine in their 33 overs. Boon made 50 off 44 balls and Speight completed a seven-wicket win with 7.3 overs to spare, which meant the full effect of the floodlights was barely witnessed.

Durham then won a championship match in two days for the first time, also at home to Derbyshire. The only cloud on the horizon was that the pitch was reported after 22 wickets fell on the first day. After the classic four-day match against Nottinghamshire a week earlier, this was another unwelcome reminder of the Jekyll and Hyde nature of Riverside surfaces.

John Morris, however, had the skill to counter the variable bounce and made 119 against his former county, passing 20,000 first-class runs. Reaching this career landmark brought him great satisfaction and gave him more ammunition with which to shoot down those who claimed he was an under-achiever. Durham won by seven wickets with Simon Brown taking nine wickets in the match. In the first innings he had Robin Weston caught at slip first ball. This was not the worst of Derbyshire teams as they had Ian Blackwell batting at eight and Dominic Cork at nine. They slipped below Durham as a result of this defeat, but would subsequently join them in division one the following year.

Cork was quoted as saying the pitch wasn't fit for first-class cricket, but summers were drier in those days and the groundsman protested that back-to-back home games with the floodlit match inbetween had left him insufficient time for watering. A pitch panel had been convened, but there was no rap on the knuckles, merely a suggestion that cracks should be allowed to open up more before filling them in.

Jon Lewis's car sponsors had been on the phone during the match asking how he'd gone on. They were apparently getting a little jittery after his two centuries because they had promised at the start of the season if he scored three they would upgrade his vehicle from a Primera to a BMW.

He was out for 59 in the next match at Cheltenham, where Morris made a cavalier 74, Boon 139 and Speak 110 as Durham amassed what was then their third highest first-class total of 552. It was a rather better effort than the 86 they had mustered on the same ground two years previously. Things were clearly going Durham's way when Morris held a smart catch at silly mid-off to see off his former Derbyshire colleague, Kim Barnett.

They were said not to be the best of pals. Brown took five wickets in the first innings and Killeen five in the second as Gloucestershire were dismissed for 202 and 223 and Durham won by an innings and 127 runs. It was the first time they had won three successive championship games and in two weeks they gone from bottom of the table into the top half. The Dutch disaster had clearly administered a sharp kick up the pants.

The Cheltenham Festival is understandably popular among the scribes, and the assembled cricket writers on the rather cramped balcony which served as our vantage point included several of our more convivial members. It was essential, therefore, to wander round to a marquee at lunchtime, despite the Dorothy Goodbody (it's a beer) awaiting evening consumption at the Butcher's Arms. Among the nostalgia-seekers, eccentrics and general cricket nuts assembled there were members of Durham's London-based fan club, the Dunelm Society. Their numbers included Stephen and Lucy Hodgson, who reported that the ECB had accepted some responsibility for the switch of venue in Holland. As compensation for having gone to Deventer, the Hodgsons had been offered tickets for the Old Trafford Test.

Also present was Gillian Edger, who harboured an ambition to be Durham's first female director. But her most pressing desire was to organise a whip round to pay a fine which the club had imposed on Betts. Sympathy for Melvyn seemed to have been heightened by the fact that his wife had recently presented him with a daughter, but it was the new dad who stood accused of throwing his toys out of the pram when warned for persistent short bowling in the nets. His absence at Cheltenham was explained by a groin strain, but he didn't reappear until the final match and it is doubtful whether soured relations were ever fully healed.

With Michael Gough going off to captain England Under 19s against Australia, Jimmy Daley opened for the first time in a one-day match against Sri Lanka A and scored 81. That booked his four-day return at the top of the order for the trip to Cardiff, but he went to the crease on the first day sporting a shiner. After a lengthy net the previous afternoon he had gone into a secondary net and top-edged a ball from physio Nigel Kent into his left eye. Kent, a demon bowler for minor league club Brandon, was on his first away trip of the season with Durham and appeared to have created work for himself.

With Morris injured, Durham gambled by selecting Steve Chapman to bat at three a year after his only previous appearance. Daley scored five and

13 and Chapman 28 and 32, but Speak's second successive high-class century, plus 97 not out from Speight, appeared to have put Durham in a strong position.

They led by 61 on first innings, but in hot weather on a dry pitch it was always likely to come down to a spin duel. Robert Croft took seven for 70 as Durham were all out for 185 in their second innings, and Nicky Phillips couldn't quite match him. With a distinct lack of bowling behind him, he took 12 of his 18 wickets for the season in this match, with six in each innings. But they were more costly than Croft's and his first innings analysis of six for 171 was then the most expensive in Durham's history. (He equalled it a few weeks later with 4-171 at Old Trafford).

Glamorgan won by three wickets with Alun Evans unbeaten on 88. It elevated him into the heavily-populated ranks of those whose career-best performances have been against Durham, but while it could have done them much harm it didn't help his career to flourish. Nor did the match help Chapman's. Norman Gifford's attempts to turn him into a first-class left-arm spinner bore little fruit as he took one wicket in the game. He made one further appearance, in which he didn't bowl, and was released at the end of the season.

Going into August, the return to Riverside in steamy weather brought nine wickets each in the match for left-arm swingers Simon Brown and Sussex's Jason Lewry. Brown passed 50 championship wickets in a season for the sixth time, but with James Kirtley giving Lewry good support Durham were on the back foot after being dismissed for 141. In the second innings they needed 283 to win and a determined 80 from Jimmy Daley, again opening, supported by a half-century from Paul Collingwood, brought victory within sight. They needed ten with two wickets left, but Lewry bowled Collingwood and Brown, and Sussex won by eight runs.

I wrote at the time: "Like a lot of the half-baked philosophy which surrounds sports teams, talk of getting into the winning habit has been exposed as little more than cliched waffle. Since winning three on the trot, Durham have been in a good position to win the next two. But they have lost them both. You don't follow a team's first-class evolution for eight years without some emotional involvement and I have never been more disappointed by a Durham defeat. Like Lord's last year, it was a fascinating contest building to a thrilling finish. But the sense of anti-climax as Lewry rattled Brown's stumps was gut-wrenching."

The defeat appeared to have dealt a huge blow to Durham's hopes of a place in the top tier, and the man who was to take over as chairman declared himself against two divisions. After retiring 12 months earlier following 20 years as the chief executive of Newcastle Building Society, it was announced that Bill Midgley was to take over the following month from Don Robson.

"It's obviously very important for us to be in division one," said Midgley. "But my concern is that we might see an elite emerging in four to five years and the money and the best players will go to them. Three up and three down should mitigate against that, but how long will it last?" Prophetic words, but at the time he probably didn't envisage Durham becoming one of the elite. Midgley described the club's financial situation as "delicate," with the next stage of the ground development having to be delayed, and his greatest contribution was probably in sorting that out.

Durham slipped below Sussex and were now two places adrift of the division one cut-off, and it didn't help when no play was possible on the first two days of the next match at Colchester. I arrived there on the first morning to find the outfield under water, so headed back in the direction I had come to the second team venue of Halstead. There was a Bentley parked near the boundary belonging to the father of Nicky Peng, who was to make his Second X1 Championship debut for Durham and would be opening the batting with Gary Pratt.

Although the torrential storms had been very localised, there was no play at Halstead either, which at least gave me the chance to interview the two highly-rated youngsters. In the amount of coaching he had enjoyed, Peng was something of a throwback to the Westons and Roseberrys. He had hit two double centuries that season, one for England Under 17s against Scotland Under 19s at Scarborough, and one for Northumberland Under 17s against Cumbria at Tynemouth, the club where he had been a member for five years.

"I hit 14 sixes at Scarborough, which they told me was a record for the ground," he said. "It was also the first double hundred in an England Under 17 match and I scored all the runs between lunch and tea. I have been approached by Northants, Glamorgan and Nottinghamshire, but I'm happy with Durham. I enjoy training with the staff and I'm getting good coaching and a good standard of cricket with the academy."

Peng was still at Newcastle Royal Grammar School, but Pratt, who had also been in the England Under 17 team, was nine months older and had left Willington Park Comprehensive with the aim of following his brother,

Andrew, on to the Durham staff. The eldest brother, Neil, had spent time on the Lord's groundstaff but a first-class career had eluded him and he was now a local club professional.

The delayed start at Colchester also gave me the chance to explore the area around Dedham, where I had chosen to stay. This is Constable country, on the banks of the River Stour just inside Essex's border with Suffolk. Flatford Mill, the subject of one of Constable's most famous paintings, is three miles downstream through pleasant pastures ideal for pre-breakfast exercise. Dedham itself is a delight, with a lovely cricket ground overlooked by an impressive church tower. A subsequent visit to Colchester, rather than Chelmsford, was therefore something to be keenly anticipated, despite it being the most inhospitable club I have visited.

I was refused admission to the clubhouse, and when I mentioned this to the local reporter, Nigel Fuller, he offered his usual colourful views in explaining that he had long since abandoned hope of getting in there. My Durham colleague, Tim Rich, somehow managed to get past the steward, but having set up his laptop in a quiet corner he was ordered out.

A young Durham opener scored a century on both visits to this otherwise pleasant ground in Castle Park. Two years hence it would be Michael Gough, but as he was still on England Under 19 duty on this first occasion, it was his deputy at the top of the order, Jimmy Daley, who continued to grow into his new role.

He made 105 after Durham were put in when play began on the third morning, while Boon made 75 and Speight thrashed a 43-ball half-century. There was some dreadful dross from Danny Law, whose loud grunting as he delivered the ball was amplified by the oaths as his wides flew past the despairing wicketkeeper. Hailed as a tremendous prospect in his England Under 19 days, when he was with Sussex, this was also the bowler who had taken a hat-trick against Durham at Riverside the previous season. Durham declared at 350 for eight then dismissed Essex for 215 in the inevitable draw, which at least allowed them to close a four-point gap and join their hosts and Middlesex in joint ninth place.

Middlesex were the next visitors to Riverside in a crucial game, in which Harmison had the satisfaction of having Roseberry caught at third slip in both innings, for 22 and 29. The opener who took the honours was Jon Lewis, although he was just about to touch a ton when engine failure thwarted him. He was two short of his third century of the season, which would have seen his sponsors upgrade his car to a BMW, when he was lbw to the second ball after lunch. Chapman, who had come in for the injured Boon, suffered the same fate to Tim Bloomfield's next ball, but in his seven not out in the second innings he had the satisfaction of driving Phil Tufnell for the match-winning six. It was the last ball Chapman faced in first-class cricket, but Durham's six-wicket win propelled them up to seventh place.

While Chapman's release would be confirmed a week later, Durham surprisingly chose this point to announce that John Morris would not be retained. At 35, he had completed his six-year contract and the club were seeking to cut costs and place a greater emphasis on youth. He had recently been left out of the one-day side and it was always a mystery, even to him, why a player of his stroke-playing ability had such a woeful limited overs record. With three games left, he said he would continue to give the club his full support in their effort to achieve division one status. But in three more championship innings he totalled 12 runs. He joined Nottinghamshire for the final two years of his career and averaged 45.71 in eight championship games in his last season.

For two Bank Holiday National League games in two days, at the Oval and Northampton, Durham handed Muazam Ali his senior debut and also brought in Marc Symington, who had returned to action two weeks earlier after a groin operation. It did not go well for either of them, and two defeats confirmed that Durham would finish bottom. From Northampton it was straight up to Scarborough for the annual Northern Electric Trophy clash with Yorkshire the following day. The two youngsters were again unable to impress in a 91-run defeat and the introduction of 17-year-old all-rounder Ian Pattison, from Sunderland, also brought no reward.

Durham had agreed to play the game because they didn't want to lose their festival place or let the sponsors down, but some of the players were not happy about the hectic schedule as they had to be at Old Trafford the following day for a championship match. Replying to 236 for four, they were all out for 145 in 32.5 overs, which at least allowed them an early getaway for Manchester. It seemed almost sacrilegious to arrive in Scarborough at midnight and leave at tea-time the next day, so I stayed over and enjoyed a pleasant early morning drive down the A64 in the morning. If there's one thing for which I have envied my Yorkshire colleagues it's their two weeks in Scarborough every year. Would I trade it, knowing I had to spend the rest of the season at Headingley? Probably not.

While Durham were at Old Trafford, Michael Gough was captaining England Under 19s in the third Test against Australia at Riverside, having scored a match-winning 95 in the first match at Edgbaston. Gary Pratt and Ian Hunter were also in the team, while four other members of the side failed to prosper in the first-class game. Of those who did, Ian Bell, Richard Dawson, James Foster and Michael Carberry, Dawson's fall from grace was just as swift as his elevation to the full England team. Gough had described the Yorkshire off-spinner as the player of the under 19 tour in New Zealand the previous winter and, as with Graeme Bridge, his struggles underlined the difficulties of nurturing spin bowlers in this country under the contrasting demands of the various types of cricket.

The consolation is that Australians don't always kick on, either. From their Under 19 team at Riverside only Michael Clarke, who made 111, and Mitchell Johnson have advanced to the Test arena. Johnson took four for 16 as England were dismissed for 84 in reply to 424. Gough and Carberry made half-centuries in the second innings, but they lost by an innings and 107 runs.

Meanwhile, at Old Trafford one of those England spinners who suffered a bigger relapse than most, Chris Schofield, wrecked Durham's promising start. Lewis and Daley opened up with a stand of 144, but from 193 for two they collapsed to 226 all out. In 43 balls either side of tea, 20-year-old Schofield took five for eight, with three of his victims caught at forward short leg.

Durham were without Simon Brown through injury, while Paul Collingwood couldn't bowl because of a side strain and John Wood bowled only seven overs because of a stomach bug. It left a huge burden on Harmison, Killeen and Phillips, and while the off-spinner turned one sharply to bowl Andrew Flintoff when offering no stroke he posed no threat to John Crawley. With even Daley and Boon having a bowl, Crawley made 158 out of 437 and Durham lost by an innings and 14 runs, despite a defiant second innings 66 from Speak. There were three more wickets for Schofield.

Durham were now 11th with two games left and Lewis's tenth championship half-century of the season held them together in the face of sustained accuracy from Warwickshire's Tim Munton. Bowling into a Riverside gale, he looked like a man wading through quicksand but quickly abandoned his usual run-up. For 22 overs broken only by lunch he bowled off six paces and took three for 37. When he returned with the wind at his back he took three for one in eight balls and finished with seven for 91 as Durham were dismissed for 255.

With opener Michael Powell surviving a very shaky start to make 117,

Warwickshire closed the second day in command on 252 for four. For the third successive match Durham were reduced to three frontline bowlers when Brown retired after bowling three overs with a recurrence of a groin strain. This merely rubbed salt into Melvyn Betts's wounds as he had expected to take Brown's place and had stormed out of the ground on being told he was not in the team.

After adding a further 11 runs on the third morning it all went wrong for the visitors as their remaining six wickets went down for 22. Wood replaced Harmison and took four for 14 in 21 balls to finish with five for 75, while Killeen had four wickets. In unusually warm weather for September, the pitch had dried too quickly and was playing funny tricks again, and when a ball from Munton which barely left the ground bowled Daley for five even a first innings lead of 30 was looking handy for Warwickshire.

Durham slipped to 56 for four, but in his last championship appearance at Riverside the tough-as-teak Tasmanian, David Boon, rode doggedly to the rescue. He was determined to leave Durham with a place in division one and he brought all his skill, experience and sheer cussedness to bear in countering the perils of the pitch.

Boon departed to a standing ovation after making 72, his second half-century of the match, and his stand of 122 with Collingwood had changed the game. Despite Dougie Brown's seven for 66, Durham reached 235 and the target of 206 proved way beyond Warwickshire on the deteriorating surface. Wood, Harmison and Killeen dismissed them for 115, with last man Allan Donald retiring hurt. He had come into the match clearly unfit, failed to take a wicket and threw in the towel when Harmison struck him on the knee. In the final analysis Warwickshire failed by the one point which separated them from Durham to achieve division one status.

Durham went to Grace Road for the final game needing to hang on to the ninth place they now occupied. Their championship record against Leicestershire was played eight, lost eight, five of them by an innings. But the Foxes were on the run. With several players injured and at least three wanting to leave, they had just suffered two successive defeats.

After a rap on the knuckles, Betts was finally recalled in place of Brown and with Lewis also injured Gough joined Daley in a new opening partnership. The weather helped as there was no play on the first day, and given events elsewhere it became clear that Durham needed ten points to be safe. Once they had dismissed Leicestershire for 322 to collect the four bowling points, with Killeen taking seven for 85, it meant two batting points would do the trick, assuming they hung on for a draw. Against an attack led by Michael Kasprowicz, Gough and Daley provided a good start with a stand of 72 and at the close of the third day Durham were 229 for four, needing only a further 21 runs.

Things were rarely straightforward for Durham, however, and early on the final day Kasprowicz removed Boon for 53 and Collingwood for 38. With two runs needed Speight cut Jimmy Ormond straight to gully, and for Tim Rich and I, the sole survivors of the original Durham corps, the sleek new press box at Grace Road suddenly seemed a mite less comfortable.

A bye followed and with one needed, Wood gambled by taking on Chris Lewis's arm following a push to extra cover. He scrambled home and the Durham fans were ecstatic. Rain washed out play in mid-afternoon, but in any case there would have been insufficient time for Leicestershire to set a target and try to force a win, so Durham were assured of the draw. Outgoing chairman Don Robson was among the first in the dressing room to congratulate them.

The hosts finished on 74 for four, Harmison's one wicket leaving him on 64, one ahead of Brown. Killeen, who played in five fewer games, had 58 and won the Player of the Year award. That final wicket for Harmison came courtesy of Darren Maddy being superbly caught by the diving Boon at second slip. "I fell over and the ball fell in," he joked. "I didn't want any more coming my way – it was a good one to finish with."

In his three seasons with Durham he played in 50 first-class games and scored 3,007 runs at 39.05. The only batsmen to have bettered that for Durham are fellow Australians and Dale Benkenstein. Boon might not have been an original thinker, but his contribution in instilling self-belief and bringing on players like Harmison and Collingwood could never be over-estimated. He would return to Tasmania two days later a deeply satisfied man, although outwardly there was no sign of emotion as he was cheered off by the Durham contingent. "I have enjoyed every minute of my 21-year career," he said. "And to finish off by helping Durham into division one is the icing on the cake."

CHAPTER 10

SPEAK AS
YOU FIND

AFTER three years under David Boon, it was clearly a gamble to hand the captaincy to Nick Speak, a player deemed surplus to Lancashire's requirements three years earlier. I did not approve of his signing, and while this former England Schools lacrosse player was a natural sportsman he had failed to justify keeping Jimmy Daley out of the team in his first season. But I had come to realise that Nick was a thoroughly likeable character and as he had produced some imaginative tactics as Boon's third season deputy, his appointment as captain seemed perfectly acceptable.

Standing in occasionally is, of course, hugely different from actually being in charge, and when many of your charges are highly promising, but unproven, academy products the last thing you need is for the curse of the Durham captaincy to rear its ugly head again. Unlike his predecessors, Speak was taking over a winning team, but it all became very reminiscent of Michael Roseberry's reign as the new captain lost eight out of his first nine championship tosses.

With the benefit of hindsight, it seems clear that, having achieved division one status, it was asking too much of a young squad to retain it. While there could be no complaints about the input from the impressive young Australian, Simon Katich, it became increasingly obvious that talent alone is not enough. Geoff Cook was sufficiently wise and experienced to have known that all along, but even for him the failure rate which lay ahead must have been immensely disappointing. After Michael Gough's spell of England Under 19 captaincy in a squad which included Ian Hunter and Marc Symington, three Durham boys had played in the Under 19 World Cup over the winter. Graeme Bridge had been vice-captain, Gary Pratt and Ian Pattison also featured, and in the summer ahead Nicky Peng and Mark Davies would also appear at that level. Yet of those eight only Davies would survive on the staff beyond his early 20s.

The drop-out rate was probably no worse than at other counties, but for the relatively new kids on the block, determined to thrive on home-grown talent, it was a dispiriting experience. Not that there was any hint of the rocky road ahead when Peng scored 98 on his debut as champions Surrey lost the opening match at Riverside by 231 runs. But more of that later.

Under the new chairman, Bill Midgley, Cook had been quietly restored to his former position of Director of Cricket, but he continued to leave the bulk of first team duties to Norman Gifford, who had been kept on for one more year as coach. Boon had been very much the man in charge, now a young Australian who had never played in England needed to find his feet quickly. Not that it was any kind of problem for the bright and eager Katich to fit into a youthful squad.

Given the preponderance of left-handers among the world's top batsmen it was amazing that, after eight years, Durham had never had an established one. They did now and it was quickly apparent that Katich was everything he was cracked up to be. It surprised me that he was jettisoned after Australia's 2005 Ashes defeat, but he fought his way back and in December, 2008, he became only the tenth batsman to carry his bat through an Australian Test innings. He scored 131 out of 268 against New Zealand at Brisbane.

Katich was a little worried about the physical demands of a county season on his arrival as he had suffered from glandular fever during the winter. "I desperately wanted to come but I knew if I wasn't right by mid-February I would have to pull out," he said. "I was back playing for Western Australia by then and getting through OK, but I still have to be careful what I eat and drink. I haven't played 30 first-class games yet and I never expected an opportunity like this to come along so soon. I spoke to team-mates like Tom Moody and Justin Langer and they were very positive about it. And David Boon said Durham had a great bunch of lads and I would have a ball. I hope to match Boony on the field, but not off it. I like a drink, but I have to be careful."

It was also the year that Shane Warne first came to Hampshire and Durham were acutely aware that first division opponents would see spin as their weakness, both in bowling it and batting against it. Leicestershire had Anil Kumble, Surrey again had Saqlain Mushtaq and Ian Salisbury, while memories of Chris Schofield's torment at Old Trafford and Min Patel's at Stockton were still fresh.

"We've talked about it until we are blue in the face," said Speak. "Graham Gooch has had a big input. We have stressed that with bowlers of this quality you have to take it to them. Spinners can't hurt you so you have to have the confidence to leave your crease."

While the usual pre-season optimism abounded, Speak gave the impression that he had plenty of fresh ideas. "There will be a picture of Boony strategically placed on our dressing room wall," he said. "He is a true champion of the game and from my point of view it was a treat to play with him. If any of the lads get above their station they will be reminded that there's a man looking down on them who played in 107 Test matches and scored over 8,000 Test runs. There will also be a picture of Simon Brown, with a gap next to him for other England players to come. And there will be pictures of people like Dean Jones and David Graveney to remind everyone of what has gone before. We have a duty to them to keep chasing that first trophy. That has to be the next goal.

"I never expected the captaincy when I first arrived, and it's a great honour. I'm a great believer in tradition and respecting the game's values and the people who went before you. At 33, the captaincy will give me a new lease of life towards the end of my career."

Speak kept in regular contact with Michael Atherton and had just taken the former England captain to task for a remark that the county championship served no purpose. "I told him it was a stupid thing to say," said Speak. "It doesn't make my job any easier when I'm trying to instil certain values into the Durham lads. He's a very intelligent man and when I asked him what he was on about he said he was just stirring the pot. I told him some players could take it as a personal statement and there are some supporters who live for the summer. There will always be a place for county cricket. It's the way it is run and played that needs to be addressed."

As will be related, very sadly in my view, those last few words would come back to haunt him, as would the following: "I'm confident I can handle the tactics. The peripheral stuff is more difficult – you need the respect of the lads. I have spoken to Athers and Graham Gooch about it a lot and I know the hardest thing will be realising when not to be around the lads because I have always been one of them at heart.

"Mike Roseberry had a tough time as captain, but he always kept trying to do the right things and never shirked his responsibility. You have to keep believing in what you are trying to bring to the club and let your personality come through. I have always been a keen student of the game, looking at what others are doing and building up a memory of what goes on. Young lads today have more distractions, but they can pick up masses by listening to people talking about the game. Unfortunately professional sport has drifted away from that. If you are asking people to make sacrifices in their lifestyle everybody has to be in it together. Last year when we won games the collective effort was tremendous. When you have done it, there's no better feeling."

One final pre-season observation from Speak which would resonate a couple of years later was with regard to Michael Gough: "He gets quite critical of himself and I'm trying to encourage him to relax a bit more and enjoy himself."

Gough was ruled out at the start because of a back problem, and he also had health problems, believed to have originated from his trip to Bangladesh with England A. His absence meant Jimmy Daley stayed at the top of the order, but wet early season conditions contributed heavily to his failure to build on his excellent start as an opener. Having fought his way back from the broken fingers suffered on early Riverside pitches, now it was damp tracks which provided yet another setback in a career which simply refused to take off. Steve Harmison soon developed shin problems and the other seamers picked up various ailments as things quickly conspired against Speak after a brilliant start.

Peng was handed his chance as the season began with five Benson & Hedges matches in ten days. Speak won the Gold Award in the first when he scored 71 out of 178 for four at Riverside against Yorkshire, who replied with 168 for nine in a match reduced to 40 overs a side. Paul Collingwood took four wickets, having been told by the captain he would be the fifth bowler in one-day games. Speak had always seen himself as something of a mentor to Collingwood, having roomed with him in his first season.

The spin worries then resurfaced as Kumble took three for 26 in ten overs and Durham lost by 20 runs at Grace Road. Speak again top-scored with 49, while Katich made one in each of his first three innings, although the third was in a ten-over thrash against Lancashire at Riverside. The visitors cruised past Durham's 53 for eight with one wicket down and 19 balls to spare with Sourav Ganguly taking three wickets and scoring 22 not out. Speak said: "It's about as disappointed as I've been in three years at Durham. I didn't think it was fit to play and neither did John Crawley, but he wanted to play because he knew they would be huge favourites in such a short game."

With the poor weather continuing, the next match at Trent Bridge was reduced to 28 overs a side and after Katich made 50 in a total of 174 for eight Durham won by two runs. John Morris was caught by Speak at cover for five and Neil Killeen bowled Paul Franks with the final ball.

Durham then booked a quarter-final spot courtesy of an astonishing innings from Ryan Robinson. Only in making 33 at Lord's in one of his nine National League innings the previous season had the Huddersfield-born all-rounder looked remotely capable of the sort of destructive hitting he unveiled against Derbyshire at Riverside. Coming in at 76 for three in the 26th over on a slow pitch, he hit 68 off 38 balls. Tim Munton, so successful on the ground with Warwickshire, had one for 11 in six overs when he returned for the 31st over and saw his first two balls hoisted over the leg-side boundary in an over which cost 24. Robinson hit Munton for two more sixes and after totalling 245 for nine Durham dismissed Derbyshire for 107, of which Michael Di Venuto made 46 before being run out.

The innings proved to be a complete one-off from Robinson. In four National League games that season he totalled ten runs, and when sent in at No 4 in the B & H quarter-final at Old Trafford he was out for ten. Katich made 62, but was one of four middle order men snaffled by Schofield as Durham slumped from 87 for one to 154 all out and lost by three wickets.

Atherton had once described a Durham bowler as the worst he had faced in first-class cricket. Although he didn't name him, it was believed to be Melvyn Betts, who on this occasion bowled him for two. With John Wood boosting the salary offer he was to be made by Lancashire by taking four for 26, the hosts were indebted to Neil Fairbrother's unbeaten 57 for rescuing them from 35 for five.

The championship programme again began at Riverside, but with no snow around this time it worked in Durham's favour. After a wet April it was a far cry from The Oval and the Surrey showboats didn't relish it, although they made a decent start in reducing Durham to 48 for four. That was when Peng walked in, aged 17 years 227 days. Although he had left school at Christmas to concentrate on cricket, he wasn't yet on a full contract and was playing only because of Gough's injury.

Peng played himself in carefully, taking 15 balls to get off the mark, then began to crack the ball through the off-side off front and back foot. Conditions were hardly conducive to fluent strokeplay and much of the bowling from Martin Bicknell and Alex Tudor was quite testing. But a four whipped off his toes showed Peng could also play through the leg side as this one scorched to the boundary. He reached 50 off 104 balls and scored his remaining 48 runs off only 41 before trying to cut a widish ball from Ben Hollioake and edging to the wicketkeeper.

Visiting captain Adam Hollioake said of Peng: "He's the best young player I've ever seen. He showed an incredible temperament as well as power and a good technique." With Paul Collingwood making 66 Durham reached the unexpected heights of 234, then Surrey subsided from 57 for two to 104 all out. There were three wickets each for Simon Brown and Neil Killeen, then Bicknell and Tudor had Durham rocking on 14 for four. But on a pitch which must have seemed a world away from the fast, bouncy tracks at Perth, Katich dug in to score 65. Peng made 23, Martin Speight weighed in with 36 and a total of 186 put the game way beyond the champions. Their first innings effort was at that time the lowest championship score made against Durham, but Surrey lowered it again by capitulating for 85. Brown had three for eight, Killeen three for 14 and there were two wickets each for Betts and Harmison.

The teams had previously met 17 times in all forms of cricket and Surrey had won them all. Durham celebrated by jumping into a hot tub. The jacuzzi-style pool had been brought in for the benefit of spectators at the following day's National League game against Surrey, who brought Durham swiftly back to earth with a 66-run victory. Harmison had been tipped as a candidate for the first Test against Zimbabwe, but he was clearly struggling and in this match took one for 66 in nine overs.

It also transpired at this time that John Morris had become Harmison's agent and had sat in on his contract talks at the end of the previous season. As the pair had since faced each other at Trent Bridge, the Durham chairman, Bill Midgley, decided to question the ethics of the situation. "Agents are going to play a big part in the game in the future, but it has to be off the pitch," he said. "I expect a lot of people will be ringing Nicky Peng at the moment, but he has grown up in this area, so let's hope his future is here."

With the Test side about to be announced, Harmison came back strongly, twice sending the middle stump cartwheeling in the opening ten overs against Lancashire at Riverside. He removed John Crawley and Andrew Flintoff, who at that stage of his career had barely scored a run against Durham. But with Ganguly making 73 and Schofield 50, Lancashire's 263 proved a winning total. In 34 overs in the middle of the second day 13 wickets went down. Glen Chapple, so often a thorn in Durham's side, took six for 42 in accelerating a collapse from 108 for two to 164 all out. Katich had grafted extremely hard for 45 and clearly did not agree with the caught behind decision which sparked the clatter of wickets.

His concentration had just been disturbed by the glint from Alan Shearer's Jaguar as Newcastle United were training next door. A piece of scruffy carpet from the press cabin was thrown over the silver motor.

Brown took seven for 51 as Lancashire were dismissed for 134, and just to confirm that this was a bowlers' pitch the 6ft 5in Mike Smethurst became the third in the match to record career-best figures. He took seven for 50 as Durham were routed for 92 and they would remain the best championship figures for a player who was released two years later. Schofield, who bowled only two overs in the match, was named in the Test squad on the final morning, along with Harmison, who was seen receiving a congratulatory handshake from Atherton before play began.

The selection of the 21-year-old Ashington lad brought reminders of the days of northern cricket clubs whistling down the pit for a fast bowler. Durham had unearthed three from former mining communities in Harmison, Betts and Killeen, with Ian Hunter about to follow, and former Durham skipper David Graveney must have taken great pleasure in becoming the first chairman of England selectors to ring a number in Northumberland.

David's uncle Tom, who left aged six, was the only other player born in the county to have played for England. Norman Gifford dismissed as "nonsense" suggestions that Harmison had a suspect temperament, saying: "You wouldn't find a more genuine lad. He wants to bowl and he doesn't shirk. He has a great heart and if the challenge is on he finds a little bit more."

As it turned out, Harmison was in the squad for the first three Tests of the summer, but didn't play, while Killeen, rarely injured in the past, had suffered a side strain against Lancashire. Neither bowler was the same force on returning to the team.

It was the second successive season that Durham's first three championship games were at home, and with the core samples from the pitch showing how damp it was just below the surface, this was clearly not good for the game. For the next one, against Leicestershire, 153 overs were lost to the weather, resulting in the inevitable draw. Hunter made his championship debut, and while wicketless he scored 63 as a nightwatchman and rescued Durham from 82 for five in a stand of 148 with Katich, who compiled a superb 137 not out.

While Katich had adapted remarkably quickly after his early B & H struggles, the reverse applied for Speak, while openers Jon Lewis and Jimmy

Daley had also struggled in the testing conditions. They got no better as Durham's accelerating misfortunes were highlighted by the fact that the next two ports-of-call were Tunbridge Wells and Basingstoke.

At Tunbrige the festival always coincides with the rhodedendrons being in full bloom. This time they were reluctant to bloom at all. Kent were bottom of the table, having spent most of the previous six weeks confined to the pavilion, and three inches of rain had fallen on the Nevill ground the previous weekend. The groundsman reported that the covers had been afloat.

Mark Baldwin was there to cover the match for The Times and had driven to the ground even though he lives in the town and could have walked. He was the first press man into our parking area and his car got stuck in the mud and had to be towed out by tractor. I arrived to be told this and, finding that traffic cones in those parts had bred like rabbits, ended up parking a mile and a half away. Had I known where Mark lived, I'd have parked in his drive.

The opinion from the deckchairs was that Kent should have fielded, but Matthew Fleming took the view that the pitch wouldn't get any better. Going in at 80 for six, the former Sandhurst man showed great discipline in abandoning his usual cavalier approach to bat for three and a half hours for 39. There were 17 Kentish mayors present on the second day and as their chains of office glinted outside their hospitality marquee it wasn't difficult to conclude that there was another mare in the middle – the nightmare being suffered by Durham.

David Masters took six for 27 and I wrote: "It's a fair bet that he'll wait a long time before he betters those figures." After three seasons with Kent, four with Leicestershire and one with Essex, he was still waiting.

Norman Gifford noted that he had been in a Worcestershire side beaten in one day at Tunbridge Wells in 1960, but that was no consolation for a team now in freefall. Robert Key was in the opposition and after his observations about the Riverside pitch in 2008 perhaps someone should have reminded him about Tunbridge Wells in 2000. While now averaging below ten in the championship, Speak philosophically accepted that, given the weather, there was nothing the groundstaff could have done about it.

Durham succumbed for 81 and 143, with nine lbws over their two innings. Some of those awarded by Ray Julian were dubious to say the least and it always surprised me how this trigger-happy umpire's joviality was sufficient to maintain his popularity with the players. He had been at Darlington for a second X1 match the previous week, where it was noticed that his car registration read: R4 LBW. There were 18 lbws in that match and my spy on the ground informed me that Julian gave 13 of them. The same spy reported a 17-year-old wicketkeeper named Phil Mustard reaching 50 amid cries from his team-mates of: "Well batted, Colonel."

As is so often the case at outgrounds, it was a travesty that the cricket was so disappointing as in all other respects Tunbridge Wells was a lovely place to visit. I take the view that there is no such thing as an ugly cricket ground, but Jon Lewis reported that when when he rang his parents back at home in Essex to say he would be playing at Ilford the next day, they said: "Oh no, we're not going to Ilford."

It's true that Essex's outgrounds are not the prettiest, but the one in the public park at Ilford produced two one-day wins for Durham, and in this one Lewis made 60 as they ended a run of four National League defeats with a seven-run victory.

Prior to heading for Basingstoke it was back to Riverside to play Yorkshire. The ground had suffered a similar fate to Tunbridge Wells a few days earlier, with the river having broken its banks in the scoreboard corner of the ground. But David Measor reported that the covers had withstood the battering and his pitch was better than he could have expected.

That didn't help Durham as Brown, Wood and Killeen were all ruled out and Harmison was now badly out-of-sorts after his flirtation with England. Ian Hunter was back in the team, along with Marc Symington, who top-scored with 36 in the second innings batting at No 10. The game was as good as lost by then, however, as Matthew Hoggard's five-wicket haul in the first innings and Darren Gough's six in the second, coupled with an innings of 94 from Michael Vaughan, carried Yorkshire to a six-wicket win.

The win took Yorkshire to the top of the table (they finished third in Martyn Moxon's final season before his switch), while Durham were about to hit the bottom following another outground travesty. They arrived for what was billed as the last first-class match at Basingstoke's May's Bounty with only Hampshire below them and Durham's goose was cooked once Speak lost the toss. England had released Harmison for county duty, but he and Brown, who had been suffering from back trouble, allowed Hampshire a flying start. They raced to 171 for two before Collingwood took two wickets and the hosts knuckled down as a couple of balls had already gone through the top of the pitch.

Although no-one reached 50, eight Hampshire batsmen scored 27 or more and with the help of 36 extras they totalled 340.

Michael Gough had suffered a recurrence of his back trouble and Durham had dropped Daley, promoting Peng to open in a team packed with bowlers, including Nicky Phillips, who batted at seven. They were all out for 83 and 93, and after batting with a runner because his sore left shin had flared up worse than ever, Harmison did not reappear for the second innings. Shane Warne took four for 34 and four for 22, and before play ended two hours into the third morning it was noted that several balls from Alan Mullally brought up huge clouds of dust. A pitch panel was convened and, having been sympathetic at Tunbridge Wells, this time Speak fully expected a points deduction. He was furious when it didn't materialise, and the strain was beginning to tell on this easy-going character.

The Friday lunchtime finish with a Sunday match to wait for allowed plenty of time for research. So I took in the ancient and modern – the oldest ground in the country on Broadhalfpenny Down and the newest at West End, Southampton, henceforth known as the Rose Bowl. The grounds were only 18 miles apart but one was two miles from Hambledon, up on the Downs in the middle of nowhere, while the other was by the M27 close to a number of spreading retail parks. Birdsong dominated the one, traffic noise the other.

At Hambledon they were celebrating 250 years of cricket. Some form of the game had been played in Kent and Sussex around 500 years before that, but Broadhalfpenny Down is known as the cradle of cricket because it was there that the modern game and its rules took shape. Hambledon regularly used to beat an All England X1 in front of huge crowds with many side stakes involved. The captain and secretary of the club was Richard Nyren, landlord of the adjacent Bat and Ball, which I visited purely in the interests of research.

Even this 280-year-old pub, it seemed, had to resurrect itself following an intervention by the modernists. The brewery which used to own it had turned all their local pubs into themed restaurants called the Natterjack, and at the Bat and Ball all the cricketing memorabilia was thrown into the attic. Fortunately, by the time of my visit it had been restored under the stewardship of the Gales brewery at nearby Horndean. I gather there has been another threat since to the long-established traditions, with Gales having been taken over by Fullers. But with a cricket-loving couple installed as managers, all is well.

It was a cracking pint at the Bat and Ball, nor was it bad at the pub in Micheldever, near the farm where I was staying. Here they had seen fit to change the name from the succinct Dever Arms to the Half Moon and Spread Eagle. It was here that I bumped into Gordon Nicholson, long-serving former secretary of football's Northern League, who at 74 had received a call the previous weekend asking him to play cricket for Bishop Auckland thirds. He was still sprightly enough to rush ahead of his wife when, on his first visit to the Micheldever pub, he realised an evening match was about to start on the adjacent cricket ground. "The first ball of the match drifted down the leg side," he said. "But the next three all took wickets." Perhaps they were anxious to get to the pub.

For the National League match at Basingstoke, Durham sent in Collingwood to open with Muazam Ali, whose audacious strokes made everyone sit up and take notice as he contributed 36 to a stand of 95. Once he was out Durham slid to 204 all out and lost by 18 runs, and as with Ryan Robinson it proved to be a one-off for Ali. He was handed his first-class debut the following week against Derbyshire and retained for three more championship games. After ducks in his first three innings, lasting a total of five balls, he was ecstatic to score seven in his fourth. But he and Robinson were released at the end of the season.

With Riverside being prepared for the one-day international, in which Marcus Trescothick and Alec Stewart took England to a ten-wicket win against the West Indies, the Derbyshire match was held at Darlington. Given the outground traumas they had already suffered that season, Durham had cause for trepidation. But Feethams was home from home, especially for Melvyn Betts, who followed his seven for 29 there against Kent by bagging seven for 30. Coupled with his nine for 64 at Northampton, he now had three of the four best analyses for Durham in first-class cricket, a situation which prevailed until Ottis Gibson came along.

Four of Betts' victims were bowled and two lbw as Derbyshire folded for 151, but there was nothing wrong with the pitch as Durham replied with 479 for nine declared. There were centuries for Collingwood and Katich, 78 for Speak and a swashbuckling 55 from Betts, who took three more wickets as Durham won by an innings and 79 runs. Simon Brown took six for 40 in the second innings, passing 500 first-class wickets.

Darlington noted the reduced amount of advertising hoardings and seating which Durham brought down compared with the early days and, amid fears for the future of outground cricket in the county, it transpired that £15,000 was now the minimum cost for a championship and one-day game. Darlington had knocked Durham down to £12,500 and received £5,000 from the borough council, plus something from match sponsors, AMEC. The rest they hoped to recoup over the bar, so it was just as well that few seemed to take notice of the sign which the football club erected on the first morning advertising their beer at £1.20 a pint. That was before the Darlington FC owner, former safe blower George Reynolds, moved them out of Feethams to a 25,000-seat stadium on the edge of town.

Mark Davies made his senior debut in the one-day match against Derbyshire and took three for 15 in a 95-run win. He came in for the injured Betts, who was in an out of the team for the rest of the season. He finished top of the championship averages with 44 wickets at 18.9, but the ten he took at Darlington had provided a lone highlight in the two seasons since his England A tour. Struggles with injury, coupled with twice having his knuckles rapped for losing his temper, curbed his enthusiasm for the Durham cause. He had previously insisted he didn't want to play for anyone else, and in many ways he was the classic case of a young man from a tight-knit community who was never likely to flourish elsewhere. But towards the end of the season it became clear that he was likely to take the Warwickshire bait, as Wood was inclined to do with Lancashire.

The Derbyshire win lifted Durham three places up the table, but it was all downhill from there. They gambled by sending in Ali and Gough to open in a NatWest Trophy tie against Hampshire in conditions ideally suited to Dimitri Mascarenhas' gentle dibbly-dobblers. He removed both and conceded only 13 runs in ten overs. Durham were all out for 91 and lost by five wickets, and although they rallied by scoring 314 at Headingley what followed was virtually the final straw. They dismissed Yorkshire for 129 and enforced the follow on, only for Michael Vaughan and Darren Lehmann to score centuries and secure a draw.

Defeat by 217 runs followed on a poor pitch at Grace Road, where Durham were all out for 93 in the second innings, with Anil Kumble recording match figures of eight for 55. The Kat offered the view that it was time to sharpen a few claws. Although not as earthy as the archetypal Aussie, Katich felt Durham needed to start answering back. He revealed that at Grace Road he had even received a few verbals from the hapless Scott Boswell, who had bowled utter tripe and prompted someone to observe that his name was an anagram of Clott's Bowels.

Kumble had resurrected the pre-season fears about spin, and they were further vindicated as Lancashire included a trio of twirlers on an Old Trafford dustbowl, on which they all bowled on the first morning. It wasn't Schofield who did the damage this time as he was clearly suffering from his England exposure. But Gary Keedy, who came on for the seventh over of the match, took ten wickets while off-spinner Gary Yates had six. Despite Katich's third century, Durham lost by six wickets in a match which featured their first pair of brothers in first-class cricket, Gary and Andrew Pratt. Wood, bending his back, took four wickets in Lancashire's first innings, as did Gough with his off-spin, and there were genuine hopes that he would make an all-rounder.

Considering that the pitch was a seamers' graveyard, I wrote that a burst of three for 29 in 11 overs by Wood was as good a spell as I had seen all season. I didn't realise until a couple of weeks later that he may have had an ulterior motive. He further impressed his future employers by scoring 44 in the second innings, although when he swept a catch to deep square leg he probably didn't impress his captain. Speak grafted for four hours for 38 not out in an effort to save the game, which was undermined by Nicky Phillips carelessly lobbing a catch to cover after scoring one.

As well as the off breaks of Phillips and Gough, Durham also turned to Katich's chinamen and there were 286.4 overs of spin in the match. This was a record for a Durham game, and I worked out that the eight matches in their first-class history which had featured most spin had all been away from home, and the only one they hadn't lost had been at Swansea in 1995.

Although reluctant to get involved in criticising his former county, Speak said: "They've got a Test match here next week and they put us on a used pitch. It turned as much as the one at Basingstoke. It's very hard for a young player like Gary Pratt to come into his first match on a pitch like that." He added that the system which allowed counties to get away with preparing pitches to suit themselves was a "shambles."

Lancashire's organisation seemed a little shambolic at the time. The match had originally been scheduled for Blackpool, where Durham had made a hotel booking, and the switch came to light only through a chance conversation between myself and a Lancashire press man. Durham had to stay in Hyde. We were also required to arrange a special press pass for Old Trafford that season, and when I rang up I got the usual recorded message: "If you want match-day information, press one; if you want marketing, press two etc." Why do they never say: "If you find all this intensely irritating swear loudly and slam the phone down?"

I was eventually informed that my pass would be left at the main gate, but on arrival there I was told it was at the ticket office, which was on the opposite side of the ground from where we park. And when I finally arrived at the press box entrance there was no steward on the door, so any Tom, Dick or lap-top burglar could have walked in. I am pleased to report that none of this has recurred.

A National League game at Edgbaston followed, in which Andrew Pratt stood up to all the bowlers and pulled off a very slick stumping off Wood. The Warwickshire Bears proved more teddy than grizzly that day, surrendering for 148 to lose by 50 runs.

Jon Lewis scored his first championship century for a year in a rain-ruined draw at home to Somerset, during which a male streaker tried to enliven proceedings. Raising two fingers to the jeering spectators, and with a cigarette in his mouth, he gave the impression his brains were somewhere close to his bare backside. He was arrested and, hopefully, charged with being boring.

Speak's determination to fight for his team's division one survival produced a five-hour vigil for 89 not out in tricky conditions at home to Kent. Martin Saggers came back to haunt Durham, taking seven for 79, but their first innings lead of 53 looked useful until the pitch flattened and Ed Smith scored 175 second time around. Letting Saggers go had seemed reasonable enough at the time, but it didn't when this uncomfortable reminder of his ability was followed by the departure of Wood and Betts.

The draw left Durham one spot below their visitors, in the third relegation place, in mid-August. It was the time of year when the annual speculation began about the following season's overseas player, and Durham were back in the Dean Jones situation. They wanted Katich to return, but wouldn't know until March whether he would be required for the Ashes series. At that stage he was the season's seventh highest run scorer in county cricket, those above him including Michael Bevan, Matthew Hayden, Darren Lehmann, Matthew Elliott and Justin Langer. The only Englishman was Surrey's Ally Brown, who had made 295 in one innings.

Gary Pratt, Nicky Peng and Ian Pattison were named in the England Under 19 squad for four Tests against Sri Lanka, but there was no place for Graeme Bridge, who had been ousted by a certain Monty Panesar. Meanwhile, Durham went to Taunton, where Speak's rags-to-riches season continued with an innings of 78, in which the main blemish was his part in running out the recalled Jimmy Daley for 34. Speak had totalled 90 runs in his first 11 championship innings, but in 11 since he had scored 400 at an average of 66.6. His Taunton effort was in vain, however, in another rain-ruined draw.

With three games left, Durham needed to win at Derby. The hosts were bottom partly because they had had eight points deducted for a pitch which was deemed to have started too wet. It was the batting which required close inspection, however, not the pitch on Durham's visit as inability to cope with swing saw 20 wickets fall on the first day. Durham replied to 167 with 144 then had Derbyshire 121 for six in the second innings when Dominic Cork walked in to join Mathew Dowman. They put on 258 before Dowman was out for 140 and Cork went on to make 200 not out.

Durham were convinced that Cork was run out on 19, and on 21 he went perilously close to playing on. The ball refused to swing in the afternoon sunshine, and by the close it was clear that Wood was going through the motions after bowling exceptionally well for the previous few weeks. Cork resumed on 105 on the third morning, and with a blaze of strokes ranging from glorious to outrageous he added 95 runs off 63 balls. His arrival at 200 coincided with Derbyshire reaching 500 for eight, prompting the declaration.

The first ball of Durham's second innings brought an impassioned lbw appeal from Cork, which was upheld by Mike Harris when some umpires might have given Jon Lewis the benefit of the doubt on grounds of height. When Jimmy Daley was another surprised victim of Harris's finger, Speak seemed to lose heart. After making his way to an untroubled 39 he tried to whip Paul Aldred through mid-wicket and was bowled.

Durham were all out for 257 and lost by 232 runs. They were now 22 points adrift of safety and an almighty row ensued in the dressing room. No explanation was ever offered, but two days later Speak was left out of the team to play Essex at Riverside in the National League. We were told he had been "rested" and I had no argument with that as the club was clearly in turmoil and needed time to sort it out. But it quickly became apparent that someone had decided Speak's position as captain was untenable. As Norman Gifford was the management man present at Derby, his report seemed likely to have been the deciding factor.

I wrote in The Northern Echo: "Durham will need to take a careful look at their cricket management following the decision to relieve Nick Speak of the captaincy. He has been unavailable for comment, but there can be no doubt that he will be devastated. He saw the job as a great honour and was prepared to work hard at it. Now he joins the list of those who will be judged as failures.

"Durham believed that what David Boon brought to the club during his three years was sufficiently well ingrained for them to be able to take a gamble on Speak. Now those who took that decision have to accept that they were wrong. Either that or they simply didn't create the right environment or provide the necessary back-up for Speak to succeed.

"Durham need a strong cricketing figurehead. It is asking too much of Norman Gifford to fulfil that role at the age of 60. Durham lean heavily on the views of Graham Gooch, but it is very much a part-time role for him and merely adds to the impression that the cricket management is a bits-and-pieces affair, which lacks a strong leader. To sort out the finances and keep the playing side moving forward has clearly been a tall order for Bill Midgley in his first season as chairman. He appears to be succeeding in the former, but where can he find another Boon-like character to help him with the latter?"

Speak had gone to ground, but our shared liking for the front bar of the Dun Cow in Durham City enabled me to have a quiet word with him. He seemed happy enough to see me and said he didn't normally buy the Echo, but his parents had come to stay and his dad had bought it and pointed out my piece. "You were absolutely right," he said.

Although he stayed on for another year, Speak did not play again that season, with Jon Lewis taking over the reins which he was to hold for four years. With two games left he had to gamble in the first when rain ruined the visit of Hampshire. Lewis led the way with 70 in Durham's 320 for nine, then Hampshire declared at 69 for no wicket and fed Durham 39 runs in three overs. Considering what they had suffered on a poor pitch at Basingstoke, it was cruel luck for Durham that they had to set Hampshire a target on a run-laden surface. A draw was no good, so Robin Smith had Lewis over a barrel in negotiating a target of 291 in 91 overs. Will Kendall made 119 not out as Hampshire cruised home by six wickets with 13.5 overs to spare.

The last match was at The Oval, which had been Durham's most barren hunting ground down the years. A little over four months after starting the season with a 231-run win against Surrey, Durham lost by an innings and 63 runs. They were officially relegated when Surrey's declaration on 453 for four allowed them only one bowling point. Openers Mark Butcher and Ian Ward put on 359, the biggest stand against Durham in first-class cricket.

Between Cork's arrival at the crease at Derby and Ward's dismissal for 144 Durham had conceded 1,075 runs and taken six wickets. They were all out for 241 and 144, with Ian Salisbury taking 11 wickets.

The following day Jimmy Daley, who had averaged 14.52 in the championship, scored 105 as Durham won the National League clash by 59 runs. He then made 54 as the final Sunday match was also won, ironically at Derby, by one run. Neil Killeen took six for 31, but he had lost the knack of taking championship wickets and became primarily a one-day bowler thereafter.

Durham had only five National League wins in total and finished seventh in division two, despite the excellent batting of Collingwood and Katich. Collingwood's aggregate of 607 was second only to Dean Jones's tally for Durham of 656 in 1992, while Katich had 598. The Australian was the only batsman with a championship average above 30, scoring 1,089 runs at 43.56. Simon Brown was the leading wicket-taker with 56, topping 50 for the seventh time in nine seasons.

It was quickly confirmed that Lewis would continue as captain the following season, but it soon became apparent that the seam attack which had threatened to become the best in the country would be sadly depleted. First Betts signed for Warwickshire, then after insisting Wood must fulfil the final year of his contract Durham accepted there was no point in hanging on to him against his wishes.

As they had given Wood a chance in first-class cricket which he would not otherwise have had, then nursed him through six injury-plagued seasons before he came good, they had a right to feel aggrieved. From his point of view he was a 30-year-old family man who had been offered better money by a bigger club, and Durham had failed to build on the progress made under David Boon.

Personally, I was sadder to see Betts go because at his best he was genuinely exciting to watch and had looked a real England prospect. He was still only 25, but he was very much a Durham lad and I suspected that he wouldn't flourish elsewhere.

Wood had four fairly undistinguished seasons with Lancashire, while Betts had three seasons of diminishing returns at Edgbaston, followed by three more with Middlesex. My last sight of him there was in a net, bowling alone off a few paces. It seemed a far cry from the day he hit Phil Tufnell for six just prior to clinching that famous win.

CHAPTER 11

MOXON ON
THE MOVE

THE signing of Martyn Moxon to replace Norman Gifford as head coach for the 2001 season was seen as quite a coup. Indeed it was, but it could not be sufficient within itself to transform the team at a time when developing the stadium to Test-match standards appeared to be the priority. Compared with what was to follow, the first four years of Moxon's six-year stay were notable for their lack of ambition on the team-building front. Signings during that time included James Brinkley, Danny Law, Gavin Hamilton and Ashley Thorpe, and there was even a brief period when the official overseas player was Arnoldus Mauritius (Andy) Blignaut.

There is a saying that nice guys never win anything. Dale Benkenstein, Geoff Cook and the rest of the team disproved that in 2007 and 2008, but if there is one other I would dearly like to see dispel the myth it is the thoroughly likeable Moxon. He undoubtedly played a part in building the Yorkshire team which won the title in 2001 and the Durham team which struck gold after his return to Headingley, and it has been his misfortune that trophies have followed his departure. Perhaps once Michael Vaughan draws a line under his England career he and Moxon will bring some sustained success back to the Broad Acres.

Yorkshire threatened to win the title in 2000, but finished third and Durham were surprised to find Barnsley-born Moxon among the 25 applicants to succeed Gifford. The former England opener was reluctant to discuss why he had fallen out with the county he had served for 20 years, although he stressed that he wasn't coming to Durham for any extra money.

"There was a difference of opinion between myself and certain Yorkshire officials," he said. "They say the cost of redeveloping Headingley won't affect the playing resources. Let's hope that's the case. The response from the public since I announced I was leaving has been humbling. It's nice to know there are a few people who appreciate what I have done and what I've been trying to do. Now I just want to throw myself into the new job. It's a tremendous challenge at a forward-looking club with huge potential."

In fact, he was leaving a club he thought was concentrating too heavily on ground redevelopment for one where the emphasis was on building up a stadium from scratch. He was seen as the outstanding candidate, but in the circumstances he had little chance of swift success. By mid-season he would find himself saying, tongue-in-cheek: "It would help if the captain could win the toss occasionally." Yes, the curse of the captaincy had struck again as Jon Lewis lost nine successive championship tosses, nor was he helped by injuries.

Danny Law admitted that part of the attraction in coming to his third county at the age of 25 was that the departure of John Wood and Melvyn Betts meant there should be plenty of opportunity to bowl. Durham wanted him to be the all-rounder they almost had in Michael Foster, and Law's desire to bowl was helped by early season injuries to Neil Killeen and Simon Brown, who was finally to enjoy a benefit season. The injuries and departures meant that of the five seamers ahead of Martin Saggers when he was released, only Steve Harmison was still standing and he had missed the England A tour to the West Indies over the winter because of his shin trouble. He had been advised to work on a slight realignment of his left foot, but wasn't right throughout the season.

Simon Katich had informed Durham in February that he would be unable to return, having been tipped off that he would be in the Ashes squad, so they signed Martin Love instead. The 27-year-old right-hander had just averaged 75.81 in helping Queensland to win the Pura Cup. He arrived on a day of snow flurries on April 18 and helped the club unveil their new sponsors, Northern Rock. The team were in the middle of a three-day match at Riverside against Durham UCCE, who were playing their inaugural first-class game.

University Centre of Cricketing Excellence seemed a wild misnomer as the students were dismissed for 67 and Durham replied with 485 for four. This was a university team which included Michael Brown, later to go very close to carrying his bat in both innings for Hampshire at Riverside, Will Jefferson, of Essex then Nottinghamshire, Warwickshire's Alex Loudon, wicketkeeper James Foster, of Essex and England, plus three bowlers with county futures in Tim Phillips, Rob Ferley and James Bruce.

For six years Durham had always started their season at The Parks, where in 1994 Oxford had been all out for 73, which remained the lowest first-class score against Durham until this match. Durham handed debuts to Danny Law and James Brinkley, the Scotland-born, Australia-raised seamer whose previous first-class career with Worcestershire had been cut short by injury four years earlier.

With Lewis, Jimmy Daley and Paul Collingwood all reaching three figures, it was the first time three Durham batsmen had scored centuries in a first-class innings. But David Boon's moustache must have been bristling at the mismatch as he had decreed that what was always a very pleasant trip to Oxford was a waste of pre-season preparation time.

Brinkley, who had been teaching at Worcester Royal Grammar School, proved an enigma. Now more of a steady away swing bowler than the tearaway of his youth, he produced two outstanding performances on helpful Riverside pitches but proved innocuous on flat tracks. He took six for 32 in the opening championship match against Gloucestershire and improved that with six for 14 against Derbyshire, also at Riverside. But he missed a few games through injury and finished the season with 31 first-class wickets at 21.38.

His effort against Gloucestershire included a spell of five for nine in 22 balls and might have produced a victory as Durham set their visitors a victory target of 300 and had them at six for one, but only ten overs' play was possible on the final day. Brinkley's previous best of six for 98 had also been on his first appearance for Worcestershire seven years earlier and he said: "Perhaps I should just sign for each county and make a debut." As he had been recommended by Moxon's former Yorkshire team-mate, Jim Love, who was then in charge of Scotland, the obvious headline was "Love is in the air," especially as Martin Love made 61 and 67. That was a good start for a man wearing six layers of clothing, but it set a trend as he made 14 championship half-centuries that season and converted only one into a hundred. Andrew Pratt scored 28 not out in both innings, having finally ousted Martin Speight from behind the stumps on merit.

It was then on to Trent Bridge, where the groundstaff began mopping up at 6.30 on the first morning and reported that they had removed 12,000 gallons before play began at 3.30. Nottinghamshire had their own weather forecaster, who said there were too many sun spots for settled weather in the next few days but we should have an excellent summer in 2007. How wrong he was!

On Durham's last championship visit to the ground, three years earlier, Collingwood had been left stranded on 97 not out. This time, again with last man Harmison for company, he went for a big hit on 95 and was caught. The hosts included Kevin Pietersen, who had been signed as much for his off-spin as his batting and was lbw to Brinkley for two, batting at number six. It was Brinkley's only wicket as Greg Blewett scored 133 out of 344 for six, giving Nottinghamshire a lead of 60. That was it as no play was possible on the final day.

While I'm a fan of Trent Bridge, where we have a superb view from opposite the pavilion and are extremely well fed, I had long since decided that at the Test match grounds I prefer to drive out of the gates and turn away from the city centre. Nottingham has some very fine pubs, such as the Lincolnshire Poacher and the Olde Trip to Jerusalem, said to be the oldest inn in England and built into the rock on which Nottingham castle stands. Hardys and Hansons beers are available there and I once stayed next to their brewery in a lovely old pub called the Nelson and Railway at Kimberley. Old mining traditions in those parts meant it was a bit lively on a Friday night, and it also involved getting through or round the city, whereas a left turn out of Trent Bridge offers an easy drive out to the Belvoir Valley.

This is not a valley in the sense of the Yorkshire or Durham dales, but it's a prosperous, rural area dotted with pretty villages and cricket grounds. In some of the more upmarket villages, like Colston Bassett, prices in otherwise delightful pubs are clearly not designed to attract impoverished cricket writers. The Peacock at Redmile, near the farm where I used to stay, increasingly became a restaurant, but a drive out to the Sugar Loaf at Ab Kettleby, just over the border into Leicestershire, is rewarded by a good balance between food and beer.

Durham had included Jimmy Daley and Nick Speak, at the expense of Nicky Peng, in the first two games. But both were injured during the Benson & Hedges series which followed, and that proved to be the end of Speak's first-class career. It wasn't the end for Daley, but he was no closer to being established than he had ever been.

He did, however, begin the B & H campaign with an innings of 70 at Liverpool as the wet April was followed by a sizzling May day. From our privileged vantage point at the Aigburth ground on the balcony of the extremely grand old pavilion, which dates back to the 1880s, we could see the Mersey shimmering in the background. We could also fully appreciate Neil Killeen bowling as well as at any time in his career. Edged catches, three of them held by Love, saw Killeen remove Lancashire's top four of Atherton, Crawley, Scuderi and Flintoff as Durham won by 54 runs. It was the first time they had beaten Lancashire in any competition since that memorable opening one-day match in 1992. It was also the first time they had faced Muttiah Muralitharan and they concentrated on keeping him out as he took one for 19 in ten overs.

Andrew Pratt's reputation continued to grow with two brilliant stumpings in a 29-run win at Derby the following day, Collingwood scoring 89. But back at Riverside Daley's 92 proved to have been acquired too slowly as Durham's 252 for three on an excellent pitch was overhauled by Nottinghamshire with five balls to spare.

An unbroken stand of 140 between Collingwood and Lewis secured a comfortable home win against Leicestershire. But Killeen broke down, and with Love having broken a finger the casualty list was becoming a big concern. It grew worse when Daley joined Speak as the victim of a pulled hamstring and had to retire hurt in the final group game at Headingley. Ian Hunter had been drafted in and took four for 48, but Darren Lehmann's 88 carried Yorkshire to 257 for seven. He produced an extraordinary shot when he stepped back to hit a straight ball from Harmison over cover for six. Despite Danny Law's unbeaten 57 off 43 balls, Durham finished 30 short. They knew they had done enough, however, to qualify for the quarter-finals.

For the resumption of championship action at Edgbaston, Speight came in purely as a batsman to replace Love at three, and Peng was at five. Both fell for four as Durham slumped to 58 for five after Lewis chose to bat on winning the toss for the last time prior to his run of nine losses. Pratt scored 52 in helping to repair the damage with Collingwood, who continued his outstanding start to the season by making 153.

In his best all-round performance for Durham, Hunter scored 31 then took four for 55. But when his 37 was the top score in a disastrous second innings the lead of 124 had been squandered. With the help of rash strokes from former team-mates wishing to get after him, Melvyn Betts took five for 22 for Warwickshire, and with Brinkley attending the birth of his first child Durham were all out for 102. Mark Wagh made 104 as the hosts reached their target of 227 with only three wickets down.

Durham had been forced to include Brinkley mainly by the injury situation, with Moxon saying: "Our only other available bowler was Nicky Hatch. He has been quite impressive but he hasn't played any first team cricket yet. We hoped to get through the match without James being called away, but it was only right that he should go to attend the birth of his daughter." Law's bowling had yet to impress, and it was because Harmison and Hunter were also wayward in the second innings that Warwickshire sped so easily to victory.

The injury crisis took an unexpected twist when it was announced that Moxon was to have a back operation. He was told he shouldn't drive for a month, so he would be staying at his Wetherby home. The first game he missed was at home to Middlesex, for whom Owais Shah scored 190 and 88 with the threadbare nature of the Durham seam attack being underlined by the rarity of spin dominating the first innings. Michael Gough recorded his best figures of five for 66 in 21 overs and Nicky Phillips had two for 101 in 31.2.

Then came a reminder of Peng's talent, 13 months after he first hit the headlines. He was still only 18 and the century he scored in this game heralded a golden phase which seemed to confirm that a glittering career lay ahead. He reached his hundred by driving Phil Tufnell wide of mid-on for four and said: "I was a bit nervous in the 90s and would have been happy to get there in singles. But I just saw the ball from Tufnell and had to hit it. He's the best spinner I've faced because he varies his flight so well. But I faced a lot of spinners with England Under 19s in India during the winter and that definitely improved my game."

Durham were set a target of 302 in 70 overs by Angus Fraser and got it down to 135 off 25 before Peng and Collingwood were both run out and they put up the shutters to earn the draw. Law finished on 36 not out but had bowled only five overs in the match. He then secured a National League win against Middlesex with an unbeaten 31, despite being bowled on 20 by Chad Keegan when Durham needed 19 off 16 balls. There were not enough men within the fielding circle and as the ball flew to the boundary off the stumps it counted as six no-balls.

The England selectors were out in force for the B & H quarter-final at Bristol, where David Graveney wore his Durham tie. Gloucestershire had won five one-day trophies in the previous two seasons and although their total of 199 did not look too daunting, a grudging pitch allowed them to impose a stranglehold on Durham's reply. Peng opened up with 32 and Collingwood followed his two wickets with an innings of 39, but Durham were all out for 133.

Three days later Collingwood was named in the England one-day squad for the first time, the day before his 25th birthday. Asked how he would celebrate that evening, he said: "I might pop in and watch some of Shotley Bridge's match at Lintz." As he had been selected for a triangular series involving Australia and Pakistan it was obviously going to be a baptism of fire, while he would miss a run of three away games in the championship.

At the time Collingwood was the leading run scorer in first-class cricket that season with 554 at an average of 69.25, having begun the season with a first-class career average of 26.19. "I've had five good years with Durham, but I knew I wouldn't get any further without lifting my standards," he said. "It's mainly about mental preparation. The 150 I made at Edgbaston was an important innings for me because I felt fresh all the way through. It showed I've learnt to switch on and off at the right times. I hope there's a lot more to come in the four-day game. I don't want to be seen as a one-day specialist."

Collingwood reported that when he rang his parents to tell them the good news his mum, Janet, said: "But we've booked to watch you at Derby." Not that she or her husband, David, would have allowed that to get in the way of seeing their son's England debut. As proud and devoted parents, they have followed Paul's career avidly and he eventually even persuaded them to board an aeroplane.

Before going off to join the England squad, Collingwood was able to contribute to two victories. First Durham's sudden discovery of spin as a potent one-day weapon propelled them to the top of the Sunday League second division through another win against Lancashire. Nicky Phillips took four for 21 and Michael Gough two for 27 as the visitors slumped from 83 without loss to 187 all out, losing by 24 runs. There was much talk at the time about balls going soft after around 20 overs and being almost impossible to hit off the square, so both sides opened with a pinch-hitter. Danny Law made a sprightly 45 for Durham in a stand of 85 with Peng, and Glen Chapple replied with 52. His opening partner, Mike Atherton, made 62 but both were expertly stumped by Andrew Pratt. Andrew Flintoff made one of his many ducks against Durham by driving Phillips straight to short extra cover.

The first of the season's three championship wins owed much to a generous declaration by Nottinghamshire captain Darren Bicknell at Riverside. Durham were required to make 315 and scored them for the loss of two wickets in 85 overs just before the start of the final hour. Martin Love made 149 not out and Jon Lewis 112, with their stand of 258 being Durham's highest for any wicket in the championship. The previous record of 206 between Wayne Larkins and Dean Jones had stood since May 15, 1992.

Lewis said: "It was a generous declaration, but I can understand why they did it. They had Middlesex eight wickets down at the end in their last match and they probably also had half an eye on the weather." Lewis scored most of his runs off the back foot in the arc between cover and third man, and added, tongue-in-cheek: "They never learn."

Despite Steve Harmison's first five-wicket haul for almost two years and an unbeaten 91 from Collingwood, Durham had trailed by 95 on first innings, then Greg Blewett made 137 not out before Nottinghamshire declared on 219 for five. Moxon had tried in vain to coax runs out of Blewett for Yorkshire two years earlier, and now the Australian had scored two centuries against Durham in the first few weeks of the season.

Moxon's influence on the spin front was clear, and while you don't take a sledgehammer to crack a nut, he was happy to take a Mallett to his trio of twirlers. Phillips, Gough and Graeme Bridge all spent four days working with Ashley Mallett, who had played in 38 Tests as an off-spinner for Australia in the 1970s. In the previous season, his third with Durham, Phillips had played in only five championship games and taken seven wickets at 59.28. Now he had a more prominent role and after working with Mallett he said: "Because he was a big spinner himself he wants me to get more revolutions on the ball. He wants me to stand tall and get through from shoulder to shoulder with more loop on the ball." He added: "It's nice to get a few games at home. I think the square has dried out more this year. Getting more overs under my belt will help my confidence."

With three successive away games spanning June 6-23, the fact that Durham were due to stage an Australia v Pakistan one-day international during that time meant they had no problems with ground preparation, and this was the first season they didn't use an outground. As it happened, the international was washed out. All 12,000 tickets had been sold and Durham announced they would increase capacity to 17,500 for the following year's one-dayer between England and India.

Durham's next stop was Derby, where the list of charges on the gate now included £2 for dogs, with canine membership available at £10. Whether they were issued with season tickets complete with photograph seems unlikely. The Derby press were eagerly awaiting the first visit of a Times reporter who always took his rather unruly labrador to matches. It had once dashed on at The Parks and accosted the Yorkshire slip cordon, perhaps thinking that some of the nutty Oxford professors over the boundary were slightly barking. I was once left in charge of Bumper, as the labrador was called, while the Times man went for the lengthy lunch to which he had been invited in a hospitality marquee. This was at Colchester, where I had previously been refused admission to the clubhouse, so I had taken along a flask and some coffee granules. Bumper ate the granules!

Phillips bowled 67 overs in the match at Derby and took nine wickets, but the cricket was fairly uninspired until Michael Di Venuto hit 86 in the hosts' second innings. Durham needed 326 to win in 85 overs and had the target down to 58 off nine overs when Peng was run out for 90. With only three wickets left, Durham opted for safety.

Among the Durham fans at Derby was Peterlee magistrate Mervyn Hardy, a member of both counties. He said: "I'm not a millionaire but I don't begrudge a penny of the money I put into county cricket because of the pleasure it gives me. Except when Trevor Jesty's umpiring." Mr Jesty had just given Michael Gough out lbw when well forward. But shortly afterwards he turned down a big appeal against Peng, prompting Mervyn to quip: "I've always said he's a top umpire."

Everyone knows that Dr Foster went to Gloucester in a shower of rain, but on Durham's first visit to the Archdeacon Meadow ground they had to endure some torrential downpours. Simon Brown had been wicketless on his first appearance of the season at Derby, and here his six for 70 was in vain as the match petered out into the inevitable draw. The downpour in the middle of the second afternoon left Gough stranded on 73, his best championship score, and he added only six the following day.

After being dogged by injury and illness the previous season, Gough said he was delighted to be a regular member of the side in both forms of the game. "I'm loving every bit of it," he said. "I'm happy to bat at six in one-day cricket because good players can play anywhere, which is what I'm aiming to do. I never expected to be bowling at the death in one-day cricket, but it's great experience."

Peng led the Valentine's Park massacre at Ilford with a scintillating century as Durham beat Essex in the Sunday League, with the 6ft 8in Darlington seamer, Nicky Hatch, making his debut. He bowled Stuart Law for four, but Peng's unbeaten 112 out of 264 for three was the highlight, despite excellent contributions from the two Essex old boys. Lewis was unbeaten on 63, while Law opened again and scored 47 then took three for 28, which seemed to mark a real turning point for him with the ball.

Law struck up a good relationship with Hatch, although on the surface they had little in common other than being tall. I had known Nicky since he was about six feet shorter, having played with his father, Mike, at Darlington. Mike had continued to bowl for the club for the best part of

20 years and his unfortunate legacy was five back operations. So I could imagine he was suffering when he climbed the steps towards me at the Rose Bowl after a five-hour drive to watch his son's first-class debut. At least he could now leave Durham to supply boots big enough for Nicky, for whom finding footwear had been a huge problem when he had size 14 feet at the age of 15.

In Harmison's absence through injury, Hatch took the first two wickets in the match, while Law had career-best figures of six for 53. His previous best had been five for 33 against Durham at Hove five years earlier. But on this occasion Durham lost by 47 runs largely because Zimbabwean Neil Johnson, who had played for Thornaby-on-Tees as a professional, scored 86 not out in Hampshire's second innings.

While the good folk of Thornaby had eulogised about his batting, they reckoned he couldn't bowl and he pretty much confirmed that in a game which reminded me of watching cricket in the early years at Riverside. Batsmen went for their shots in the belief that the death ball might come along at any time. Peng, however, again looked a potential match-winner until, running out of partners, he holed out for 49. Ian Hunter's decline since his excellent showing at Edgbaston had continued and he emerged from the match without a wicket or a run, while sending down ten wides.

Collingwood rejoined the side after scoring 20 runs in four innings for England. He said: "It was a big disappointment. I went through a similar thing with Durham in my first two years when there were times when we wondered where our next win was coming from. Hopefully I will have learned from that. I was made to feel very welcome straightaway and Duncan Fletcher was brilliant. He has a very dry humour. Whenever I was batting or bowling it was a difficult situation, but that's international cricket. I knew we were coming up against the best two one-day sides in the world. It's a hard school and hopefully I've learned from it."

Durham had to play Hampshire again three days later, this time at home in a C & G Trophy match. It was a measure of how much Riverside pitches had improved that the visitors scored 262 for five in 50 overs and Durham won by seven wickets with 9.4 overs to spare. Johnson's unbeaten 113 proved to have been too pedestrian as Peng made 119, Love 51 and Collingwood 59 not out. It was Durham's first win against first-class opposition in the premier knockout event since 1992.

Peng reached his 110-ball century with a swept six off Dimitri Mascarenhas and said afterwards: "This was my most memorable innings for

Durham because we were chasing a big score in an important match. Martin Love was playing such good shots it took the pressure off me. I have tried to learn from the way he just strokes the ball because sometimes I try to hit it too hard."

After missing the first five games with a side strain, Simon Brown suffered a recurrence of his old knee trouble in the next match at home to Warwickshire and was out for the rest of the season. Mark Wagh followed his century against Durham at Edgbaston with another one, but Durham were saved from defeat by Peng and Speight. They finished on 284 for eight, still 119 behind, after Peng withstood a hostile barrage from Vasbert Drakes to make 70. Speight, who had been doing just enough to retain his place as a batsman, finished unbeaten on 67.

Speaking of Peng, Moxon said: "There was an outstanding hour and a half's cricket when they weren't holding back and he took it on the chin and counter-attacked whenever he could. When he gets to a higher level he is going to come across more of that sort of thing and it will stand him in good stead."

Nicky Phillips had been spotted on his hands and knees stalking two ducks which appeared on the pitch, but he suffered a hand injury against Warwickshire. It ended his season, halting the improvement he had been showing through extra bowling and he never rose to such heights again. With Brown also out, Ian Hunter now considered too risky and James Brinkley in Canada with Scotland, Neil Killeen had broken down on his second team comeback. So Mark Davies came in for the Sunday League visit of Glamorgan and made a vital contribution with the bat.

It had been noted that pitches nearer the Riverside pavilion tended to be less reliable, and so it proved again as Glamorgan were all out for 145 and Durham were 98 for seven when Davies joined Jon Lewis. They put on 30 and Lewis finished unbeaten on 46 in the two-wicket win. Glamorgan captain Steve James, tuning up for a future career with The Sunday Telegraph, wrote in his column in a South Wales newspaper that the pitch was a "disgrace," adding: "I could not believe I managed to glove one of those seaming balls when everyone else seemed to miss them." Groundsman David Measor pointed out that the pitch had sweated under the covers during wet weather and added: "Nobody hates it more than me when we have an unsatisfactory pitch and I think it's wrong that a professional cricketer should mouth off about it."

Davies retained his place for the C & G Trophy tie against holders

Gloucestershire at Bristol and Durham brought in another 20-year-old bowler in Graeme Bridge. It was the left-arm spinner's first senior one-day appearance and he won the Gold Award as Durham sensationally knocked out the one-day kings. Seven weeks after losing their B & H quarter-final on a used pitch at this venue, a much better surface allowed Durham to make 232, with Lewis unbeaten on 65. Gloucestershire made an untroubled start in reply, reaching 92 for one before Davies applied the brakes with one for 31 in ten overs, while Bridge took three for 44.

He was unable to celebrate as he had been given the task of driving the kit van back to Durham, but he said: "The atmosphere in the dressing room afterwards was the best I've known. A lot of people seem to get lost in second team cricket after playing for England Under 19s and I don't want that to happen to me." Skipper Lewis added: "We were what we want to be, which is like Gloucestershire. They have set the standard in defending totals."

I also had to drive back rather than celebrate the win, which was unfortunate after spending the previous evening in a pleasant spot called Old Sodbury.

Richard Montgomerie, who had played for Oxford University in Durham's inaugural first-class match nine years earlier, scored his fifth championship century of the season and passed 1,000 first-class runs in mid-July on his way to 156 for Sussex at Riverside. With Bridge having to bear the brunt of the work into a strong wind, there was also a century for Umer Rashid as Sussex totalled 442. Harmison had one for 80 in 22 overs on the first day but finished with the first six-wicket haul of his career following a spell of four for two in 14 balls.

Amazingly, this was matched by Chris Adams taking four for six in four overs. First the Sussex captain caught Jon Lewis at slip for 99 off Mark Robinson then he removed Peng and Collingwood off miscued pulls, bowled Speight with an in-swinger and had Law stumped down the leg side by Matt Prior. Adams followed up with 90 in the second innings, and despite four wickets for Bridge the target was way beyond Durham, who lost by 133 runs.

Mark Davies took four for 13 as Sussex succumbed for 144 in the Sunday match, Durham staying level with Worcestershire at the top of the second division as Love's unbeaten 75 carried them to a seven-wicket win.

Andrew Flintoff finally came good against Durham with an unbeaten 72 as Lancashire cruised to a seven-wicket win in the C & G quarter-final. The highlight of a disappointing performance by Durham was Andrew Pratt stumping Glen Chapple for the second time since the all-rounder had become a pinch-hitting opener. The ball from Danny Law was two feet wide of leg stump, but Pratt had the bails off before you could say Robbie Williams, whose concert at Old Trafford was the reason for this high-profile match being transferred to Blackpool.

Durham were inserted in the sort of sticky atmosphere in which Simon "Chubby" Brown would have swung the ball prodigiously, but the only Chubby Brown in Blackpool that day was the blue comedian at the Winter Gardens. It would have taken more than the Teessider's tasteless jokes to have cheered up Durham's three coachloads of supporters.

Durham recalled Jimmy Daley and James Brinkley for the trip to Lord's, but with former Durham University pair Andrew Strauss and Ben Hutton scoring centuries Middlesex won by an innings and 74 runs. Martin Love had the dubious distinction of becoming Phil Tufnell's 1,000th first-class victim and the electronic scoreboard immediately flashed up: "Well done the Cat," with a drawing of a feline face. The claws were sharpened to exploit the dry, cracked pitch and when another ball kept horribly low to bowl Collingwood it was all over bar the miaowing.

David Graveney was at Lord's to attend an ECB disciplinary meeting in his role as chairman of the Professional Cricketers' Association. When the meeting ended he donned his selectorial hat and rushed off to watch Owais Shah just as he was being given out lbw by Ray Julian to a ball which might have had a passing acquaintance with leg stump.

The coffee at Lord's was not to the liking of scorer Brian Hunt, and even less to the liking of the irate MCC member beneath his window, who was showered by the dregs.

Peng had shown recent signs that his purple patch was fading, but he scored 66 in the second innings at Lord's then lit up Worcester with a spectacular century before the floodlights came on in the top-of-the table one-day game. In easily the most memorable floodlit game I have seen, Peng's 121 helped Durham to 274 for seven in what was then a 45-over competition and Worcestershire won by seven wickets with 14 balls to spare. Graeme Hick made 87 and Vikram Solanki an unbeaten 91.

Andrew Pratt had been promoted to open and contributed 36 to a stand of 102 with Peng, who reached his century off 94 balls. A third one-day hundred of the season for someone who was still only 18 was an astounding achievement. Yet he never scored another, and it has always seemed to me that the most likely explanation was that he stopped doing things naturally. Golfers call it paralysis by analysis, although whether he had the desire to work it out is open to doubt.

Moxon had requested that Peng should continue to play first-class cricket rather than join England Under 19s for the series against the West Indies, and the selectors had decided he should play in the first Test then be released from the second. He scored 50 and Pratt his career-best 86 in the next one-day match at home to Derbyshire, but once he started switching from Under 19 to county duty Peng's championship form disappeared. There was one further one-day classic, an innings of 92 at Cardiff.

The three-day finish at Lord's had at least allowed an early getaway from London and I spent a pleasant day reacquainting myself with the area around Ombersley, north of Worcester. I had previously stayed in the Crown and Sandys Arms next to the attractive cricket ground, which is large by village standards and has been used for county second X1 matches. The pub had since become too bistro-ish for my old-fashioned taste, but as the championship match following the floodlit game was to be held at Kidderminster the opportunity to stay at the Wenlock Edge Inn in Shropshire was too good to miss.

Set back about 200 yards from the precipitous Edge, with its spectacular views, this pub in my experience has always offered the perfect blend of good real ale (the local brew is Hobsons), unpretentious, freshly-cooked food and comfortable accommodation. It's about three miles from the utterly charming little town of Much Wenlock, where the annual games were said to have inspired the modern Olympics and some of the old regulars in the George and Dragon would doubtless tell you all about it.

The Wenlock Edge Inn is about a 20-mile drive from Kidderminster through rolling countryside passing by Bridgnorth, where it was tempting to catch a steam train on the Severn Valley Railway as the terminus is very close to Kidderminster cricket ground. The end opposite the pavilion is known as the railway end, which sounds rather prosaic considering the charm of the Severn Valley line. There's a pub on the platform called the King and Castle, which is a re-creation of an Edwardian station waiting room, and the prices of beers such as Wyre Piddle are also designed to take you back in time.

As for the cricket, I always remember it for the Law-Hatch double act. With all the frontline seamers injured, they opened the bowling and took three wickets each, the highlight being when Nicky Hatch had Graeme

Hick lbw first ball. In reply to Worcestershire's 227, Durham were 176 for nine when Hatch joined Law and they put on 84. It has remained the third highest last-wicket stand in Durham's first-class history. Hatch was unbeaten on 21, Law made 64 then took five for 52 as Worcestershire folded for 147. While otherwise impressive, Andy Bichel bowled poorly at his Queensland team-mate Martin Love, whose second half-century of the match carried Durham to a seven-wicket win. After taking five wickets in his first seven championship games for Durham, Law had added 30 in the last five.

"I thrive on bowling," he said, but pulled out of the next match, at home to Derbyshire, because of his girlfriend's pregnancy problems. Ironically, the man whose good start had been interrupted by attending a birth, James Brinkley, stepped in to take six for 14 on an extraordinary day. The first day had been washed out and on the second 18 wickets fell between lunch and the fifth over after tea, with 24 going down in total. It was tempting to suggest that someone should invent an anti-perspirant for pitches as, once again, this one was said to have sweated under the covers.

The umpires' obligatory call to Lord's prompted the ECB to send up pitch inspector Raman Subba Row, who had visited Riverside 12 months earlier and saw Ed Smith score 175 for Kent after 15 wickets had fallen the previous day. Subba Row dropped into the press box to inform us he wasn't allowed to speak to us, although we gathered from his amiable chat that no action would be taken.

In truth, the shambles had as much to do with the batsmen's inability to play the swinging ball as 13 of the first innings victims fell to edged catches and three more were out shouldering arms. Brinkley came on with Derbyshire on 46 for one after Ian Hunter bowled three overs for 26 runs, and 20 overs later the visitors were all out for 95.

Brinkley had Michael Di Venuto well caught in his first over by Sunderland lad Gary Scott, who was making his debut 19 days after his 17th birthday. Brought in as an off-spinning all-rounder to bat in Law's slot at No 6, he remains Durham's youngest first-class debutant. He scored a useful 25 in the second innings, but it was four years before he appeared again. His career only briefly threatened to take off before injury sidelined him in 2007 and a year later he was released.

Of the rest of Brinkley's victims, four were caught off the edge and the other was yorked. "The pitch is fine," he said, a quote which was lifted by Ted Dexter in his Daily Telegraph column, with the ex-England captain adding: "He would say that, wouldn't he?" There was also a career-best for

Derbyshire's Graeme Welch, who took six for 30 against his native county. Di Venuto held five slip catches in the Durham first innings, added a sixth in the second before he scored 111 in easing conditions as Derbyshire reached a target of 224 with four wickets standing. It was Sod's Law that, on winning the toss for the first time in ten championship games, Jon Lewis's decision to bat had backfired.

Another oddity about the match was that when umpire Nigel Cowley retired feeling unwell Derbyshire provided three deputies while John Steele umpired at both ends. First 12th man Adrian Marsh did the job at square leg, then physio Craig Ranson and finally scorer John Brown, a qualified umpire.

Andrew Pratt had top-scored for Durham with 68 not out in their second innings and he followed up with 86 off 72 balls in the one-day match, which Durham won comfortably to stay in the running for promotion. In fact, they went back to the top with a 17-run win in a home floodlit game against Hampshire, in which Love and Collingwood shared a stand of 166 in 28 overs.

Against the same opponents two days later Law scored his only championship century. He was last out for 103, and as it came five years after his previous best of 97 for Sussex he admitted: "I have under-achieved a lot with the bat, so to finally get a hundred means a lot." He shared what was then Durham's record seventh-wicket stand of 127 with Brinkley, who made 65 as Durham recovered from 92 for five to make 323.

Hampshire replied with 312, Brinkley taking four wickets and the rest falling to Graeme Bridge. He became the first spinner to take six wickets in an innings at Riverside, bowling unchanged for 35.1 overs to finish with six for 84.

Word had obviously gone round that Peng was vulnerable against short bowling, and in this match he was felled by Neil Johnson and retired hurt. Suffering from mild concussion, he batted in the second innings but was out for a duck as Durham were dismissed for 202. Losing the toss had been crucial for Durham on unsatisfactory pitches at Basingstoke and the Rose Bowl, but now for the second successive season Hampshire faced a fourth innings run chase on a good Riverside surface. Needing 214 in 53 overs, they cruised to a seven-wicket win.

Having opened for four games without success in Michael Gough's absence, Jimmy Daley moved down to No 4 in the penultimate match at Hove and in difficult conditions grafted for five and threequarter hours for

89. The ball swung in the sticky heat and Sussex had left enough grass on to encourage their four seamers. Gary Pratt, opening on his first appearance of the season, made eight and nought, falling in both innings to the third frenzied lbw appeal in an over from James Kirtley. Peng scored two runs in the match, but Daley's diligence laid the platform for victory, especially as Harmison produced his best spell of new ball bowling for two years.

Coming up the Hove hill, he removed four of the top six as Sussex succumbed for 117, but in their second innings they began their pursuit of 316 by racing to 84 without loss. That was when Gary Pratt served notice of the fielding talent which was to bring him fame by swooping from mid-wicket to run out Richard Montgomerie. Sussex were all out for 265, giving Durham their first championship win against them after losing eight and drawing one.

Peng's 92 was not enough to save Durham from a one-day defeat at Cardiff, after which he and Gary Pratt rejoined the England Under 19 squad for the third Test. Peng had been captain in the first before being released from the second, when Pratt made 188.

Durham made 369 in the final championship match at home to Worcestershire thanks to centuries by Lewis and Collingwood, who passed 1,000 first-class runs for the first time. But after his first ball duck at Kidderminster, Graeme Hick replied with 200 not out, equalling the highest Riverside score made by Darryl Cullinan. It also gave Hick the unique record of completing championship hundreds home and away against all the other 17 counties. His batting was more metronomic than magnificent against some ordinary bowling, but he made his runs out of a total of 356, with two batsmen run out by Gary Pratt.

Hick edged Harmison to Andrew Pratt in the second innings as Worcestershire slumped to 63 for seven after being set a target of 251 in 55 overs. Steve Rhodes and Chris Liptrot then held out for 28 overs and the draw left Durham next to the bottom, their worst finish since 1997.

There was jubilation the following day, however, as results elsewhere went in their favour and they clinched promotion in the one-day league by beating Worcestershire by nine runs. Durham had cause to be grateful for the presence of the Sky cameras in confirming that Andrew Pratt's latest piece of leg-side brilliance had stumped Hick for two. It needed 30 seconds of tension accompanied by the theme music from Jaws for the third umpire to make the decision. After being 83 without loss the visitors had swum into treacherous waters and never quite recovered.

Skipper Jon Lewis, who made 76 not out, said: "It's the finest hour in my five years here. There has been progress and it's nice to achieve something you can put a label on." With 373 runs at 41.4 Lewis had edged ahead of Peng in the league averages, the latter's 495 runs coming at 41.25. In the championship Love had 1,364 runs at 50.52, while Collingwood averaged 48.9 and there was then a big gap to Lewis on 28.71. There was an element of the local hero in the voting for the Player of the Year as the members gave the award to Andrew Pratt, who had pulled off seven stumpings in the championship and 11 in one-day games. Having made his second team debut in 1994, he had had a long wait behind Martin Speight to become recognised as one of the best wicketkeepers in the country.

It was announced at the end of the season that Speight and Nick Speak would be released, while Graham Gooch's consultancy role was to end as he would be taking over from Keith Fletcher as coach of Essex.

Moxon summed up his first season by saying: "Our one-day form has been very good. In the championship injuries haven't helped, although they meant that we needed everybody and we now know we have a squad of 20 who can compete at this level. Our last two performances, when we won at Hove and almost beat Worcestershire, showed what we are capable of. The attitude and application of the players has been fantastic and overall I'm delighted."

CHAPTER 12

FLEDGLINGS IN A TEST NEST

GOING into the 2002 season Durham knew that Riverside was to become the country's first new Test ground for 101 years, with Zimbabwe as the visitors in June, 2003. Paul Collingwood had played in 11 one-day internationals in India and New Zealand over the winter, winning three Man of the Match awards, while Steve Harmison and Nicky Peng had been in Adelaide as members of the inaugural ECB Academy. Peng had also captained England at the Under 19 World Cup in Australia and New Zealand, where Gary Scott was also in the squad.

While Scott was one of those who seemed to think his natural talent would sustain him, Collingwood at this stage was saying: "I reckon there's still 20 per cent improvement in me and I know what I have to work on. This time last year I was returning from playing club cricket in Australia and I could not have foreseen how well things would go. Coming back from 3-1 down to draw the series in India was one of the greatest things I have been involved with. But I still have to keep improving. Even my fielding needs work because I don't hit the stumps often enough. I'm not taking anything for granted. The World Cup is a massive goal, but I wouldn't say I'm well established in the team."

Chairman Bill Midgley took many of the plaudits for driving forward the application for Test match status in the face of opposition from some of the counties who already enjoyed that privilege. But with work still to be done on the ground, including the building of a long-awaited indoor school, it was clear that team-building still revolved around local talent. With Phil Mustard, Gordon Muchall, Mark Davies and Chris Mann promoted from the academy, the only outsider added to the full-time staff was Ashley Thorpe, a 27-year-old Australian all-rounder with a residential qualification after playing for seven years in the local leagues.

Of the 23 staff members, 17 were from the North-East and the only players over 30 were the captain, Jon Lewis, and Simon Brown. Mann, whose father, Harry, had played for 35 years for the Marsden club near

South Shields, already had a history of back trouble and his ailments meant he never played a first team game. The rest proved amazingly susceptible to injury, and as that even applied to Martin Love and his replacement, Brad Hodge, the season turned into a disaster.

Brown was said to be raring to go after missing most of the previous season, but he suffered a side strain in the first match and it proved to be the end of his career. In the second match Jimmy Daley suffered his seventh broken finger and that also spelt the end for him. With their departure an emotional bond was severed because they were the last survivors from the squad of 1992. Brown had carried the attack for years and was known for staying fit, but eventually the burden resulted in a spate of injuries. In 141 first-class matches for Durham he took 518 wickets at 28.3, while Daley played 93 games and scored 4,196 runs at an average of 27.97.

In some respects Daley was lucky to have an 11-year career, although when he scored 88 as a shy 18-year-old debutant at Taunton he looked an England player in the making. Broken fingers and politics held him back and we will never know how good he might have been. In the end there was a suspicion that he wasn't tough enough. Having seen Dean Jones and David Boon defy damaged digits, Daley retired on 57 in his final innings at Derby when he looked like winning the game. After a mini-collapse he re-emerged with two wickets standing and four runs needed to win, but seemed reluctant to command the strike and allowed the indomitable Dominic Cork to seize the moment yet again. The two-run defeat was very damaging for Durham and that was the last we saw of Daley.

He announced in early August that he was calling time on his career. He planned to set up a fishing and hunting business in his girlfriend's homeland of South Africa, which was quite an adventure for a lad who had emerged from the flight to Zimbabwe in 1992 with such a ghost-like pallor that he was probably telling himself he would never get on an aeroplane again. First-class cricket had certainly broadened his horizons, but eventually he returned from South Africa to his birthplace and continued to score bucketloads of runs for Eppleton in the Durham Senior League.

Some broken fingers, of course, are worse than others and Martin Love suffered a particularly bad one in the sixth match when fielding in the slips. Six weeks later he still hadn't recovered, so Durham drafted in his fellow Australian Brad Hodge and after playing one game he broke his left thumb in the nets. Martyn Moxon was said to have been apoplectic. It seemed to sum up a season of astonishing casualties, and they still hadn't finished as a groin injury forced Jon Lewis to miss the last six matches.

Paul Collingwood and Danny Law played in only five championship matches, spinners Nicky Phillips and Graeme Bridge both missed half the season with broken fingers, Nicky Hatch had an Achilles problem and Nicky Peng went into a steep decline after a tremendous start. Of those six only Collingwood would truly recover. The encouraging progress made in 2001 by Law and Phillips hit the buffers through these injuries, Hatch's injury was never properly sorted out until he had an operation after emigrating to Perth, and Peng's decline proved terminal. Bridge survived for a few more, largely frustrating, years. But as with the previous left-arm spinner, David Cox, his lack of athleticism counted against a wholehearted, enthusiastic and likeable lad.

The result of all these mishaps was that Durham finished 47.75 points adrift at the foot of division two after 11 defeats out of 16. After the previous season's promotion in the one-day league they won only two of their first 11 games and three wins from the last five came too late to save them from relegation. In the final season of the Benson & Hedges Cup they won two out of five and in the C & G Trophy Gloucestershire beat them by eight wickets at Bristol with 24 overs to spare.

Just as in the 1995 season, when they lost 13 out of 17 championship games, Durham had gone on a pre-season tour to South Africa and it was tempting to say they might as well have gone to South Shields. Yet out of all the gloom emerged three bright lights in Muchall, Davies and Gary Pratt, while another was rekindled. This was Michael Gough, who missed most of the first half of the season but finished with 616 championship runs at 51.3.

That put him second in the averages to Love, who just before his injury scored 251 at Lord's and finished with 576 runs at 82.28. But the top run scorer was Gary Pratt with a mere 713, and with Neil Killeen as the leading wicket-taker with 35 Pratt's runs and brilliant fielding were enough to see him succeed his brother as the members' choice as Player of the Year.

James Brinkley didn't feature at all and requested his release in mid-season to return to teaching, while the injuries meant there were plenty of opportunities for Marc Symington and Ashley Thorpe to demonstrate they were not the all-rounders Durham so desperately needed, given the demise of Law. Symington was considered a tough little character, but at 5ft 8in his medium pace was never going be a huge threat. As he averaged only 16.6 with the bat, he was also released.

This was the season when Durham's home-grown policy started to look futile in the face of other counties trawling the planet. Durham and Warwickshire had been the only ones to vote against the introduction of two official overseas players the following season, and some of the others were already pushing back the boundaries. As if to rub Durham's noses in their home-grown dirt, it was often the imports who stood between them and victory.

It all started in the first match with Sven Koenig. As an EU passport holder courtesy of his Italian mother, the 28-year-old South African was keeping Ben Hutton, grandson of Sir Len, out of the Middlesex team which arrived at Riverside. It is a reasonable assumption that Koenig's jubilant celebrations on completing a dour debut century did not go down particularly well with the Durham faithful. Nor did they help his concentration as he was out next ball.

Middlesex at the time were becoming the Chelsea of cricket as they had four other South Africa-born players on their staff, plus two born in Australia, one in Kenya, one in Pakistan and one in Ireland. Their official overseas man, Queenslander Ashley Noffke, impressed sufficiently in this match for Durham to keep tabs on him and they signed him a few years later.

After several years of steady improvement, this was also the season when Riverside pitches started to suffer from the grass roots breaking about an inch and a half below the surface. It resulted in very bland pitches and was a mystery which took a few years to resolve. In this instance there was no assistance for Mark Davies on his championship debut, while Brown's career ended when he broke down in his 19th over. Phillips got through 27 overs in the first innings, previously unthinkable at Riverside in April, but he also broke a finger in stopping a fierce straight drive by David Nash.

Replying to 347, Durham batted poorly with Gordon Muchall, also making his debut, top scoring with 48 out of 160. Following on, Martin Love made an unbeaten 101 out of 213, but with neither Brown nor Phillips able to bat Middlesex needed only 27 for a ten-wicket win.

The pain inflicted by imports was to continue with Syed Mohammad Ali Bukhari at Derby, followed by Neil Carter at Edgbaston, and was brought to a coruscating climax by Craig Spearman. Carter, a South African with a Scottish mother, took five for 31 then smashed 23 off one over in a crushing one-day defeat for Durham. Spearman, a former New Zealand Test player with a Welsh mother, truly was the Bristol bomber as he cracked a 75-ball century in the C & G Trophy hammering. Then in the final championship match of the season he hit 89 and 114 not out in a ten-wicket win for Gloucestershire.

First came Mohammad Ali, as he now wished to be known after appearing for several teams in Pakistan as Syed Bukhari. Aged 28, he qualified for a British passport by virtue of an English wife and had been taken on by Derbyshire on a match-by-match basis. Coming in at No 9, he set about Bridge, hitting 12 fours in his 35-ball half-century. His whippy left arm also delivered the ball at sufficient speed to inflict the break which ended Daley's career. The Derbyshire team also included Andrew Gait, a South African with an English father.

Peng made 108 for Durham, who were 174 for two chasing a target of 235 when Daley retired in the second innings. In the end Cork took the last four wickets for six runs in 21 balls. All fell to edged catches, two to Michael DiVenuto and two to Luke Sutton, with Steve Harmison departing first ball to give Derbyshire their two-run win.

The B & H Cup produced little of note other than more injuries and Bridge being dismissed only once while scoring 98 runs in four innings off 104 balls. Mark Davies had missed the end of the previous season with a collapsed lung, something he had suffered previously, and in the third B & H game against Yorkshire it looked as though he hadn't appealed when he had Matthew Wood lbw. It transpired he was too breathless to shout and he was taken to hospital and kept under observation for a few days. Michael Gough, who had missed the start with a back problem, now developed a foot injury, and amid growing talk that he would be in the squad for the first Test against Sri Lanka Steve Harmison suffered a side strain. That happened at Trent Bridge, where Kevin Pietersen was lbw to Neil Killeen for two but then took two for 36 in nine overs as Nottinghamshire won by five runs.

In the final group game at home to Derbyshire neither side could progress and the greatest interest surrounded the arrival of the Sri Lankans for a three-day match. In extremely chilly weather they had stopped off on their way north to buy some thermals and wore two pairs each in the Riverside nets.

The B & H jinx which had afflicted two other Australians, Dean Jones and Simon Katich, continued as Love totalled 70 runs in five innings and he also joined the casualties, along with Andrew Pratt, so that Durham had only 11 fit men to face the tourists. Phil Mustard and Ashley Thorpe made their first-class debuts and Mustard fearlessly served notice of his stroke-playing ability by contributing a run-a-ball 75 to an eighth-wicket stand of 130 with Collingwood.

Collingwood's 190 would remain his highest first-class score until his double century in the Adelaide Test which England went on to lose in 2007. With the Sri Lankans clearly struggling to warm to their task, the match also produced career-best bowling for Symington, whose four for 27 included the scalps of Mahela Jayawardene and Aravinda da Silva. Despite also including Kumar Sangakkara, who a few years later would play one of the finest innings I have seen in county cricket, the Sri Lankans replied to 469 with 167 all out. They fielded nine of the team who contested the first Test a week later and, following on, scored 282 for four with Russel Arnold making a century.

Advancing into mid-May, there was no need of thermals on a trip south to Cardiff. Before its transformation into a Test arena, the old Sophia Gardens had a certain rustic charm and this was a trip I always enjoyed once I'd discovered the best places to stay. After a pleasant drive down the M50 past Ross-on-Wye, it was always well worth detouring to Tintern to spend the night before the match at Parva Farmhouse. This is, in fact, a small and very quaint hotel overlooking a lovely stretch of the Wye in a wooded valley. A couple of pints in the very cosy Moon and Sixpence just along the road perfectly whetted the appetite for the delicious dinner in the Parva's intimate restaurant. After a pre-breakfast jaunt through meadows to the old station, or along the riverside promenade to Tintern Abbey, the hour's drive to Cardiff could be undertaken in good spirits.

As at Nottingham, I prefer to come out of Sophia Gardens and turn away from the city centre, which takes me eight miles north-west to Groes Fan. I had previously stayed out this way at St Brides-Super-Ely, near St Fagan's, famous for its village cricket team and the Welsh Folk Museum. But the bed and breakfast at Groes Fan, in a detached house called Smokey Cot, provided exceptional value, as did the nearby Creigiau Golf Club for nine holes late on a summer evening.

Darren Thomas, hardly one of the sultans of swing, plunged Durham into dire straits with a spell of seven for 19 on the first afternoon. He had taken eight for 50 for England A against Zimbabwe in Harare three years earlier, but like Melvyn Betts never really kicked on from there. Thomas's final figures in this innings of seven for 33 elevated him into the pantheon of those with career-best county championship performances against Durham and he never did better them.

With the ball suddenly swinging in rising temperatures after lunch, six of his victims were caught in the arc between wicketkeeper and gully. Love made 71 out of Durham's total of 162, while in the second innings 19-year-old Simon Jones took three wickets in nine balls to undermine a promising fightback. He ended a stand of 140 when he removed Muchall for 77, then Collingwood departed for 99 when he shaped to hook Michael Kasprowicz, changed his mind and gloved a catch to the wicketkeeper.

After most of the third day was lost to rain, there was a High Noon start on the fourth and the James gang came out with all guns blazing. Skipper Steve James scored 121 as Glamorgan reached their target of 201 with five wickets standing.

A back injury forced Jon Lewis to miss a championship match for the first time for four years, so Collingwood took over the reins for the first time for the visit of Gloucestershire and there were ten North-Easterners in the team. Michael Gough and Gary Pratt made light of Lewis's absence with an opening stand of 71, almost twice the previous best of the season. Only Peng of the top eight failed to reach 30 as Durham made their highest Riverside total of 470 for eight declared. It seemed a fair bet that a pair of Pratts making their best scores in the same innings would be unique in the annals of first-class cricket. While Gary would go on to beat his 66, Andrew would not surpass his 93, which ended when he ran himself out an over before the declaration.

Perhaps Pratt senior had been alerted to the threat from Phil Mustard by his young deputy's 75 against Sri Lanka, but after following up with two more good innings Andrew's batting declined. In this instance his innings was ultimately no avail because Durham were denied by rain and Jack Russell when they had Gloucestershire by the throat. After being dismissed for 132, the visitors closed on 261 for eight in their second innings, still 77 behind, with Russell unbeaten on 78. Ian Hunter had looked Durham's best bowler but broke down with an abdominal injury.

It was a typically dogged effort by Jack Russell, whose ever-present hat had blown off during the Durham innings. It was a comical sight as he seemed unsure whether to chase his cherished lid or get to the stumps to collect a throw-in. Professional instincts prevailed, but other members of the breed could not have looked more unhappy had they been parted from a bone.

Next came the trip to Lord's, where a sparser than usual gathering witnessed Love's 251 and Muchall's maiden century, possibly because of the Queen's Golden Jubilee celebrations. Lewis returned in place of Collingwood, who had a knee injury, and the captain opted to bat down the order, only for Gough to duck into the last ball of the first day's fifth over from Abdur Razzaq. It hit one of the screws on the back of the helmet, causing a nasty cut as well as briefly knocking him unconscious. He was taken off, but once it became clear there was no serious damage some banter ensued in the media centre about whether Gough had been prone or supine. When I asked (jokingly) if he had been prostate the reply was "he didn't look too gland." I related this in my Durham Diary, and in possibly the most annoying piece of sub-editing I have suffered the word gland was changed to grand.

During his memorable innings of 127, Muchall dominated his stand of 251 with Love as Durham amassed their highest first-class total of 645 for six declared. Owais Shah made a century as Middlesex replied with 465, but after bowling 167 overs it was asking too much of tiring bowlers to dismiss their hosts again. On a very flat pitch, Middlesex held out on 194 for five after following on.

As the Queen's jubilee coincided with my own, my wife, Annie, had accompanied me to London. Having failed in our application for tickets for the Buckingham Palace concert, we watched it on a large screen in nearby Green Park. Other than that the celebrations largely passed me by, and when we moved on to Edgbaston for a one-day match it struck me that I was missing something, such was the amount of bunting in the streets of Birmingham.

There were no flags flying for Durham, however, as they followed their 645 at Lord's by being dismissed for 72, this being the occasion of Neil Carter's five for 31. Martyn Moxon said: "I don't want to make excuses but you have to wonder if fatigue played a part. We spent a lot of time in the field against Gloucestershire and again at Lord's. Ideally we would have brought in some fresh legs, but James Brinkley has had a toe injury and there wasn't really anyone else available." It was virtually the only time Brinkley was mentioned that season.

Another disaster swiftly followed when Love broke and dislocated a finger in trying to take a slip catch in a rain-ruined game at home to Worcestershire. Danny Law was back and scored 68 as Durham achieved first innings parity before Neil Killeen took four wickets, including Graeme Hick for a duck, in reducing the visitors to 60 for five. That was how it finished and for the third successive championship game Durham had to settle for a draw after victory had beckoned.

The rules said they couldn't replace Love unless they were ruling him out for the rest of the season. Another oddity was that the next match was away to Worcestershire and this time Hick scored 315 not out as Durham were hammered by 308 runs. The one bright spot was another good innings by Law, who scored 72 not out. But his bowling was back to where it had been in the first half of the previous season.

The thrashing seemed to highlight Durham's habit of making a complete pig's ear of the best trip of the season for their fans. Worcester was the obvious choice because the two-division format meant there was no trip to the deep south in 2002. High on the list of previous disappointments were Taunton 1994, Hove 1996, Cheltenham 1997, Canterbury 1998 and Tunbridge Wells 2000.

On this trip to Worcester it was reassuring to discover the ladies' tea room in its usual fine fettle, but the best old pub in the city, the Cardinal's Hat, had closed down, although I believe it has reopened since. At that time it was surrounded by places with loud music and flashing lights advertising alcopops at £1.80. Not that it mattered greatly to me, as I discovered these atrocities on a fleeting visit before moving out to Great Malvern. Worcester itself does have plenty of attractions, but I prefer to head west, somewhere close to the Malvern Hills. In glorious weather I tramped those enticing hills on the unscheduled Saturday off and spent the night in a disappointing hotel.

I have since discovered a couple of excellent farmhouse bed and breakfasts along the Elgar Route. Pomp and Circumstance? I don't know about that, but it's certainly an area which feels reassuringly civilised. It also boasts a good selection of pubs nearby such as the Talbot at Knightwick, famous for its home-brewed beers named This, That and T'Other. The Admiral Rodney at Berrow Green has also proved very soothing after watching yet another mauling at the hands of Hick.

On to Northamptonshire, where in my experience more over-priced, sub-standard beer is sold than anywhere else in the country. Or perhaps it isn't sold, but stays in the barrel too long. The only explanation I can think of is that the London commuters in the pretty villages care more about the food and wine than the ale.

Durham arrived at Wantage Road to find that the groundsman had brought forward his end-of-season scarifying by three months. I exaggerate, but the pitch appeared to have been roughed up at both ends on a spinner's length to suit Jason Brown and Graeme Swann. The umpires' attitude was: "We'll see how it plays," but as half the playing time was lost to rain they had no cause for complaint. Durham made 352 and forfeited their second innings after Northants declared at nought for none. Graeme Bridge then took four wickets and Nicky Phillips picked up three after a mauling by Swann, whose 73-ball century guided the hosts to a one-wicket win.

With the floodlit one-day international against India, involving Collingwood, due to be held at Riverside, Durham went to Darlington for the visit of Derbyshire. The arguments about outground cricket were fuelled by the fall of 20 wickets on the first day. Durham still had 17 overs to bat in their second innings and reached 63 without loss.

Harmison was back for this game, while both spinners were retained and Bridge top-scored with 49 in Durham's 191. Just when he seemed to have established his superiority over Phillips, he dislocated a finger and did not reappear until the final match. Derbyshire had three men run out, two of them by Gary Pratt, in being dismissed for 96, of which Michael Di Venuto made 57. There was also a last-wicket stand of 20 between Kevin Dean and Lian Wharton.

Pitch inspector Phil Sharpe was quite happy with the surface and at 206 for six in their second innings Derbyshire were threatening to get somewhere near their target. Then Phillips came on for his first bowl of the match and took three for none in four overs to wrap up an 89-run victory for Durham. Mohammad Ali, so threatening at Derby, neither danced like a butterfly nor stung like a bee on this occasion as he took one wicket in each innings and bagged a pair with the bat.

It was Durham's fifth win at Feethams, but with the Darlington club, like Hartlepool, struggling to maintain borough council support there has been no more first-class cricket at the ground.

There were to be no more wins as Durham lost six of their seven remaining games. After deciding to write off Martin Love, they brought in his fellow Australian Brad Hodge and saw him score 21 and 44 in an eight-wicket defeat by Nottinghamshire at Riverside. He then broke his left thumb in the nets and as this coincided with Jon Lewis's groin injury and Collingwood was ruled out by a trapped nerve in his neck, Durham were now rudderless.

The captaincy went to the slightly eccentric Nicky Phillips. He was an unlikely leader, but Moxon seemed mystified by repeated media questioning about whether the Sussex reject would be continuing in the role, which he did until Hodge returned and took over for the final match.

The batting was further weakened by Muchall's absence on England Under 19 duty and the top six for the visit of Glamorgan to Riverside included Ashley Thorpe and Ian Pattison, making their championship debuts. Michael Gough returned to the team and for the rest of the season rose majestically above the general malaise, starting with innings of 30 and 37 in totals of 124 and 114 against Glamorgan. Michael Kasprowicz had match figures of 11 for 105 and was clearly far too good for Thorpe, batting at three. Mark Davies's first five-wicket haul was to no avail as Durham lost by ten wickets and the match finished at 3.25 on the second day.

In their second innings Gough and Gary Pratt shared an opening stand of 77 before Durham equalled their worst case of losing all ten wickets for 37 runs. They had gone from 46 without loss to 83 all out at Old Trafford in 1993. The last six batsmen dismissed by Kasprowicz and Robert Croft all made ducks and chairman Bill Midgley said: "It's not just losing that's the concern, it's the manner of this defeat. We will be putting in 2,000 seats this winter and starting work on the indoor school, but it's pointless spending money on developing first-class facilities if we are not getting the performances on the field. We have a policy of developing young local players, but if they don't perform we are going to bring in some older heads from outside."

In a floodlit one-day match at Headingley, Darren Lehmann suffered a rare failure against Durham when he became Gary Pratt's tenth run-out victim of the season and the youngster then scored 84 not out. His stand of 88 with his brother, Andrew, just about kept Durham afloat but they lost by 28 runs.

Amid all the gloom, Harmison was named in the England squad for the second Test against India and made the interesting observation that his time with the ECB Academy the previous winter had done little for his cricket but had made him a better person. "The academy wasn't really for me and I didn't particularly enjoy it from a cricketing point of view. But it was really worthwhile because it made me a more rounded person and it was brilliant in improving the way I look at the game and prepare for it. I would love to go on the Ashes tour this winter and I hope I can stake my claim this week. I think I have a better chance of playing than when I was in the squad two years ago."

Harmison duly made his Test debut, along with his academy pal Robert

Key, at Trent Bridge, emerging with match figures of five for 120 from the draw. Durham, meanwhile, needed Gough's maiden championship century to make a game of it at Colchester. He made 103 out of 259, with the rest of the top five totalling 49 between them. Gough said: "I've waited five years for this. I have worked really hard recently on my fitness and my cricket and it's nice when the sacrifices pay off. I have had some bad luck with injuries, but also my mind has not been totally focused on the game. I'm just trying to enjoy it, I'm on a good trot and long may it continue."

Captain Phillips ran himself out for a duck, but in the second innings he cut and carved outrageously to make an unbeaten 58 before shouldering the responsibility for preventing Essex reaching their victory target of 322. He took four of the six wickets to fall, but three of them came too late to make a difference and he conceded 103 runs as John Stephenson's unbeaten century saw the hosts home.

Durham achieved first innings parity at home to Northants then, after an opening stand of 62 between Gough and Gary Pratt, subsided for 136. The visitors won by seven wickets, and despite Hodge's return the batting woes continued as he top-scored with 48 out of 132 at Trent Bridge. For the second time in a fortnight Usman Afzaal scored 103, but rain prevented Nottinghamshire from completing their sixth win in eight games since sacking Clive Rice as Director of Cricket. Afzaal's languid strokeplay earmarks him as one of the most gifted players of his generation, but the word was at Nottingham that he laboured under the impression that he was the bee's knees. Moves to Northants, then to Surrey, suggest he is a difficult man to fit into a team environment.

Hodge showed his one-day class with innings of 77 and 91 not out in victories against Somerset and Nottinghamshire, with the latter match featuring 19-year-old Will Smith, the future Durham captain. But in the penultimate championship match, at home to Essex, Hodge made only two in the first innings as Gough became the third player to carry his bat for Durham after Wayne Larkins and Jon Lewis. He made 75 out of 187 after centuries by Mark Waugh and Aftab Habib had carried Essex to 463. Despite Hodge scoring 56 and Ashley Thorpe 95 in the second innings, Essex won by ten wickets.

With an Ashes tour beckoning, Harmison finished the season with his first five-wicket haul for 14 months at Bristol. Gloucestershire's Jonathan Lewis showed no inclination to get into line, preferring to offer a horizontal bat from a healthy distance towards square leg and eventually offering

Andrew Pratt his fifth catch. Despite Harmison's five for 65, Gloucestershire made 359 in reply to Durham's 216, of which Hodge made 73.

Gough and Gary Pratt then shared their seventh half-century stand in six matches and this time went on to three figures. But no-one else passed 40 and the total of 312 left Gloucestershire needing 171, of which Craig Spearman made embarrassingly short work. While only 41 runs were scored off the bat at the other end, the New Zealander sped to a 94-ball century and finished on 114 in a ten-wicket win.

All that remained was for Durham to be dismissed for 79 in the final one-day game at Taunton, losing by 175 runs. After the joy of the previous season's promotion, relegation was already confirmed and the only consolation was that Neil Killeen finished as division one's leading wicket-taker with 30.

Afterwards Martyn Moxon assured fans he was on the trail of a player who would help the youngsters. "We have had extensive talks with him and I think it's someone who would excite the members," he said. His target was Craig White, who opted to stay with Yorkshire, and Durham signed 37-year-old Vince Wells, from Leicestershire, instead. Further evidence of their need to continue watching the pennies came with the announcement that, with two overseas players allowed in 2003, Martin Love would be joined by South African Dewald Pretorius. He had played for the South Northumberland club that summer and had taken a hat-trick for Durham in a friendly against Scotland. But it was not exactly a signing which reeked of ambition.

CHAPTER 13

THE RICKSHAW ROLLS IN

JUNE 5,6 and 7, 2003, saw the staging of Riverside's first Test, and shortly afterwards came the first hint that the Durham focus might switch more towards team-building ambitions. As Dewald Pretorius was required to join the South Africa squad, Durham signed Shoaib Akhtar for the second half of the season. Was he the Rawalpindi Express or Rickshaw? The answer was both as he shunted from one extreme to the other, but there was no doubt he excited interest. Never before had stumps been so spectacularly splattered by yorkers at Riverside.

If Shoaib's signing signalled a shift of thinking on the part of chairman Bill Midgley it didn't last long because on July 10 he quit. It was known that the 2,000-seat stand in the ground's south-east corner, which was opened just before the Test match, had been funded by the development of a health club in the opposite corner. But as this wasn't part of the original plans some members took exception to it, and when Midgley felt that the criticism had become too personal he abruptly walked out.

He had played his part by balancing the books and helping to bring international cricket to the unlikely venue of Chester-le-Street, and he was also credited with a surprising role in giving the green light to Twenty20 cricket. He had gone to a meeting of county chairmen the previous year determined to oppose the introduction of this crash, bang, wallop version of the game. The voting was expected to be tight, but when he rose to speak Midgley suddenly changed his mind, deciding that the game needed to reach out to a wider audience after all. His words persuaded a few others and Twenty20 was duly born.

Durham were ill equipped for it and, whatever their outgoing chairman's wishes, the cricket management did not seem inclined to embrace this unwelcome interruption in the championship programme with full seriousness. They were riding high in the table until they were unsettled by the shift in tempo and lost their next two games on the resumption of four-day action. They recovered to remain in contention for promotion with three games left, but lost them all as the traditional batting woes resurfaced.

The ever-present Bob Jackson, who had been vice-chairman, took over the reins but insisted it would be a temporary measure as he was determined to bring in someone with real clout. That man would eventually prove to be Clive Leach, but ten months elapsed before his arrival, leaving Durham treading water with Martyn Moxon continuing as coach and Jon Lewis as captain.

As Yorkshire had gone from champions to relegation and had lost the services of their Australian coach, Wayne Clark, Moxon had been approached to return. But with one year left on his three-year deal, Durham were already negotiating with him over an extension of his contract and he opted to accept that. With Chris Hassell no longer chief executive at Headingley, the reasons for Moxon's resignation appeared to have been removed. But he said: "The fact that Durham were wanting to extend my contract, particularly given the season we had last year, shows a lot of faith in me. I think that deserves some loyalty on my part. I feel there are exciting times ahead here with the young players developing well. I left the Yorkshire job unfinished and I don't want to do the same again. I feel no bitterness towards Yorkshire and I wish them well. But I desperately want to beat them, because we haven't done it yet in my time here."

As it happened, Durham pulled off a championship double against Yorkshire and improved their tally of four-day wins from one to five. But the Tykes finished 24 points ahead of them, almost entirely through their greater accumulation of batting points. Durham improved on 2002 by finishing fourth from the bottom in both tables, but significantly three Australian left-handers scored two hundreds against them. Phil Jaques was one, while the others, Mike Hussey and Michael Di Venuto, would both become Durham targets once the ambition started to grow. Another left-hander who scored two centuries against Durham, two weeks apart towards the end of the season, was the more unlikely Mark Wallace, the Glamorgan wicketkeeper.

At the start of the season there was every reason to hope that Durham could build a top four of Michael Gough, Gary Pratt, Gordon Muchall and Nicky Peng to sustain them for years to come, with help from Paul Collingwood when available. Pratt continued his improvement in 2003, but the others didn't and the biggest disappointment was Gough, not least to himself. Although he was still under contract for 2004, he announced he would be taking a year off because he had stopped enjoying the game. The decision proved terminal as he worked in his father's sports shop, played football for Spennymoor and cricket for Hartlepool before umpiring became his life.

A bigger than usual clear-out at the end of the season meant it was also the end of the road for Nicky Phillips, Danny Law, Ian Hunter, Nicky Hatch, Ashley Thorpe and Chris Mann. Vince Wells was due to stay for a second season, but decided against it, ostensibly for business reasons.

Over the winter Collingwood and Steve Harmison had become the first Durham pair to represent England. Their opponents on Harmison's one-day international debut in Brisbane were Sri Lanka, and his first victim was Kumar Sangakkara, caught by Collingwood. Martin Love had also graduated to international level, sparked by scoring two double centuries against England in a fortnight, for Queensland and Australia A. He made his Test debut, aged 28, in the fourth Ashes Test and went on the subsequent tour to the West Indies, delaying his arrival in Durham.

Collingwood had also played in the World Cup in southern Africa, where England's decision not to play Zimbabwe in Harare had severely hampered their prospects of progress beyond the group stage. It had also left a slight question mark over whether Zimbabwe would turn up for Riverside's inaugural Test. Their captain, Andy Flower, had turned his back on the country, leaving Heath Streak in charge and he led out the team 11 years after his sensational performance against Durham at Bulawayo as a 17-year-old schoolboy. He opened the bowling with Andy Blignaut, who would briefly return to Riverside with so little distinction the following year. Harmison took six wickets in the match, including the final one to clinch victory by an innings and 69 runs, but Collingwood was unable to compete for a place because of injury.

He had suffered a shoulder injury in a pre-season match at Old Trafford and it seemed the cruelties of 2002 were to continue as one of Mark Davies's lungs collapsed on the same day. Both played in only four championship games, and Love in only seven as shortly after his late arrival he broke a thumb during a C & G Trophy hammering by Lancashire. Pretorius also missed a game though injury during his brief stay and, having opposed the increase, Durham fielded two overseas men in only three of their first 13 matches.

While waiting for Love, Durham had signed veteran Indian seamer Javagal Srinath, who had just completed his international career at the

World Cup. He showed only glimpses of his class during his three games for Durham. He felt the cold and generally looked jaded, and at the end of his stint he announced his retirement from first-class cricket.

Durham were denied the usual chance to ease their way into the season against a bunch of students, coming up instead against some top-class swing bowling from Richard Johnson at Taunton. This sadly injury-plagued bowler was at the peak of his form at the time and six weeks later took six for 33 in Zimbabwe's first innings in the Riverside Test.

Whatever confidence Gough had gained from his excellent finish in 2002 visibly drained away as the season's first few overs saw him continually beaten by Johnson. The bowler eventually found the edge and took five of the first six wickets. Jon Lewis, who had continued his roller-coaster Durham career with a disappointing 2002, scored two half-centuries in the match but his team lost by six wickets and lost a quarter of a point for failing to bowl 16 overs an hour.

With Johnson rested, Durham won the Sunday League game courtesy of some scintillating strokeplay by Pratt and Peng, who shared a stand of 164 in 23 overs. Pratt, now 21, oozed class as he hit his first senior hundred off 79 balls, equalling the Durham record set by Dean Jones on their very first day as a first-class county. Peng made 92 and Pretorius took four for 31 on his debut.

After playing in four Ashes Tests, Harmison was awarded a central contract just prior to the next game at home to Gloucestershire, when it was clear that the root break problem was still resulting in bland pitches. This one suited neither Harmison nor Pretorius, who had been timed at 92mph but came under fire from Phil Weston. The Durham-born left-hander had made the switch from Worcestershire over the winter and as a 6ft 3in blond he must have felt like Snow White. The dwarves among his team-mates now included the 5ft 7in South African Jonty Rhodes, who made a cultured 60 before becoming Pretorius' only victim.

Durham had been demoralised by a last-wicket stand of 65 and before you could say Jack Russell they were five for three. As big an irritant as ever to Durham, Russell scored 65 and dominated that final partnership with Mike Smith, who was never exactly a master bladesman. Durham were saved by rain as, following on, they were one run ahead with only four wickets standing. Lewis again made two half-centuries and Gough scored 73 in the second innings, but it was his top score in a season which he ended with a championship average of 23.77.

That was slightly better than Vince Wells, who scored a swift century against a poor attack at Derby but was otherwise unable to prove Leicestershire wrong for letting him go. He had been an excellent servant to them as the sort of all-rounder Durham had been seeking to develop for years. They appreciated his contribution "in the dressing room", but in persevering with him in the team they put him ahead of Danny Law, who was jettisoned after five games. At that point he had a batting average of 6.62 and the end came when he bagged a pair at the Rose Bowl.

As with Michael Foster, who was finished by injury, Law's failure to blossom into the all-rounder he could have been was a big disappointment. The talent was obvious, but he gave the impression of being a bit of a Jack The Lad. When he was released, Moxon said he had no complaints about Law's temperament or work ethic, adding: "In the end he just wasn't quite good enough."

Law also suffered the ignominy of a first ball duck against Scotland, who marked their debut in the National League with a four-wicket win at Riverside. Paisley-born Majid Haq looked an extremely useful off-spinner in taking four for 36. He was said to be one of many youngsters with Asian backgrounds coming through in Scottish cricket, and Durham had just taken one of them, 16-year-old leg-spinner Moneeb Iqbal, into their academy. They persevered with him for six years before letting him go. Sadly, the slightly tubby Haq also failed to kick on as even Scotland prefer their cricketers to shed excess poundage and look like athletes. Clearly, there is no room for the Colin Milburns of this world any more.

Peng made a dashing 158 against Durham UCCE at the Racecourse, to which Alex Loudon replied with 172 in a match in which 18-year-old Liam Plunkett made his first-class debut. He suffered a knee injury, spoiling his chance of playing on his native Teesside when Durham decamped to Stockton to play Worcestershire. The visitors scored 395 with Law taking one for 100, but at least his victim was Graeme Hick, who had pulled Law's first two balls for six and four but fell for a modest 30.

Several years earlier I had written that after death and taxes, rain at Stockton was life's biggest certainty. It did not go down well, unlike the bacon butties and home-made cakes we always enjoyed there. This occasion was no different as half the first day was lost to rain, the third was washed out and play began at 1.30 on the final day and was abandoned after two more interruptions. Perhaps it was something to do with the hospitality that pitch inspector Phil Sharpe returned for a second day as

Worcestershire made 395. In hindsight, it was also a warning about what was to happen at the same venue three years later, effectively killing off Durham's use of outgrounds.

The greater intimacy of these grounds is one of their attractions, which always seems to promote more banter, and on this occasion it was good to find that the humour in critics' corner was still alive and well. As Durham had not bowled particularly well and Graham Onions had just taken six wickets in the second team, someone asked me: "When are we going to get Onions in this team? Then we can have tripe and Onions." With Phil Mustard now pressing for a first team place, the quips about Mustard and Onions were starting to flow, and there was another bowler in the second team called Kean, so there were several instances of caught Mustard bowled Kean.

Srinath took three for 70 on his farewell appearance at Stockton, his wickets coming in a spell of three for nine in 11 balls after the score had reached 250 for three. Durham declared at 146 for three and were left with a target of 250 in 67 overs when Worcestershire forfeited their second innings. While Gordon Muchall was making an imperious 74 they looked like cruising it, but a rain interruption didn't help and after tea they slumped from 135 for one to close on 151 for seven.

Against Derbyshire at Riverside, Lewis made his sixth half-century in seven championship innings and Martin Love cruised to a classy 54 in his first innings after his arrival. With Harmison now unavailable, Pretorius led the attack and took four for 96 as Michael Di Venuto rose like a colossus above the rest of the shambolic batting on the second day. Durham had lost their remaining four wickets for 21 at the start of the day, then the left-handed Tasmanian scored 150 out of Derbyshire's 244. No-one else passed 20 and Shahid Afridi reinfoced his reputation as a slogger by falling second ball when trying to launch Nicky Phillips into the stratosphere.

After Graeme Welch took five for 60 against his native county in the second innings, Derbyshire needed 223 to win and sent in Afridi to open. He thrashed 14 off the first over he faced and blazed to a 37-ball half-century before holing out for 67. Going into the final day, Derbyshire needed 64 with four wickets standing but Pretorius took three of those to wrap up a 30-run victory for Durham.

They were then dismissed for 86 in their C & G Trophy tie at home to Lancashire, with Love unable to bat after breaking his right thumb when attempting a slip catch. This was May 28, two weeks earlier than the season-ending injury he had suffered the previous year. Durham had beaten Berkshire at Reading in the first round with Vince Wells taking six for 20 and scoring 63 not out against a team which included a South African named Tyron Henderson. This was the same man who would blast them to defeat in the Twenty20 semi-final in 2008.

Wells missed the Lancashire C & G match with a back injury and Durham also decided to send Law, Gough and Andrew Pratt in search of form in a four-day second team match at Blackpool. They gambled by bringing Mustard in to open at Riverside but he was out for a duck as they plunged to 26 for six. Peng made 44, Neil Killeen 18 and no-one else scored more than five against an attack of Anderson, Martin, Chapple and Mahmood.

Mustard and fellow Wearsider Ian Pattison were retained for the championship match at Headingley, where the captain stepped up the example he had been setting all season and duly had his reward. Lewis passed John Morris's record total of 5,670 first-class runs for Durham on his way to 124, while Pattison went in at 51 for four and made what would remain his best score of 62 in a total of 280. Mustard cracked a disbelieving Darren Gough for two off-side fours in making 23. After batting throughout the first day to finish on 120, Lewis said: "One of the advantages of being the wrong side of 30 is you have seen a few ups and downs. The younger lads can lose a bit of self-belief, but they have talent and they must give themselves the best chance to succeed by working hard."

Pattison was continuing to look the part with the ball, having figures of one for seven in 5.3 overs when he fell down in his follow through and dislocated his shoulder so badly he was out for the rest of the season. The consolation was that Plunkett, making his championship debut, returned from an initial mauling by Yuvraj Singh to take four wickets in nine balls and finish with five for 53. All out for 220, Yorkshire were 60 behind, despite 105 from Michael Lumb and 56 from Yuvraj.

Plunkett's father, Alan, had played at the Yorkshire second X1 venue of Marske, while Liam was a product of the Middlesbrough club. "I came to Yorkshire's indoor nets a few times, but they didn't pursue it," he said. "I was batting a No 3 at the time, but Geoff Cook must have seen something in my bowling when he invited me to Durham."

Plunkett had bowled with good pace and extracted some testing bounce. But balls began to go through at increasingly variable heights in the second innings and after Lewis scored 66 out of 200 for Durham the target was way beyond the Tykes. Once a ball from Plunkett had shot through at ankle height to bowl Yuvraj the once-deep reserves of Yorkshire grit seemed to have been exhausted. Pretorius took four for 15 and, in the absence of Pattison, Durham turned to Gordon Muchall's medium pace. He took three for 26 and Yorkshire were all out for 93.

It was the first time Durham had beaten their neighbours in the championship and afterwards Moxon was quick to ask: "Where's the cup?" There was no sign of the 4ft Durham Light Infantry Trophy, which had traditionally been at stake in these encounters. Someone at the DLI had now decreed that it would be contested in the Twenty20 meeting, thereby rendering the trophy subject to even more mickey-taking by the rival press corps.

It was now almost time for Riverside's Test baptism and when Steve Harmison was interviewed on Radio Five Live prior to the match he hinted that Durham had put county cricket on the back burner while pursuing their international aspirations. Lack of ambition in their signings was probably one reason for his observation, another was that there was still no sign of the indoor school being built. Bureaucratic bungling attached to the Lottery funding appeared to be the reason for the latest delay, much to Bill Midgley's annoyance. Nor was he pleased about Harmison's remark, saying a few days later: "We hope we have re-educated Stephen to the fact that it was an unfortunate statement. There's not one shred of evidence to support his claim, except that we took a match to an outground. We have said all along that the great advantage of having international cricket is that it will give us more resources to put into the county game."

While the Test was taking place Durham were at an even newer ground, the Rose Bowl, where there was another successful debut by a Middlesbrough player. Opening the innings because Michael Gough was unable to travel because of a family illness, James Lowe made a dogged 80. In the few subsequent opportunities he was given he never looked like repeating it.

The injury jinx continued with Pretorius straining a hamstring after four overs in his final appearance before meeting up with the South African squad. He couldn't risk aggravating it and didn't bowl again as Simon Katich reminded Durham of the class he showed in 2000 by making 135. He had slipped below Martin Love in the Australian rankings and said: "I just didn't make enough runs last year, but I plan to get back up there. Getting a few wickets might help. I've done a lot of bowling since moving

Tasty duo or hot dogs? Headline and caption writers have relished the Onions and Mustard combination.

Champagne moment. Gary Pratt and Paul Collingwood celebrate England's 2005 Ashes triumph. Pratt earned his moment of fame as 12th man for running out Ricky Ponting at Trent Bridge, while Collingwood was called up for the final Test.

Magic moment: Ottis Gibson bowls James Bruce to complete his ten-wicket haul against Hampshire at Riverside in 2007.

All smiles. Geoff Cook with the 2007 Friends Provident Trophy at Lord's.

One for Dale's diary: Dale Benkenstein with the cup as the Durham squad celebrate their Lord's triumph against Hampshire.

Were you there? The Durham fans celebrate a six at Lord's.

Cheer up, Cooky. Geoff Cook wipes the champagne from his eyes as Durham celebrate winning the 2008 LV County Championship.

Bubbly bunch: The Durham squad celebrate winning the championship: standing: Jon Lewis, Alan Walker (coaches), Luke Evans (behind), Gareth Breese (front), Mitch Claydon, Lee Goddard, Kyle Coetzer, Will Gidman, Mark Stoneman, Ben Harmison, Liam Plunkett, Graham Onions, Phil Mustard, Will Smith, Garry Park, Scott Borthwick (front), Callum Thorp, Gordon Muchall, Nigel Kent (physio). Seated: Neil Killeen, Paul Collingwood, Steve Harmison, Dale Benkenstein, Geoff Cook, Mark Davies, Michael Di Venuto.

from Western Australia to New South Wales." He duly took three wickets with his left-arm chinamen when Durham followed on 221 behind, but with the help of rain they held on for a draw on 137 for nine.

Katich added that he was surprised to see so few players he knew in the Durham team but said he was pleased to see things were progressing well at Riverside. "I've been watching the Test up there on television. The set-up here is also very good and I'm sure they'll get a Test here in a few years." Durham probably didn't want to hear that.

After the Riverside banquet came the fast food. Preparations for the Test meant Durham had little opportunity to promote the launch of Twenty20, which followed a few days later. James Bailey, the marketing manager, said he had wanted to send out a remote control car with a plastic duck on the roof to escort a batsman off if he was out for nought. I assumed he was joking as James was from an impeccable cricketing background. His father, John, had captained Durham from 1968-71, while John's brother, David, had played for Lancashire. James added: "The ECB looked at a lot of ideas, but decided they wanted to keep it as close as possible to proper cricket."

The visitors for the first match, Nottinghamshire, had run a male beefcake poster campaign featuring four players stripped to the waist and plugging the event as a "Girls' Night Out." Chris Cairns was one of the quartet but was injured after the posters went up and took no part.

Durham sent in Peng and Mustard to open and had Ashley Thorpe at No 4. With 109 runs in nine championship innings behind him, Peng's 49 off 29 balls launched the reply to 157 for seven and Thorpe's unbeaten 38 completed a six-wicket win with five balls to spare. Durham lost the other four games, although Pratt's 62 not out took them close at Derby, as did Mustard's 61 at Old Trafford.

Love had returned to action in the middle of the Twenty20 series, but not before his replacement the previous September, Brad Hodge, returned to haunt Durham with Leicestershire. His exhilarating strokeplay in scoring 64 almost emptied the bouncy castle. While songs like Another One Bites The Dust were played when a batsman was out, Durham were no longer singing Love Is All Around. No sooner was he fit again than their overseas batsman was named in the Australian squad for a two-Test series against Bangladesh in July.

The blow was softened by news of Shoaib Akhtar's signing. He was in the country for the one-day series also involving South Africa and had just completed his duties with Pakistan, having missed the first game because he was completing a two-match ban for ball tampering. He had also been suspended the previous year for throwing, but a visit to experts in Perth had shown that his arm was straight at the point of delivery. "They discovered that whereas a normal person's joints move about 20 per cent, my elbow can move 42 per cent," he said. "It's the same with all my joints."

At the World Cup the previous winter Shoaib had become the first bowler to be timed at over 100mph, clocking 100.2 with a ball to Nick Knight at Cape Town. He was said to be very pleased with himself because of that, and his time with Durham certainly confirmed him as a narcissist of the first order. They probably inflated his ego at the outset by sending him in at No 3 on his debut in the final Twenty20 game at Old Trafford, where the teams were greeted on to the field by someone wearing a giraffe's head. Shoaib was out first ball, skying a catch to mid-wicket, but he spent the rest of the summer doing enough to make sure he was invited back the following season, which proved a big mistake.

Nowhere was the contrast greater than in his two performances at The Grange in Edinburgh — most definitely express on the first occasion and rickshaw on the second. If there were any flying Scotsmen in the 2003 team seeking a National League double over Durham they were swiftly shunted into the sidings as Shoaib reduced them to six for five. The only member of the top five he did not remove was the Indian Test star, Rahul Dravid, who was bowled by Neil Killeen. Majid Haq followed his excellent bowling at Riverside by making 55 and James Brinkley chipped in with 21 as the Scots recovered to reach 153, but Durham won by 114 runs. On Shoaib's return to The Grange the following year he was said to have been out in Edinburgh until the early hours and was powerless to prevent a six-wicket defeat.

Just before the resumption of four-day action at Worcester, England released Harmison as he was not required for one-day duties. So the two expresses bowled in tandem and while the Rawalpindi version intially looked notably quicker than the Ashington one it was the latter who carried the greater threat. With both teams still in Twenty20 mode, Harmison took four for 50 as the hosts were dismissed for 218, but Durham then folded for 120. On a moderate pitch Shoaib's match figures of three for 61 were not especially impressive in the context of the game. But Durham had a chance of reaching their target of 297 until Gary Pratt was cut down by a dubious decision for 85. They lost by 31 runs.

This was Pratt's purple patch and he looked destined for a different kind of stardom from that he would briefly achieve as England's 12th man when he scored a magnificent 150 in the next match at home to Northants. It was his only first-class century, and it wasn't enough as the infestation of Australian left-handers crept further under Durham's skin. The visitors had three in their top four in Mike Hussey, plus EU passport holders Phil Jaques and Jeff Cook. With Shoaib again failing to impress, Jaques made 109 and 81, while Hussey's unbeaten 72 in the second innings carried his team to a target of 206 with only two wickets down.

Jason Brown took seven for 69 in Durham's second innings, becoming the first spinner to take a seven-wicket haul at Riverside. The best previous figures at the ground by a twirler were Graeme Bridge's six for 84 against Hampshire two years earlier. But, as with David Cox when James Boiling was preferred with no benefit, Bridge was now being kept out by Nicky Phillips, whose failure to justify the selection resulted in his release. In this particular match Phillips had match figures of two for 146. He was then replaced by Bridge until both played on receptive pitches at Cardiff and Northampton, where Phillips was again comprehensively out-bowled by Jason Brown. There again, so was Graeme Swann, who went on to play for England while his off-spinning colleague faded from view.

Hussey also made 112 not out in Northants' comfortable one-day victory, which followed the departure of Bill Midgley. This news would have meant little to Shoaib, but in one of the greatest matches seen at Riverside he then provided a vivid example of how quickly one man can turn a game. His electrifying burst in the second innings came after he bowled only 14 overs in four wicketless spells on the first day as Yorkshire reached 340 for six. But when he was handed a soft wicket off the second ball the following morning he smelt blood and suddenly found the energy to bowl an 11-over spell.

He also removed Darren Gough and Ryan Sidebttom then became increasingly frantic in his efforts to dislodge Steve Kirby. One ball of fearsome pace and lift flew down the leg side for four byes, prompting a shout of "well batted extras" from a Yorkshire fan. The barrage included a beamer, which was also down the leg side but prompted Kirby to fling down his helmet and march after Shoaib. Craig White, who was on his way to 135 not out, intervened.

The Durham innings brought a battle of Goughs. Darren was on the verge of an England recall and eventually had Michael caught at slip for 54 to claim his only wicket. Gary Pratt also got out immediately after scorching to a 46-ball half-century, then a fluent 50 from Bridge helped Durham avoid the follow-on. They trailed by 121, but the game turned on a burst of three for none in 11 balls from Shoaib. The third victim was Yuvraj, caught behind for a duck. Shoaib then retired for what had become regular attention to blisters, but although he took only one more wicket Yorkshire were all out for 129 and Durham needed 251 to win.

Everyone chipped in and Mustard's fearless 34 took them within sight, but he also managed to rile the fiery Kirby, who at one stage angrily ripped off his sleeveless sweater then followed up a bouncer by running down the pitch to eyeball the unflappable batsman. When Mustard was run out by a deflection at the non-striker's end, Shoaib went in with 19 needed and smashed a short ball from Gough wide of long-on for six, then drove him back over his head for four and sliced the winning runs to third man.

Martyn Moxon said: "It's always nice to win against your old club and it shows we are making progress. It has been a tremendous game with no quarter asked and it has gone down to the wire. It shows our youngsters what is required to win a game which goes the full distance."

A twisted ankle then forced Shoaib to miss a game on a run-laden track at Derby, which was ruined by the third day being washed out. Wells made 106, Peng 99, Lewis 77 and Mustard 70 not out in a total of 501 for eight declared before Di Venuto's 143 ensured Derbyshire would not have to follow on. Lewis, who passed 1,000 runs for the season, set them a target of 251 in 55 overs and they finished on 204 for seven.

Two home games followed in which resounding victories lifted Durham into promotion contention. The youngsters were continuing to blossom as Muchall, Pratt and Peng all made half-centuries and Bridge chipped in with 42 in a total of 345 against Somerset, who were in freefall at the time. But as Muchall's 65 was his first innings of substance for ten weeks, and several of his fours came off the edge, he was the one who had to make way for the return of Martin Love.

Shoaib was back for the Somerset match and again he was initially in rickshaw mode. But when Somerset resumed on 83 for four on the third morning the gift of an early wicket prompted the same response as against Yorkshire. Three more swiftly followed and Somerset were all out for 139. Declining to enforce the follow-on, Durham made 168 to lead by 374.

For the second time in the day, Shoaib then took four wickets in 15 balls and whatever the future held his place in Riverside folklore was secure. Somerset were five down with only two runs on the board and when Neil

Killeen took his second wicket courtesy of Ian Blackwell's edged slog they were eight for six. There was an element of good fortune about Shoaib's first two wickets as Jamie Cox gloved a leg-side catch to Mustard and Michael Burns was pinned lbw by a shooter. With several players injured, Somerset also included a couple of novices in Tom Webley and Wes Durston, plus Aaron Laraman at No 6. There was little resistance until No 11 Nixon McLean top-scored with 14 and they were all out for 56 in 19.4 overs. It was the lowest first-class total against Durham, eclipsing Durham University's 67 two years earlier. Shoaib had four for nine and Killeen four for 30.

Love returned from Australia, having made a first-ball duck in the first Test against Bangladesh and a century in the second at Carins. Now the Pakistan Cricket Board had changed their minds about excusing Shoaib from their three Tests against Bangladesh. He had also taken five for 35 in the one-day match against Somerset, although Blackwell's unbeaten 79 carried the visitors to a four-wicket win.

Even the big-hitting Blackwell, who joined Durham for the 2009 season, could not match the feat of Kevin Pietersen, who became the only player to have cleared the Don Robson Pavilion. It was one of three sixes in an over from Graeme Bridge, who would have his revenge by clean bowling Pietersen with a perfect left-arm spinner's ball at Cleethorpes the following year. At Riverside the future England captain thrashed 72 off 57 balls before cutting Shoaib fiercely to backward point. Pietersen had done enough to ensure a four-wicket for Nottinghamshire.

Love's maiden ton in his fifth Test was the last chance he got as Damien Martyn returned to the Australian side after injury. Durham weren't to know that and, having been down this road before with Dean Jones and Simon Katich, they decided not to ask Love back for a fourth season. Shortly after his return they announced in mid-August that they had signed Herschelle Gibbs, the dashing South African opener, for the 2004 season. As they also wanted Shoaib to return it was clear they were raising their sights, even if it meant courting two controversial characters. Gibbs had been suspended for his part in the Hansie Cronje match-fixing scandal, even though he failed to abide by the agreement he allegedly made to get out for fewer than 20.

Love never did add to his five Test caps, although he made 300 not out for Queensland against Victoria on his way to passing 10,000 runs and breaking Stuart Law's run-scoring record for the state. Although he reappeared in England for Northants in 2005, Love continued to be plagued by brittle fingers, then had a knee reconstruction and also missed some cricket when afflicted by Bell's palsy.

In his first match back for Durham he came up against fellow Queenslander Michael Kasprowicz at his best. Just as on Durham's previous visit to Sophia Gardens, it seemed the spinners would decide the outcome on a dry pitch and Robert Croft took six wickets when Durham batted first. Not for the first time, Nicky Peng impressed his future employers by showing the sort of four-day application Moxon had been preaching. He combined the necessary periods of vigilance with glorious strokeplay in making 133 out of 355, rekindling hopes of a glittering future. Mark Wallace then made the first of two hundreds in a month against Durham as Glamorgan replied with 455, with Phillips and Bridge sharing nine wickets.

With everything apparently set up for Croft, he opened the bowling in the second innings with Kasprowicz, but it wasn't working as Durham eased to 119 for one at tea on the third day. Then disaster struck, starting when Love tried to whip a straight ball to leg and was lbw to the fifth ball after the break. In 9.2 overs of mayhem Kasprowicz took nine for 22 and Durham were all out for 174. There were three more lbws and the last two were bowled as Kasprowicz was rewarded for fast, straight bowling and finished with nine for 36, the best first-class figures against Durham. At least he had expunged the hapless David Follett from the record books. Needing 74 to win, Glamorgan knocked them off in 14 overs for the loss of two wickets.

Love admitted that it was "a bizarre statistic" that in his first 44 championship innings for Durham he never got out between 78 and 251. His two innings of between 100 and 200 were both unbeaten, while his 251 against Middlesex at Lord's in 2002 was the first of four double centuries he made in 15 months, including the two against England for Queensland and Australia A. The fourth came against Hampshire and raised the Durham record to 273. It was also the highest individual innings at Riverside and took Durham to their record total at the ground of 515.

Love's 364-ball masterpiece seemed to drain the stuffing out of Hampshire, who were next to the bottom of the table and subsided meekly to defeat by an innings and 115 runs. Katich made 16 and two, while Neil Killeen took a career-best seven for 70 in their second innings.

Durham were now third in the table, and with Paul Collingwood back after his pre-season injury they also won three successive one-day games.

Shoaib also returned from the Bangladesh series for the last three championship games, but it all went wrong at Northampton. Durham were all out for 190, then Mike Hussey scored 187 and Phil Jaques 147 as they shared a record second wicket stand against Durham of 268. Graeme Bridge was handed an unwanted 23rd birthday present by recording the most expensive analysis in Durham's first-class history, taking three for 180. Northants amassed 538 for seven declared and won by an innings and 85 runs.

If that didn't kill the promotion challenge, defeat by 126 runs at Bristol did. Jonty Rhodes scored a hundred in both innings, while Love made 98 and 97. It was another bizarre statistic that in seven championship innings against Gloucestershire he never failed to reach 50, but he never went on to three figures.

It was during this match that Collingwood heard, to his surprise and delight, that he had been awarded a central contract. His parents were at Bristol, and his father, David, a former Shotley Bridge captain, said: "People used to ask me if I thought Paul would play for England, but at the time I just wanted him to play for Shotley. Anything else was a bonus." At the same time Liam Plunkett and Mark Turner, a paceman from Sunderland, were named in the England squad for the Under 19 World Cup in Bangladesh.

Cricket's penchant for throwing up the unusual continued into the final game. It was strange enough that Mark Wallace, who had previously scored one century, should score his second in a month against Durham, but for Michael Kasprowicz to achieve another nine-wicket haul was incredible. Weirder still was for two batsmen in Glamorgan's second innings to be out hit wicket. Wallace trod on his stumps when his foot slipped as he set off for a single, then a fourth-wicket stand of 231 between Michael Powell and Matthew Maynard ended as soon as Maynard completed a 97-ball century. Having already hooked Shoaib for one of his three sixes, he attempted a repeat. The ball struck his helmet and as he fell he dislodged a bail. Powell went on to make 198, and after trailing by only 23 on first innings Durham were now out of the game.

They succumbed for 118, Kasprowicz taking nine for 45, in the middle of which he was belted for 15 in an over by Shoaib, who went in at 44 for seven and hit 37 off 27 balls. The last five batsmen were all bowled and Kasprowicz's haul meant he had taken 35 wickets in his last three matches against Durham.

Gary Pratt passed 1,000 first-class runs for the season while making 59 in the first innings, but only he, Love (59.84) and Lewis (38.06) averaged more than 30 in the championship. In seven matches Shoaib took 34 wickets at 17.05, but with both spinners averaging around 40 it was no surprise when it was announced that West Indian Gareth Breese had been signed for 2004. An off-spinning all-rounder, he had captained Jamaica and played in one Test, in India. As his father was Welsh, he had an EU passport and this was the first indication that Durham were prepared to follow other counties in making such signings. Moxon explained: "We have made progress, but we have to keep moving forward. We have a policy of encouraging local talent, but there are areas we need to strengthen and decided we are prepared to go down the EU route to do it."

CHAPTER 14

THE TIPPING POINT

IT was mid-season in 2004 before Clive Leach was installed as chairman, by which time it was too late to do anything about the disaster which was unfolding. But whatever he had in mind, there is no doubt that returning to the bottom of the championship, following the previous season's progress, further fuelled a determination to turn wooden spoons into silverware.

Although little was seen of him, the former Metropolitan Police commissioner Sir John Stevens was the club president when Leach took over as chairman, aged 69. Born in Bombay of British parents, he spent the first five years of his life in India before being educated in Suffolk. He had batted in the middle order and bowled left-arm spin for Warwickshire in 39 matches from 1955-58 before becoming the Bishop Auckland professional from 1959-65. During that time he played in 66 matches for Durham with a top score of 98 against Cumberland and best bowling of six for nine against Staffordshire.

Leach's business career had seen him become head of Yorkshire and Tyne Tees Television and he was living in a village between Leeds and York when Durham approached him. On taking the reins, he said he planned to give himself a bit of time to learn how things worked at Riverside and in the ECB before making any moves. But, with his television background, within a couple of years he was playing a big role in securing the lucrative contract which gave Sky a monopoly of cricket coverage. He shrugged off the inevitable criticism with a fairly unsympathetic attitude towards anyone not wishing to attach a dish to his home. Leach had helped to get the best possible deal for the game, and it's probably safe to say that a similarly ruthless approach was applied to driving Durham from bottom to top in four years.

On taking over, he said: "I'm in favour of two divisions because it adds an element of competition and a bit of spice. I'm a strong believer in competition in everything in life because it encourages people to sharpen up."

The new chairman quickly decided that the club needed to be restructured at board level and an extraordinary general meeting was called on August 24, at which the members voted overwhelmingly in favour of Leach's plans. As in 1992, it was felt that Durham could pioneer a more efficient means of running a county cricket club. It didn't bring success on the field for the first 13 years, but it would in the next four. Leach brought in two other successful businessmen and they formed a new company, Durham County Cricket (Holdings) Ltd, with Bob Jackson continuing to be chairman of the actual cricket club, backed by the directors who were in place before Leach's arrival. The holdings company took on the assets and liabilities, including £1.8m of debt which had been incurred in building the stadium, and borrowing powers were increased.

After playing in 42 one-day internationals, Paul Collingwood had made his Test debut in Sri Lanka over the winter, and he and Steve Harmison had subsequently also gone on the tour to the West Indies. Collingwood played only in the one-dayers, but Harmison recorded his career-best figures of seven for 12 in the first Test at Sabina Park, Jamaica, in March and two months later he reached number one in the world rankings.

His only appearances for Durham, however, were in two one-day games and while he was ascending to the summit the county's fortunes with overseas bowlers were hitting rock bottom. Shoaib Akhtar's arrival was delayed partly by injury and partly by accusations that he had feigned it. He had apparently suffered a stress fracture in a rib cage during a heavy defeat in Pakistan's series decider against India in early April. He was unable to bowl in the second innings, but then went out and wielded the bat to great effect, leading to the accusations of feigning the injury. Even the captain, Inzamam-ul-Haq, voiced his doubts and seemed to question Shoaib's attitude.

Durham were told that the bowler was delaying his arrival in order to clear his name, and after a scan he was cleared of faking injury but was cautioned about his conduct. He arrived in England on May 10 and travelled to Taunton the following day to play in a four-day match, in which he looked out of sorts. He then bowled five overs in a one-day match and missed the next two championship games because he wasn't fit. We were told that he was unavailable for interview under instruction from the Pakistan Board, but a Press Trust of India report quoted him as saying: "I have asked the county to play me selectively for the rest of the season. I have advised them to look for a back-up player because I want to take proper rest between matches."

A Pakistan Board spokesman was quoted as saying: "He was going to England, where he would rest and after two weeks he would send us his bone scan. But he played a match and breached the promise. It is quite surprising that one is unfit in Pakistan and by reaching England gets fit overnight."

Durham were also unsure at that stage how long Shoaib would be staying as Pakistan were to play in the Asia Cup from July 16–August 2, and he would probably be required to team up early with the squad for the ICC Trophy, starting on September 8.

As it turned out, once he had declared himself fit he played in one more championship game then fell ill. He performed poorly in a one-day match in Edinburgh and finally in a floodlit one at Hove, after which he was summoned to the Asia Cup. Durham waved him a less-than-tearful farewell, and given the problems he caused it is amazing that two other counties dabbled with him in later years with a predictable lack of reward.

The unsettling nature of this episode was hugely compounded by what surrounded it as three stop-gap signings proved totally ineffective. Then when it seemed things couldn't get any worse, they did. That was when Durham welcomed the 21-year-old Australian paceman Shaun Tait for the final month of season. He was the winner of the Bradman Young Cricketer of the Year award and was known to be genuinely quick. Unfortunately, he totally lost his run-up on arrival and in two games he took none for 176 in 18 overs, including 26 no-balls. Durham dare not risk him after that, but bowling coach Alan Walker continued to work hard with him and he went home to take a stack of wickets and earn a place in the 2005 Ashes squad. Tait was quoted in Australia as saying some uncomplimentary things about Durham, which was totally out of order.

The overseas batsman was present throughout the season. But it wasn't Herschelle Gibbs, the South African signed amid great anticipation the previous August. Delayed by a new Twenty20 Cup in South Africa, Gibbs kept Durham in the dark about his likely arrival date and they secured the services of Western Australia left-hander Marcus North for the start of the season. He had married a North-East girl and had returned to continue his role as club professional for Gateshead Fell, who agreed that Durham could have him for as long as necessary. He totalled 60 runs in four innings in the first two championship games, and at that stage Durham were still hoping Gibbs would arrive in time for the C & G Trophy tie at home to Sussex on May 5. They had heard he had a hamstring injury and a few days later came the news that he had been ordered to rest by the South African board. They had a tour to Sri Lanka starting on July 14 and wanted Gibbs to take two months off because of "severe physical and mental fatigue."

Although worse was to follow weather-wise, that summer was the wettest to date of Durham's 13 seasons in first-class cricket and given the combination of damp conditions and the continuing problem of root break on the square, the batsmen's former phobia about playing at home resurfaced. The pitches did not suit stroke-players such as North and Gareth Breese, who both played much better away from home. Eight visiting batsmen scored championship centuries at Riverside, but Durham didn't manage any. Gordon Muchall progressed, but just when it seemed Gary Pratt was an established fixture in the side he slipped backwards and was eventually dropped, as was Nicky Peng.

The Player of the Year was Mark Davies, who was the first bowler in the country to 50 championship wickets before a side strain kept him out for the last two months. But the search for a seam-bowling all-rounder proved as frustrating as ever as Martyn Moxon's gamble on signing his old Yorkshire colleague, Gavin Hamilton, failed to pay dividends. Moxon had also hoped to land Ryan Sidebottom, but he opted for Nottinghamshire instead.

Hamilton had played in one Test in South Africa in 1999 following an outstanding season with Yorkshire, but had developed a bowler's equivalent of the golfing yips at the start of the 2002 season. He had suddenly sent down nine wides for Yorkshire against the Leeds/Bradford students, and in the two years since he had explored every possible means of rectifying the problem. A debut for Durham against Durham UCCE provided a pressure-free opportunity to bowl and in the second innings he took three for 30 in 12 overs. That was three times as many first-class wickets as he had taken in the previous two years, but by the end of April he was injured and was out for three months.

Having made way for Phil Mustard for most of the 2003 season, Andrew Pratt was preferred behind the stumps in the opening game against the students and top-scored in both innings with 67 and 68. The only other remarkable feature of the game was Lee Daggett taking eight for 94 in Durham's first innings. He hailed from Ramsbottom, but neither Lancashire nor Durham showed much interest in him and he was eventually taken on by Warwickshire.

In Shoaib's absence, Durham had signed the former West Indies Test paceman Reon King for the first two championship games, which proved to be a mistake. They began on a tricky pitch at the Rose Bowl with Shane Warne, in his first season as captain, correctly offering the view that Michael Clarke, the young Australian batsman he had brought with him, was a Test star of the future.

Clarke showed his class in making 75 out of 221 after Durham had been dismissed for 128 in the sort of sunny weather which highlighted that southern counties enjoy an advantage in their pre-season work. Peng followed his 49 in the first innings with 66 in the second before becoming one of five victims for Warne and Hampshire needed 112 to win. Davies had taken six for 53 – then his career-best – in the first innings and now he and Liam Plunkett bowled their hearts out in reducing the hosts to 52 for seven. But when they had to be rested Durham turned to King, who conceded 21 runs in 3.2 overs as Dimitri Mascarenhas took Hampshire home by three wickets.

Gareth Breese had been unable to make his debut because of last-minute confusion over his registration. It had already been resolved that he had to appear for Jamaica as an overseas player after signing for Durham, and he had effectively accepted that his Test career was over after one game. The fact that his registration was queried at Lord's did not go down well at Durham considering the number of EU-qualified players at other counties.

For the first home game against Nottinghamshire the earth tremors behind the press box told us that work had finally begun on the indoor school. But the local products seemed to be doing fine in any case as both Pratts, Peng, Plunkett and Graeme Bridge all made around 50 in a total of 350. But the visitors replied with 523 and Hamilton cut a disconsolate figure when Russell Warren hit him for five fours in his second over then he bowled a wide and a no-ball in his third. Warren went on to make 120, while King struggled with his run-up, running through the crease a dozen times.

After Durham folded for 93 in their second innings, with Charlie Shreck taking six for 46, Moxon said: "We planned our staff around having two top-quality overseas players until August. But now everything is up in the air. Everything has been meticulously planned according to what we can spend, but with so much international cricket to get two quality players for any length of time is very difficult. Having Reon King has not worked out, but that can happen. We went into it with the best of intentions."

On a day when there was scarcely a breath of wind at sunny Riverside, Breese made his debut in the one-day match against Nottinghamshire and created quite a stir. He scored 25 and took three for 37 in a 26-run win, during which Kevin Pietersen – helmetless on the slow pitch - was run out by Gary Pratt.

Breese's championship debut at Derby coincided with that of Graham Onions, replacing King, but the rain returned and play didn't start until noon on the third day. With Michael Di Venuto having withdrawn from the Derbyshire captaincy following a back operation, this match featured centuries by two Western Australia left-handers. Chris Rogers, Di Venuto's replacement, made 156 and Marcus North replied with 119 for Durham in the inevitable draw.

In terms of extracting full value from my usual stay at the Lathkil while visiting Derbyshire, the weather was a mixed blessing. The Peak District deserves to be cloaked in sunshine, but at least the lack of cricket on the first two days created more time for exploration. Having previously sampled the delights of Chatsworth, for the culture on this occasion I turned to Haddon Hall, and for refreshment to the Quiet Woman at Earl Sterndale. Set in one of those almost gorge-like valleys, this pub is such a throwback that one fears for its survival at a time when so many are going out of business. Like the wonderful Falcon Inn in Littondale, North Yorkshire, this is the sort of pub which deserves a preservation order. Unfortunately, on my most recent visits to both there was a lack of warmth and cosiness which hinted that they were starting to suffer.

The sign outside the Quiet Woman is of a headless female, the legend being that a long-gone landlord had decapitated his wife in order to halt her endless chatter. Another Peaks pub which is a reminder of days of yore is the Barley Mow at Kirk Ireton, where the ale is served from casks behind a wooden counter. Then there's the Three Stags Heads at Wardlow with its flagstoned parlour bar. This was popular with bikers the last time I called, and will be too basic for many tastes. But if you seek greater comfort the Devonshire Arms at Beeley is extremely civilised, as is the Chequers at Froggatt Edge. For a spectacular view, the pub attached to the Monsal Head Hotel would take some beating.

Martyn Moxon probably needed a stiff drink when he realised he would have to draft in his 41-year-old bowling coach, Alan Walker, for the C & G Trophy visit of Sussex. Liam Plunkett was the latest casualty, suffering from sore shins. Walker hadn't played in the first team for six years and he survived only until the sixth over of this match. In his heyday bowlers weren't expected to do any more than stick out a boot if they couldn't bend down to pick up the ball, but in attempting a sliding stop he pulled a calf muscle and limped off.

Ian Pattison conceded 26 runs in his first three-over spell, then returned to take three wickets, but the visitors' 245 was beyond Durham's reach by the time Walker went in with a runner at 175 for nine in the 45th over. He proceeded to thrash an unbeaten 23 off 15 balls in a stand of 48 with Neil Killeen. It was never going to be enough and Killeen was run out with eight balls left and 23 still needed.

Speaking of his injury, Walker said: "At first my groin and shoulder hurt, then about two balls later I realised my calf had gone. It was more embarrassing than anything. When you're young you just think you can run these things off."

The crisis persuaded Durham to bring in a Pakistani seamer named Tahir Mughal as an overseas player until Shoaib arrived. He had impressed Geoff Cook in one match for the academy the previous year and was now in his third season with Silverdale, near Stoke, in the North Staffordshire and District League. Bowling at little more than medium pace, he posed no threat with the new ball at home to Essex, but returned later to claim two wickets in a rain-ruined draw. Gordon Muchall began a return to form by making 94, his highest score since his century at Lord's two years earlier. Mark Davies greatly impressed Graham Gooch, the Essex coach, in taking five for 30.

Paul Collingwood, just back from the West Indies with the England squad, was made available for Durham and was joined by Shoaib in the team which headed for Taunton. Shoaib looked distinctly rickety as 19-year-old James Hildreth set about him on his way to a 112-ball century. He had appeared over the winter in the Under 19 World Cup in Bangladesh with Plunkett, Mark Turner and Ben Harmison, but this was only his second championship appearance.

Richard Johnson followed his six-wicket haul at Taunton the previous year by taking seven for 69as Durham trailed by 140 on first innings and Somerset continued to dominate on the third day. When Hildreth came in and drove Shoaib for four it fired up the lethargic Pakistani and instead of resting, as usual, after four overs, he carried on. He bowled off a short run to Jamie Cox and fed him singles, but Hildreth met good length balls with audacious strokes while watching ferocious bouncers fly over his head. Shoaib lengthened his follow through so he could eyeball Hildreth, then another bouncer flew wide of Andrew Pratt for four byes. Hildreth went on to make 72, Cox scored 124 and Somerset declared on 310 for five, setting a target of 451.

Andrew Caddick, Durham's old nemesis, took four wickets in reducing them to 95 for five, and a three-day defeat was on the cards when Breese joined Peng, whose good start had vanished in a run of three ducks in five innings. As Caddick tired, Peng crusied to 70 not out at the close, when the total was 174 for five.

On the final morning Caddick put everything into the first hour and Peng took the brunt of it, surviving with no little skill. He had added four runs in 57 minutes when he suddenly hit three fours in four balls off Johnson. Then Caddick summoned one last effort to nip one back and pin Peng lbw for 88, ending a stand of 131. Durham still needed 225, but the pitch remained sound, while Caddick and Johnson were virtually a spent force. Andrew Pratt chipped in with 25, Shoaib made 46 and Neil Killeen 35 before he was bowled by Nixon McLean with 18 needed.

Last man Mark Davies, who had been at the back of the dressing room with skipper Jon Lewis, admitted he was "terrified" when he joined Breese. He was perilously close to lbw first ball and Somerset thought they had run him out when the gap was three runs. But this was Breese's day and by scrambling that single to mid-on he retained the strike. He played and missed at the first three balls of Johnson's next over and cut the fourth for the winning boundary. It was the 24th four of his 348-minute innings and he finished on 165, having previously made only one first-class century, for Jamaica eight years earlier.

Since his encouraging one-day debut, Breese's off-spin bowling had not looked worthy of keeping Graeme Bridge out of the team. But this was such a high-class innings that his place was secure and he said: "I'm just really happy to contribute to a Durham win. It was a total team performance. The camaraderie has been really good. I have made a lot of half-centuries, so it's really good to convert one like this. I was really nervous with three runs needed and nearly ran Mark out. It was very tight."

Durham's 453 for nine was 110 more than they had previously scored in a fourth innings and it remains one of the five most unforgettable days in their first-class history.

More records tumbled the following day at Worcester, where Durham's total of 319 for three was their best in the one-day league and Collingwood's 72-ball hundred was the fastest one-day century by a Durham player. Marcus North also made a century and Durham won by

94 runs, with Moxon saying: "Saturday's win was a massive springboard for what has happened today. It has given a tremendous boost to everyone's confidence."

The confidence did not, however, extend to batting at Riverside. Durham were back there three days later and after Michael Powell hit a rapid 124 in Glamorgan's 393, Durham were all out for 220 with Muchall's 93 the only significant contribution. Even though Michael Kasprowicz was required by Australia to cull Zimbabwean rabbits instead, Durham lost by 201 runs in a match for which they had drafted in 22-year-old Sunderland University student Pallav Kumar. Born in India, he had lived for seven years in Carlisle and had played for the town's cricket club for four seasons, while also appearing in three matches for Cumberland. He played a few games for Durham seconds in 2003 and stayed on for the rest of 2004, but was then released.

Against Glamorgan, Kumar replaced the injured Shoaib and when he opened the bowling he was pulled for three early sixes. He later took three wickets and was retained for the next match at Trent Bridge, where Durham fell foul of another Hussey.

Whereas they had suffered at Michael's hands the previous year, this time his brother David blasted seven sixes in his unbeaten 166. Durham were in control until he put on 120 for the last wicket with fellow Australian Stuart MacGill. It was a record tenth-wicket stand against Durham and undermined Davies's figures of six for 78. Killeen also bowled well with no reward, but Durham showed little faith in Kumar when Nottinghamshire needed 291 to win in the fourth innings, despite the fact that he had Pietersen caught at second slip for a duck in the first innings.

At 221 for seven Durham were slight favourites, but Nottinghamshire lost no more wickets and Chris Read remained unbeaten on 108 after being caught off a no-ball on seven. The bowler was Collingwood, who was amazed by Allan Jones's call as he had never been in the habit of over-stepping.

May ended with Shoaib back in the team for a Sunday League match at Riverside against Derbyshire and he took four for 15 as they were shot out for 82. They were 41 for nine until Luke Sutton, who made 43, was joined by West Indian Daren Powell, who had been playing for Belper Meadows and had just joined Derbyshire as a temporary overseas player. Although wicketless, Mark Davies delivered the most economical completed spell for Durham in the one-day league by conceding only ten runs. Durham won by seven wickets, but this was an early taste of how one-day pitches at Riverside would yield increasingly fewer runs over the next two years.

It could not have done Durham's case much good in bidding for international cricket when New Zealand visited in June for a one-day match and dismissed England for 101 in 32.5 overs with James Franklin taking five for 42. Steve Harmison took the three Kiwi wickets to fall in their seven-wicket win. Although Martin Saggers didn't play in that match, he had made his Test debut at Headingley, where Gary Pratt and Peng helped Collingwood with 12th man duties. That was because, after a hectic first six weeks with barely any time off, the fixture computer had suddenly left Durham kicking their heels.

Their batting frailties on home turf continued with totals of 150 and 214 in a 320-run defeat by Yorkshire, for whom Anthony McGrath and Darren Lehmann scored centuries. It was the start of a golden run against Durham for McGrath, while Lehmann was used to plundering runs against them. More amazingly, off-spinner Richard Dawson had match figures of nine of 115, while Breese had one for 152. He would have his revenge at Scarborough in September, but until then things continued to go badly, with the next defeat coming in the one-day league in Edinburgh. There were only four Scots in a team which featured a young Yasir Arafat alongside Asim Butt, Sridharan Sriram, Australian Paul Hoffman and the big-hitting Zimbabwean Ryan Watson. There was no sign of Paisley-born Majid Haq.

Durham handed a debut to Scotland-born Kyle Coetzer in the next match in Cardiff. He had captained Scotland in the Under 19 World Cup the previous winter, and had also spent some time with the Western Province Academy as both his parents were South African. But his father had come to Aberdeen 22 years earlier to work in the oil industry, and in his second year with the Durham Academy Kyle was determined to commit his future to them.

The first and last days at Sophia Gardens were washed out and inbetween Durham amassed 466 with Marcus North making 219 after dropping down to No 4. Breese, promoted to open, scored 76 and Coetzer an impressive 67. With Shoaib ruled out by a virus amid rumours that the new Pakistan coach, Bob Woolmer, was coming to see him, Glamorgan replied with 258 for seven.

There was to be one final undistinguished appearance from Shoaib in a floodlit match at Hove. Sussex were the first county to install permanent lights in 1998 and they proved far more adept at playing under the Brighton illuminations than Durham as Matt Prior hit 119 in a 99-run victory. Shoaib had one for 65 in his nine overs and the match reinforced the impression that floodlit cricket is a waste of time in this country other than on perfect, warm evenings. The only time Durham had experienced one of those was in the high-scoring game at Worcester three years earlier.

It now transpired that Woolmer wanted Shoaib for the Asia Cup and as the ICC Trophy would follow Durham said farewell to the man from Rawalpindi and signed Andy Blignaut as a temporary replacement. As he had worked as a male model, he was probably a worthy successor to Shoaib in the vanity stakes. He certainly didn't live up to what Geoff Cook had said about Zimbabweans offering blood and guts back in 1992.

Blignaut was one of 15 players who had been sacked by the Zimbabwe board and he had signed a three-year contract with Tasmania, where he was expected at the end of August. Chiefly a seam bowler, he had hit the headlines with a 27-ball half-century against Australia in the 2003 World Cup, but he did not arrive in Durham in time for the Twenty20 Cup.

Still ill-equipped for this competition, Durham again won only one of the first four games, the victory coming courtesy of a remarkable spell of four for seven by Neil Killeen at Grace Road. In the opening game at Trent Bridge there were tasty contributions from Mustard and Onions, but it was clear Durham were not going to be the hot dogs of the competition. By the time they also won the last game at home to Yorkshire hopes of progress had gone.

The shift in tempo back to four-day cricket again proved problematic as Durham were bowled out for 93 by Derbyshire at Riverside, with the unheralded Mo Sheikh taking four for nine. Jon Lewis carried his bat for 35. Davies again improved his career-best figures with six for 44, but Blignaut bowled 11 no-balls in 11 overs in the first innings and had match figures of two for 91. Durham lost by 165 runs. It was their third successive three-day home defeat and they had not played on a Saturday since the outstanding win at Taunton ten weeks earlier.

Davies, with 50 wickets at 18.76, had suffered the side strain which ended his season, and the return of Liam Plunkett to share the new ball with Blignaut at Grace Road proved a disaster. Jon Lewis's decision to put Leicestershire in probably hastened the end of his four-year captaincy reign as Brad Hodge scored 262 out of 634 for nine declared. It was Hodge's third double century of the season, but Leicestershire had slipped a long way since their title days and went into the match with only Durham below them.

Durham lost by an innings and 26 runs and it had clearly been a mistake to bring in a player for a few weeks with no recent cricket behind him and probably unsettled by events back home.

"My parents still have their farm," said Blignaut. "It's a lot smaller than it used to be, but at least they have a roof over their heads. I was born in Zimababwe and I love the place, but even if things did settle down I can't see myself playing there again." He had been a highly-rated cricketer in his homeland, but he never did recover his form and his stay in Tasmania was brief. He later played a bit in South Africa.

It was impossible to believe that any other first-class county would have gambled on such an assortment as Tahir Mughal, Pallav Kumar and Andy Blignaut, and Martyn Moxon seemed aware of this. "What we have to get right next year is the balance of youth and experience," he said. "We have been trying to do that, but the financial situation has meant our potential signings have been limited. I'm confident that will change. I've had several chats with the new chairman and I'm very impressed with him. He hasn't come here to be second best and he's working hard to create the finance to bring a few players in."

With nothing left to play for other than pride, the season's only remaining highlights were at the seaside – first at Cleethorpes, then Scarborough.

Nottinghamshire had played two championship matches at the Lincolnshire club in the early 1980s and first went back there for a one-day match in 1999. As Durham's visit was on a Sunday, I took expert advice to get there early and go to Steel's for a coal-fired fish and chip lunch. It was said to be as good as the Magpie café at Whitby, and indeed it was. So much so that when I met up with my frequent companion at Durham matches, Ray Parker, and eulogised about it he persuaded me to go back afterwards. Otherwise Cleethorpes was not my bag of chips. Having parked at the cricket ground and walked along the seafront to Steel's, I overheard someone say to her companion: "I prefer this place to Skeggy," which didn't seem to say a lot for Skegness.

It was a pleasant day at a hospitable club and the game provided an excellent advert for the dwindling spectacle of outground cricket. The most memorable moment came when Graeme Bridge bowled Kevin Pietersen with an absolute beauty. Two months short of becoming England-qualified,

Pietersen had raced to 30 off 22 balls when he played back and shaped to turn Bridge to mid-wicket, only to be beaten by the spin. Despite a healthy total of 229 for seven, Bridge had figures of three for 14 in nine overs and Nottinghamshire's three spinners were unable to match him as Marcus North's unbeaten 121 carried Durham to six-wicket win.

Durham's one annual floodlit match at Riverside was another damp squib enlivened only by Ricky Ponting making a match-winning 83 not out for Somerset. On a miserable rain-interrupted evening no-one else could hit the ball off the square, but Ponting was simply superb.

Rain also blighted the championship clash, when the Friday start seemed to promise Saturday cricket for the first time since Durham were at Taunton. The ground was so wet, however, that despite afternoon sunshine no play was possible. While awaiting the next pitch inspection one member decided to vent his wrath in the press box. "If Sky TV were here they'd be playing," said our vexed visitor, adding: "My mates have gone to watch Burnmoor seconds."

This was the match in which Shaun Tait's nightmare began, with his long delivery stride producing four no-balls in his first over. He said he had had no such trouble before, but with his confidence shattered he finished with none for 113 in 12 overs, including 21 no-balls. If that was the fastest century of its kind for Durham there was a quicker one with the bat from Richard Johnson. Going in at 243 for eight in reply to 231 midway through the final day, he lashed nine fours and six sixes in his 63-ball hundred, the fastest scored against Durham.

With only one day off, largely taken up by travelling, Durham had little time to work with Tait but felt obliged to play him at Colchester. This time he took none for 63 in six overs, but there was only a day and half's play because of rain. The occasion was marked by Jon Lewis scoring a gritty century on the Castle Park ground where he had played some club cricket in his youth. He already knew that Durham had lined up an overseas player to take over as captain, but the innings proved his determination to fight to the end. He said: "I don't like giving up. It's tough and there have been an awful lot of disappointments this season. But I still enjoy it, even if I do have a few tantrums."

While not admitting that there was to be a change of captaincy, Martyn Moxon did admit at Colchester that negotiations were well underway with an overseas batsman for 2005. He was not prepared to drop further hints, other than that the man concerned had not played Test cricket. Being fairly certain that they would want him to be captain, and that he would be an Australian, I worked out on the long drive home that it had to be Mike Hussey. The only alternative seemed to be Michael Di Venuto, but he was said to be committed to Derbyshire after having to miss that season through injury when they had appointed him captain.

Hussey had made a triple century in each of his three seasons with Northants, captaining them in the last two, yet at 29 he didn't seem at the time to figure prominently in the Australian selectors' thinking.

With Hussey on the horizon, the skies suddenly cleared and for the festival lovers among us the cumulo nimbus had a spectacularly silver lining at Scarborough. In sublime first day weather the old stagers salivated at the return of the art of leg spin as Mark Lawson took five wickets, while Gordon Muchall batted beautifully for 142 not out. Lawson and Dawson featured prominently for Yorkshire, but by some strange quirk it was again the visiting off-spinner who belied previous form to win the match. It had been Richard Dawson when the counties met at Riverside, and here he was presented with his county cap but was upstaged by Gareth Breese.

The Jamaican went into the match averaging 65.6 with the ball, but against a depleted team who had Ismail Dawood top-scoring at No 6 he emerged with match figures of ten for 151. Breese was the first Durham bowler since Melvyn Betts four years earlier to take ten wickets in a match. He also scored 68 in Durham's second innings as they won by 210 runs, the only blot in the continuing sunshine being that it was all over in three days.

Liam Plunkett, named in the England Academy, finished the season strongly with career-best figures of six for 74 in another rain-ruined draw at home to Hampshire. Then he won a one-day match against Sussex with the bat. With five balls left to score 14 runs he drove Robin Martin-Jenkins for four, six, four.

Confirmation that Hussey would be captain in 2005 came on the first day of the final match at home to Leicestershire, which Durham lost by six wickets. How different things would be when they went to Grace Road for the opening match seven months later.

CHAPTER 15

LIFT-OFF

DURHAM had suffered enough at the hands of Husseys, so getting into bed with one was the ideal solution. As Mike Hussey was a month short of his 30th birthday when he took over the Durham captaincy it was a reasonable assumption that a Test career was going to pass him by. One former Australian star had labelled him "a good player on slow pitches," which was surprising as he had been good enough to captain Western Australia, playing on some of the fastest pitches in the world at Perth.

Hussey signed a two-year contract with Durham, but inbetween agreeing the deal and taking up the reins he made such a successful start to his one-day international career that he quickly propelled himself into the highest echelons of the world's batsmen. He was, therefore, available to Durham for only one season and had to miss six weeks of that through international duties. But what a season it was.

It helped enormously that Dale Benkenstein arrived at the same time. This was a further indication of the increasing ambition within the Durham hierarchy, acknowledging that local youngsters needed more experience around them for the club to achieve any success. It wasn't immediately apparent, but there can be little doubt that Benkenstein was the greatest signing they had made. There have been perhaps five better batsmen from Australia, Hussey among them, but in terms of overall input the title-winning captain edges ahead of David Boon.

Benkenstein was 30 when he arrived. He had captained Natal for eight years and given it up the previous winter, saying: "I decided it was time to help a younger man come through. Hashim Amla is the captain now and he's someone you're going to hear a lot about." He wasn't wrong there, and Durham fans were left hoping that his judgement would be proved right again in handing over the reins to Will Smith for the 2009 season.

Having to carry the label of "Kolpak signing" was a small price to pay for Benkenstein for the opportunity to live and play in Durham. A court ruling in favour of a Slovakian handball player named Kolpak had established that European sports clubs could sign anyone from a country with a trade agreement with the EU. Suffering at the hands of other counties who had exploited this encouraged Durham to follow suit and Benkenstein said: "I realised it could give me the chance to do something I'd always wanted to try. I got in touch with an agency who fixed me up with a second team game for Durham. I was fortunate enough to score a hundred, they were keen and so was I, so I'm here on a three-year contract."

The contract was subsequently extended twice and even after ending his three-year captaincy reign he was still committed for a further three years. He hoped to devote a little more time to his wife Jackie, a former South Africa hockey international, and their three children.

Benkenstein had played as a club professional in northern England at places like Pudsey St Lawrence, Kendal and Burnley, where he appeared alongside a young James Anderson. Dale's father, Martin, had played for Rhodesia, but they left when it became Zimbabwe, when Dale was six.

"Most of the top players in South Africa have come up through a very strong school system," he said. "I learnt the game at Michaelhouse School then played for Durban High School Old Boys and Natal, where we had Malcolm Marshall as the professional for two years when I first started. He was great for me at that stage. He had an incredible mind for the game."

He had played in 23 one-day internationals, but was no longer in the South Africa squad and, unlike Hussey, accepted that a Test career had passed him by. He was quite happy to play under Hussey, having enjoyed the break from captaincy back home. But as things turned out, he proved the perfect man to take over.

Another new signing with less obvious credentials was Callum Thorp, who had played with Hussey for the Wanneroo club and whose swing bowling was considered by the new captain to be well suited to English conditions. He was also 30 and qualified because he and his sister were the first members of their family to be born outside England. His father worked as a printer in London then ran a window cleaning business in Perth for 30 years, prompting some members of the English press to label Callum a window cleaner when he took four for 58 for Western Australia in a two-day game against England in October, 2002.

He remained something of a mystery in that he had been at the Australian Academy at the age of 27, when most of the others were in their late teens. If that meant he was a late developer, it had done nothing for his career in Perth. He had a history of back trouble and had played only six first-class matches for Western Australia, with whom he was no longer involved.

Given all the injury problems they had had with bowlers in the previous two years, Durham had decided they needed at least seven seamers. But Thorp started out at the bottom of that list and made no impression in his first season. At that time it would have required a huge leap of faith to imagine him taking the first seven wickets in Kent's second innings in the title-clinching victory at Canterbury.

In addition to Hussey, the second official overseas player was the Queensland seamer Ashley Noffke, who had impressed at Riverside when bowling for Middlesex. His two seasons there had been cut short by a back injury, and a different back problem had now surfaced, forcing him to miss the first six weeks of Durham's season.

It was not considered a matter of huge concern, however, as everyone was available for the first four championship games, including Steve Harmison, who had played no four-day cricket in 2004. Noffke's absence, in fact, gave Liam Plunkett the opportunity to start the season as he had finished the previous one, while Mark Davies was also fit again.

At the start of the Ashes summer Harmison had slipped down the world bowling rankings from top spot to ninth after the winter series in South Africa, but said: "I don't think I bowled as badly as the statistics suggested. Jacques Kallis was happy to spend 260 balls making a hundred and left anything he didn't have to play at. But there's no way the Aussies are going to leave me. They'll come at me like the West Indies did and I'm looking forward to the challenge.

"It will be good to start playing for Durham again. It's important to get enough bowling and have your rhythm, but I have no doubt the challenge of the Ashes series will lift me. With Durham the competition for places can only be good for us and I have no doubt we can win promotion. In the first four games I will be playing against teams who will be up there, so hopefully we can make a good start."

Durham won all four of those games, which included their first championship victories against the two remaining counties they hadn't beaten, Leicestershire and Lancashire. Debuts are rarely any more dream-like than the one made by Hussey at Grace Road. He won the toss, pulled the first ball – an Ottis Gibson long hop – for four and went on to make 253. He wanted Jon Lewis in the team, and with Phil Mustard starting behind the stumps, there was no room for either of the Pratt brothers. Lewis contributed 50 to an opening stand of 93, then Gordon Muchall made 82 and Hussey was on 165 out of 325 for three at the close of the first day.

With their overseas men, Dinesh Mongia and Charl Willoughby, not yet available, the cracks were really starting to show in the Leicestershire side and Gibson was required to bowl 44 overs in the innings, finishing with three for 121. It looked like a season too far for his new ball partner, Phil DeFreitas, who had none for 84 on a pitch offering the bowlers some help. That was the remarkable thing about Hussey's innings and he said: "I have made big scores before in good conditions, so it was nice to nick and nudge and graft to that total. I never really felt in, but we worked well in partnerships, rotating the strike well. I don't have any particular technique for maintaining my concentration. I just love batting and want to stay out there as long as I can."

He batted for ten minutes short of ten hours before driving a catch to long-off shortly before declaring on 523 for eight. A week after his 20th birthday, Plunkett then capitalised on the fact that Hussey had ground Leicestershire down by destroying their top order. He took the first four wickets, plus the last, as they were dismissed for 123. Plunkett again removed both openers in the follow-on, then Harmison took over, finishing with four for 30 as victory was achieved by an innings 216 runs. It was all very different from the occasion of Harmison's debut nine years earlier, when Leicestershire won by an innings and 251 runs at Riverside.

Speaking of his captain, Martyn Moxon said: "For a coach an innings like Mike's is worth a million words. It makes such a difference when players can see someone of his quality showing them how it's done. Liam Plunkett was excellent. He has worked hard on remodelling his action to prevent a recurrence of his back trouble. He has fine-tuned it and he bowled beautifully."

In little more than the twinkling of Hussey's blade, Durham had suddenly left Leicestershire behind after years of subservience. While never a great fan of Grace Road, I had come to enjoy visits to a surprisingly pleasant county, usually staying somewhere off the A6 heading south-east towards Market Harborough.

Unfortunately, in my experience the pubs come second to neighbouring Northamptonshire's for serving bad beer. On tasting one rancid pint I returned it to the landlord, who took a sip and said: "Ah yes, you've obviously got a good palate." Another example was at the Bell in Gumley, where the friendly landlord was most embarrassed about one of his barmaids serving me something from the bottom of a barrel. This was just after I told him I'd been partly responsible for getting the pub elevated to a main entry from the also-rans in the Good Pub Guide. It's not often I write to the GPG, but I felt moved to do so having been so impressed on my first visit to the Bell.

It had been recommended by the hostess at my B and B down the road in Foxton, famous for its canal locks, and she said I should tell the landlord I was there for the cricket as he was a big fan. On enquiring after him at the bar I was told he'd been in a hospitality box at Grace Road all day and had taken himself off to bed. Even without him on that occasion the beer, food and general ambience appeared spot on. Other than that first pint, willingly replaced, it was still as good on my return.

The Nevill Ams at Medbourne, reached via a footbridge over a duck-filled stream is a lovely pub, as is the Griffin at Swithland. This is not quite so rural, but gives the impression of being an excellent all-rounder and evokes an air of prosperity. It is north of Leicester in some surprisingly up-market country west of the main road to Loughborough, where I once stayed at the Swan in the Rushes. That was in the days before I realised that, no matter how good the beer or how enormous the breakfasts, down-to-earth boozers were not necessarily the most comfortable places in which to rest one's head.

In Noffke's absence Durham had signed Victoria bowler Mick Lewis, who was playing club cricket on Merseyside, as a temporary replacement. He made his debut in the Sunday match at Grace Road. Ottis Gibson had Hussey lbw for one, but Durham won by nine runs.

There was no place for Lewis, however, at home to Worcestershire and the decision was vindicated by Mark Davies taking six for 32. Wicketless in his first six overs after coming on first change, he suddenly took six for nine in 41 balls as the visitors declined from 75 without loss to 171 all out. On a pitch offering a good deal of seam movement, Paul Collingwood then scored 129 in taking Durham to 271 for four before the last six wickets went down for 15 runs.

The procession continued as Worcestershire slipped to 78 for six before Chaminda Vaas began to strike boundaries. He had put on 54 with Jamie Pipe when Harmison claimed the first hat-trick in first-class cricket for Durham. He bowled Pipe then spreadeagled Matt Mason's stumps with the perfect yorker and hit David Wigley's leg stump via an inside edge. Alamgir Sheriyar, who had taken a hat-trick against Durham 12 years earlier, lasted five balls before Harmison bowled him. He finished with five for 61 and said: "I didn't get to bowl here last season in a championship match, so I wanted to put on a bit of a show for the fans. This place is close to my heart and put me on the world stage, so every time I come back here I want to do well."

There was no doubt that Collingwood's superb century had set up the seven-wicket win as no other batsman in the match reached 50. He had scored only five championship centuries at that stage of his career, but this was the first of six in one season and underlined how far he had progressed.

Durham had never won their first two championship games before and the sensational start continued with a 138-run home win against Surrey in the one-day league. Benkenstein scored 63 and took four for 16 with his dibbly-dobblers. With Plunkett also taking four wickets, Surrey were all out for 86. Graham Thorpe made 33 of those and there was a reminder of his 200 not out against New Zealand at Christchurch three years earlier as Durham announced they had signed Nathan Astle to cover for Hussey during the one-day internationals. Astle had hit a double century off 153 balls in that Christchurch Test, beating Adam Gilchrist's record by 59 balls. Astle had hit 11 sixes when he was out for 222. It was an innings he had never threatened to repeat, but Durham were hoping he would prove a useful Twenty20 acquisition.

The other stand-in, Mick Lewis, took five for 48 in the next one-day match at home to Sussex, but it was washed out with Durham in a precarious position on nine for two in reply to 182. Had a further 2.3 overs been bowled, they would have lost under the D/L calculations. This might have been seen as a sign that things were going Durham's way, but the bubble did burst in very disappointing fashion in the C & G Trophy tie at home to Derbyshire.

After a delayed start Durham made 234 and Derbyshire were 132 for five overnight with 13 overs left. The following day Graeme Welch took his score from 15 to 50 before being bowled by Harmison with 44 needed off five overs. But Ant Botha, who had played under Benkenstein for Natal, took 17 off an over from Neil Killeen, who then tipped the balance back in Durham's favour by taking two wickets and conceding only three runs in the 49th over. That left 14 needed off the last over and Botha collected seven off Harmison's first three balls. Last man Kevin Dean, another left-hander, was then on strike and when Harmison went round the wicket and tried a yorker he got his line slightly wrong and Dean helped it to fine leg for four. He scrambled a single off the next ball and with one needed off the last ball to tie Harmison again went for the yorker and Botha calmly paddled it just behind square for his fourth four to finish on 34 off 26 balls.

With Bangladesh due to visit Riverside for a Test match which would barely scrape into the third day, Durham went to Stockton to play Somerset, for whom Andrew Caddick's heroic deeds were not enough. Perhaps still trying to prove he was better than Harmison, he took six wickets in both innings to take his tally against Durham in the championship to 71. And they hadn't had to face him from 2000–2003.

While Caddick registered his seventh and eighth five-wicket hauls against Durham, Collingwood claimed the first of his career as Somerset made 252. Things were looking bleak for Durham on 160 for eight, but they were rescued by the Teesside twosome rising to the occasion in their own backyard. Plunkett made 74 not out and Davies 62, sharing a stand of 124, only three short of Durham's ninth-wicket record. Somerset's lack of support bowling was again exposed as they scored most of their early runs off Simon Francis and Aaron Laraman. Supposedly an all-rounder, Laraman took one wicket in the match with his gentle medium pace, scored eight runs and invited ridicule in the field by wearing a woolly hat.

England coaches Duncan Fletcher and Troy Cooley were present on the third day, when rain restricted play to 30 overs. They were checking on Harmison and Marcus Trescothick, and the former removed the latter in both innings, for 21 and 20. Although Ian Blackwell played very impressively for 87, it was otherwise a one-man show for Somerset from Caddick, who scored 54 in the second innings to set Durham a target of 244. He than took all six wickets to fall, but with Hussey and Benkenstein both making 51 the stage was set for Gareth Breese to finish the task, just as he had at Taunton a year earlier. He remained unbeaten on 79, so at the time his two highest scores were both against Somerset.

What a difference a year makes. At the same stage in 2004 Durham had drafted in Tahir Mughal, now they decided to rest Mark Davies, even though he was top of the national averages. Mick Lewis replaced him at Old Trafford and had a spell of three for nine in 14 balls on the first day, with Stuart Law and Andrew Flintoff among his victims. After pulverising Durham at Grace Road in the final match of the previous season, Brad Hodge had moved to Lancashire and had been preferred to Hussey in the Test squad for the Ashes series. Hussey caught him at second slip for eight to give Harmison the second of his three wickets, and with Plunkett also taking three Lancashire were dismissed for 199.

That included a ninth-wicket stand of 73 between James Anderson and Gary Keedy, and it had become a talking point at this early stage of the season how batting was becoming much easier down the order because balls were going soft around the 40-over mark. Hussey provided further confirmation, however, of his expertise against the new ball as he became the fourth batsman to carry his bat for Durham. He scored 144 out of 338, the key partnership being one of 139 for the seventh wicket with Phil Mustard.

Having got off the mark at Grace Road with a straight six off David Masters, Mustard opened his account here by hitting Keedy for six over long-off. He provided wonderful entertainment as he failed to connect with a few early lunges at Muttiah Muralitharan, but once he had reached 20 he seemed to sort out which balls he could hit. He took 14 off one over from the Sri Lankan wizard and went on to make 77.

The national press were there in droves to watch Flintoff, who was making his comeback after his first ankle operation. He cracked nine fours to reach 42 not out and Lancashire were 135 for five at the close of the second day, four runs behind. If the game were to turn Flintoff would have to win his battle with Harmison on the third morning, but he was controversially adjudged lbw for 55. "I think he would have been disappointed with the decision," admitted Harmison as Flintoff had been well forward when given out by Steve Garratt, who was on the umpires' reserve list at the time. A former Nottingham policeman standing in only his second championship match, he copped some flak from the Lancashire press and it was suggested he would be the most unpopular man in town but for Malcolm Glazer's recent acquisition of Manchester United.

In his last game before joining the England squad, Harmison took six for 52, his best figures for Durham, and his tally from four games was 27 wickets at an average of 14.52. "In my first four years with Durham we hardly won four games in two seasons, so to win four out of four is very special," he said. Durham had needed 35 to win and Hussey clinched the nine-wicket victory with 26 not out, taking his average to 107.6, despite his Riverside failings.

He began to put those behind him with an innings of 66 in a 51-run one-day win against Yorkshire, in which Mustard cracked a 25-ball half-century. The Tykes stayed on for the four-day game and again there were runs down the order with Richard Dawson making 86 and Mustard 78 off 70 balls. Chris Silverwood thrashed his career-best 80 off 66 balls in Yorkshire's second innings in a ninth wicket stand of 108 with Anthony McGrath, who remained unbeaten on 133. Mick Lewis took five for 80 and Durham needed 245 to win. With half of the last day lost to the weather, they finished on 226 for eight, Hussey top-scoring with 61.

That was his last game before flying back to Australia for a five-day training camp prior to coming straight back to England for the one-day internationals. He was rarely dismissed, although his 31 not out in the opening match against Bangladesh was not enough to prevent a shock defeat in Cardiff. England and Australia still contested the final, in which Hussey was unbeaten on 62 in a tied match at Lord's.

Astle and Noffke both made their debuts in a one-day match at Tunbridge Wells, where only Peng, with 50, and Mustard, 32, topped 20 in Durham's 189. Kent were coasting at 170 for three in the 38th of the 45 overs until Astle suddenly took two wickets. Noffke then came back for his final two overs and took two for three, enabling Durham to win by one run.

It is never a good idea to upset an umpire, but Durham must have managed it the next day in another one-day game at The Oval. Roy Palmer, his hair dyed blond at the age of 62, remained statuesque in response to all Durham's appeals then gave four of them out lbw and one stumped. Few were happy about the decisions as they lost by 43 runs.

As this was the last match at The Oval before the opening of the £22m stand at the Vauxhall End it was also the last to be covered from the old press box. We had an excellent view of the arch over the new stand, and the word at the time was that there were plans to grow vines along it. So the planners must have had grape expectations.

Arriving at Worcester on June 1 for a four-day match, Durham found that Shoaib Akhtar had just flown in, even though his stint at New Road wasn't due to start for a month. The home press had to go off and interview him during play, leaving me smirking in a corner. The following year's Wisden Almanack reported: "Shoaib often looked uninterested, and there were constant rumblings about dressing-room unhappiness at his lack of commitment. After the season John Elliott, Worcestershire's chairman, complained: "Players like that are no good to our club. In fact, Shoaib has been no good for any club he's been at."

Durham's visit was ruined by rain, although Paul Collingwood scored

103 not out in the second innings before heading off for the one-day internationals. It meant the last three of his seven championship centuries at the time had all been against Worcestershire. Noffke took four for 75 in the home innings.

Benkenstein's first taste of championship victory as captain came against Essex at Riverside, where he and Muchall scored centuries against an attack which included South African paceman Dale Steyn and New Zealander Andre Adams. They made a bigger impression with the bat after Noffke and Davies took four wickets each in dismissing Essex for 106. There was one wicket in the second innings for debut boy Mark Turner.

Going in at No 3 as a nightwatchman in the second innings, Steyn improved his career-best from 11 to 82. He played and missed at least twice an over and got away with some comical swipes, but managed some good leg-side shots until the frustrated Noffke unsettled him with short bowling from round the wicket. Adams then hit 11 fours and five sixes in a 76-ball century. He was finally bowled by Davies, who finished with five for 86 to stay top of the national averages with 31 wickets at 13.9. Having arrived in second place, Essex lost by an innings and 79 runs, and on previous evidence with five wins and two draws Durham were as good as promoted.

A fifth win in the one-day league followed, but this was when the decline of one-day pitches at Riverside accelerated as Derbyshire were dismissed for 82 with Benkenstein taking four for 17. Gary Pratt's unbeaten 23 on his first appearance of the season took Durham to a five-wicket victory, but Derbyshire's Director of Cricket, David Houghton, complained about the pitch. The visiting press also had a light-hearted grouse when I told them this was the last match to be covered from our old cabin and it would take the high road the following day to act as Scotland's press box. "Oh no," they said. "That means we'll be back in it soon."

The trip to play "Kolpakshire", as Northants had become known, was ruined by rain. If an innings of 80 by Mustard was the highlight, the lowlight was the left-arm dross bowled by one of the hosts' South Africans, Charl Pietersen. Amazingly, he was still keeping Monty Panesar out of the team when Northants visited Riverside for the last match.

Liam Plunkett had been out for three weeks with a heel injury and it provided an indication of how disruptive injuries would be to him. His excellent early season form had vanished as he bowled nine wides in three overs in a disappointing one-day match at Arundel, which Durham lost by seven wickets.

With a promotion double looking possible, Durham rested Noffke, Davies and Jon Lewis in the Twenty20 Cup. Gary Pratt and Gary Scott played throughout an event which had been expanded to eight games, but Durham won only twice. Despite Mark Ealham blasting 34 off one over from Neil Killeen at Riverside, they overhauled Nottinghamshire's 179 for nine with six wickets and three balls to spare. Astle had been a disappointment, but both he and Muchall scored 64 in this game, while Scott made a swift 31 in the win at Headingley. At Old Trafford a Mal Loye century sparked his golden run against Durham.

At the start of his captaincy run, Benkenstein had been able to do no wrong, but on the return to championship action his final game at the helm brought what he called "a wake-up call." In Hussey's absence, Peng had been promoted to the top of the order, without success. So for the visit of Lancashire Scott was given a chance to open and put on 72 with Jon Lewis, only for Durham to collapse to 167 all out. Loye then scored 200 and Dominic Cork 102 not out in a total of 530 before Durham succumbed for 135 to lose by an innings and 228 runs.

Jon Lewis didn't bat in the second innings, having broken his left collar bone when falling awkwardly in the field. His season was over, but it gave Scott a chance to continue opening, alongside Hussey, who marked his return by scoring 97 under the Derby floodlights as Durham won a one-day game by six wickets.

Collingwood was also back and made his best championship score of 190 at Derby on the day when England began the Ashes series by slumping to 21 for five. He shared Durham's record fourth wicket stand of 240 with Benkenstein, who made 98. No-one else passed 18 in a total of 371. Collingwood, who sped from 48 to 153 in the afternoon session, had once said that Kevin Dean was the bowler he least liked to face in county cricket, but the left-armer was missing from this match after falling off a buggy at Derbyshire's golf day.

A Derbyshire reporter had told me the previous year that Dean was the only English bowler playing at the time who had taken more than 100 first-class wickets at an average of less than 24. A trawl of the records unearthed one other – Martin Saggers. As Dean never seemed to be quite the same after his buggy tumble, and Saggers' average declined with age, they were both overtaken, average-wise, by Mark Davies. At the end of the

2008 season he had 223 first-class wickets at 21.17. Melvyn Betts took exactly that number of wickets at 27.73, which is the next best average of anyone with more than 100 for Durham.

Derbyshire were dismissed for 161, but Noffke suffered a recurrence of his back trouble, ending his season, and Davies was also starting to suffer. He took three for four in the first innings and none for 64 in the second as Derbyshire, following on, reached 539 for seven declared. Michael Di Venuto made 203, creating a remarkable trilogy. There had been three instances of second innings double centuries against Durham, and all were by Derbyshire players. The first was Mohammad Azharrudin at Chesterfield in 1993 and the second by Dominic Cork at Derby in the 2000 game which ended Nick Speak's captaincy.

Paul Collingwood couldn't quite reach the landmark, although his purple patch continued when he reached 181 not out on the first day at Taunton. He looked displeased to be given out lbw by Roy Palmer without addition in the first over the following morning, but followed up with Durham's fastest first-class century in the second innings. He was on six overnight, scored off 16 balls, but needed only a further 57 balls to reach his hundred, beating Wayne Larkins' 88-ball effort against Sussex at Durham University in 1993.

Collingwood had become the first player to score two hundreds in one championship game for Durham, but at 29 he had still played in only two Tests, in Sri Lanka 19 months earlier. He had seen Andrew Strauss, Ian Bell and now Kevin Pietersen leapfrog him, and briefly Robert Key, but was clearly thumping loudly on the selectors' door after the defeat in the first Ashes Test. At the time he had scored 591 runs in his last five championship innings at an average of 197, but he said: "I don't see why they should change the Test team after one bad game when they have played well for two years. My turn will come.

"It's good to be part of such a good Durham team. We've always had good players but we haven't really been a good team. Everybody is sticking his hand up now and contributing. I'm learning my own game mentally. It comes down to yourself to sort it out if you know what standard you want to get to."

Gary Scott made 61 not out in the second innings before Durham declared on 208 for one, then Gareth Breese continued his love affair with Taunton by completing match figures of nine for 138 as victory was achieved by 207 runs. Breese had also made 51 in Durham's first innings total of 476 for nine. Scott wasn't called on to bowl his off-spin because he had strained a hamstring. Graeme Bridge was also injured at the time, continuing the litany of misfortunes which seemed to prevent any young Durham spinner from progressing.

Somerset's scorer, Gerry Stickley, was awaiting a hip replacement at the time and was relying heavily on a crutch. So resident reporter Richard Latham went to a joke shop and asked for a Long John Silver parrot. "There's one right behind you," was the reply and it spent the next two days perched on Gerry's shoulder. "I get the feeling it's watching everything I write down," he said.

The victory equalled Durham's record of six championship wins in a season and it was still only late July. The only slight cloud on the horizon at that point was that Andrew Pratt had grown disenchanted with his lack of first team opportunities and had been released at the age of 30. Two years earlier he had been the best gloveman in the country, but Phil Mustard was eight years younger and considered a better prospect with the bat.

With three teams to go up, Durham were 37 points ahead of fourth-placed Essex, their next opponents at the new venue of Garon Park, the home of Southend Leisure and Tennis Centre. It had never been used for a second X1 match, never mind a first-class game. This was the 100th Southend Festival and it had been switched from the usual venue of Southchurch Park because of vandalism.

"Festival cricket – what's it all about?" was the question posed on the front of the brochure, and the thought occurred that they ought to visit Scarborough to find out. Garon Park, named after a Lord Garon who set it up, turned out to be in a rather bleak landscape two miles inland on the edge of town. A couple of years later it was reported that the trees planted there had died, and while Durham's promotion prospects were not killed off they certainly withered.

Winning the toss on a ground which no longer even staged club games created a dilemma. When Essex's groundsman began his preparations three weeks earlier he had been able to put his hand down the cracks. He had repeatedly flooded the square, so it was damp, but Durham chose to bat thinking the pitch might not last. In fact, it got better and they got the worst of it as 15 wickets fell on a drab first day, when some of the 2,000 spectators would have been there just to tick off a new venue.

Durham had recalled Mick Lewis from his club duties with Huyton to replace Noffke and he took four of the wickets as Essex closed the first day on 102 for five in reply to 196. Alastair Cook, who was 20 at the time, moved on from his overnight 47 to become the first player to score a century at the ground in earning a 49-run lead.

Collingwood had been summoned to Edgbaston for the second Test, but was released from the squad and for the second innings at Southend he replaced Nicky Peng, the player nominated in advance to stand down. It could not have helped Peng's state of mind that, having been left out on the flat tracks at Derby and Taunton, where he had made runs in the past, he recorded a duck on the first day on a damp strip at Garon Park. His Durham career was nearing its end.

Durham were 13 for two shortly after lunch on the second day when Collingwood went in and immediately played like a man in prime form. He cruised to 46, but sport often finds an extraordinary way to bring participants back to earth just when they feel they can do no wrong. In advancing to hit James Middlebrook for what he thought would be the boundary to bring up his 50, Collingwood could scarcely believe the salmon-like leap with which Andre Adams plucked the ball out of the air high to his right at mid-wicket.

The recovery was underway, however, and Benkenstein continued it with a masterful innings of 124 as Durham's total of 347 left Essex needing 299 to win. Cook fell for 44, becoming Mark Davies' 47th victim of the season. But attempts to manage Davies' back problem ended when he had to retire after bowling five overs, and confirmation of the feared stress fracture meant he missed virtually a season and a half of cricket. Scott's hamstring had gone again, and with Graham Onions bowling poorly Durham's limited resources were insufficient to cope with the technical excellence of Andy Flower. A video recording suggested he was lucky to survive a very tight run-out call when nine were needed for victory, but he remained unbeaten on 132 as Essex got home by two wickets.

What had threatened to be a shambles had, in fact, turned into a very good game and had opened up the promotion race with Essex threatening the northern stranglehold imposed by Durham, Lancashire and Yorkshire. While defeat was a disappointment, the quality of the contest at least raised the profile of an uninspiring venue. Other than an excellent fish restaurant tucked under the cliff at the southern end, I saw little to entice me back to Southend. There are some lovely inland villages such as Rickling Green, with its Cricketers Arms, but I tend to think of Essex as an estuary county. I first sniffed the salt air and mingled with an unpretentious breed of yachting folk at Burnham on Crouch, where the lovely old White Harte provided waterside accommodation within a reasonable distance of Chelmsford. The Crouch Vale beers were also very quaffable.

After the mid-1990s Essex always used to send Durham to Colchester, and while it was difficult to detach myself from the delights of Dedham, it was always worth a short trip down to Wivenhoe on the estuary of the River Colne. There stands the Rose and Crown, another old pub with nautical décor and good real ale. And finally to Southend, where the kiss-me-quick promenade overlooks the open sea. But by heading south you soon turn the corner into the Thames estuary, where the Crooked Billet awaits on the water's edge at Leigh-on-Sea.

This is in danger of turning into a lament for venues left behind in the second division. When Durham first came into the first-class game they saw the Essex way as the blueprint to follow. Yet, despite the home win at Southend the counties went their separate ways at the end of the season and Essex continued to struggle to escape the second division.

Hussey, who had been summoned for an Australia A tour to Pakistan, bowed out much as he began, making 146 against Leicestershire at Riverside. Dinesh Mongia replied with 164 in a rain-ruined draw, while Durham won the one-day contest on another sub-standard pitch on which Mick Lewis took four for 13 as Leicestershire were dismissed for 113.

Lewis also had to go home early, to give evidence in the David Hookes trial. The former Test batsman was in his second season as Victoria's coach when he lost his life, aged 49, in an incident outside a nightclub. Lewis was a witness, and having had 18 months to get over the shock he now struck me as the most laid-back character I had ever interviewed.

As he had done quite well, I chiefly wanted to ask if he would fancy coming back for a full season. Slumping in a chair with a bare foot on the table in one of the lavish hospitality boxes, he replied: "Yeah, that would be fun."

Had he enjoyed his two short stints with Durham? "Yeah, we all enjoyed each other's company and made each other laugh."

Why was he a late developer in the game? "I enjoyed my Friday and Saturday nights too much."

There were a few warning bells here. As we had seen with Shoaib Akhtar, performing well during a short stay is no guarantee of a full season's effort from someone of questionable dedication. Lewis did return, but with only partial success.

Much the same could be said of the two other Australians Durham brought in to replace Hussey and Lewis, Jimmy Maher and Brad Williams. Although it was Collingwood, the official vice-captain, who took over the reins, it was Benkenstein who played the biggest part in ensuring promotion was secured. He scored 126 at Scarborough, where rain allowed only one innings each, and 162 not out in another draw at home to Derbyshire.

Collingwood also scored 112 in the second innings in that match and took the admirable step of coming up to the media centre for a better view before deciding when to declare. It was a ticklish problem as the pitch had got flatter throughout the match after Ian Hunter returned to haunt Durham with five for 63 in the first innings. They remained his best first-class figures.

Offered a target of 280 in two sessions, which gave them 66 overs, Derbyshire threatened to pull off their first win of the season. With Steve Stubbings making 101, they needed 11 off the final over, bowled by Williams, but managed only eight and finished on 277 for six.

Meanwhile, Ronnie Irani had also made a generous declaration at Colchester, but for him it backfired as Somerset knocked off the runs, virtually ending Essex's promotion challenge. Durham needed only a draw in the final game at home to Northants, and they secured that with the help of more rain. Maher totalled only 18 runs in four championship innings, but did his bit in clinching second place in the one-day league. He scored 70 in an eight-wicket home win against Kent and 48 in a seven-wicket triumph at Headingley, where Gordon Muchall made his maiden one-day century.

That was the last opportunity for Gavin Hamilton, who had been given the chance to prolong his career by opening the batting in the last few one-day games. He had abandoned his efforts to rediscover his bowling accuracy, and as Martyn Moxon always insisted he signed him as an all-rounder, it looked like a very generous gesture to allow him this final chance to prove his worth with the bat.

His lack of success prompted Hamilton to retire, while Nicky Peng turned down the offer of a one-year contract and opted to join Glamorgan. Gary Pratt accepted his offer of a one-year deal, but there was to be no resurrection of a career which had promised so much yet reached a strange peak with his running out of Ricky Ponting in the fourth Test at Trent Bridge. Pratt was available only because he couldn't get into the Durham team and there was a perception that England were finding any excuse to send on their specialist fielder.

He was also required for the final, decisive Test at The Oval, when Collingwood was called up as a replacement for the injured Simon Jones. Both Durham players, along with Harmison, played a full part in the triumphal celebrations and after the visit to 10 Downing Street Collingwood said: "We gave Mr Blair some stick about his fridge." "Why was that, Paul?" I asked. "Because he had no beers in it."

Pratt was asked by Steve James, writing a piece for the Sunday Telegraph, whether he had felt embarrassed about being so prominent at the front of the open-top bus then going to Downing Street. Pratt was quoted as saying: "No, I was pissed."

He said all the right things about his involvement with England whetting his appetite to become a Test batsman. But it was Liam Plunkett who really caught the selectors' eye, finishing with 51 championship wickets and earning a place in the England one-day squad to tour Pakistan. Harmison's 27 wickets at 14.51 in those first four games saw him top the county's bowling averages, while for the first time Durham had three men with more than 1,000 runs. Hussey averaged 76.71, Benkenstein 62.26 and Collingwood 55.15. There had never been such days.

CHAPTER 16

SKIN OF THEIR TEETH

THE 2006 season suffered disruptions before it had even begun for Durham and in the end they needed Nottinghamshire's implosion in their final match to survive in division one of the championship by half a point. Such are the margins between success and failure. Had they been relegated then, it's hard to imagine Durham would have been champions two years later.

They learnt in March that Mike Hussey would not be returning for his second season of captaincy. He was now firmly established in Australia's Test and one-day teams and the board wouldn't let him come. He said he had unfinished business at Riverside, but the reality was that a glittering international career lay ahead.

Liam Plunkett had also embarked on an international career over the winter, making both his Test and one-day debuts at Lahore. It was the Test in which Paul Collingwood established himself with innings of 96 and 80, and as Steve Harmison brought the Durham contingent up to three, Collingwood observed: "Perhaps we're the new Surrey." Sadly for England, it was also the series in which a rejuvenated Shoaib Akhtar briefly returned to his best and proved the difference between the teams in Pakistan's 2-0 win.

The Lahore Test set an unfortunate trend for Collingwood in that he scored his runs in a losing cause. Plunkett did as well as any of the four seamers, taking two for 125 as Pakistan piled up 636 for eight declared.

Durham wanted somebody for the full season to replace Hussey, and with so many demands on international players they opted to bring back the jovial Jimmy Maher. The Queensland captain arrived shortly after scoring his career-best 223 in the Pura Cup final in Brisbane, where he eventually fell to his new Durham team-mate, Mick Lewis. It could have done little for Lewis's confidence, however, that Queensland had scored 900 for six shortly after he took none for 113, the worst analysis in one-day international history, as South Africa knocked off 438 to beat Australia at

232

Johannesburg. It ended his brief international career, which might at least have been good news for Durham.

Durham had promoted Gary Scott, James Lowe, Ben Harmison and Kyle Coetzer to the full-time staff and brought in South Africa-born Garry Park as the reserve wicketkeeper. He had been in England for six years and had studied at Cambridge's Anglia Ruskin University, where he was coached by the former Durham wicketkeeper, Chris Scott, who recommended him. Perhaps the biggest surprise, however, was that Durham had signed 37-year-old Ottis Gibson.

He was well known to Martyn Moxon as they had done their level four coaching together. But ahead of what was to be his final season as Durham coach even Moxon could not have anticipated the extraordinary impact Gibson would have. Apart from his deeds on the field, he was always an absolute pleasure to deal with and is supremely worthy of a potted biography here.

Born in Barbados, he was one of five children and recalls his mum being his biggest fan. "From Barbados Under 19s to the senior team she never missed a ball I bowled," he said. "From as early as I can remember we would be out with the other kids, all trying to be the next Malcolm Marshall or Joel Garner. We had no running water or electricity and we had to do our playing before 6pm because after that we would be inside trying to read our schoolbooks round a kerosene lamp. Mum allowed us to have fun, but she insisted we did our schoolwork.

"When I was growing up in Sion Hill we would organise matches against lads in the next village. Now it's all organised for them. There's the same amount of cricket going on in the schools, but you don't see boys meeting up and doing it themselves. They need to do it off the cuff, playing in the streets and developing shots like you see in India. All my flair came from that. Too many coaches try to curb natural instincts."

Gibson played for Glamorgan in 1994 and was selected for the West Indies' tour of England the following summer. He made the first of his two Test appearances at Lord's, which was also the scene of the first of his 15 one-day internationals. "It's very easy to get bracketed as a one-day player and perhaps that's what happened to me," he said. "It's frustrating, but it's gone."

Gibson also played for three South African provinces, where he came up against Dale Benkenstein. Durham's new captain was very happy to have him on board, especially when they combined heroically to stave off relegation in a stand of 315 in the last match at Headingley.

Gibson gave up playing for Barbados because he felt if he wasn't going to play Test cricket he should give younger players a chance. He moved to England in 2001, did his level three coaching certificate and became an ECB national coach for the North-West of England. But after taking his level four he was told there had to be cutbacks for financial reasons and he went to play for Leicestershire for two years. Now he had signed for Durham, but they almost lost him before he arrived as he had been interviewed for the England bowling coach's job following the departure of Troy Cooley to Australia. The job went instead to Kevin Shine.

Durham's season began at Canterbury, where they surpassed the previous year's start by reaching 401 for five on the first day. With none of the England men available, Gordon Muchall rose to the challenge of extra responsibility by becoming the first Durham-born batsman to score a double century. His 219 equalled Marcus North's score at Cardiff two years earlier and the only higher scores for Durham were by Hussey and Martin Love.

Phil Mustard kept control of his swashbuckling strokes long enough to make 130 in a total of 575. Kent were still awaiting the arrival of their South African all-rounders, Andrew Hall and Justin Kemp, while Durham didn't risk Mick Lewis because of a hamstring strain. With Mark Davies still recovering from his back trouble, it opened the door for Graham Onions and Callum Thorp. After his disappointing first season, the Australian was said to have looked a different bowler when he joined Durham for some pre-season work in Sharjah.

After Kent reached 230 for two on the placid pitch, Onions came good on the third day. He took three middle order wickets as the hosts folded for 340 and when they followed on he knocked back Rob Key's off stump in the first over. Onions also swiftly removed David Fulton and Kent were all out for 179, giving Durham victory by an innings and 56 runs.

In his last three appearances in 2005, Onions' figures were one for 198 in 39 overs, but Durham had worked on making his action stronger and more consistent, while he had also benefited from a spell at Dennis Lillee's academy in Chennai.

Muchall's three previous championship centuries had been spaced over four seasons, but he immediately followed his double ton by making 102 against Lancashire at Riverside. No-one else passed 40 until Benkenstein made 88 in the second innings. The lack of support meant it was in vain as Mal Loye and Stuart Law had indulged their liking for the Durham bowling, both scoring centuries in a 128-run victory. Durham had dropped five slip catches, with Maher the main culprit.

Mick Lewis came in for the start of the C & G Trophy, in which Durham began with home wins against Northants and Warwickshire on pitches showing a marked improvement from the one-day surfaces blighted by the root break problem. Collingwood also featured and Durham looked a well-balanced and skilful one-day side.

In a championship match in which both teams had the words Northern Rock on their shirts, Maher provided the rock around which Durham built a total of 348 against Middlesex. His 106 was well supported by 78 from Mustard. It was a day of hard labour, particularly for Hayley Harmison, who presented Steve with his third daughter, preventing the paceman from making his comeback after injury. His old sparring partner, Melvyn Betts, played in the match but bowled only nine overs because of back trouble and his career was as good as over. When he arrived at the crease in the first innings I observed to the other press men that he used to be able to bat a bit. No sooner had the words been uttered than Onions splattered his stumps, first ball.

Onions took four wickets and Thorp had three for 19 in 15 overs as Middlesex were all out for 242. Then Jon Lewis grafted for 346 minutes before falling for 99 for the second time at Riverside when he sliced a catch to gully. If Middlesex weren't already ground into submission, their task was monumental once Onions clean bowled both openers, Ed Smith and Ben Hutton, in the second over. Onions took two more wickets as Durham won by 135 runs and with two wins out of three they were looking a first division force.

Harmison returned for a C & G Trophy tie at Old Trafford, but was the only bowler to command respect as Loye made another ton, as did Brad Hodge in a total of 307 for five. Durham were all out for 182.

Ahead of the second Test against Sri Lanka, in which he was expected to replace Plunkett, Harmison also played in the championship match at Trent Bridge. But rain reduced it to one innings each, Muchall top scoring with 88 in Durham's 404. He was run out and it was as though someone had pulled the plug. At that stage he had 432 runs in six innings, but by the time he was dropped for the final two games he added only 323 runs in a further 20 knocks. As with Gary Pratt, the decline was swift, inexplicable and apparently irreversible.

Pratt had started the 2006 season in the team, but by the time he got to

Trent Bridge, the scene of his most famous moment when running out Ricky Ponting, it was obvious that ecstasy had turned to agony. He spent two hours trying to work out why he couldn't locate the middle of the bat. He made 26 off 95 balls, mostly off the edge, and there was to be no return to his impressive form of 2004.

Speaking of Pratt's struggles, Martyn Moxon said: "Sometimes it's like that for a batsman. We all have to endure it at some point, but at least he didn't give it away. There was a bit of reverse swing going on, which put a bit of doubt in his mind. He was trying not to plant his front foot in case the ball came into him and he was lbw, but it kept going the other way. We need to clear his head and we've been back in the nets trying to get his footwork back to what it needs to be."

An ignominious home defeat by Sussex followed, with Mushtaq Ahmed claiming match figures of ten for 37 as Durham capitulated for 110 and 80 to lose by an innings and 39 runs. The visitors' other Pakistani, Rana Naved-ul-Hasan, had match figures of nine for 70. The ground had been under water the day before the match, but that offered no excuse for Durham being mesmerised by the googlies which earned most of Mushtaq's wickets. They were 47 without loss when he came on in the second innings and took three wickets in four balls in his first over. The match was all over in 145.2 overs, and was the shortest completed match in Durham's first-class history, other than when Kent forfeited their second innings at Riverside in 1995. This was also the occasion when they lost half a point for bowling their overs at fewer than 16 an hour.

Harmison took four wickets before disappearing on international duty, but the family name was not lost to the Durham team as 20-year-old Ben became the first Durham player to make a century on his first-class debut since John Glendenen in 1992. It was at the same venue, The Parks, to which Durham had returned for the first time since 1997. It didn't earn Harmison junior a run in the side, but when he next appeared seven weeks later and scored 105 against West Indies A at Riverside he became only the second player to have hit centuries in his first two first-class matches in England. The other was Alan Fairbairn for Middlesex in 1947.

Also making his first-class debut against Oxford UCCE was the Scottish leg-spinner Moneeb Iqbal, who bowled poorly in the first innings but took four for 36 in the second. And it was in The Parks that wicketkeeper Garry Park became the 100th player to represent Durham in first-class cricket. He came behind Harmison and Iqbal in alphabetical order. Mark Davies made his first appearance of the season and bowled 12 overs in each innings without discomfort, while Gary Scott made his only first-class century.

It was a huge pleasure to re-visit Oxford, except that huge planes from RAF Brize Norton passed alarmingly close to my bedroom in the farmhouse I stayed in near Witney. On visiting the local pub, we were immediately asked if we were there for Aunt Sally, to which my colleague, Ray Parker, replied: "No, but we'll have her if she's available." It turned out to be a pub game, played out the back, in which batons are thrown at a wooden skittle, known as a doll. There's a thriving league in that area, but you won't find it anywhere else.

In Oxford itself I took the chance to nip into the Eagle and Child, where the Inklings used to bounce literary ideas off each other in the 1940s. They included J R R Tolkein and C S Lewis, and it was said that Colin Dexter, creator of Morse, also used to drop in. It wasn't difficult to imagine them, lubricating their creative minds in one of the dimly-lit nooks and crannies. There was usually an E Morse in the Oxford UCCE team in 2006, but he was doing exams during Durham's visit. His name was Ed, not Endeavour.

Steve Harmison was able to fit in the C & G match at home to Yorkshire and had to face the final ball with three runs needed. Facing his Ashes opponent, Jason Gillespie, he swished at an attempted leg stump yorker and an inside edge sent the ball to the boundary. Craig White and Jimmy Maher both scored unbeaten centuries.

The Benkenstein-Gibson double act first came into its own at Edgbaston, where on the first day the pitch appeared to be far from a Birmingham belter. In muggy conditions, which helped the ball to swing, Warwickshire collapsed from 103 for one to 208 all out, Gibson taking four wickets, and Durham were 73 for five at the close. They advanced to 359 the following day with Benkenstein unbeaten on 144, while Gibson contributed 81 to a seventh-wicket stand of 148.

Onions chipped in with a useful 40, and with a lead of 151 it looked all over when Warwickshire were 154 for seven in their second innings. But on a hot, sunny day it was Tony Frost who plunged Durham's victory hopes into a deep freeze. Dropped on five, the wicketkeeper went on to make 96 and with No 10 batsman Heath Streak scoring 37 Warwickshire reached 310.

Needing 160, Durham were 62 for two at the close of the third day. But at lunch on the final day they were 140 for eight. Benkenstein, on 22, took a single off the first ball after the break and three balls later it was all over. Onions edged Lee Daggett to Frost, then Mick Lewis recklessly completed a king pair by driving the next ball into the hands of cover. Durham had lost by 19 runs and Daggett, the ex-Durham student from Ramsbottom, had taken six for 30.

This was Daggett's first match at Edgbaston and he said he had no complaints about Durham showing no interest in him after he had taken eight for 94 against them for the university. "They had a crop of good young bowlers coming through at the time," he said. While that was true, it was notable that at Edgbaston they had two Australians in their attack, Lewis and Thorp, who between them took three wickets in the match and scored two runs. Thorp also dropped a catch, while Jimmy Maher put down two and failed twice with the bat.

So it wasn't a good game for the Aussies and perhaps they were reminded of their countrymen's steely reputation when Benkenstein said: "If it's going to be tough you have to get stuck in. We needed one solid stand up front, but batsmen kept getting in then getting out. We just needed two batsmen to knuckle down, even if it took three hours."

Thorp had been the one to make way for Steve Harmison and had come back in for this match when Harmison was withdrawn by the England hierarchy as he was about to board the Durham bus. His first England assignment of the summer was to be against Ireland in Belfast, a match for which some media men were advised their usual press card would not admit them. They were told they must contact a Mr C Lyon and were given a phone number which got them through to Dublin Zoo.

Maher continued to look better in the one-day arena and made another C & G century in a 28-run win against Nottinghamshire at Trent Bridge. Again there were fears of snatching defeat from the jaws of victory as Chris Read hit 135 to revive the hosts from 95 for eight in reply to 280 for six. He reached 50 off 62 balls then hit six sixes in blasting his remaining 85 runs off 49 deliveries.

Read, of course, had been able to cut loose in carefree fashion because this revamped competition had, as widely predicted, already rendered a lot of matches a waste of time. With nine group games to be played, only the winners of the two groups would go through to the final. Durham had won five out of seven at this stage, but trailed Lancashire by two points as well as on run-rate. The situation stayed the same after they beat Scotland at The Grange, where Thorp took six for 17, the best one-day figures for Durham since becoming a first-class county. So Durham went into the final game at Derby with very little chance of overhauling Lancashire and duly lost, despite another Maher century.

They still finished second in the group, and the fact that there were no semi-finals, producing so many dead matches, caused a big enough outcry for the situation to be rectified in 2007. Not that it mattered to Durham then, as they finished top of the group.

With an Elton John concert to be staged at Riverside, Durham debunked to Stockton, where the only Rocket Man they care about is George Stephenson, who brought the railway there. If first-class cricket had helped to put the town more firmly on the map it wasn't going to last as the lengthy deliberations of a pitch panel astonished the locals and seemed to draw a line under Durham's use of outgrounds.

Durham had found their own Rocket Man in Ottis Gibson and it wasn't so much the pitch as his devastating spell of swing bowling which sparked Kent's collapse from 82 for one to 179 all out. He took three for none in 14 balls, but Durham found themselves light in the seam department after deciding they needed a second spinner. They handed Moneeb Iqbal his championship debut at the expense of Thorp and this was to backfire when Mick Lewis suffered a groin injury and bowled only six overs in the match.

Durham replied with 221 and when Gibson quickly reduced Kent to 24 for three in their second innings, still 18 behind, the visitors took the view that the pitch was like the cobbled streets of Canterbury and they might as well slog. They sent in James Tredwell, whose 47 off 44 balls changed the game. Durham's gamble on Iqbal backfired as his first three overs cost 33. Darren Stevens hit 70 off 60 balls, but the real fireworks came from the South African, Justin Kemp. He thrashed the fastest first-class century against Durham off 56 balls, seven faster than Richard Johnson's effort at Riverside two years earlier.

He was finally caught at long-off for 118 to give Gibson his first five-wicket haul for Durham. Iqbal did at least have the consolation of picking up two late wickets, but Kent's total of 411 left Durham needing 364 to win.

Maher made 99 and the target looked reachable until Benkenstein was run out for 70. Gareth Breese made 31, but otherwise there was little resistance once the captain had gone and Durham were all out for 268. Mustard tried the Kent approach by going down the pitch and swinging wildly at Tredwell, only to be stumped by the width of Stockton High Street.

Although there had been some low bounce on the first two days, the Stockton volunteers who had worked so hard to put on a good show could scarcely believe that a pitch panel was convened in the first place. The club chairman, Ray Waite, was astonished that it took them three hours to reach a verdict, saying: "They're just trying to justify their existence. It's very disappointing after we have bent over backwards. It's hard work, but we do it for the club and because people enjoy it. The people who have come up from Kent seem to have been impressed."

It was suggested by a Durham member that if points were to be deducted for the standard of the pitch they should be added back on for the quality of the bacon butties. I can also vouch for the cakes being as good as those at Worcester, and they have since been sadly missed, as have the ladies who served them.

As the club's telephone was mysteriously incompatible with my laptop, I had to file my reports about the furore surrounding the pitch from the groundsman's house. I had the nerve to ask only because I'd known Colin Gray from his days as Darlington's groundsman. Despite the pitch being marked "below average" he told me had been complimented by the ECB's pitches consultant, Chris Wood, who had driven up from Hove. He might have been better advised to drop into Trent Bridge, where Middlesex were in the process of being bowled out for 49.

Wood could apparently see from the Stockton soil profile that damp conditions drying out too quickly in the recent heat had caused a slight problem an inch below the surface. In the circumstances, he felt Gray had done a good job. There was no points deduction, but the Kent captain, Robert Key, was adamant there should have been, just as he would be at Riverside two years later. Andrew Hall, who was once shot by a mugger in Johannesburg, apparently claimed he was too scared to leave his Stockton town centre hotel at night.

The pitch was no better at the Rose Bowl, Durham's next port-of-call, where an extraordinary all-round performance by Thorp won the game. First he almost trebled his previous best score in serious cricket after going in at 108 for seven. He hit Shane Warne for three sixes in making 75 to lift the final total to 234 and also scored a useful 28 in the second innings while collecting match figures of 11 for 97. It was the best all-round performance in Durham's first-class history, beating the one other instance of a player taking ten wickets and totalling more than 100 runs. That was Gareth Breese with ten for 151 and 103 runs at Scarborough in 2004.

With Mick Lewis ruled out, Durham brought in Mark Davies. He had been feeling his way gently back to fitness in the second team, as well as playing at Oxford, and had experienced no problems. But after taking one for nine in eight overs his back stiffened up and that was it for the season. The pitch suited the gentler seamers and Benkenstein bowled in his absence, taking three for 16 as Hampshire succumbed for 104 in their second innings to lose by 227 runs. They lost five wickets in 11 balls with their score on 83, then Warne blasted two fours before being bowled by Thorp when swinging across the line. Warne was about to return to Australia for a shoulder operation.

After Elton John at Riverside came Sri Lanka for a one-day international, which featured all three of Durham's England men. It also confirmed that groundsman Dave Measor had got Riverside's one-day pitches back on track as the tourists passed England's 261 for seven with eight wickets and 7.3 overs in hand. Mahela Jayawardene made 126 not out and Liam Plunkett had none for 46 in 5.2 overs. He was a fixture in the England team in the early part of the summer, but in his only appearance for Durham a side strain suffered against West Indies A ended his season in mid-July. England coach Duncan Fletcher had wanted him to play to get some batting practice and Durham agreed to restrict his bowling, but he broke down in his seventh over.

Collingwood, meanwhile, performed for England as though determined to justify the MBE he had been awarded after scoring seven and ten in the deciding Ashes Test. He made his maiden Test century at Nagpur, scored 186 against Pakistan at Lord's, and performed so consistently he was named one of Wisden's five Cricketers of the Year.

Durham again flopped in the Twenty20 Cup, their two wins out of eight both coming, surprisingly, against Lancashire. The player they desperately wanted to come good in this event, Phil Mustard, totalled 55 runs in six innings as a No 3 and was then sent in at No 7 in a desperate situation against Derbyshire and thrashed 67 not out. That was the best individual score Durham had managed in four years.

The midsummer madness had its usual disruptive effect as Durham lost the subsequent game at Riverside by 145 runs against Yorkshire, for whom it was the first championship win of the season. It also set in motion the train of results which would result in them meeting in the final match at Headingley with relegation apparently at stake.

On this occasion it was Anthony McGrath's liking for Riverside which proved decisive as he scored 140 and 61. Durham's top four batsmen totalled 107 runs in two innings and it proved to be the end for Jon Lewis, who had averaged 22.18 in nine games. He did, however, have the honour of being easily the county's leading run-scorer in first-class cricket with 7,854. Benkenstein fell in the 90s in both innings, while Jason Gillespie took six for 37 in Durham's second innings after coming into the match with 15 wickets at 41.47.

Durham brought in James Lowe to replace Jon Lewis at the top of the order for the next three games and also introduced Ben Harmison to championship cricket, starting at Lord's. Just as they had been on their last visit, four years earlier, they were thwarted after enforcing the follow-on. Nick Compton made 190 in Middlesex's second innings total of 503, but Durham still had a chance to win.

It looked as though they had fallen foul of the delicate balancing act between introducing new blood and pressing for victory. From a position where they needed 110 in 20 overs with six wickets left they sent in Harmison and he scored two off 33 balls. In a last throw of the dice, Phil Mustard then thrashed 16 off eight balls, but once he holed out at long leg Durham settled for a draw, finishing 53 short on 220 for seven.

Gareth Breese had scored his first century since his Taunton epic two years earlier in the first innings, while Benkenstein scored 125 and 47. It was at the fall of his wicket in the second innings that Harmison went in, and while the captain may not have been in a position to tinker with the batting order it was indicative of a cautious approach in such situations. He would generally put the avoidance of defeat before risk-taking in pursuit of victory, and in the end the lifting of the 2008 trophy meant no-one could argue with that.

The Mustard and Onions combo was full of relish in this match as the bowler took a career-best five for 45 in the first innings and the wicketkeeper, who had just become a father, held nine catches in total.

The match was played in stifling late July heat, and instead of my usual policy of staying outside London and travelling in by train, I stayed within walking distance of Lord's in a B and B which was very handy for Ye Olde Swiss Cottage. I'd just been served my first pint of excellent hand-pulled Sam Smith's at the extraordinary price for the capital of £1.72 one evening when they announced they were closing. Other parts of London had been crippled because of power cuts caused by excessive use of air conditioning, but this was because of a problem with the water supply. The local gardens did look very parched, but Lord's was as lush as ever with its unrestricted water supply.

A century of the highest class by Owais Shah gave Middlesex victory in the opening Pro40 League match, and after five energy-sapping days at Lord's Durham had one day off before resuming, still in muggy conditions, back at Riverside. Nottinghamshire swinger Charlie Shreck reduced them to 37 for six before Mustard and Thorp put on 125. They were the only batsmen in double figures, but the total of 195 earned a first innings lead of 56. Unfortunately only half a day's play was possible out of the first two and it was one of those occasions when Durham bowled out the opposition almost too quickly. It meant they had to go back in when batting was still difficult and they were all out for 157. Conditions had eased on the final day and, needing 214, Nottinghamshire were guided to a six-wicket win by Stephen Fleming's unbeaten 89.

Durham were then thrashed by an innings and 133 runs at Hove, where it would have been no surprise to see a camel appear in the parched outfield. They had played in the desert on the pre-season trip to Sharjah, but such arid conditions were unheralded in their first-class existence. Chris Adams scored 155 and Moneeb Iqbal, in his last appearance, had figures of none for 132 in 21 overs. Durham wanted him to learn from Mushtaq Ahmed, who again tormented them with eight wickets in the match. Attempts to prevent him dominating resulted in Ben Harmison being stumped while almost shaking hands with the umpire and his first five championship innings had brought a total of 15 runs.

He shaped much better in making 29 in the second innings, and it proved a big turning point as he finished the season strongly, although he couldn't bowl his brisk medium pace because he was yet another to have succumbed to a stress fracture of the back.

Durham's second innings was in similar tatters to Brighton's west pier when Mustard went in at 79 for five in the second innings and hit a 95-ball century. He was last out for 103 and at least provided some entertainment for the coachload of Durham fans who had made the trip. Benkenstein said of Iqbal: "Mushy could see he has a bit of talent and had a chat with him. It takes time to learn the art of spin bowling. There's a big difference between bowling good balls and bowling people out. Winning is important, but we are also trying to bring through young players and Durham are a step ahead of a lot of counties in that respect."

The difficulty in developing spinners was underlined in the next match at home to Warwickshire. Five years after making his debut as an off-spinner, Gary Scott took his first two championship wickets bowling medium pace. He bowled both Alex Loudon and Dougie Brown, but his figures deteriorated from two for seven in 3.3 overs to two for 39 after seven. He bowled a few more spells before the end of the season, but took only one more wicket. He had also been promoted to open as Lowe had recorded two golden ducks in totalling 36 runs in six innings. Scott fared better, making 34, while Ben Harmison scored 65 to restrict the first innings deficit to 30.

Lovers of the Outer Hebrides will know that Harris has more to offer than Lewis. But after Warwickshire's South African spinner Paul Harris took six wickets, Durham's Mick Lewis took three quick wickets to reduce the visitors to 25 for four in their second innings. His prospects of returning for another season had begun to look as bleak as a Western Isles peat bog, but this burst turned the game. It opened the door for Neil Killeen to clean up after coming in for Ottis Gibson, who had had a groin operation. Killeen took five of the remaining wickets for 29 runs, and Durham were left with a target of 214. They got them for the loss of three wickets, with Jimmy Maher unbeaten on 101 and Ben Harmison on 61. Maher made only two championship hundreds, but both resulted in home wins, the other having come against Middlesex.

The victory appeared to have halted the slide towards relegation, but after a two-week break from championship action an innings of 150 by John Crawley put Durham on the back foot at home to Hampshire. Onions had been called into the England squad, so Gibson was rushed back and proved expensive. Shane Warne declined to enforce the follow-on and finally had so many runs to play with he could buy his own wickets at great expense. His Victoria team-mate Mick Lewis, in his final appearance for Durham, hit the leg-spinner for three fours and two sixes in an over.

Lewis signed off with 38 off 17 balls before Warne had him caught to finish with five for 135. Despite Ben Harmison's 75 in the second innings, Durham lost by 174 runs and were back in trouble with only visits to Old Trafford and Headingley to come.

The newly-signed former New Zealand off-spinner Paul Wiseman was brought in for his debut on another arid strip against Lancashire. These dustbowls seem all the more remarkable in the light of the two very wet summers which followed. At 37, Wiseman was resigned to his Test career being over and had just signed a two-year contract for

Durham after helping Walkden to the Bolton League title. He was a British passport holder by virtue of his father coming from Sheffield. "I have signed on the understanding that I will help to develop young spinners like Moneeb Iqbal, and there are one or two others coming through," he said. "I have done a bit of coaching and I want to pass on my experience and knowledge."

Garry Park made his championship debut as a No 3 batsman in place of Gordon Muchall. Amid rumours that Durham were to sign Michael Di Venuto for the following season, Maher dug in to score 95 off 288 balls as Durham laboured to 255 for four on the first day. Maher and Scott, who made 55, shared Durham's first century opening stand in the championship for three years, which was Sod's Law for Muchall, who had suffered from regularly being exposed to the new ball too soon. Park got over an uncertain start to make 45, but then global warming's impact on the eccentricities of the English weather were highlighted by the second day's washout being followed by sun stopping play.

It happened at 5.43pm on the third day, with the sun shining straight down the pitch. Being from Durham, umpire Peter Willey might have said it was glishy. He and Nigel Llong returned at 6pm and decided, to the disgust of the Lancashire members, that there would be no significant change in time for play to resume. Only the previous day the Lancashire press were bemoaning the fact that yet again wet weather could deprive them of the title.

Mal Loye, having grown accustomed to making centuries against Durham, stood paralysed at the crease for several seconds after holing out for 78, but another thorn in their flesh, Dominic Cork, made 154. He had made seven first-class centuries and three were against Durham. He denied them what might have been a crucial bowling point as Lancashire declared on 482 for eight. Durham closed on 69 for one in their second innings, with Park unbeaten on 34.

Durham were relegated in the Pro40 League, despite winning their final game by six wickets at home to Essex, who won the title because their only challengers, Sussex, lost at Trent Bridge. Mustard was promoted to open for the first time in the one-day league and booked the slot for the following season by scoring 84 off 86 balls.

For the final championship match Durham went to Headingley half a point ahead of their hosts, having led them by 37.5 at the halfway stage. They were 8.5 behind Nottinghamshire and one of the three would join Middlesex in going down. It was the first season in which only two were relegated.

Durham gained only one bowling point on the first day, while Yorkshire picked up their full hand of five for batting by reaching 473 for three. Darren Lehmann, the man Durham had first encountered during Victoria's tour in 1991, came into his final match for Yorkshire averaging 66.66 over his seven seasons, nine better than anyone else had achieved for the county.

With Graham Onions, back from bowling in the England nets, posing the only threat, Lehmann converted his 26th first-class century for Yorkshire into a triple. In an innings of supreme power and placement he went on to make 339, falling two short of the Yorkshire record set by George Hirst at Leicester in 1905. Lehmann was bowled aiming to hit Wiseman to long-on. It was an anti-climactic end to a stupendous innings, the second highest against Durham after Brian Lara's 501 and the total of 677 for seven declared was also the second highest against Durham behind the 801 for four Warwickshire made in that match. The wicket meant Wiseman emerged from his two introductory games with figures of one for 230.

Michael Lumb, also playing his last innings for Yorkshire prior to his move to Hampshire, contributed 98 to a stand of 358, one short of the record stand for any wicket against Durham, set by Mark Butcher and Ian Ward at the Oval in 2000.

Durham looked doomed, but were handed a lifeline by the news that Nottinghamshire had been dismissed for 165 in reply to Sussex's 560 for five declared at Trent Bridge. Durham's nemesis, Mushtaq Ahmed, was now doing them a huge favour and after claiming four wickets in the first innings he took nine for 48 in the second as Sussex clinched the title in an innings win which left Nottinghamshire with one point.

No sooner had it become clear on the second day that an opportunity had presented itself for Durham than they lost three wickets in four balls half an hour from the close. They needed maximum batting points and a draw to edge half a point in front for Nottinghamshire, but from 175 for two they slipped to 203 for six at the close. Scott and Park both made 77, but after being promoted to No 5 Mustard fell lbw second ball to Deon Kruis and Ben Harmison edged the next one to wicketkeeper Simon Guy. Finally Gareth Breese was bowled by Adil Rashid for six.

Dale Benkenstein was on 24 and Ottis Gibson seven overnight. By the time rain arrived in mid-afternoon on the third day both had completed centuries. It was only the second of Gibson's career, the first being 101 not out for the West Indies against Somerset at Taunton in 1995. This one was rapturously received by his team-mates, shortly after they cheered with relief when he hit the six which took the total to 400, clinching the fifth batting point.

Nottinghamshire might have suspected collusion, but Yorkshire could not afford to show obvious signs of complacency as the pitch liaison officer, David Hughes, had stayed on to act as a match referee and ensure everything was above board.

Gibson revealed that he had coached Adil Rashid when the leg-spinner was in the England Under 15 team and said: "Facing him in this situation was a bit spooky. He bowled quite well, but I didn't want him to get me out. There's a very good atmosphere in this Durham team. Benks is an awesome batsman and a very good leader, and we just need a bit more from everyone else. I have always been capable of scoring runs, but it only takes one rush of blood to get you out and that's what I've been guilty of."

On the final day Gibson joined the exclusive club of those who have achieved the first-class double of 5,000 runs and 500 wickets, but both batsmen were out shortly after reaching 150. They had put on 315, easily beating the championship record for any wicket for Durham, the 258 put on by Martin Love and Jon Lewis against Nottinghamshire at Riverside in 2001. But the drama wasn't over because with only 22 needed to avoid the follow-on Benkenstein fell for 151, top-edging a sweep at Mark Lawson to be caught behind. In the next over Gibson offered no stroke to a googly from Rashid, which bowled him for 155.

Only eight more runs were added as Rashid also took the last two wickets and Durham were obliged to go in again, 159 behind with 48 overs to survive. Kruis quickly removed Maher and Scott, and an hour after his dismissal Benkenstein was back at the crease. In an alliance of South African steel, he put on 67 with Park, who then showed amazing confidence as he repeatedly swept the spinners and finished unbeaten on 100 out of 181 for three.

In four innings Park had scored 256 runs and been dismissed only twice, so his lack of opportunities over the next two seasons was a big disappointment to him, prompting his move to Derbyshire. But there were no negative thoughts at the end of the 2006 season as seventh place meant Durham had achieved their highest finish. They had also given a strong hint of what was to follow in the 50-over competition, even though they were still not very good at the shorter forms of the game.

Graham Onions finished the season with 50 championship wickets, while Gibson had 49 and Phil Mustard and Ben Harmison had made encouraging strides. But Gary Pratt, James Lowe and Graeme Bridge were released, while seamer Mark Turner opted to join Somerset, and after nine years' service Jon Lewis was handed a coaching role. Among his new charges was to be Will Smith, the Luton-born former Bedford School and Durham University captain, who had featured in the relegated Nottinghamshire team and had declined the offer of a new contract at Trent Bridge.

The members voted Benkenstein Player of the Year for the second successive season after he scored 1,427 championship runs at 52.85. Next came Maher with 948 at 34.92.

CHAPTER 17

COOK DISHES UP
SUCCESS

AFTER six years with Durham, Martyn Moxon was lured back to Yorkshire just before the daffodils started to bloom. As he had continued to live in Wetherby, 15 miles from Headingley and 70 from Chester-le-Street, it had always seemed likely that he would go back eventually. The timing had much to do with his daughters' schooling, but it came as something of a surprise as Yorkshire had been looking all winter for a replacement for David Byas as Director of Cricket. When asked about it a few months earlier, Moxon had laughed it off, but the chance to form a Barnsley brotherhood with new skipper Darren Gough proved irresistible.

The news came at roughly the same time of year as the announcement about Mike Hussey 12 months earlier, and again with the season only six weeks away Durham felt they had insufficient time to cast their net far and wide. Instead they simply reinstated Geoff Cook to first team duties after ten years of concentrating on youth development, although for most of that time he retained the title of Director of Cricket.

All those years earlier, when appointing David Graveney as Durham's first captain, Cook had observed that sometimes people relish the chance of a second crack at captaincy so they can apply what they learnt before and make a better job of it. Now the same applied to him as first team coach. After the struggles of the first few years some might have felt he was lucky to survive on the staff, and at almost any other county he probably would not have done. After all, only Hampshire, with Tim Tremlett, had kept one man in such a prominent managerial position since 1992, and some had four or five coaches in that time.

Cook had the advantage that, from the outset, he knew far more about the first-class game than those who were employing him. That may have helped to safeguard his position, but in the end the value of keeping faith with him was underlined in resounding fashion. There had been a time when he seemed to want to hide away, but now he was comfortable as an older and wiser figurehead. The timing was good because he was working alongside a captain he greatly admired with a squad in which he had achieved the perfect balance between youth and experience. It didn't quite fit with Cook's ideology of the early years, but still no-one could argue that Durham weren't doing their bit for English cricket.

Graham Onions had impressed with England A in Bangladesh over the winter, but Liam Plunkett endured a frustratingly inactive few months with England. He performed well in the one-day series win in Australia, but then had a minor role in the World Cup, culminating in figures of one for 71 in seven overs when recalled for the final game against the West Indies at Bridgetown. Kicking his heels in the Caribbean meant he missed the start of Durham's season and he was to spend the next two years blowing hot and cold. He played in the first three Tests of the 2007 summer against the West Indies, but a perception developed that there had been too much tinkering with his action, aimed at injury prevention rather than pace. It looked like yet another example of different coaches creating confusion where once a clear head had relied successfully on natural talent.

There were also signs of this with Onions, and for these bowlers the 2007 and 2008 seasons were remarkably similar. They played 11 championship matches each in 2007 with Plunkett taking 38 wickets and Onions 36, both at around the 30 mark. Then in 2008 Onions took 16 wickets in five matches and Plunkett 16 in seven. The only disappointing aspect of the final championship triumph was that neither was in the team, despite being fit.

The new arrivals for the 2007 season were Michael Di Venuto, Will Smith, Mitch Claydon and Will Gidman, the brother of Gloucestershire's Alex. The Yorkshire press joked that it was an unkind parting shot for Moxon to sign Claydon for Durham as he had not impressed in his one season with Yorkshire. A burly Australian seamer, he was already 24 and back trouble would disrupt his first season with Durham, as it had done with Yorkshire. As Callum Thorp had proved, however, it can be unwise to write off such people.

Two official overseas men were still allowed, but Durham began the season by insisting they would try to make do with one, Di Venuto, partly because of the disruptions caused by the comings and goings in the previous two years.

Di Venuto's arrival re-affirmed a sentimental link Durham had maintained with Tasmania since the days of David Boon's captaincy and the left-handed opener arrived on the back of Australian domestic cricket's newest participants winning the Pura Cup (formerly Sheffield Shield) for the first time. At 33, Di Venuto had played for Tasmania for 15 years. He had appeared in nine one-day internationals, but any chance of a Test career had gone and Durham had an eye on the future in signing him as he held an Italian passport. That meant he would not have to be considered an overseas player once he decided to retire from first-class cricket back home.

He had spent one season with Sussex before joining Derbyshire in 2000 and had rivalled the likes of Graeme Hick, Bill Athey and Mal Loye for regularly plundering runs off Durham. "I was at Sussex when David Boon was with Durham and I've been interested in them ever since," he said. "I know he really loved his time at Durham. I needed a fresh challenge and Derbyshire were looking to go down a different route, signing an all-rounder. As soon as Durham came into the picture, I knew that was where I wanted to play. As a club on the way up with big ambitions, they fitted the bill perfectly."

Durham began the season in lovely weather at Worcester, where the river had burst its banks four times over the winter, and would flood the ground twice during the summer, which was unprecedented. Despite his century in the final match at Headingley the previous September, Garry Park was left out of Durham's 12 and Gordon Muchall was reinstated at No 3. The World Cup was still underway, but Steve Harmison had opted out of one-day international cricket and was available for Durham. It was the first time he and his brother, Ben, had appeared in the side together and it helped to inspire Steve to two spells of sustained pace and accuracy.

For the third successive season, Durham got off to a cracking start on the back of someone making a big score. Mike Hussey and Muchall had scored double centuries at Grace Road and Canterbury, this time Di Venuto made an unbeaten 155 out of 313. He became the fifth batsman to carry his bat for Durham and three weeks later he did it again, making 204 out of 407 against Kent at Riverside. He also went close to following Paul Collingwood as the only Durham batsman to make centuries in both innings of a championship match, only to fall for 83 second time around at Worcester.

As he had spent the winter feeling like King Canute, the New Road groundsman thought 225 would be a good score. So, despite the failures of the other batsmen on a glorious opening day, Di Venuto had put Durham in pole position and Onions, Harmison and Ottis Gibson took three wickets each in dismissing Worcestershire for 191. Then an unbeaten century by Benkenstein put the game beyond Worcestershire and, even though the pitch had become very docile, Harmison took five for 63 to clinch victory by 241 runs.

Durham moved on to Grace Road for the opening match in the national cup, in which Friends Provident had taken over sponsorship from Cheltenham and Gloucester. That Leicestershire's decline was continuing was evident from their capitulation for 138, which included an unbeaten 72 from John Maunders. Phil Mustard was now established at the top of Durham's one-day order and he hit 66 as they knocked off the runs for the loss of two wickets in 28.1 overs.

Gareth Breese was under pressure to justify his place ahead of Paul Wiseman, but the Jamaican couldn't buy a wicket in the early games, while Adil Rashid enjoyed a five-wicket haul at Headingley. Durham were all out for 274 and Yorkshire replied with 414 on the back of opener Joe Sayers surviving for nine hours and 13 minutes to carry his bat for 149. Superb bowling by Matthew Hoggard then destroyed Durham's second innings and it needed Onions' career-best 41 to make Yorkshire bat again. They won by nine wickets.

Di Venuto and Benkenstein apart, the batting had yet to fire, so Kyle Coetzer was rewarded for good form in the second team with a place in the side to play Durham University at the Racecourse. In his determination to succeed with Durham, his relationship with Scotland had deteriorated and he had been overlooked for the World Cup. After beginning his first-class career with an innings of 67 at Cardiff in 2004, he had played in six more matches that season but hadn't featured in the two years since, so this was a make-or-break season. He unveiled his new-found attacking prowess against the students and scored 153 not out at a run-a-ball.

Durham also brought in Plunkett and Mark Davies for their first appearances of the season, but it was Neil Killeen who took the bowling honours with four for 22 in the students' second innings. In losing by 163 runs they seemed to confirm the fears of their coach, Graeme Fowler, that the number of Kolpak signings in county cricket had greatly undermined the purpose of university centres of cricketing excellence. The steady flow of Durham UCCE players into county sides had ceased.

Derbyshire's one-day domination over Durham continued in the Friends Provident Trophy with Simon Katich marking his return to Riverside by scoring 81 before fellow Australian Ian Harvey completed the four-wicket victory with an unbeaten 60. For the next FPT match, however, all the England men were available and Durham's trio upstaged Lancashire's in a 57-run home win. Paul Collingwood scored a high-class 74 and fielded superbly, Plunkett plundered 33 runs and removed Mal Loye and Brad Hodge, while Steve Harmison chipped in with 14 not out and two wickets. Plunkett drove both Andrew Flintoff and Sajid Mahmood over long-on for huge sixes, while Coetzer also surprised both bowlers with some audacious strokes in his swift 35.

For the next championship match, at home to Kent, Plunkett was included and Ottis Gibson was left out. Although Plunkett justified his selection by looking comfortably the best bowler in the match, this was to have a big bearing on the rest of the season. Gibson was unhappy about being dropped but adopted the mantra: "Don't get bitter, get better" with sensational results. Callum Thorp also stood down, to make way for Park as an extra batsman as Collingwood was available to bowl. But for Thorp there would be no way back, partly because of injury.

Collingwood was out third ball, bowled by Yasir Arafat, but it proved a minor irritation as Coetzer supported Di Venuto's double century with an innings of 74 after replacing Muchall. The pitch was so good Durham scored at five an over for much of their innings, then Rob Key followed up by making 169 as, for the first time at Riverside, both sides achieved maximum batting points. The first rain of the season arrived on May 10 after Di Venuto and Collingwood had both raced to half-centuries in the second innings. After the break four wickets went down for 29 runs before Benkenstein made 77 not out and Park 61 prior to a declaration on 319 for six.

The match was heading for a draw when Kent had only three wickets down with 21 overs left, but Plunkett suddenly took three wickets to take his haul to eight in the match. Harmison did the rest and after removing Joe Denly for an excellent 92 there were still 13 overs to go when last man Robbie Joseph went in. He had had a miserable time with the ball, with match figures of 14-0-113-0, and after a fearful blow on the helmet from Harmison it was decided Joseph needed stitches in a cut ear. He retired hurt and Durham had won by 157 runs.

The lovely early season weather had now vanished and there was no play until 1.45 on the second day at Edgbaston. As Breese hadn't taken a wicket in three games he was left out and made only one more championship appearance, in which he didn't bowl, until he was selected for the final two games of the 2008 season. With the three England men required for Test duty, Gibson returned but it was Onions who had Warwickshire rocking on 23 for four. While the rest of the top five could barely lay bat on ball, Kumar Sangakkara effortlessly took charge of the recovery as though he were playing on a Sri Lankan shirtfront.

He scored 48 of the first 56 runs, four of which were leg byes, before Alex Loudon began to plunder the bowling after taking nine overs to get off the mark. Playing his first innings for Warwickshire, Sangakkara then seemed content to switch to a supporting role. As a dapper left-hander, there was more than a hint of Brian Lara about him, and the dazzling quality of his strokeplay was at least the equal of Lara's on this ground 13 years earlier. Loudon contributed 105 to a stand of 229 and Sangakkara made 149 before Onions wrapped up the tail with the new ball. Despite a spell of none for 56 in the middle, he finished with eight for 101, the second best first-class figures for Durham until Gibson twice surpassed them.

Onions had been overshadowed by Harmison and Plunkett in the previous match and said: "With those two in the team I was not getting the amount of overs I like to bowl. I did well in Bangladesh with England A, when the captain kept throwing me the ball all the time and I was thriving on that."

With rain returning on the final day, Durham replied to Warwickshire's 335 with 274 for six. Benkenstein was unbeaten on 93 and he followed up with 97 not out the following day as Mustard's maiden one-day century helped Durham to a four-wicket win off the last ball in an FPT tie at Northampton.

For the visit of Yorkshire to Riverside in late May, Durham brought in Claydon and Wiseman. But they took only one wicket each in the match as Gibson began his golden run by taking seven for 81 in the first innings. At the time they were his best championship figures – but not for long. He also scored 71 as Durham replied to 393 with 481, Coetzer making 91. Five wickets for Onions and three more for Gibson then sent back Yorkshire for 218 and Durham won by six wickets. After five games they were second in the table, 4.5 points behind Yorkshire, and Martyn Moxon said he would be happy for the table to remain exactly as it was. He added: "I expected Durham to do well this season. They have a strong squad and they played very hard for two days at Headingley and all the time here."

There were signs that the Scots had enjoyed a few drams too many after winning an FPT match at Old Trafford as they were comfortably beaten at Riverside, then Durham soared to the top of the group by amassing their highest score in one-day cricket. The desire to maintain their strong start had seen them draft in New Zealander Scott Styris as their second overseas player. But he made only 19 in a total of 332 for four at home to Worcestershire. Will Smith, who had failed to capitalise on good starts as an opener in the championship, struck a 104-ball century batting at No 3 and took 116 off the last ten overs in partnership with Benkenstein, who was unbeaten on 94. Durham won by 143 runs.

Styris, who had signed for two months, arrived with a knee injury, which prevented him from bowling as much as Durham had hoped. He made his only significant contribution in the FPT win at Headingley, where he produced a one-day master class after Mustard's 77 had looked in danger of going to waste. Styris hit only two fours in his first 50, but he scored his last 42 runs off 15 balls before being caught on the square leg boundary for 98 off the last ball of the innings.

Durham eased home by 53 runs, then began a series of home games in which the members might have been tempted to have pacemakers fitted to regulate their pounding hearts. First came evidence that four-day cricket can witness just as much drama as the shorter version when Durham held out for a draw at home to Lancashire. Mark Davies returned to form with seven wickets in the match, but the value of experience was underlined when Wiseman joined Gibson with Durham on 171 for seven in the second innings. They survived together for 20 overs before Gibson fell for 54, becoming Muttiah Muralitharan's eighth victim of the match. There were nine balls left when Davies was out, but Onions survived the rest of the over and Wiseman blocked out Muralitharan's final over as the tension rose to a gripping climax. The New Zealander had survived 92 balls for seven.

More Riverside drama followed as Durham reached their first one-day semi-final with a one-wicket FPT win against Nottinghamshire, who scored 238 for eight. With 21 still needed off four overs when last man Neil Killeen went in, Gareth Breese emerged as the hero, clinching victory when he hit the last two balls of the 49th over for four to remain unbeaten on 68. Mustard had launched the reply with 77, taking his FPT tally to 426 in eight innings.

Durham were at home to Essex in the semi-final, which followed straight after Riverside's most high-profile Test to date against the West Indies. Rain restricted play to 40 overs on the first two days, then Shivnarine Chanderpaul and Paul Collingwood both made centuries as England won by seven wickets.

Plunkett had been dropped after playing in the first three Tests, and he was to play a massive role in guiding Durham to the FPT final on a pitch for which preparation time had been restricted by the Test and the weather.

There had been more rain overnight and the start was delayed until 12.10. Essex were put in and the ninth ball, from Gibson, did just enough to take Alastair Cook's edge on the way to Mustard. The next two dismissals resulted from Mark Pettini and Varun Chopra batting as they might at Chelmsford as they drove Neil Killeen to extra cover and mid-on respectively. With Ronnie Irani and Ravi Bopara injured, depleted Essex were unable to recover as Killeen and Gibson shared the wickets in reducing them to 26 for six then Plunkett did the rest. Against desperate batsmen he didn't need to bowl particularly well to take four for 15 and Essex were all out for 71.

The visitors had an opening attack of Australian Andy Bichel and Martin Saggers, on loan from Kent, and when they had Durham rocking on six for three it was clear that victory would be no formality. Bichel took four wickets and Durham were 38 for seven, just as Essex had been, when Plunkett joined Gibson. Only one run had been added when Gibson was dropped at mid-on by Danish Kaneria off Graham Napier, who followed up with a no-ball. Plunkett drove the resulting free-hit for a straight six, which proved a huge turning point. Through sensible strokeplay, rather than desperate hitting, Plunkett scored 30 in the unbroken stand of 34 which carried Durham to Lord's.

He paid tribute to his partner by saying: "It was good to have Ottis in the middle when I went out to bat. I felt the pressure when I was watching the wickets go down, but once you step out into the middle you have to relax. I have done some work with Ottis on my run-up and have bowled better as a result."

There were no complaints from Essex about the pitch and Benkenstein said: "It was slow but it wasn't doing a hell of a lot – just enough to find the edge or earn lbws. We thought we could knock off the runs without too much trouble, but they came out and really fought. It was unbelievable to get into that position. Teams from the south come up here and don't know what a good score is, so it's best to put them in."

Strangely enough, he would adopt the same policy 12 months later in a semi-final against Kent, only to see his bowlers put to the sword by fearless batting.

Durham's championship challenge began to unravel at the Rose Bowl, where they were involved in controversy as their first taste of four-day cricket under floodlights cast a dark shadow over their victory chances. Geoff Cook described the 40 minutes of floodlit action as "slapstick cricket" after Chris Tremlett threw the bat at everything and enjoyed some outrageous fortune.

Hampshire switched on the lights for the first time in championship cricket at 5.30 on the third day and Benkenstein immediately objected to the umpires. He said he had not been told beforehand that this could happen, and from his experience of similar situations in South Africa he knew it was difficult for outfielders to pick up the red ball. The captain spoke to the umpires several more times as Tremlett survived three chances, two of them from steeplers which the fielders failed to see clearly. Eventually play was suspended with 16 overs still to be bowled, but with Tremlett having advanced rapidly to 62, Durham were 253 adrift after leading by 56 on first innings thanks to Di Venuto's 124.

The start was delayed until 1.35 on the final day, but Shane Warne declared, giving Durham 66 overs to make 254. Not many other county captains would have taken such a gamble, but after an opening stand of 91 Durham began to crumble as Warne took five of the first seven wickets to take his match haul to 11. The score was 201 for seven with 12 overs left when Tremlett was recalled and six balls later it was all over as he had Plunkett, Davies and Onions caught in the slips.

Durham began their Twenty20 programme with a six-wicket defeat at Old Trafford, where Mal Loye scored 80 not out. For the second game, on Monday, June 25, their coach left Riverside for Derby in mid-morning following assurances that it wasn't raining at their destination. En route it was clear that there were going to be serious flooding problems in south Yorkshire, and following news that Chesterfield was virtually cut off it was obvious on arrival at Derby that there could be no play.

The journey back took more than twice as long as usual in the coach, and rather than take my car through the floods I headed south at the gridlocked M1 junction, then went across country to Stoke and headed up the M6 in evening sunshine. All this in forlorn pursuit of a game of Twenty20 cricket!

The bad weather continued as the home match against Nottinghamshire failed to start, the visit to Grace Road was abandoned after 4.4 overs and the Saturday evening match at Headingley was reduced to a ten-over farce. The home match against Lancashire survived intact, but Loye's 89 put the game well beyond Durham and their only joy was in beating Leicestershire at home in a 13-overs-a-side contest. It had been hoped that Styris would make a difference in the Twenty20, but he played in only three games because of a calf strain, while DiVenuto suffered a nasty finger injury in the field in the home defeat by Lancashire and was out for a month.

He missed three championship games in which Durham displayed their usual Twenty20 hangover. They began by reaching the crazy score of 151 for eight at lunch on the first day at The Oval. Plunkett's radar was on the blink, but Steve Harmison took seven wickets in the match, including the four which Surrey lost in reaching a target of 154. They were, in fact, 50 for four but Rikki Clarke's unbeaten 68 saw them home.

Harmison had bowled with good pace and aggression and had persuaded England coach Peter Moores to allow him to play in Durham's next match, against Sussex at Horsham, which would end three days before the first Test against India started. It had been stated a few weeks earlier that Harmison would require a groin operation, but he had bowled without pain at The Oval and it was felt he would get through safely to the end of the season. He broke down after five overs at Horsham, however, and any hope Durham had of salvaging something from the match went with him as they lost by an innings and 102 runs.

This was the occasion of Mark Stoneman's debut, a month after his 20th birthday, but the left-handed opener found it tough going against Rana Naved-ul-Hasan and Jason Lewry. Ben Harmison was also brought back into the team, but twice fell cheaply to Mushtaq Ahmed, who took nine wickets in the match. Chris Adams scored 193 out of Sussex's 517, but Durham's feeble batting meant the match was over inside three days at this lovely rural retreat.

The night before the match I had stayed in one of my favourite farmhouses near Ockley and wished I had continued to commute from there. My recollection from the 1992 visit was that Horsham was a sufficiently pleasant town in which to spend a couple of nights. I wasn't wrong, except that the lady running the B and B I alighted upon said my visit coincided with her birthday and she wished to have a couple of days free from cooking breakfast. She recommended a Wetherspoon's pub en route to the ground for a value-for-money breakfast. That was how, on a try-anything-once basis, I found myself suffering the hugely dispiriting experience of eating lukewarm hash browns and baked beans while someone on the next table drank a pint of lager at 10am.

I think it was the lager I really objected to, but my image of Horsham as somewhere to match Much Wenlock as a small country town in the ancient civilisation mould was shattered. The mistake was amplified when I discovered that the lovely girls at the cricket club served a far superior breakfast, which was gratefully sampled the following morning.

Harmison had his groin operation and in his absence Durham's resurgence was inspired by Ottis Gibson at the same time as the news leaked out that they were trying to sign his fellow West Indian, Shivnarine Chanderpaul. It was intended he should take over as soon as possible from Styris, who had struggled with injuries. He stayed for one more match, in which he scored two and 17 at home to Hampshire, leaving him with an average of 21 from ten innings. This game also marked the end of Will Smith's season in the first team. Having been signed as an opener, he had averaged 20.89 in the first ten matches and stood down to make way for Di Venuto's return, with Stoneman given the chance to continue.

The Hampshire game lost a day and a half to rain, but will forever be remembered for Gibson's ten for 47 in the first innings. Another remarkable feat was totally overshadowed as Michael Brown carried his bat for 56 and was unbeaten on 126 in Hampshire's second innings as they hung on for a draw on 262 for nine.

Benkenstein had looked like a reckless gambler on the first day when he chose to bat in conditions tailor-made for the gentle swing and seam of Dimitri Mascarenhas, who quickly removed the top four. Durham were 29 for five when Ben Harmison joined his captain with a total of 16 runs from six innings behind him. But a stand of 156 ensued and Benkenstein went on to make 114 in a total of 252. If ever an innings epitomised his man-for-a-crisis value to Durham this was it as he doggedly concentrated on survival until lunch then played fluently in the afternoon. With the outfield extremely lush after all the rain, his shots would normally have been worth many more runs in late July and he had only six fours in his century.

Shane Warne went wicketless, continuing to look less impressive at Riverside than at the Rose Bowl. When he came on for his third spell the public address man began to introduce him as "Mike", much to the crowd's amusement, and Gibson began to make his mark on proceedings by driving two successive balls from Warne for six.

The second day was washed out before Gibson wrote his name indelibly in the record books on the third. Relying on swing more than seam, he had five batsmen caught off the edge. Two others were bowled, two were lbw and Nic Pothas drove a return catch. Gibson had five for 31 from 12 overs at lunch and eight for 40 after 15 overs. But he enjoyed no further success in his next two overs and would surely have been taken off had rain not intervened. It gave him almost a two-hour break and on the resumption he completed his perfect ten with the second and third balls. James Bruce was the final victim, pushing forward to ball pitched in the perfect spot. It moved away just enough to beat the bat and hit off stump, sparking joyous scenes.

It was an unforgettable moment as the ecstatic Gibson continued his follow through on a curving run towards cover, his right arm wheeling in celebration of its momentous achievement, with his team-mates in pursuit. The only other person to have taken ten wickets in an innings for Durham was Alf Morris, a bespectacled seamer, who took ten for 130 against Yorkshire seconds at Barnsley in 1910. Born in West Hartlepool, his statistics seemed to confirm his reputation as the best bowler to have played for the county in their Minor Counties history. He played as a professional for Burnmoor and Sunderland before the war and afterwards in the Bradford League. Gibson was only the third bowler to perform the feat in the county championship in the last 50 years, and the first since Richard Johnson took ten for 45 for Middlesex at Derby on 1994.

Gibson said: "I wasn't going to bowl after lunch, but the captain said at my age I wasn't going to get many more opportunities to take all ten. It couldn't have worked out better, because both times I started to feel tired I got a break. I've got the ball as a memento and I'll get Shane Warne to sign a copy of the scoresheet – and you won't be finding it on e-bay tomorrow. In my young days I was quick and I still like to rough people up when I have the chance. But in conditions like this I know it's best to let the ball do the work."

Gibson had recently been linked with the West Indies coaching job and added: "I am trying to give the young guys here a lead. If they're not listening at least now I can say to them 'this is what I've done, when did you ever take ten-for'?" He also took the first two wickets in Hampshire's second innings after they were set a target of 359 in 75 overs, Stoneman having made his maiden half-century in Durham's second innings. The declaration was notably more cautious than Warne's at the Rose Bowl, and with Gibson unable to add to his tally Hampshire finished on 262 for nine. Had last man David Griffiths not survived for 5.3 overs, Michael Brown would have become only the seventh man in history to carry his bat through both innings of a first-class match. Paul Wiseman took five for 65 in Hampshire's second innings.

Chanderpaul, who had averaged 148 in the Test series against England, made his Durham debut in a Pro40 League match against Surrey at Guildford, making 80 not out as a target of 249 was reached with seven wickets and four overs in hand.

It had transpired that Chanderpaul would have to depart at the end of August for the World Twenty20 Championship in South Africa, and he failed to shine in his first four-day match, against Warwickshire at Riverside. Maiden championship centuries by Kyle Coetzer and Ben Harmison, however, helped Durham to a first innings lead of 235, only to see it wiped out by centuries from Ian Westwood and Kumar Sangakkara. Their second wicket stand of 219 appeared to have made the game safe for Warwickshire, but four wickets each for Gibson and Wiseman had them back in trouble at 355 for nine when Lee Daggett joined James Anyon. Daggett made 33 in a stand of 71 and Durham needed 192 to win with 36 overs left. They sent in Mustard, whose 33-ball half-century equalled the record for Durham's fastest first-class 50, jointly held by Ian Botham and Martin Speight.

Against a side who were tumbling down the table on their way to relegation, Mustard and Di Venuto had 49 on the board after five overs and put on 157 before Mustard fell for 76. Chanderpaul helped to pick off the rest of the runs, with Di Venuto unbeaten on 91 when victory was secured with 5.5 overs to spare.

Amazingly, the fastest 50 record was broken only six days later by Lee Goddard, a 24-year-old wicketkeeper from Dewsbury who had played briefly for Derbyshire and been taken on in mid-season. He reached the target from 32 balls in a three-day match against Sri Lanka A, in which Steve Harmison captained Durham. He was reported to have worked extremely hard to get fit in his desperation to play in the Friends Provident Trophy final but was under orders to feel his way back gently in this game. The new ball was shared by Onions, who had lost form, and Luke Evans, a 20-year-old seamer from Sunderland who stood 6ft 7in. He was making his first-class debut along with Will Gidman.

Just over three weeks after his operation, Harmison then bowled seven overs in a Pro40 defeat at Canterbury, from which Durham arrived back at base at 2am to start a four-day match against Surrey on the same day. It had been brought forward to a Monday start because of the FPT final the following Saturday. Harmison bowled nine overs in the first innings before succumbing to a back problem which ruled him out for the rest of the season. He had paid a cruel price for his over-strenuous efforts to prove his fitness for Lord's.

After a day was lost to rain, Jon Batty's unbeaten century enabled Surrey to hold out for a draw on the last day and Durham travelled to London on August 17 for the biggest occasion in their history the following day.

Given the choice of four days at Scarborough or Lord's, I would opt for the seagulls, the whelk stall, the terraced wooden seating and the Tetley's Bitter any time. Although Lord's is always special, it can be almost eerily quiet during a county championship game. But when 6,000 Durham fans travelled down for a one-day final they didn't need the invitation I'd seen on the new scoreboard at The Oval to "make some noize." I would rather have sat among them than in the almost hermetically-sealed space age media centre, but when I wandered out to sample the atmosphere I was quickly asked by a steward to return to my seat.

It was abundantly clear, however, how much the fans were enjoying themselves. Ahead of the game Dale Benkenstein had said: "I understand how much passion there is here. From talking to people like Steve Harmison and Paul Collingwood I know that the people involved in the club have been through some tough years. Other counties have been there and done it, but there haven't been too many highlights for Durham, so I understand how important it is getting to centre stage. This really makes a big statement for cricket in the North-East."

Amid all the excitement and fears of possible stage fright, the captain also displayed the value of a wise, experienced head when he added: "Finals are there to relax and enjoy. It's a reward for the hard work involved in getting there. It's not a case of putting pressure on yourself to win, but it is an opportunity to bring the best out of yourself. You often get career-best performances in finals."

Durham even took their own brass band to Lord's. Fittingly, Tom Moffat was president in Durham's 125th year and he was also chairman of the Tavistock Riverside Band. It had started life as the Pelton Fell Colliery Band in 1878, had struggled on after the pit closures, and for the last few years had been playing out of Durham's headquarters. Those of us still working there an hour after close of play had occasionally heard them strike up in rehearsal.

"There'll be no prouder man than me at Lord's," said Moffat, who had launched a president's appeal in the hope of raising £50,000 towards a nursery ground. "I said in the appeal letter that it would be 60 years next June since I received a card from the secretary, Jack Iley, telling me I had been selected to play for the county colts against the Durham Coast League at Castle Eden." He still had that card among his mementoes, which included a 1946 photograph of a Wearmouth team in which he appeared alongside Phil Mustard's grandfather.

Speaking of the band, Moffat added: "We've just had a £10,000 grant for new instruments from the Coalfields Regeneration Trust, which was set up to sustain the history and heritage of coal mining. They are one of top brass bands in the country. They were granted rehearsal facilities at Lord's prior to playing at the Royal Albert Hall two years ago."

On this occasion they struck up between innings, by which time Durham had every reason to blow their own trumpets.

Although he travelled with the squad, Harmison was mortified to miss a match for which Collingwood was available, while Shane Warne and Kevin Pietersen were in the opposition. But Hampshire were lacking a key man in the Australian seamer, Stuart Clark, whose 21 wickets in the competition at under 12 had helped them to the final. He had taken six for 27 in the home win against Surrey which clinched top place in the group and three for 38 in the semi-final against Warwickshire.

Clark had been replaced by Daren Powell, the West Indian paceman, so both he and Chanderpaul were making their first appearances in the competition. Powell's only contribution, while conceding 80 runs, was to have Michael Di Venuto very well caught by the excellent Michael Carberry at mid-wicket for 12. But Mustard had already given Durham a flying start as, from the moment Warne invited them to bat, the underdogs strutted the hallowed turf like supreme champions. They out-Shaned Hampshire as they imposed their own will, skill and sheer bravado on the game to win by 125 runs.

Mustard made 49 off 38 balls before he was controversially adjudged lbw, and Durham's faith in Kyle Coetzer was rewarded with a classy innings of 61. His pick-up off Sean Ervine into the top deck of the Grand Stand over square leg was rivalled as shot of the day only by a sweep from Chanderpaul which barely rose more than ten feet off the ground as it flew over the boundary. In making a masterful 78 off 79 balls, the West Indian looked likely to carry Durham to at least 320, but he was run out in the

38th over in a mix-up with Collingwood, whose struggles to locate the middle of the bat scarcely mattered.

Benkenstein had no such problems as he ensured his side's total would be the highest in a domestic one-day 50-over final. Going in with 12 overs left, he applied the sweetest possible icing to the cake with an unbeaten 61 off 43 balls, which included three sixes. And if the cake needed some glowing candles Durham had just the man to supply them in their most spectacular form.

Ottis Gibson needed only nine balls to confirm his status as a Durham legend. He faced seven with the bat and smote 15 not out to lift the final total to 312 for five, then he took wickets with the first two balls of Hampshire's reply. They were perfectly pitched on off stump, slanting away from left-handers Michael Lumb and Sean Ervine, who both edged to Di Venuto at second slip. Gibson had cemented his place in Durham folklore, and if the game wasn't already over it would be shortly afterwards.

Pietersen had arrived at none for two and if anyone could retrieve the situation it had to be him. He made 12 before a ball from Gibson skidded through a shade low, homing in on the pads like a heat-seeking missile. Pietersen almost doubled up in his attempt to dig it out. It looked a little too theatrical, but he quickly straightened up and turned for the pavilion with barely a glance at the inevitable raised finger.

Plunkett and Collingwood also took three wickets each as Hampshire were dismissed for 187 and the only blemishes on a glorious occasion for the Durham hordes involved the weather and the appeal system. The latter had been introduced to the competition as an experiment, but Durham would not have expected any joy from the third umpire on this occasion, Trevor Jesty. He could not have been expected to overturn the lbw decision against Mustard, who had almost reached the pavilion gate when alerted by his team-mates that the replay showed the ball had pitched outside leg stump. The rules said referrals should be immediate, and Durham reacted swiftly when a drive from Pietersen brushed Gibson's hand then hit the non-striker's stumps with John Crawley out of his ground. After seeing the replay most commentators agreed it was out, but Jesty maintained the competition's record of referrals having a 100 per cent failure rate.

Rain brought an anti-climactic end to play on the Saturday with Hampshire in a hopeless position on 158 for five after 32.3 overs. Most Durham supporters returned home on the specially-chartered train, wondering why the Duckworth/Lews method could not have been used to crown their heroes on the day. There was more rain the following morning, but play resumed at 12.30 and it was all over inside nine overs.

Mustard was the FPT's highest run scorer with 484 at an average of 44 and also led the way in the Pro40 League with 409 runs at 58 and a strike rate of 159 per 100 balls. He was also the leading wicketkeeper in the championship with 62 catches and three stumpings. His only disappointment was a batting average of 25.96 in the championship, but he had done enough to earn a place in England's one-day team over the coming winter.

After Lord's, Mustard lit up the next two home Pro40 matches with 78 off 40 balls against Leicestershire and an unbeaten 66 in another easy win against Yorkshire. The second division title was clinched with a 70-run win against Glamorgan at Riverside, where Durham paraded the Friends Provident Trophy in front of 2,000 fans but did not receive their second piece of silverware. That was because it had been taken to Taunton, where Somerset would have finished top had they not lost to Middlesex.

One man who had not featured at Lord's was Mark Davies. In fact, he watched the Durham innings then travelled across London to watch his brother, Andrew, playing for Middlesbrough at West Ham. Such was Durham's glut of seam bowling talent at the time that they had allowed Davies to go on loan for a month to Nottinghamshire, where he took what was then a career-best seven for 59 against Northants before his stay was cut short by a hamstring strain.

Neil Killeen had played at Lord's, but his season was ended by a similar injury and it was Gibson who continued to take the bowling honours. He took 11 wickets in a five-wicket home win against Worcestershire, which revived hopes of winning the championship. They were instantly dashed, however, on a poor pitch in Blackpool's Stanley Park, where 18 wickets fell on the first day. Glen Chapple was in his 14th over with figures of none for 26 when he began the carnage which earned him a final analysis of seven for 53, then Gibson took eight for 68 in Lancashire's first innings.

While Chanderpaul had gone to the Twenty20 World Championship, Lancashire had drafted in VVS Laxman and from 44 for three chasing a victory target of 169 he steered Lancashire home in partnership with Stuart Law. The match finished in two days, and having taken only three points from it, Durham trailed leaders Sussex by 16.5 points with two games left.

Sussex came to Riverside for the penultimate game, with Durham expecting a trial by spin as the visitors included Saqlain Mushtaq as well as

Mushtaq Ahmed. But Durham left more grass on the pitch to nullify the threat and backed their own seamers. A maiden century by Mark Stoneman took them to 316 in reply to 291, then Gibson quickly reduced Sussex to 27 for three. They advanced to 85 before Davies weighed in with two wickets, then a burst of three for none in five balls by Plunkett ended their resistance and they were all out for 131. Stoneman followed his 101 with 46 not out in securing the nine-wicket win and Benkenstein said: "To score those runs against the new ball on this pitch at 20 shows a lot of character. I asked for commitment and our bowling in the second innings was outstanding."

Chris Adams, the Sussex captain, had no complaints about the pitch, saying: "We use the conditions at Hove to favour us and Durham got this right tactically. They look like a proper team now. They know what they are doing."

Lancashire had now gone to the top and were 8.5 points ahead of Durham, who still trailed Sussex by 2.5. Lancashire's final game was at The Oval, Sussex were to entertain bottom club Worcestershire and Durham had to go to Canterbury, where news came through that Gibson was to be England's bowling coach in the one-day series in Sri Lanka.

Chanderpaul had returned following the West Indies' early exit in South Africa, but he provided an exaggerated imitation of Durham's efforts in mid-season, when they had struggled to readjust to four-day cricket after the Twenty20 Cup. He made only four before dancing the pitch and trying to launch James Tredwell into orbit, only to edge to slip.

Gibson's three wickets in Kent's first innings took him past Simon Brown's 1996 record of 77 first-class wickets in a season for Durham. While Surrey were piling up runs against Lancashire, the news from Hove wasn't good, but Benkenstein's determination to battle to the end saw him score 117 in a match in which no-one else passed 54. Paul Wiseman took four wickets as Kent were dismissed for 160 in their second innings and Durham knocked off the 52 needed to win for the loss of two wickets.

It was all over at 12.20 on the third day, and Gibson said: "It's great to be champions for a day." Sussex duly overhauled them by 4.5 points the following day, but second place easily beat Durham's previous best of seventh, achieved when they so narrowly survived in division one in 2006.

Benkenstein had become the first player to pass 1,000 first-class runs in three successive seasons for Durham, while despite missing three games Di Venuto scored 1,329 championship runs at 66.45. Chanderpaul averaged a surprisingly modest 37.33 in his four games, but such was his overall impact in passing on his experience to the others that Durham signed him up for whatever time he was available in 2008.

Steve Harmison topped the bowling averages with 32 wickets at 16.37 in his six games, but there was no doubt that the Player of the Year was Gibson. He had taken an incredible 57 wickets in the last seven games to finish with 80 in the championship, and only Mushtaq had more.

At 38, it seemed certain Gibson had played his last game. If the England one-day coaching role in Sri Lanka had not led to a permanent position, there was the possibility at that time that he might be offered the job of West Indies coach. Given the choice, he said he didn't know which way he would turn, but as the season ended he was happy to reflect on his achievements. He had already been named Player of the Year by the Professional Cricketers' Association and the new editor of Wisden, Scyld Berry, had decided that Gibson would be one of the almanack's five Cricketers of the Year. I was asked to interview him for the piece in Wisden and the 90 minutes I spent with him in the team hotel at Canterbury provided one of the most enjoyable interviews of my career.

He explained how, even in his final year, being left out of the third match of the season against Kent had been such a disappointment that he had repeated to himself "don't get bitter, get better" every day for the rest of the season.

"Every time I went on the field I tried to do everything that was required for the team and I just got better. People appreciate that, and if the other players see your efforts they raise their game. I had some fantastic catches taken."

He also felt his success was the end product of putting everything into practice which he had learnt as a coach over the previous six years. That included things like physiology, which he believed had helped his fitness during a season in which he played in every competitive game except the home match against Kent and the FPT tie against Lancashire.

"There have been times when I've been in at 8am for a massage to get ready to bowl," he said. "That's the mindset I adopted and perhaps it's one reason for my success. I can talk to the young lads about bowling and about game situations, but when I'm playing I can set the standard and impress on them that when the game is on the line you have to run in and be aggressive. You have to weigh up what the conditions will allow you to do on that day. Sometimes the in-swinger and out-swinger both work, and that's what happened against Hampshire."

Gibson felt that coaching had taught him how to create more variations, particularly in changing the angle of delivery. He lost count of the number of times he took a wicket in the first over of a spell, saying: "Batsmen would love to have a ball to leave or a free hit, so you have to make sure you don't give them a loosener. The first over has to be a challenge to the batsman. In the final at Lord's I said I wanted the first over. I wanted to lead and set the tone. I knew where I wanted to bowl those first two balls, and I got them in the right spot, slanting across the left-handers and asking them questions."

With Gibson's help, England surprisingly won the one-day series in Sri Lanka and he was rewarded with a full-time post. It meant Durham would see him no more, other than on his frequent social visits. But his deeds in the 2007 season will long remain the stuff of legend.

CHAPTER 18

THE CROWNING GLORY

IN what would be a final, triumphant season as captain, Dale Benkenstein insisted that Durham truly believed they could win everything. This was despite the potentially damaging loss of Ottis Gibson and fears going into the season that they could be without Phil Mustard for large parts of it. Having two players dropped by England, however, worked in Durham's favour. Steve Harmison was available for most of the season and, much to his disappointment, Mustard lost his place as England's one-day wicketkeeper, which he had held throughout the winter.

Far from winning everything, it seemed on the first day of the final match that Durham would be left with nothing. They lost in the semi-finals of the Twenty20 Cup and the Friends Provident Trophy, and achieved third place, their highest finish, in the one-day league.

They went into the final championship match at Canterbury ten points behind Nottinghamshire, who were at home to Hampshire, and two behind Somerset, who faced Lancashire at Taunton. At lunchtime on the first day the decision to take the Sky cameras, and the trophy, to Trent Bridge looked fully justified as Durham had taken only two Kent wickets after putting them in on a damp pitch. Nottinghamshire, meanwhile, had Hampshire reeling on 96 for six.

The current began to turn in the afternoon, and by the third evening it was as though a tidal bore had swept up the Trent as Nic Pothas repaid his old pal, Benkenstein, for walking when the Hampshire wicketkeeper had claimed a catch at Riverside which didn't appear to carry. Durham had lost that match by four runs, but all was forgiven when Pothas's second innings century swept Hampshire to the victory which left Nottinghamshire eight points adrift. Somerset had also stumbled badly, allowing Durham to complete a sensational double, having also won the Second X1 Championship under the captaincy of Gordon Muchall.

It seemed a result pitch had been prepared at Taunton, but Somerset were on the back foot after being dismissed for 202 when batting first. In the end Lancashire needed 183 to win and an opening stand of 151 between Mark Chilton and Paul Horton set up an eight-wicket win.

Muchall's inability to break into the first team for any championship game underlined the strength of Durham's squad. Some others, like the long-serving Neil Killeen and Gary Scott, might have felt marginalised, and it was a disappointing season for Kyle Coetzer and Garry Park. Even for Graham Onions and Liam Plunkett there were frustrations as they played only half a dozen championship games each and were left out of the last three. But the squad always gave the impression of being one big happy family.

After his 2007 season was blighted by injury, there was no role for Scott, who was released seven years after making his championship debut shortly after his 17th birthday. Another slow bowler in whom much was invested, Scottish leg-spinner Moneeb Iqbal, also toppled off the bumpy road which all young tweakers have to travel.

While the lack of a home-grown spinner remained the biggest failure in Durham's production line, the mantle of expectation fell on Sunderland lad Scott Borthwick, of whom Benkenstein claimed after pitching him into Twenty20 action at Old Trafford that he was made of stern stuff. The captain also said the 18-year-old leg-spinner was as good a batsman as bowler.

Of the youngsters who featured regularly, Ben Harmison's seam bowling improved significantly, but neither he nor Mark Stoneman added to the maiden championship centuries they scored in 2007. Mustard's batting average also declined, and in terms of winning games the input of Neil McKenzie, the South African Test opener, and Shivnarine Chanderpaul, who shared the overseas player's duties, was slight. The latter again impressed sufficiently, however, to be invited back.

McKenzie began with a match-winning knock of 77 in the opening Friends Provident Trophy game at home to Yorkshire, but averaged only 19 in eight championship innings before going off to star in the Test series against England. Chanderpaul made runs in two rain-ruined draws - 93 at Taunton and 138 at home to Sussex – helping him to a respectable average of 37.36.

So, if there were few individuals making huge strides, it was clearly a team effort which enabled Durham to take the final step to the title. There were two Players of the Year, Will Smith earning the members' vote and Steve Harmison gaining the accolade from his team-mates. Otherwise only Callum Thorp improved significantly on 2007, his 50 championship wickets proving more crucial than the 39 which carried Mark Davies to the top of the national averages. Astonishingly, Davies took 30 of those wickets in three games at an average of 6.56 and Durham lost two of those matches – at Old Trafford and Basingstoke. In the final three games of the season he took only three wickets, but he was still in the team ahead of Onions and he also earned selection ahead of his team-mate for the England Development squad to tour India and New Zealand.

The big difference from Durham's past was that they failed collectively only once, in the face of superb bowling by Jimmy Anderson and Andrew Flintoff in the second match, when Benkenstein was attending the birth of his third child. Otherwise someone always rode to the rescue, which showed the value of having a gritty, experienced performer like Paul Wiseman at No 8, even though it was not a season for spin bowlers.

Despite an early spate of run-outs and tricky conditions, Michael Di Venuto finished with 1058 championship runs for the season and Smith's tally, after coming in for the fourth match, was 925 at an average of 51.38. The only other Englishman to have averaged 50 for Durham was Paul Collingwood with 55.15 in the promotion season of 2005.

Di Venuto also made a masterful 138 in the final FPT group game at home to his former Derbyshire colleagues as Durham overcame a stuttering start to their defence of the trophy to sneak into the quarter-finals. Gareth Breese's 34 not out then carried them to a dramatic one-wicket win against Nottinghamshire, but the semi-final defeat by 83 runs against Kent was a huge disappointment.

The South African duo, Shaun Pollock and Albie Morkel, played in that match and had combined figures of 17-0-126-0, while totalling 27 runs, although they did contribute heavily in the Twenty20, for which they had been signed. Their acquisition was indicative of Durham's determination to cast off the mantle of having the worst record of all the counties in this event. The mega-bucks potentially on offer to the winners via the proposed Champions League might also have influenced the signings, but the best-laid plans were almost scuppered by a repeat of the 2007 weather. Only one of Durham's home games was not rain-affected, but overall they showed a marked improvement by winning six out of ten, with one tie, one defeat and two no-results.

The Twenty20 highlight came at Old Trafford, where Morkel's five sixes in the last nine balls he faced was the most astonishing feat of hitting in

Durham's history. He carried them to a target of 181 with an over to spare after the game had looked lost.

Then came the farce of the home quarter-final, which was eventually played 15 days after the scheduled date and only four days before the finals day. Durham were due to play Yorkshire, but received word from the England and Wales Cricket Board at 3.30 on the afternoon of the game that it should not go ahead because Yorkshire had fielded an ineligible player, Azeem Rafiq, in a group game against Nottinghamshire.

Durham objected and began to let people into the ground while negotiations went on, and it was only ten minutes before the scheduled start that the 6,000 spectators were told the match was off. Yorkshire were thrown out and Nottinghamshire re-instated, but on Yorkshire's appeal it was decided to award them the match but not the points.

As Nottinghamshire didn't have the points either, it opened the door for Glamorgan to proceed as one of the two best third-placed teams. They were euphoric after removing Di Venuto, Mustard, Collingwood and Chanderpaul inside seven overs, but Durham recovered through Smith's 37-ball half-century then took 47 off the last three overs to win comfortably.

Unfortunately, they never got to grips with their semi-final against Middlesex and on a glorious day in front of a packed house at the Rose Bowl they were blasted to defeat by the burly South African all-rounder, Tyron Henderson. It was another big disappointment to follow the FPT semi-final defeat, which made it all the more remarkable that Durham were able to muster the strength and character to land the title which remains the most cherished by true cricket lovers.

In the one-day arena, there were other lowlights, notably two floodlit farces at Derby. Despite going on to win the cup, Durham had lost to their bogey side, Derbyshire, in the group stage of the 2007 FPT, and the jinx continued in the 2008 day-night match. The original starting time of 2.30 was brought forward an hour in case play was halted by a low sun. That is exactly what happened at 6.45 with Durham looking likely winners after an opening stand of 76 in reply to 236 for six.

Play resumed after 15 minutes with the sun behind a cloud and the floodlights having no perceptible impact. Durham immediately lost Di Venuto and McKenzie to successive balls from Graham Wagg. Then at 7.25 the sun re-emerged and play was suspended for a further 55 minutes, at which point storm clouds were gathering and Durham knew they needed to get ahead of the required run-rate under the Duckworth/Lewis method.

In the bizarre blend of natural and artificial light they kept losing wickets and it wasn't until the floodlights took full effect that Ben Harmison and Neil Killeen put on 39 for the last wicket. Killeen was run out off the last ball, going back for the second run which would have tied the scores.

There was again a suspension of play when Durham went back to Derby for a Twenty20 match, which was reduced to 18 overs a side. But this time they comfortably reached their target of 119 through an unbroken fourth-wicket stand of 91 between Benkenstein and Albie Morkel. Derbyshire had already announced plans to realign some of their strips, and the following winter they decided to rotate the whole square through 90 degrees.

The FPT defeat at Derby was followed by back-to-back games at Old Trafford and Headingley, and when both were lost Durham's grip on the trophy was not exactly vice-like. But the revival started with a six-run win at home to Lancashire. When the sides had met at Old Trafford Onions bowled the last over with 12 needed and Steve Croft struck the last ball over extra cover for the required six to clinch a one-wicket win for Lancashire. This time 11 were needed and Onions conceded only four.

Two wins against Scotland put Durham back in the frame, then came the decider at home to Derbyshire, in which Di Venuto eclipsed his previous one-day best for Durham of 66, scoring 138 off 135 balls as they totalled 298 for seven to win by 117 runs. This was the only group game in which they won the toss and Gareth Breese cashed in on Derbyshire's plight by taking five for 41, his best one-day figures for Durham.

His batting then clinched the quarter-final win, in which Di Venuto again featured prominently by making 70 as Durham threatened to coast past Nottinghamshire's 188 all out. But they lost five wickets for 12 runs before last man Mark Davies went in with 12 needed. Breese finished it with a straight six off Darren Pattinson off the last ball of the 49th over.

Expecting Kent to be wary of the pitch after Essex were dismissed for 71 in the previous year's semi-final, Durham found exactly the opposite after putting their visitors in. An opening stand of 96 laid the platform for Martin Van Jaarsveld to register his fourth hundred of the competition as Kent amassed 301 for four, with Joe Denly also making a century. The only bowler to pose problems was Steve Harmison, who took all four wickets to fall. Durham battled back from two for two after nine balls to give themselves a chance, but the last five wickets went down for ten runs.

In the NatWest Pro40 League Durham fared better away from home, twice winning comfortably with the help of Paul Collingwood against

Middlesex at Uxbridge and at Worcester, while also scrambling home under the Trent Bridge floodlights.

Defeats at home to Somerset and Sussex proved costly, with Marcus Trescothick hitting 124, the highest 40-over score at Riverside, as Somerset made 286 for eight. Durham needed 100 off 10.3 overs when last man Steve Harmison joined Liam Plunkett, whose one-day best of 72 came off 42 balls. He was run out when 19 were needed off two overs.

The home match against Lancashire was washed out and Durham went into the final game against Gloucestershire at Riverside in danger of finishing third from the bottom, which would have meant a play-off to avoid relegation. Gloucestershire were all out for 119, and with the ball seaming around after wet weather Steve Kirby's three quick wickets reduced Durham to 29 for four. But Benkenstein hit six fours in his 25 to turn the tide and Di Venuto finished the match with two successive fours off Richard Dawson to complete his half-century off 67 balls.

The victory left Durham in third place, but their highest finish in the one-day league was of minor significance alongside the meat and drink of the championship. They began the campaign at home to Surrey and as the visitors finished well adrift at the foot of the table, this was a game Durham could have been expected to win in fine weather. But there were long breaks for rain on the first and third days, and in hurrying to a declaration after lunch on the last day, Durham allowed Saqlain Mushtaq to take five for three in 14 balls before setting a target of 270 in 53 overs. At 45 for three Surrey opted for safety. Di Venuto had been run out in the game's first over and, through no fault of his own, he was run out three more times in the opening month.

The title looked a distant dream when Durham then lost by 232 runs at Old Trafford, despite Davies taking what was then a career-best seven for 33 as Lancashire were dismissed for 143. Durham were shot out for 114, of which Mitch Claydon made 40 in his only championship appearance. He was brought in ahead of Thorp in place of Onions, who was on England A duty, but Claydon and Steve Harmison between them had match figures of two for 194, while Jimmy Anderson and Andrew Flintoff took 16 for 119.

With Benkenstein attending the birth of his son in South Africa, and McKenzie at a wedding, the Durham middle order featured Coetzer, Collingwood and Park, who totalled 33 runs in two innings between them. Park did spring a surprise by clean bowling Stuart Law and Flintoff with his bustling medium pace, but it was not a sign of things to come. That was

Park's only championship appearance of the season after playing only twice in 2007. Despite his century at Headingley in the final game of 2006, Durham's 100th first-class player had come to be seen as a bits-and-pieces squad man, and at the end of the season he opted to join Derbyshire.

Still searching for form after his latest lay-off, Flintoff bagged a pair in that match. Davies had him caught at slip first ball as 20 wickets inexplicably fell on the first day. This was on the ground where the same teams had amassed 923 runs for the fall of 19 wickets two years earlier.

In the second innings Flintoff studiously blocked the first ball to the cheers of the locals, which he acknowledged with a raised bat. Four balls later the same bat was swishing furiously as he departed, his timber rearranged by the unheralded Park. Paul Horton restored sanity by making a century, however, and when Durham had 12 overs to survive as they began their pursuit of a target of 323 on the second evening six of them were delivered in fast and furious fashion by Flintoff.

He took all the wickets in reducing them to 28 for three, culminating in a ferocious over to Collingwood. While it was later suggested that Freddie no longer had the man who was then England's one-day captain near the top of his Christmas card list, the brimstone probably stemmed more from his own batting failures. He also knew that if Durham were to have any chance of reaching their target, they needed a big innings from Collingwood. But he was also struggling for form at the time, and even had he been in prime working order he would have done well to survive that torrid over. He edged the last ball to the wicketkeeper, Luke Sutton, the same combination having already seen off Coetzer.

When DiVenuto, the acting captain, was run out early the next morning Durham crumbled. It cut short another pleasant trip for me, in which I had accidentally stumbled on the village where Flintoff was fighting a planning battle. It had been reported that he had followed the example of several Manchester United footballers by buying an old country house then applying for permission to knock it down and build something bigger on the site. The reports were probably exaggerated, but whatever his initial plans were they had to be scaled down.

It was in the village of Mottram St Andrew, between Alderley Edge and Prestbury, that area of Cheshire much favoured by Sir Alex Ferguson's overpaid acolytes. Among all the millionaires, I secured bed and breakfast for £25 a night in a farmhouse where the comfort and service could not be faulted. Possibly because of the competition between the many restaurants, there was also good value to be had in Prestbury, where the impressive Legh Arms also served immaculate Robinson's Unicorn at a very competitive price.

Mottram itself seemed to comprise a few strung-out clusters and the only pub had become an Italian restaurant. Still, the village was handy for Flintoff's next appearance as he strained a side against Durham and it was five weeks before he made his comeback, in a second team match against Durham, at Alderley Edge. The cricket ground struck me as one of the more attractive assets of this highly fashionable spot, where the old stagers probably wonder what they have done to attract the influx of footballers' wives and girlfriends.

Harmison's return to form after being dropped by England in New Zealand during the winter was a gradual process. But Durham's was immediate after their humbling at Old Trafford, with Benkenstein and Onions back for the visit of Yorkshire. Onions fully deserved his match figures of eight for 98 as the Tykes were thrashed by 295 runs. The lethal ball with which Onions had Jacques Rudolph caught behind for a fourth-ball duck in the second innings brought huge admiration from the watching England selector, James Whitaker. But just when it seemed he was knocking on the door again, Onions suffered a heel injury, which totally disrupted his season. He was out for six weeks and couldn't regain his rhythm on his return.

McKenzie returned against Yorkshire, but he and Coetzer totalled only 25 between them and it proved to be the Scot's last game. Di Venuto batted magnificently for 184 and 45 not out on a pitch favouring the seamers. Yorkshire were 212 behind on first innings, but Benkenstein declined to enforce the follow-on then made good his plan to bat the visitors out of the game by making 86 not out.

Over the previous two seasons first Muchall then Coetzer appeared to have nailed down the No 3 spot, but neither had sustained the form and now it was Smith's turn. A pattern had emerged whereby the incumbent had struggled on early season pitches, and the man coming in as conditions eased seized his opportunity.

At 25 and with one year left on his contract, Smith had been out in the cold, and it looked like a case of the seagull has landed as fortune suddenly smiled on him. Dropped at first slip on five at Hove, he revealed after making a century that there had been other droppings which signalled his change of luck. A seagull had splattered him on the evening before the match and he said: "All the lads said then I would score a hundred. When I was on 99 it almost happened again. It landed a foot away and I thought the luck might have turned against me, especially as the total was on double Nelson."

Nelson (111) and any multiple of it is considered bad luck by cricketers, but Smith drove Robin Martin-Jenkins through mid-on to reach his hundred shortly after seeing the redoubtable Benkenstein depart for 110. They had come together with the score on 11 for four and put on 205.

"Batting with Dale was fantastic," said Smith. "He has been in that situation so many times and his hundred was pure class. Last year I tended to get a bit giddy when I got to 30 and looked to play more shots. I know that showed a lack of experience and to have Dale at the other end was a big help. This century has made me realise that I should be scoring more and I hope to be with Durham for many more years." Little did he suspect at the time that he would be captain the following season.

Thorp replaced Onions at Hove and also made an immediate impact in the seven-wicket win, which confirmed Durham's title credentials. It was the champions' first home defeat since the final match of 2004. Ben Harmison took four wickets and Steve three as Sussex were dismissed for 214, then Durham recovered from 11 for four to total 301.

The only resistance from Sussex came in an astonishing blitz from their acting captain, Matt Prior. Producing an array of immensely powerful strokes, he was almost impossible to bowl to towards the end of his unbeaten 133 in a second innings total of 212. Prior drove a mighty straight six off Steve Harmison and reached his century by cutting successive balls from the resurgent paceman for two more sixes. Harmison already knew all about life's vicissitudes, but here they were in a nutshell as he had just taken a hat-trick. It could have been quite an aristocratic treble, but after Rory Hamilton-Brown and Robin Martin-Jenkins were caught by Mustard, a rather proletarian prod saw Mushtaq Ahmed's stumps spreadeagled.

On the way down to Hove I had gladly repeated the previous year's night-before stay in a very comfortable converted farmhouse at Chelwood Gate. I needed only to cross the road for a pre-breakfast jaunt in Ashdown Forest, reminding me of the inland delights in Sussex I had discovered with the rest of the travelling press corps during Durham's early first-class life. At that time one of our favourite pubs was the Shepherd and Dog at Fulking, about eight miles north-west of Brighton, near the Devil's Dyke.

With its pretty garden by a stream cascading from the South Downs, which rise majestically from here, the pub offered good Harveys beer, excellent food and old-fashioned ambience once the sun had gone down. According to the Good Pub Guide it is now a Badger dining pub, refurbished with modern tables and chairs, providing further depressing evidence that nowhere is sacred (my words, not the GPG's).

A non-drinking radio man would invariably drive us out there, but in later years I opted to stick with the rich and varied fare of Brighton. There are times when walking or jogging along the promenade at 8am that I seem to be the only normal person around. Perhaps I flatter myself. There are people on roller blades, others doing tai-chi or yoga, while the dishevelled vagrants emerge from their sleeping bags to test the discarded cider cans for whatever dregs can be extracted.

All human life is there, perhaps, and it includes the eccentric boxer, Chris Eubank, who once jogged past me accompanied by his minders. We used to say "it's never dull with Durham," referring purely to the cricket, but it would apply to Brighton seafront as well. In order to be close to it, I had booked into the Imperial Hotel on the 2008 visit, partly because it seemed to offer the best value at £50 a night. On arrival, I discovered that didn't include breakfast, so as the first morning was warm and cloudless I opted for alfresco scrambled eggs at a beachside café. You wouldn't think they could do much wrong with scrambled eggs, but this stodgy heap would have got my day off to a very bad start had it not been such a beautiful morning.

Victory at Hove was a huge fillip and Durham would have had the title sewn up well before the final match had they not lost twice to Hampshire, both times narrowly and in controversial circumstances. Having to play at Basingstoke fanned the flames later in the season, but in the four-run defeat at Riverside there were thinly-disguised allegations of chicanery.

Durham began the fourth day needing 109 with four wickets standing and their chance looked to have gone when Benkenstein, after initial hesitation, accepted Pothas's word that an edge had carried. The video recording suggested that it hadn't. A last-wicket stand of 57 between Steve Harmison and Mark Davies ended agonisingly short when Davies drove wide of off stump at Shane Bond and edged to Pothas, who held his tenth catch of the match.

Harmison's unbeaten 36 equalled his best score for Durham, and he also recorded his most expensive analysis for the county in taking six for 122 as he shouldered a big burden in the second innings. He shared 16 wickets in the match with Thorp, while Bond took nine in his last appearance for Hampshire before returning to New Zealand.

For once Durham came back from the Twenty20 break with no sign of a hangover from the slogfest and completed the double over Yorkshire. They won by eight wickets at Headingley to climb into third place with a game in hand on the top two. Making his first championship appearance of the season after a side strain, Liam Plunkett took three wickets in each innings and scored 68 not out, putting on 143 for the eighth wicket with Phil Mustard, who made his season's best of 92.

The bad weather started to blight proceedings on July 11 as the first four sessions at home to Somerset were lost. Harmison then reduced the visitors to 42 for three and would have had four wickets in seven balls had a confident first ball lbw appeal against Zander De Bruyn been upheld. Poor bowling by the rest allowed the South African to coast to a classy 152-ball century before Somerset declared as soon as they collected the fourth batting point 30 minutes into the third morning. Durham collapsed from 68 without loss to 145 for six before Plunkett's second successive half-century avoided the embarrassment of following on against a modest attack.

Somerset's declaration on the final day left Durham to score 285 in 52 overs. After slipping to eight for two they settled for a draw. This set out the risk-free strategy for the rest of the season, with everything apparently geared to ensuring they were in position to strike for gold in the final match.

Durham surged to the top at the halfway stage with their fourth win out of eight, a ten-wicket triumph against Surrey at Guildford. Chanderpaul made only five on his first appearance, but Will Smith's magnificent 201 not out underpinned Durham's 410 for a lead of 190. He became only the third Englishman after John Morris and Gordon Muchall to score a double century in the championship for Durham, while Jon Lewis had done it at Oxford.

Surrey looked to have escaped when they were 261 for three at lunch on the final day, but Jon Batty ran himself out immediately afterwards and they collapsed to 323 all out. Not for the first time against Durham, Usman Afzaal oozed class with his wristy flicks and steers. But as usual he failed to see the job through. Needing 134, Di Venuto and Mark Stoneman had no need to hurry and quietly helped themselves to unbeaten half-centuries.

Although tree-lined on three sides, and with a railway embankment visible among the poplars and beeches at the opposite end from the pavilion, the Guildford ground would not get into my top ten. But while acknowledging Surrey's prowess down the years, it would be heartening to think that the beautiful village grounds have contributed just as much as the rather soulless Oval. The area south and west of Dorking is a treasure trove of idyllic villages. From my digs near Ockley, the drive to Guildford took me through Forest Green, Holmbury St Mary, Abinger Hammer and Shere. Shere delight? Well, it certainly beats battling through London traffic or jostling with the unsmiling throngs emerging from the Oval or Vauxhall tube stations.

After interference from the weather and a first innings deficit of two, Durham declined to take any risks on the final day in the battle of the top two at Trent Bridge. Chanderpaul batted for 54 overs before striking his first boundary on his way to 53 as Durham crawled to 257 for eight from 128 overs before a draw was declared.

The visit of Kent followed wet weather and although the pitch appeared quite dry and hard it offered just enough seam movement, which, allied to swing, allowed the bowlers to wreak havoc. Only 4.1 overs were bowled because of more rain on the first morning then 15 wickets fell in two sessions. A pitch panel was convened and after seeing 23 wickets fall on the second day before the last ten overs were lost to bad light they decided no action need be taken.

Kent's first innings 78 was the second lowest total ever recorded against Durham in the championship and their captain, Robert Key, described the pitch panel as "a bit of a muppet show." Although he did not feel Durham had deliberately prepared a poor pitch for their 43-run victory, he added that it was "absolutely ridiculous" that no points were deducted and that he would have said the same had Kent won. They were brave words by Key, who had let it be known he wished to speak out and did so in front of the Sky cameras. While I might have agreed with his general sentiments about pitch panels, which rarely seem to justify their expense, overall I felt Key was taking a risk and it was no surprise when he was fined £1,000.

His attitude was in stark contrast to that of the more diplomatic Geoff Cook at Blackpool 11 months earlier. After that match finished in two days, Cook said: "We have no complaints about the pitch." This also contrasted with David Graveney's view 15 years earlier when, after hearing groundsman Harry Brind's words at The Oval, he said: "It proves even the man at the top is guilty."

Graveney was questioning whether it was right for counties to prepare pitches to suit their own attack, but the greater debate occurs when questions arise about whether a pitch is actually fit to stage first-class cricket. In such cases, unless it can be seen that the problem has arisen through deliberate intent, such as over-watering, pitch panels always err on the side of caution. While pitch inspectors are a necessary safeguard, the convening of panels occurs too frequently in relation to the number of guilty verdicts they produce.

After the Kent match umpire John Holder said the ball had swung throughout and sometimes "slipped" off the seam, but he felt there had been no extravagant movement or uneven bounce. The vast majority of victims were bowled, lbw or caught off the edge, with Geraint Jones holding six catches behind the stumps in Durham's second innings. Mark Davies consistently hit the right spot and earned his first ten-wicket match haul (his figures were ten 45).

After 11 games Durham were a point behind Nottinghamshire with a game in hand when the leaders came to Riverside on August 12 and not a ball was bowled in four days.

Things were beginning to look grim when a winning position was surrendered at Basingstoke, which was staging its first match since Durham lost in two days there in 2000. Having apparently consigned outgrounds to the history books, Hampshire had switched the game because of an REM concert at the Rose Bowl and, following rain, the pitch was soft.

Unsure what to expect, Durham opted to bat and Smith's 70 helped them to 156 before Hampshire collapsed from 48 without loss to 96 all out with Davies taking a career-best eight for 24, which were the best figures in the country that season. Steve Harmison had returned to England duty, allowing Onions to make his comeback, but the spongy surface didn't suit the quicker bowlers and Onions and Plunkett were wicketless in the match.

Although the pitch was easing, Durham's 179 in the second innings looked more than enough when Hampshire slipped to 77 for five in pursuit of 240. But two dropped catches proved costly and Sean Ervine played and missed with amazing regularity in making the unbeaten 94 which saw them home by two wickets.

After two half days' play at home to Lancashire the final two days were washed out, Durham reaching 280 for three in 95 overs with Smith unbeaten on 144. His unbroken stand of 184 with Benkenstein was 15 more than the previous Durham record for any wicket against Lancashire.

With Harmison back, Durham left out Plunkett and Onions for the last three games. At Taunton the first day was washed out and a tedious draw ensued against opponents who had managed to produce a bare, dry pitch in the hope that their spinners could win the game. They couldn't because neither Ian Blackwell nor Michael Munday caused any problems.

On a surface designed to nullify his threat, Harmison bowled skilfully to take five for 84 and dismiss Somerset for 224. Against one of their title rivals, Durham won the bonus points battle 8-3 when they replied with 400 for seven, Di Venuto (135) and Chanderpaul (93) sharing a stand of 174. With Benkenstein making 62 not out, a swift half-century by Paul Wiseman ensured Durham achieved maximum batting points with 15 balls to spare.

It was a similar story at home to Sussex the following week as there was no play on the first day because of a waterlogged outfield, but strenuous efforts to produce a dry pitch resulted in a bland surface. Chanderpaul went into the match with 50 runs in seven innings in all cricket at Riverside since his arrival in July but was untroubled in scoring a sublime century, the hallmark of which was his perfect placement.

He and Gareth Breese, making his first championship appearance since the middle of the previous season, put on 182. They failed to add to that on the third morning as the search for quick runs saw the remaining six wickets go down for 55 and Durham fell 20 short of maximum batting points.

Sussex's last man, Jason Lewry, who had reached 600 first-class wickets for Sussex in Durham's innings, became Harmison's 600th first-class victim when he was bowled immediately after the third batting point had been secured. Durham led by 78, and with a possible 78 overs left they batted out time in tedious fashion on a sunny afternoon, not wishing to risk a defeat which would have effectively ended their title chances.

And so to Canterbury for the final game, knowing that Nottinghamshire had crushed Surrey the previous week and were hot favourites to win at home to Hampshire. They were even hotter favourites when they reduced their visitors to 96 for six, but Nottinghamshire themselves collapsed dramatically on the second day and led by only eight on the first innings.

As Hampshire piled up runs on the third day, and with Somerset struggling at home to Lancashire, it became steadily clearer that the title was there for the taking for Durham. Thorp and Breese, former flatmates, emerged as the unsung heroes of the innings victory. Thorp took a career-best seven for 88 in Kent's second innings and Breese hit 121 not out as Durham reached 500 for the first time since the final face-saving match of the 2006 season at Headingley.

While he had been signed primarily for his off-spin, Breese had always looked a class batsman. It was a mystery why he hadn't scored more runs after his heroic innings at Taunton in 2004, and he was as disappointed by it as anyone. Always a good team man, he derived a quiet satisfaction from his part in this Canterbury tale, which came shortly after the birth of his first child. He also heaped praise on Thorp, who took all the wickets as Kent, trailing by 275, slumped to 58 for five. "It was nice to take the slip catch which gave Callum his fifth wicket," said Breese. "He had some injury problems last season, but I'm really elated that he has shown what he can do this year."

Durham suffered a temporary setback when both Davies and Harmison were injured and with Justin Kemp and Ryan McLaren adding 101 Kent closed the third day on 159 for five, while Hampshire had reached 376 for five at Trent Bridge to lead by 368.

Thorp was on 48 wickets at the time and said: "I don't care about getting to 50 as long as we take the last five. The ball wasn't swinging much. I got Rob Key with my first ball through a lack of pace because he played too soon, then when I held the return catch from Joe Denly I was protecting the crown jewels. I got Darren Stevens through extra bounce, but I didn't put any extra effort into it, I was putting everything I could into every ball as it was."

Given our four-strong presence of the early years, it seemed a shame that the only other North-East media person there was Martin Emmerson, doing ball-by-ball commentary for Radio Newcastle and enjoying sufficient feedback to confirm the interest back home. At this point, with the weather finally set fair, it was clear that it would take something close to a miracle to deny Durham the title. There was therefore extra work to be done for the following morning's Northern Echo, and while I was ploughing on with that the deputy editor, Chris Lloyd, a cricket fan, rang to outline his extensive plans for Monday's edition, once the championship had been secured on the Saturday.

While I told him, quite sincerely, that it would be a pleasure to oblige, all this delayed my departure for a new port-of-call. I had been staying in a house in Whitstable named the Pearl Fisher, an end-of-terrace property which looked fairly undistinguished externally. But it provided further evidence of the joys to be found by scratching beneath the surface, or taking the road less travelled. I could easily have opted for the Premier Inn on the edge of town, but tucked away in this side street I had a wonderful bedroom named Old Saybrook after the Connecticut town where Katharine Hepburn lived. Doubtless there are great similarities between Old Saybrook and Whitstable, while my hosts were obviously fans of the actress as the room was, in part, dedicated to her. The attention to detail in ensuring every comfort would have put most hotels to shame.

Pearl Fisher was fully booked on the Friday night, so I was taking pot luck with a farmhouse in the village of Aldington, near Ashford. This proved a little further away than I realised, being 20 miles south.

At least I could leave the cricket ground and follow my preferred option at the larger cities of turning away from the centre, because even at Canterbury the traffic had become horrendous. But it was dark by the time I left, so the views offered by a very pleasant drive had to wait until the morning. The route was directly south on the very straight B2068 past the village after which the St Lawrence ground's Nackington Road End is named. The farmhouse was in prosperous, rolling arable land dotted with the occasional old oast-house, and by the time I'd checked in and found the nearest pub, on the western fringe of the village of Sellindge, it was almost too late to eat.

The combination, however, of being in celebratory mood and being confronted by a landlady who was a temptress in the nicest possible way persuaded me to eat, drink and be merry for a very memorable couple of hours, which made the journey worthwhile. But even in this ecstatic state it was clear that plans to detour via the old port of Hythe the following morning, simply to see it for the first time, would have to be abandoned. The priority was to get to the ground early in the hope of speaking to Durham's number one fan, Jim Kay, among others.

It was still necessary to rise early enough to work off the evening's over-indulgence and make room for the inevitably hearty farmhouse breakfast. Anyone connected with Durham cricket would have wanted this auspicious day to dawn bright and sunny, so it was initially dispiriting to open the curtains to be confronted by fog. Surely the title could not be snatched away in a swirl of mist?

I ventured out regardless and as I climbed the narrow lane towards the village the sun began to burn off the mist, the church spire came more clearly into view and all was well with the world. With blue sky above and the fog still clinging to the hollows it was a lovely, pastoral scene to herald a great day.

Arriving at the ground an hour before the start, Jim Kay was virtually the first person I saw. While I was talking to him, the man who took the photograph on the front cover of this book, Barry Goodwin, came by. I made sure he was available for Northern Echo purposes that day, got him to take a quick snap of Jim, then bumped into a few more Durham fans arriving in high excitement. For me, everything was falling perfectly into place, now we just needed the team to apply the finishing touches to their season's work.

It emerged that Harmison had cracked a bone in his left wrist when going for a sharp catch in the gully, but he kept steaming in and took the last three wickets in very quick time after Thorp had taken the first two. Only six runs had been added to the sixth-wicket stand of 107 when Kemp sliced low to gully, where Benkenstein held a good catch.

Durham were then held up by Ryan McLaren and Yasir Arafat, and it was while enjoying the sunshine during a quiet lap of the ground that I saw a Durham man of advancing years, Bob Robinson, leaping around like a young buck after Arafat edged a drive to Di Venuto at second slip.

The end was swift as James Tredwell shouldered arms and was bowled by Harmison, Robbie Joseph edged to Di Venuto and Martin Saggers was bowled first ball. Kent were all out for 204 and Durham won by an innings and 41 runs, with the other major contributors being Di Venuto with 90, Smith with 81 and Mustard with 83 off 114 balls. When runs had been desperately needed in the final game of the previous two seasons, Benkenstein had obliged with typically gutsy centuries. On this occasion all that was needed from him was his calm, astute leadership.

He deserved all the praise that was coming his way, but it was also typical of him that he should deflect much of it on to Geoff Cook, describing him as "the heart and soul" of the club. While Geoff would celebrate as heartily as anyone, this description should not be taken to imply a boisterous nature. When asked for a comment he had always been much more likely to speak with carefully-considered diplomacy than produce an off-the-cuff rant.

In devoting the last few words of this book to him, however, it is worth looking back first on what he had to say 12 months before the Canterbury climax. Durham's clinching of the Pro40 second division title in 2007 coincided with the news that the two finalists in the 2008 Twenty20 Cup would qualify to compete for a mind-boggling $5m prizefund in an eight-team tournament in India. Cook said: "The finance involved will produce an unhealthy bias towards Twenty20. The ECB try to keep a balance to the whole structure of the game, but this is a threat coming from outside, which is quite frightening. This external money will put an onus on the competition which will imbalance the whole season."

My reporting of this in the immediate aftermath of Durham's Pro40 triumph apparently did not go down too well in the dressing room, probably because the headline said: "Twenty20 mars Durham joy." But while all players in any sport are entitled to celebrate winning even the lesser trophies, it seemed important at the time to stress the mounting threat to the game's traditions.

If you've read this far, you are presumably not in thrall to the iPod shuffle, nor do you zap manically between TV channels or generally indulge in the sort of bite-sized chunks of which Twenty20 cricket is a further example. Cook's words rang true when the vulgarity of the Stanford Challenge became acutely apparent and the Champions League collapsed in disarray after the farcical exclusion of England's beaten finalists, Kent, because one of their players had appeared in the Indian Cricket League. The outlawing of the latter by the Indian Premier League merely added to the tacky tastelessness of the whole shebang.

So it was with wonderful timing that, as Middlesex won the Twenty20 Cup while still floundering in the second division of the main event, Durham rose above the dreadful nonsense to win the championship.

For the final words, I go back to the quote from Cook I used in chapter one: "I have been in the game for 36 years and the things I have stood for are based on traditional values of behaviour, team ethos and individual ambition. The culmination of all this has always been to win the county championship, so for us to do it with as nice a group of lads as you could possibly have means this is one of the sweetest moments of my career. After 96 days of cricket this season we had to come out and play really well to give ourselves a chance of winning this title, and we did that when it really mattered. It's a tangible reward for players who have shown stamina, professionalism and desire to perform for a club that tries to do them proud."

About the Author

Tim Wellock began his own North-East cricket career in the Durham University team which won the UAU in 1972. He then played for Tynemouth, Darlington and Sedgefield before finally indulging his love for village greens at Aldbrough-St-John, near his home. A former deputy sports editor of The Northern Echo, he has been a freelance sports journalist since 1987 and has followed Durham for The Northern Echo, home and away. He has also covered Durham's home games throughout their first-class existence for the Daily and Sunday Telegraph and the Press Association. He has also done some broadcasting for the BBC radio stations, Tees and Newcastle.